Films Were Made

A look at films and film makers
in the East of England 1896 – 1996
through films in the
East Anglian Film Archive, University of East Anglia

Volume 1
The Region at Work

David Cleveland

Published by
David Cleveland
Manningtree
Essex

PO Box Manningtree 7608

ISBN 978-0-9558271-2-9

British Library Cataloguing-in-Publication Data
A catalogue record for this book is available from the British Library.

Designed by Ken Rickwood

Printed in Great Britain by Print Wright Ltd, Ipswich

Contents

The cover picture is of Leslie Gillham filming ***"Around Orfordness"*** *in 1960 with his 16mm Bolex camera, and the title page is of a BBC Look East film cameraman at work about 1960.*

Introduction

Since 1896 people have operated motion picture film cameras in the East of England recording and making films in the counties of Bedfordshire, Cambridgeshire, Essex, Hertfordshire, Norfolk and Suffolk. Only a fraction of the films made have survived, but those that have show us what life was like, what film makers were making, and what we were watching and doing. These may be local films, home movies, cinema films, television films, educational films, publicity films etc. This book looks at some of these films and the people behind them, and is based on films preserved in the East Anglian Film Archive at the University of East Anglia. This is a unique and wonderful collection of material reflecting local history in the form of moving images of the past.

The Archive, based in The Archive Centre, has been building up the collection since 1976 and now holds over 100,000 items made and preserved on motion picture film. This book looks at only a small number of films held in the Archive, though it does try to cover a variety of subjects through the decades. During the 1970s and 80s video tape began to take over, though many film makers continued to use film into the 1990s. By then other methods were coming along, but recording on tape, discs, files and hard drives is another story.

I am producing this book myself, as I want to put down for future use what I have learned about the films and film makers of the region. This book could not have been written without the help of a large number of people across the region who have given me information over a period of 30 years or more about films and film makers, in many cases their own films, and about how films were made and how and where they were shown. There are so many fascinating films, that this is only part one, for it is hoped that Volume 2 will be published next, subtitled *Local History*.

Illustrations taken from film frames in this book are of variable quality, and have been reproduced for the purpose of explanation. I would like to thank the many people and organisations over the years who have allowed me to reproduce stills. Some however, I have been unable to trace or contact.

After the opening chapter of this book all photographs are in black and white, even though many of the films are actually in colour. This is done because of the high cost of printing colour images. Films with their titles in bold exist in the East Anglian Film Archive.

David Cleveland
Director, East Anglian Film Archive 1976 - 2004

Facing page: "Empire Cinematograph No 1" manufactured by Robert Rigby for W. Butcher & Sons, London. The cost of this machine in 1907 was £16:16:0 (£16.80). This hand turned projector was designed for use in "small theatres" where films were only part of the programme.

What's it all about?

What is motion picture film and how does it work? It is worth just recalling how moving pictures got on to the screen before the days of digital electronic methods.

Motion picture film used in the commercial cinema, as well as other applications, developed from photography, where a layer of light sensitive particles in the form of an emulsion is coated on to a strong base of transparent material in darkness, exposed in a camera to the scene coming through the lens, and then developed in chemicals to form a physical image on the film. The image is negative, that is the black and white tones are reversed. From this negative a positive print is made to view. This is a simple description, but in reality, many different skills and processes are involved.

The flexible clear base of cinematograph film, 35mm wide, was first made of cellulose nitrate or celluloid (a trade name). It was used in the cinema industry until production of nitrate film base ceased in the UK in 1951. Celluloid was a very durable film stock which had good translucent properties. However it was highly flammable, and had to be handled carefully. Nitrate film also has the propensity to decompose with time.

Safety film, though put on the market as early as 1909, was only used by the cinema industry where 35mm film prints were shown outside the commercial cinema circuits, such as in schools or village halls. After 1951 all 35mm film base was acetate, or safety stock, which does not burn easily. The film itself, whether nitrate or acetate, is a shiny plastic, which is made flexible by ingredients at the time of manufacture. The emulsion is applied to one side, which then appears as the dull side of the film.

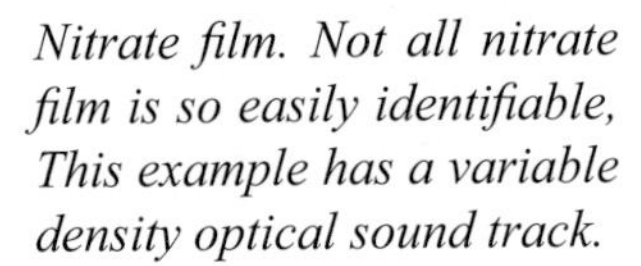

Nitrate film. Not all nitrate film is so easily identifiable, This example has a variable density optical sound track.

Safety film. Sometimes only an "s" is visible. This has a variable area optical sound track.

The emulsion contains the picture. The emulsion is a coating of gelatin holding a compound of light sensitive silver halides. When light falls on these, a latent image is formed of the scene. That means all the information is there, but is not yet visible. The film is then developed in a chemical solution, which turns the exposed silver halides into dark metallic silver, revealing the image. After fixing and washing, we now have a permanent black and white picture.

35mm motion picture film has holes down the side which engage with the machinery of the camera, printer, and projector, and these are called perforations. There are four perforations per frame on each side of 35mm film.

A can of 200 feet of unexposed film, enough for two minutes filming at the sound speed of 24 frames per second. Ilford's Pan F was a 1950s fully panchromatic film with medium speed and contrast and practically grainless.

35mm silent film. Note the individual frames, the frame line, and the perforations. There are 16 individual frames to every foot of 35mm film. This is from ***"Barking Pageant"*** *in Essex about 1912, a local news item.*

To get motion, the individual pictures have to be taken in quick succession, and shown in quick succession. The unexposed film, kept in darkness, is loaded into the camera, where there maybe as much as 300ft, enough for five minutes of filming in one of the early wooden cameras. This is transported through the camera mechanism by sprockets with 'teeth' which engage the perforations. Behind the lens is the 'gate', a place where the film is held stationary momentarily while the film emulsion (which is on the side of the film facing the scene) is exposed to the image coming through the lens. It is then moved on by the camera mechanism and another portion of unexposed film is held in the gate, and that is then exposed and then moved on, and so on. To stop light reaching the film while it is being moved a revolving shutter closes off the light coming through the lens. In the silent film days 35mm film cameras were normally turned by hand, and the average speed was about 16 individual pictures, or frames, per second, though this did increase gradually in the 1920s.

The exposed film, coming out of the camera in a light proof container, was then sent to the film laboratories where it was developed, fixed, washed and dried. The image on the negative is now seen in the form of individual still photographs, separated by a frame line, normally a clear line between the pictures. This negative is then put into a film printing machine, and pressed up against another piece of unexposed film stock, this time a 'positive' stock. A light is shone through the negative which exposes the negative picture on to the new film stock. This is really re-photographing the film again, but under controlled conditions. The exposed positive film stock is then passed to the laboratory developing machine where it is processed in the same way as the original camera negative. When developed, because the original film was negative, the copy comes out positive, that is with the tones the correct way round. The individual still photographs are now separated by a black (normally) frame line. We now have a recognisable scene on the film, ready to show on the screen.

The positive, or print as it is known, is put into a projector. The projector does roughly the same as the camera. There is a sprocket to pull the

35mm hand turned camera of 1909. Note the box to hold the unexposed film at the top right, and the box at the bottom to hold the exposed film. The loops of film above and below the gate take up the intermittent motion achieved by claws engaging the perforations and pulling the film through the gate at about 16 individual frames per second. In this photograph the film is stationary in the gate with the shutter open, and a picture can just be seen on the back of the film. The door must be kept tightly closed during filming to stop light fogging the film and ruining it. Film running through a camera at less than 16 frames per second will produce speeded up motion on the screen.

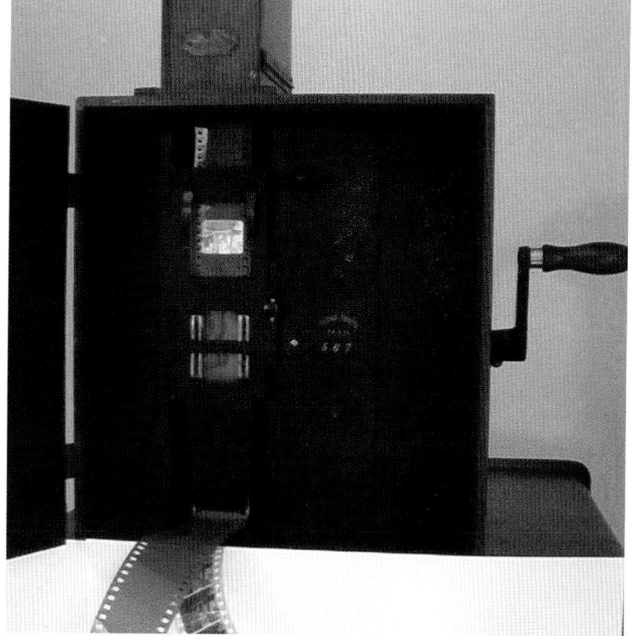

An early 35mm film printing machine of about 1905. The negative is in contact with the emulsion of an unexposed positive film stock. Light is shone through the negative and the picture is exposed on to the print stock. This can be seen in the aperture of the printer. The negative can be seen behind the print stock in the lower part of the photograph. The exposed print stock is then developed in the normal way, and a positive picture emerges. This contact printing from a negative to produce a positive is carried out in darkness, and is the basic method used today. Modern printing machines are motorised and can run at high speed. For film preservation optical printers are used which re-photograph each frame.

film down from the reel to the gate, where it is held stationary while a bright light is shone through the frame projecting it on to the screen. A shutter covers the light while a sprocket, revolving intermittently, moves the film down bringing into the gate the next frame, and holding this stationary while the light is shone through, and so on. This happens at approximately 16 frames per second with silent films or 24 frames per second with sound films. The individual still photographs projected on to the screen at these speeds are merged in the brain to produce a moving picture of the scene, just as the camera recorded it. Motion picture film on the screen is an illusion.

To produce the film with the shots in the right order, editing has to take place. A 35mm print is made of the complete camera negative, often called a 'rush print', as it was rushed through the laboratory so the cameraman, director, film maker etc, could see a print as quickly as possible. This rush print was then 'cut' by the film editor. This means the shots were cut up individually then joined together in the right order to form the film. This 'cutting copy', or 'work print', which is full of joins made by the editor, and probably damaged by repeated handling and viewing, was then used as a guide by the 'negative cutter', who would get out the original negative (untouched so far, so free from scratches, dirt etc.) and cut the shots in the order exactly matching the 'cutting copy' prepared by the film editor. The negative is now 'cut'. The cutting copy is no longer needed. A new 'graded' print is made from the cut negative on the printing machine. This is developed and we have a join free positive print ready to show. This is the basic procedure, but in the early film days

35mm negative and 35mm print. This film, ***"Cromer Lifeboat"****, of 1942, was made in the sound era, and a space to the left of the picture is for the sound track which has not been added yet.*

the negative was not always cut, but individual shots printed separately, and 'assembled' to form the final positive film ready for projection.

One foot of 35mm film contains 16 separate pictures. This means that in the silent film days, at roughly 16 frames per second, a foot of film went through the projector in one second, or 60ft in one minute. But projectionists often turned the projector handle too quickly, not only because it was very easy to do, but to get on with the story, to get through the film quicker, to possibly even get amusement from the slightly speeded up actions of the actors. When motors began to be fitted to projectors the speed was regulated by a rheostat. Projectionists could easily set the machine running faster than the film was taken, and this was often done. Towards the 1920s, the cameramen turned the cameras at a faster rate, partly to keep up with the projectionists, and by the mid 1920s films were being shown at anything up to 20 or even 22 frames per second. When sound on film was introduced, the speed had to be set exactly for cameras and projectors, without variation. This was fixed at 24 frames per second.

In the silent film days sometimes the positive films were tinted – that is an individual shot or title, or sequence of shots, was dyed a colour, sometimes just to add interest, at other times to reflect the mood of the scene. That is why tinted films (and toned, another method of colouring shots) have many joins in the print. Tinting really belongs to the silent era, when tinting and toning as a way of colouring the image overall was used extensively until sound tracks and improved printing methods came in with sound films. However, some sound trailers, advertising, and early feature films were lightly tinted (so the tint was not dense enough to spoil the sound track), but by then pre-tinted stock was available, so no dipping in baths of dye was necessary.

Sound films have a smaller frame area than the silent ratio, principally to make room for the optical sound track down the left hand side. When making a sound film the sound was recorded on a separate piece of film running in synchronisation with the camera. So in the studio there was a camera taking the pictures, and in another area a 'sound camera' recording only the sound track. For some early sound newsreel work, where less bulky equipment was necessary, a special newsreel camera was made which recorded the sound track down the side of the picture all in one go, but this made the film difficult to edit, and the sound had to be transferred as it was out of synchronisation with the picture.

The sound track is a visible photographic record of the modulations of sound. These optical tracks come in two main types, variable area where there are clear and black areas which vary with the sound, and variable density, where the track looks grey with light and dark patches which correspond to the sound. The sound track is "read" by shining a thin beam of light through it. As the sound track runs continuously (without intermittent motion as in the case of the picture) the light coming through the track varies with the dark and light modulations of recorded sound. This varying light falls on a photo electric cell or diode, which coverts it into electrical pulses. These are amplified and sent to a loudspeaker for us to hear.

A scene from ***"Bury St Edmunds"*** *1913. Note silent full frame and overall tint.*

A 35 mm release print. The picture area is reduced to incorporate the sound track.

A Vinten Model 'H' 35mm studio and location camera (c1937) with the author pointing to the 'gate'. This camera could hold 1000ft of film, enough for 10 minutes of filming at 24 frames per second. Films running at a higher rate through the camera, say 64 frames per second, produced slow motion on the screen when run at the normal 24 frames per second.

Because the sound track must run continuously, it has to be isolated from the gate of the projector where the film is moved in jerks 24 times a second. Therefore a loop of the film below the gate takes up the excess of the intermittent movement, followed by a smoothing sprocket or roller. Twenty frames below the picture gate the film is "read" by the thin beam of light from a bulb called an exciter lamp – because the light excites the sound track. Therefore, it will be realised, the sound track has to be twenty frames in front of the picture. So if a gun is fired, the image of smoke at the point of firing is in the gate being projected, while lower down in the projector, twenty frames ahead, the noise of the gun is being reproduced which is heard in exact synchronisation.

During production of a film, the sound tracks were kept separate, in level synchronisation, until the time came to produce the final prints, when the cut picture negative and the fully dubbed sound negative (dialogue, effects, commentary, music etc all mixed together) were printed together to produce release copies for showing – with the sound pulled up the necessary twenty frames by the film laboratory.

About 1950 magnetic recording tape and 35mm fully coated magnetic film began replacing optical sound tracks during the film production process. The final cinema release copies however, still had to have optical sound tracks. Eventually Dolby Digital Sound replaced the optical sound track with the information displayed between the perforations. An optical sound track was still incorporated in 35mm prints though, for those cinemas without Dolby, and as a back up should things go wrong.

Motion picture photography in colour took a long time to achieve. At first, to get colour on the screen, the 35mm black and white prints were hand coloured, an expensive process as each small frame had to be laboriously painted. About 1905 Pathe in France developed Stencil Colour. This was a mechanical method of colouring existing black and white prints. Cut out areas in blank 35mm film corresponding to the colours decided upon in the scene were made. These stencils were then run on a machine together with a black and white

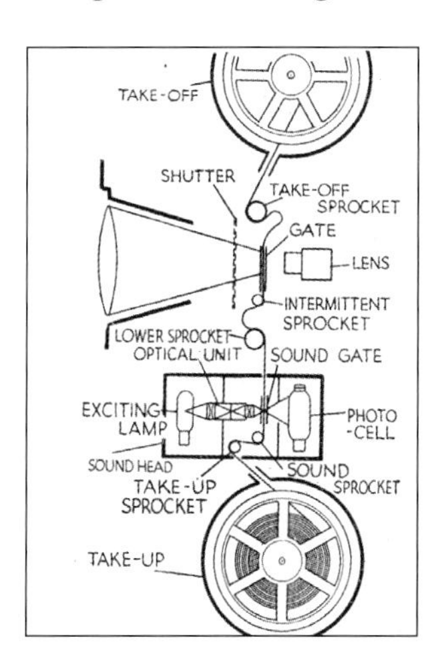

Layout of a sound projector.

"Moment of Perfection" *1954, an advertisement for canned vegetables. This was one of the last films made in the three colour Technicolor process.*

"Blickling Hall" *1929, a short stencil colour film.*

print of the film, and the colour applied through the cut out holes on to the film. A stencil could be made for the green parts of the scene to be coloured, another for the blue parts, another for the red parts and so on, depending on the amount of money available. Once the stencils were made, many black and white prints could be coloured this way, and they would all be the same. Stencil colour ceased being used when sound films came in at the end of the 1920s.

Actual filming in colour proved difficult. There were many systems in the silent era, most only being able to record two colours, normally the greens and reds in a scene. Technicolor (and some other systems) eventually managed to have full colour by the use of three black and white films in the camera, one recording the red information, one the blue information, and one the green information in a scene. Then came the complicated part of producing a full colour print from all three monochrome films. This was done not by normal photographic means, but by a system of printing by dye transfer, a bit like colour paper printing.

At the same time in the early 1930s as Technicolor perfected their three colour process, Dufaycolor became available. Marketed by Spicers of Sawston, in Cambridgeshire, this system used normal black and white film with the base covered in diagonal lines of red, blue and green stripes. These stripes, crisscrossing one another thus formed small dots of colour. The film was exposed in the camera the wrong way round, with the base side, covered with the coloured dots, facing the lens. The image came through the lens, through the coloured dots, through the film base, and was recorded in black and white tones in the panchromatic emulsion. Panchromatic means the monochrome emulsion was sensitive to all colours. Dufaycolor, although reproducing all colours, was never a great success, though a number of short films used this process in the 1930s. The mosaic of dots making up the colour were faintly visible on the screen.

The real breakthrough came in 1952 with the availability of the new Eastman Colour negative film. In this colour film, the emulsion contains basically three layers capable of recording the red information, the green information and the blue

A 35mm colour negative and rush print from ***"The Broads, Britain's Newest National Park"*** *1989.*

information in the scene. These layers contain silver halides and dye couplers (chemicals which produce a dye when the silver halide is developed) and during processing the silver is bleached out leaving just the coloured dyes. We now have a full colour image. The unexposed film could be loaded in any 35mm motion picture camera, and the laboratories could easily develop and print the film. It was as simple to use as black and white film. A colour negative is recognisable by the orange cast the whole film has. This is put on deliberately to correct the colour when printing the film for release.

The films that come into archives are often ex projection prints, which have been well run. These will be dirty and need cleaning, and may be scratched, or have frames or longer sections of image missing. The conservation of these films, and the copying on to modern film stocks for a further century of life is part of a motion picture film archive's work. From masters and copies, digital access copies can be made.

A 35mm optical sound track negative, used with a picture negative to make a print.

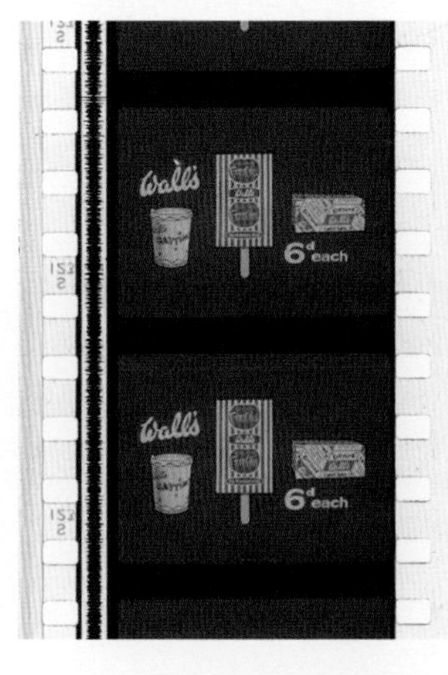

A 35mm colour print with optical sound track ***"Cinema Adverts"*** *1960.*

Narrow Gauge Films on Safety Base

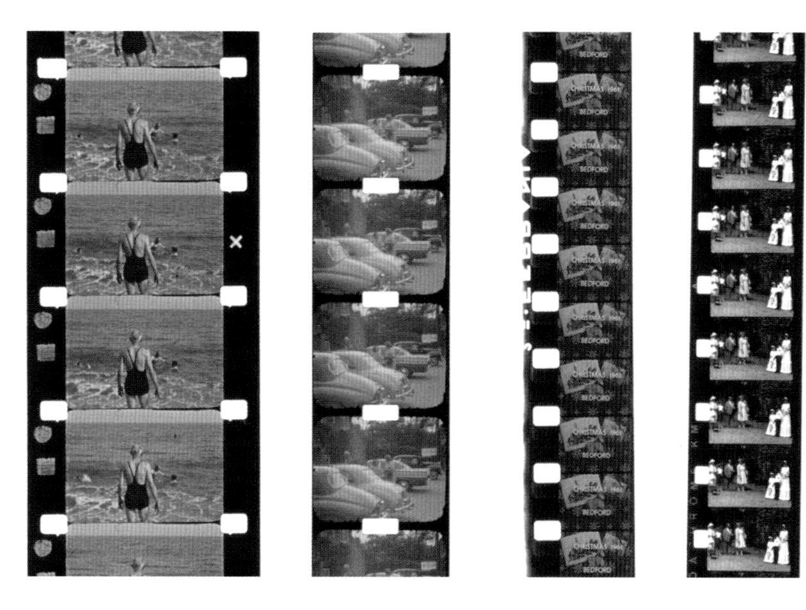

The popular sizes of narrow gauge films: 16mm, 9.5mm, Standard 8 and Super 8. The image area of 9.5mm is almost as big as 16mm, but frames on Standard 8 are only a quarter of the area.

There were other gauges of film besides 35mm, the main ones being 9.5mm, 16mm, and 8mm. Film has always been described in millimetres for the width, and feet for the length. These narrow gauges of film were intended for non professional film making and presentation, in other words for amateur use. They were always on acetate film stock, never nitrate. So 9.5mm, 16mm, and 8mm film stocks are 'safety' – that is non flammable film.

Introduced in 1923, 16mm was a film making outfit consisting of camera and projection equipment. It became much more successful than 9.5mm mainly because the larger size picture area coupled with well made (and expensive) equipment produced high quality images, so that serious film makers began to use the gauge. Most cameras held 100ft of 16mm film, enough at 16 frames per second for four minutes of filming. The film came on metal spools, which could be loaded in daylight, only the first foot or two being fogged by light as the film was threaded into the camera. The black and white film was of the reversal type. This means that after exposure, when the film was sent back to the manufacturer for processing, the film was developed directly to a positive image. This cut the cost considerably for

A 1920s advertisement for Kodak's 16mm.

Kodacolor filter.

***"Walton Carnival"** 1935 in Kodacolor.*

the amateur film maker as there was no negative and positive print to be made. However it did mean there was no other copy - the film that ran through the camera was the same film that ran through the projector, so if the film got damaged or ripped, then that was it – it could not be replaced. For those that wanted to make more professional films, a 16mm negative film stock was available. This meant that after development, a 16mm negative film existed. From this, and after editing, a join free print could be made. If this print became damaged, then another print could be made from the negative. For wider distribution, several prints could be made from the negative.

A 16mm Kodachrome film on double perforated film stock. Reversal film has black edges.

Colour became available for the amateur quite early compared with the cinema industry. In 1928 Kodak marketed Kodacolor for the 16mm user. A special glass filter with red, green and blue vertical stripes was fitted over the camera lens. The film, though normal black and white reversal, had vertical embossed stripes in the base of the film (the shiny side). The film was laced in the camera the opposite way to normal, that is with the shiny side facing the scene, so the emulsion was at the back. The image came through the lens,

*A frame from a Dufaycolor film **"Cromer and Norfolk Broads"** 1934.*

*A frame from a Kodachrome film **"Friends of Kelling"** 1963.*

and was 'directed' by the embossed lines (acting as miniature lenses) through the base of the film on to the emulsion behind where the shades of the colours were recorded in the monochrome emulsion. After processing the film looks just like a normal black and white reversal film. A similar tri-colour filter was fitted to the projector, and the film laced opposite to normal, with the emulsion facing the projector lamp. This meant that the light went through the image in the emulsion, through the base of the film and the embossed lines on the base which 'directed' the appropriate black and white shades through the vertical coloured stripes within the filter. It sounds complicated, but the picture did come out in colour on the screen.

Although Kodacolor was successful, its time was limited. In 1934 Dufaycolor was available for the 16mm user. This black and white film had a mosaic of coloured dots on the base of the film, so no filter was necessary on the camera. It was loaded in the camera in a similar way to Kodacolor, with the base of the film facing the lens. So, like Kodacolor, Dufaycolor reversal amateur films appear the wrong way round if viewed normally through the base. Dufaycolor was also available for a short time in the late 1930s on 9.5mm.

A 16mm reduction print from a 35mm original, with variable area sound track on the right.

In 1935 Kodak launched Kodachrome on 16mm (and shortly afterwards on 8mm). Kodachrome was a reversal colour film which recorded all three colours in a single emulsion. There were no filters, no mosaic of coloured dots. It was very easy to use, just load in the camera in the normal way and shoot. After exposure the film was sent to the Kodak laboratories for processing to a direct positive image in full colour. Between 1935 and 1938, there was a tendency for the Kodachrome colours to fade somewhat, leaving a pink image only. This was corrected, and Kodachrome after 1938 retains its rich colours.

During the Second World War 16mm, with its compact and portable projection equipment, was used extensively to get news and entertainment films to those in the services, and information films to the public in places that were not equipped with heavy 35mm projectors. Also 16mm was cheaper to use than 35mm. Some instructional and training films were shot on 16mm.

During the 1950s and for the next thirty years or so, 16mm was used by film makers for commercial and sponsored films. From 1955, and through the 1960s and 1970s television used 16mm for news and documentaries as cameras were light and easy to use, and above all it was economical. Television continued to use 16mm for some work even after video had taken over, as directors liked 'film quality'. So 16mm was a success story.

In December 1922, 9.5mm was launched at first as 'home cinema'. Small and relatively cheap projectors were available to show short, cut down versions or excerpts of cinema films which could be bought over the counter for a few shillings. From 1924 cine cameras for 9.5mm became available which held one minute of film. The black and white reversal film was bought at a price which included processing. The film, mostly from Pathescope, the British firm that promoted 9.5mm, came in a metal cartridge, which was just dropped in the camera, and filming could begin. After exposure the film was processed direct to a positive, and the one minute of film sent back to the film maker. The gauge of 9.5mm, with its centre perforation, was aimed at the enthusiast with limited pockets, and

A 1930s advertisement for 9.5mm.

was popular in the 1930s and 1940s. It declined in the 1950s, eventually ceasing with the demise of Pathescope in the early 1960s. A large catalogue of shortened cinema films on 9.5mm listed silent and sound films available for use at home either by hire or outright purchase.

In 1932 Kodak launched "Cine Kodak 8". This was a cheaper version of 16mm, for the film was cut in half longitudinally, thus halving the cost. The individual pictures were a quarter of the size of 16mm, though quite adequate for home film shows, where usually only a three or four foot picture would be shown.

Cine Kodak 8 camera film came on metal spools holding 25ft of 16mm wide film with double the amount of perforations. This was laced into the camera and one side only of the film exposed. When the roll ran out, it was taken out, turned over, and re-loaded into the camera, so that the other side of the 16mm wide film could be exposed. When this had finished, the film was sent to the laboratories

A Bell and Howell Standard 8mm camera of 1955. The 16mm wide film is ready to load. Only half of this is exposed on the first run, then the reel is reloaded and the other side exposed.The spool holds 25 feet of film.

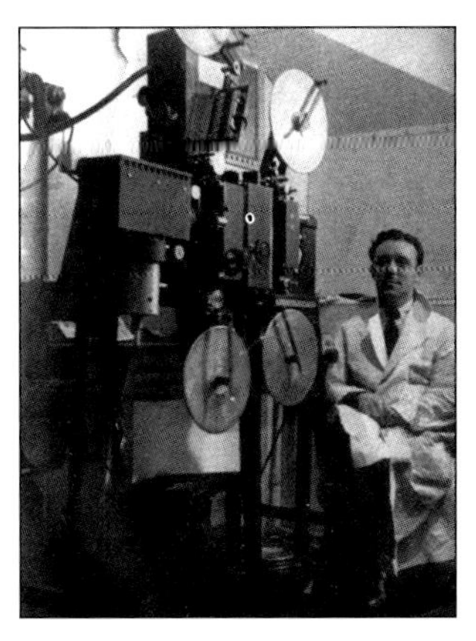

A Lawley film printing machine. This is a reduction printer for making 16mm copies of 35mm cinema films. The operator, photographed in 1947, is Gordon South-Butler at Kays Film Laboratory in London.

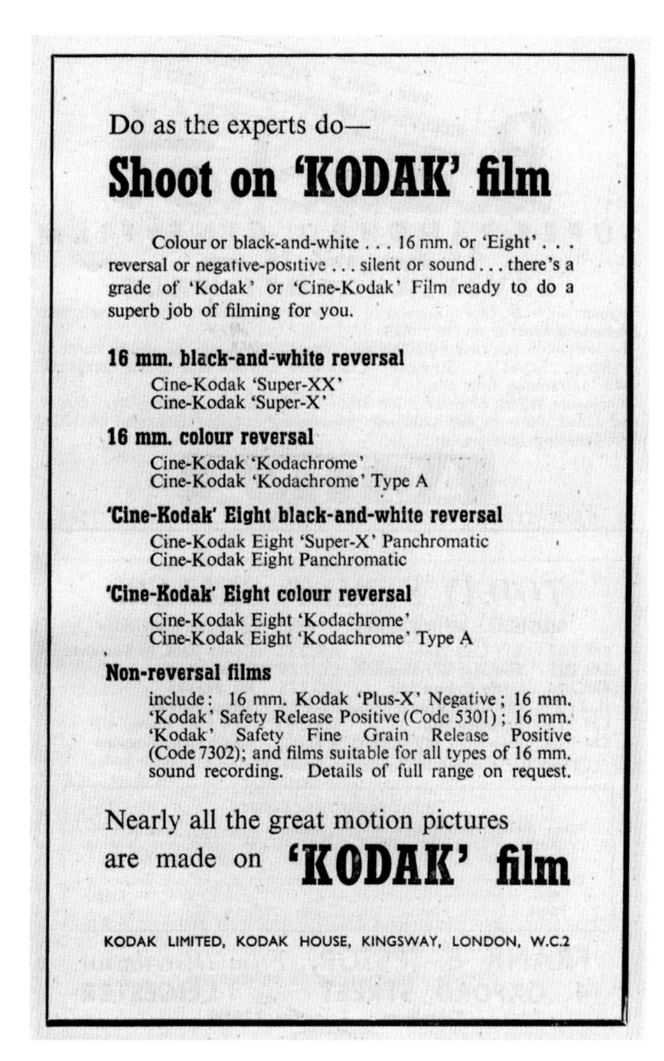

A Kodak advertisement of 1949 for the various camera films for 16mm and 8mm.

for processing. Black and white reversal film, and Kodachrome, included processing in the purchase price. After reversal processing the 16mm wide film was slit in half, and the two subsequent 8mm lengths joined together, producing fifty foot of 8mm film. At 16 frames per second this lasted for four minutes.

The big advantage of 'Standard 8', as we know it today, was that colour film was available. Kodachrome was something quite new when it arrived in 1935. It was a brilliant (in every sense of the word) colour reversal system, providing good quality colour images projected at home. The thrill for the cine enthusiast was when the yellow packet came back from Kodak and fell on the doormat. The film was ready for projection, but most amateurs could not wait, and opened the packet and pulled out a few feet to 'see if there was anything on it'.

In 1965 Kodak re-designed 8mm film as a boost to the market. The film was still 8mm wide, but the perforation was smaller and the picture area bigger. This gave slightly better quality. The advantage of Super 8mm, as Kodak called it, was that it was easier to use. There were no spools of film to fiddle about with, just a plastic cartridge which just dropped into the camera, the door closed, and you were ready to shoot. The cameras ran at 18 frames per second, so 50ft of film lasted three minutes twenty seconds. There was an improved range of colour film stocks available, and from 1973, sound cameras. For Super 8 sound, the film in the cartridge carried a narrow magnetic stripe down one side. The camera either had a microphone on top, or an external one. As you filmed, so the sound was recorded in synchronisation. A Super 8mm sound projector was required to play the film back on. Some had facilities to record sound, such as commentary or music or both. An external mixer enabled tracks to be mixed and recorded on to the magnetic stripe. Sound films, just like those in the cinema, were now possible at home and for the local cine club.

So, on all these sizes of film, people made their films. Cameramen and camerawomen loaded their cameras, took exposure readings, set the aperture of the lens so the right amount of light came through the lens to expose the scene correctly on to the film, and either turned the handle, wound up the clockwork motor, or pressed the button on battery driven cameras, and filmed. This was just

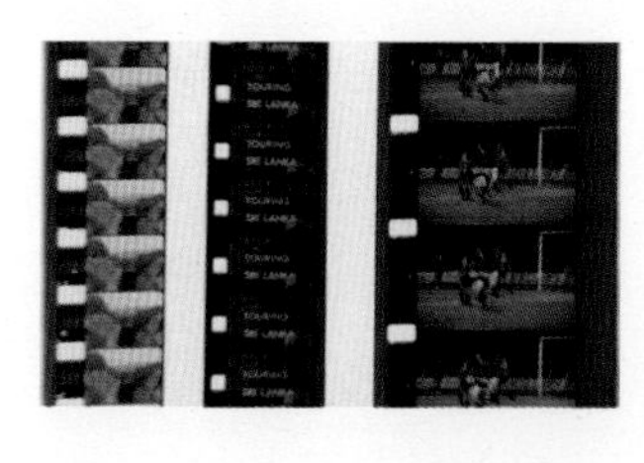

Standard 8mm, and Super 8mm with magnetic stripe. The 16mm has a stripe track on the right and a balance track on the left which enables the film to wind evenly on the spool.

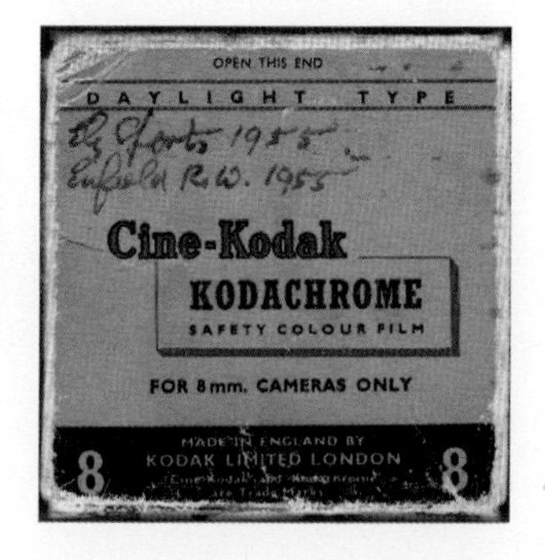

It was always exciting when the processed film dropped through the letter box.

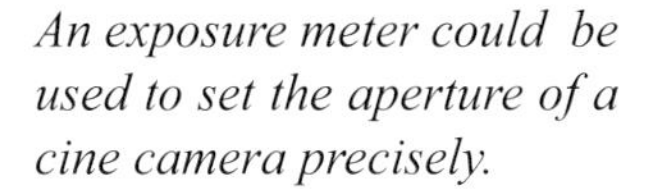
An exposure meter could be used to set the aperture of a cine camera precisely.

A typical 16 mm optical sound on film projector of the 1950s.

the beginning of film making. Because the film in the camera might only be of a minute's duration (9.5mm), four minutes (16mm and 8mm) or possibly six or ten minutes (35mm), each shot had to be carefully planned, and if possible rehearsed. Cine film was expensive, and every time the camera started, it was money running through the machine. You stopped as soon as you had the shot. Film making, whether professional or amateur, was a disciplined process. It had to be thought out.

Once the film had been developed, editing began. This was a physical job of cutting up the film, and joining it in the right order to tell the story. Titles might have to be filmed and cut in. Film was joined by 'cement' splices. These were made by scraping away a small amount of the emulsion so that two bare bits of film slightly overlapped one another. A little film cement was applied, and this welded the two films together. This took time, about 20 seconds or so for the weld to set. Later adhesive tape was used, but this does not keep well, as it can dry out and fall off, or become sticky with time and destroy part of the image on the frames either side of the join. Also tape joins, particularly on the small gauges of Standard and Super 8mm, can be seen on the screen. Cement joins are usually permanent, but film cement is becoming more difficult to obtain.

Next the sound track had to be compiled. For the amateur this often meant using a tape recorder running roughly in synchronisation with the film. From the late 1950s there were devices on the market to link the projector and tape recorder together to make 'lip sync' sound films. A skilled projectionist was needed to make it work correctly. An alternative system was to have a thin coating of magnetic 'stripe' applied to the side of the already edited film either by a company specialising in this work, or by purchasing a home stripe applicator kit. On projectors with magnetic heads, the sound track could then be recorded and played back.

Often short films for the cinema, or educational, advertising, and sponsored films, were shot silent, and the sound track compiled at the studio afterwards. This normally consisted of commentary, music from a library, and sound effects. These would then be dubbed into a complete finished sound track called the 'final mix'

Once the film and its sound track was completed, the laboratories would run off copies of the film ready for showing. It is often the case that it is one of these prints that has survived, or been carefully kept. The original cut picture negative and sound negative, and intermediate duplicating materials, were often left at the laboratories and forgotten about.

With television production on film, the processes are the same, except that only one good print was required for transmission, and this usually had a separate magnetic sound track on the same gauge of film running in synchronisation. There was no point in going to the expense of having a sound negative made and a combined optical sound print. Sometimes, particularly on news and current affairs programmes, the original reversal was cut and transmitted – complete with all the joins. There was no time for a print to be made. In fact in news in black and white days, the negative was shown, and electronically reversed so the picture appeared correct.

With amateur films on 16mm, Standard 8mm, Super 8mm and 9.5mm, it was the original camera

A 16 mm viewing machine of a type used for editing television films.

An open reel tape recorder linked to an 8 mm projector for synchronised sound.

A viewer capable of running Standard 8 and Super 8 films, used for editing.

film (reversal processed to a positive image) with all the joins made during editing which ran through the projector when the film was shown. Amateurs lovingly looked after their films, for if they became scratched or damaged, there was nothing they could do about it.

Copies could be made of 16mm, Standard 8mm, Super 8mm and 9.5mm films by the reversal method, but the quality did drop, and it was expensive. The film maker who knew he or she wanted to distribute the film used negative film stock in the 16mm camera, and positive join free copies were then made by the laboratories once the negative had been cut. If colour, there were film duplicating and printing stocks available, both reversal and negative positive.

Throughout the East of England region people were using movie cameras from 1896 to the late 1990s. During this time feature films were made in the region, short subjects for the cinema, advertisements, newsreels, documentaries and entertainment films. Cameras were exposing film during the making of educational, instructional, promotional and industrial films. Companies had film units, television had crews working across the region, and people were making record films of everyday life. Amateurs were recording their lives, their family, their hobbies and interests. Cine clubs, experimental film makers and co-operatives were making films, and on top of all this, people were coming to the region from other parts of the country, or even from abroad, to shoot part or the whole of their film.

Without realising it, all these film makers were recording the way of life of the region, and the physical nature and structure of the East of England. The following pages attempt to document some of these films and their makers.

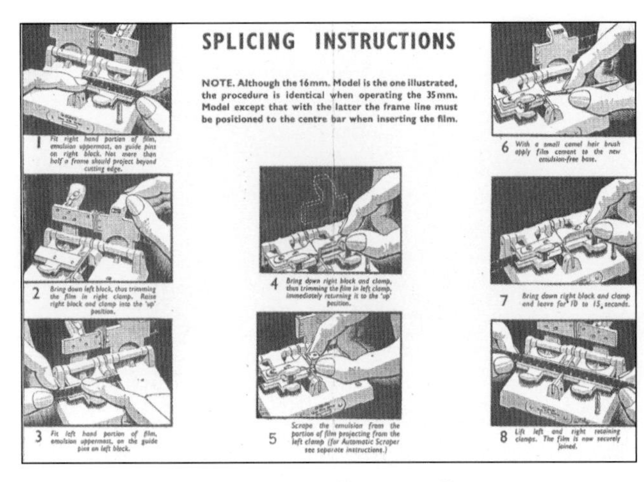

SPLICING INSTRUCTIONS

NOTE. Although the 16mm. Model is the one illustrated, the procedure is identical when operating the 35mm. Model except that with the latter the frame line must be positioned to the centre bar when inserting the film.

1 Fit right hand portion of film, emulsion uppermost, on guide pins on right block. Not more than half a frame should project beyond cutting edge.

2 Bring down left block, thus trimming the film in right clamp. Raise right block and clamp into the 'up' position.

3 Fit left hand portion of film, emulsion uppermost, on the guide pins on left block.

4 Bring down right block and clamp, thus trimming the film in left clamp, immediately returning it to the 'up' position.

5 Scrape the emulsion from the portion of film projecting from the left clamp (for Automatic Scraper see separate instructions.)

6 With a small camel hair brush apply film cement to the new emulsion-free base.

7 Bring down right block and clamp and leave for 10 to 15 seconds.

8 Lift left and right retaining clamps. The film is now securely joined.

How to join triacetate film using film cement..

Colchester Cine Club ready for a film show with 16mm, Standard 8mm and Super 8mm machines. Left to right Colin Noon, John Jones, David Lewis.

Birt Acres film taken in July 1896 of sailing trawlers being towed by steam paddle tug out of Great Yarmouth harbour. This one is YH 120 Thrive, *39 tons, and built in 1868.*

The Beginning

Birt Acres, one of the pioneers of motion picture film, is credited with what was probably the first film shot in the East of England. It is an historic recording in more ways than one.

It was in early July 1896, that Acres or his assistant at the time, Arthur Melbourne Cooper, shot this short film of sailing trawlers being towed out of Great Yarmouth harbour by a steam paddle tug. The historic part of "**Yarmouth Trawlers**" (the East Anglian Film Archive title for this film) is that offshore trawlers were to disappear from Yarmouth in only a handful of years, Lowestoft becoming the trawling centre. Yarmouth was to become known for the landing of herring from the steam drifters, which took over from the sailing drifters. The smacks that pass the camera, which looks inland towards the bend in the River Yare, are easily identified by their port of registration numbers, indicated for Yarmouth by YH. We see YH 120, named *Thrive*, owned by William Buckle of 67 South Quay, and YH 723 named *I Will*, owned by A. Bland, 57 Georges Road, Yarmouth.

It seems that, though only running about a minute, this film was shown at the Royal Aquarium in March 1897 - "introducing the Cinematograph with local pictures of fishing boats leaving Yarmouth Harbour". This was not the first showing of "animated pictures" as films were known, in the region. The first show that has so far been found was at Ipswich on September 14th 1896. "The Cinematograph, the 'animated pictures' which have caused such a furore in the metropolis, delighted the audience in spite of certain little hitches in the arrangements of a first nights performance" said the report in the East Anglian Daily Times the next day.

The "marvellous Cinematograph" as it was advertised, was new, a novelty, and was included in the stage show as a 'turn', for the real star of this music hall programme at the Tivoli Theatre of Varieties in Tower Street, Ipswich, was Charles Coborn, a singer most famous for his song "The Man Who Broke The Bank at Monte Carlo". The show opened with Miss Frances Coventry, a singer; then "The Two Daniels" with songs and dances; Mademoiselle Zeba "graceful and clever performance on a revolving table", and comedians Will Percival and Mabel Breeze. Charles Coborn then came on and sang several popular and comic songs until he was "obliged to retire and make way for the Cinematograph". It may be that the Yarmouth trawlers film was shown, but the contents of the film show are not recorded. The cinematograph was described as "in good working order", with "entire change of views" the next day.

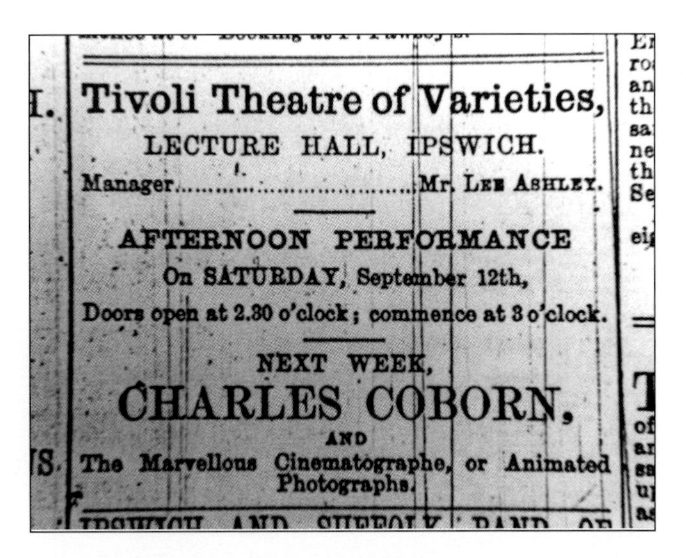

Tivoli Theatre of Varieties,
LECTURE HALL, IPSWICH.
Manager..............................Mr. Lee Ashley.
AFTERNOON PERFORMANCE
On SATURDAY, September 12th,
Doors open at 2.30 o'clock; commence at 3 o'clock.
NEXT WEEK,
CHARLES COBORN,
AND
The Marvellous Cinematographe, or Animated Photographs.

The Tivoli Theatre advertisement from the East Anglian Daily Times which includes the programme for the week of September 14th 1896.

The survival of Acres' trawler film is due to Ray Henville who in 1996, exactly 100 years after it was made, took some old films he had kept behind a shed in his garden to the National Film and Television Archive for identification. These had been purchased by Mr. Henville along with some electrical equipment some time before. This is often how these early films have been found, through collectors and hoarders not wanting to see things thrown away. This is the story of many of the films mentioned in this book.

Animated pictures were shown at first in music halls and theatres as an extra turn, in presentations to mechanical, photographic and scientific groups, at special shows in halls in the big towns, and then in set ups, some very elaborate, at fairgrounds.

The sailing trawler, often called a smack, seen here is the "I Will", 51 tons, and built in 1877.

Robert Paul, the other pioneer, with whom Acres had collaborated in developing moving pictures, had had success with his Theatographe in London, and this was taken by Mr. P. Shrapnel to Tudors New Circus in Auckland Road, Cambridge on October 5th 1896. "A most agreeable surprise awaited those who visited the Circus last Monday night, in the form of Paul's Theatographe; for though most had heard of the marvellous invention, a very small number had any idea what it was, and the majority must have been surprised by the reality. The Theatographe or Cinematograph, consists of pictures, or rather photographs, which are reflected by means of limelight on to a sheet. Each one of these living pictures is depicted by means of a series of 1,000 or even 2,000 photographs which have been taken in such quick succession that there is no perceptible break in the movements of the objects taken. The effect is really marvellous."

Tudor's New Circus really was new, as it had opened on August 31st that year on a site overlooking Midsummer Common. William Tudor, a juggler and horse rider, had presented shows for the previous three years, but now he had a new brick building with six emergency exits, dressing rooms, and a stable. Both the entrance and the interior had gas lighting. The building could house

TUDOR'S NEW CIRCUS,
AUCKLAND-RD., NEWMARKET-RD.,
CAMBRIDGE,

First time in Cambridge,
PAUL'S THEATOGRAPHE,
The Greatest Success of the London Season, from the Alhambra and Empire. Animated Pictures. The Latest Scientific Marvel,
CENIMATOGRAPHE,
Under the Management of Mr P. Shrapnel. NEW PICTURES NIGHTLY.
First appearance of
FLO EVERETTE'S CLEVER PARISIAN PETS.
THE LEAURANCE TROUPE
(Five in number), the only Troupe of Lady Trick and Fancy Bicyclists in the World.
THE 3 ROYS,
Scientific and Comical Skaters.

NOTICE.—TUESDAY, October 6th, 1896.
GRAND FASHIONABLE NIGHT,
Under the Distinguished Patronage and presence of Wm. C. Hall, Esq., J.P., the Worshipful Mayor of Cambridge, Mrs Hall, and Party.

Look out for October 5th, Paul's Theatographe, the Latest Cenimatographe.—See Special Bills.

DAY PERFORMANCES EVERY SATURDAY AT 2.30.
Prices of Admission: 2s., 1s.; Gallery 6d.

Robert Paul's Theatographe was presented at Tudor's New Circus in Cambridge in October 1896.

700 people on the ground floor, with another 700 in the gallery. The ring was 40ft in diameter.

Mr. George Gilbert began his fourth season on Boxing Day 1896 of Gilbert's Modern Circus within the Agricultural Hall in Norwich with a variety of acts. Here too animated photographs were shown on January 11th 1897, and in the programme was a film of Yarmouth beach also attributed to Birt Acres, but now sadly lost. The Agricultural Hall was home to a variety of occasions, from corn sales to fat stock shows (there is film of one of 1920 called "**Xmas Beef**" showing cattle in the main hall which was later to become a television studio), from roller skating to a tight rope walker.

It was probably here in 1901 that a film of Norwich streets was shown. Denis Gifford in his "The British Film Catalogue - Volume Two, Non Fiction Film" lists "**Tramway Ride Through The Streets of Norwich**" released in July 1901 by the Warwick Trading Company.

The film is taken from the top of a tram travelling through the city, with the camera operated at certain points which the cameraman thought were interesting. First there is a lengthy shot of the Dereham Road as the tram approaches the bottom of Grapes Hill. The tram itself is not seen, but the single line track stretches out in front, with a passing set of lines ahead. Dereham Road was narrower at this time, with larger front gardens for the houses. The camera then stops, and starts again at Charing Cross. This part of Norwich has changed completely, and it is difficult to recognise anything, but the following scene is unaltered today. This is Bank Plain with what was the Royal Hotel on the left, and the Agricultural Hall ahead.

The camera continues towards the Agricultural Hall entrance, and then swings round towards Prince of Wales Road.

The tram now reverses, and as we travel backwards we see Prince of Wales Road, the road between Castle Meadow and Orford Place (Red Lion Street), and finally St. Benedicts. The most attractive thing about these shots is not only that it is so early in film terms, but that we see ordinary people going about their business without the knowledge that they were being filmed, and that audiences would still be watching them over a century later.

At Yarmouth, about 1902, comes a similar record of daily life, though this time it is an industry, the fishing industry. As we have seen, Yarmouth quickly went over to the harvest of herring, particularly in the autumn when these fish passed this part of the coast in huge numbers.

*Bank Plain in 1901 from "**Tramway Ride Through The Streets of Norwich**".*

*Girls gutting herring at Yarmouth in 1902 from "***Yarmouth Fish Quay Scenes***".*

A short film, this shows sailing drifters and steam drifters coming into the harbour, and scenes on the quay. In the background of "**Yarmouth Fish Quay Scenes**" can be seen the swills, those particularly shaped double baskets which only Yarmouth used to contain the herring. The fish were gutted and packed into barrels in the open for the overseas markets, this work being done by Scottish fisher girls who travelled down from Scotland for the season. There is one shot in the film which shows how the catch of each boat was assessed. While still on the boat, the herring are seen being counted by hand, in what were known as long hundreds - a typical old fashioned method by which 130 fish or more equalled a hundred! The men counted in "warps" that is four fish, two in each hand - a method which ceased to be used about 1908 when the quarter-cran basket was legalised as a measure. Next the girls are seen at work gutting the herring; a caption stating that each girl does sixty-five a minute, but this seems a bit optimistic, though perhaps the quickest girls did reach one a second.

This was a time when Pageants were in vogue – re-enactments of historical events of towns and cities. Bury St Edmunds was one town that went in for this is a big way. When, in July 1907, two thousand performers took part in the "**Bury St. Edmunds Great Historical Pageant**", consisting of seven episodes in Bury history from the time of Boadicea to the founding of Edward VI's Grammar School in 1550, Ronald Bates recorded scenes from each episode. With these shots he produced a film running twenty-five minutes for the Gaumont Company.

Ronald Bates had an electrical shop and business at 34 Abbeygate Street in Bury St Edmunds, and was fascinated by film. He put on film shows, was involved with the first cinemas in the town, and made films. He may well have shot the 1913 film "**Bury St Edmunds**", a film distributed by a company using the Isle of Man symbol – but more about that later. It seems though, that Bates had a movie camera, and just acted as cameraman. Mrs. Bates had the pageant film restored in the 1950s, and copies exist in both the BFI Archives and the East Anglian Film Archive.

The pageant film was shown first in Bury, then on September 7th 1907 at Newmarket Town Hall. The show ended in tragedy however, for just before the interval there was a fire, the audience panicked, and three lives were lost.

Fires were common in the days when 35mm film was made of celluloid, or nitrate as it is often

Ronald Bates, who filmed the Great Historical Pageant of 1907.

The Gaumont Co.,

The success of Harry Lauder, at the London Hippodrome and Empires, Swansea and Cardiff, during the past week has been PHENOMENAL, completely surpassing every previous performance of the popular comedian.

Crowded Houses Nightly. Operator mobbed for Interviews.

Congratulations from every quarter. Cheered to the echo.

"I Love a Lassie."

The house was carried away, and the town infected with the popular air.

We are prepared on behalf of HARRY LAUDER to receive offers for the hire of this highly Popular Star Comedian's most favourite productions (of which we have the entire rights as ***Chronophone Subjects*** for Exhibition) in districts not affected by the Moss Stoll Circuits.

Uncle's Legacy.

The latest out.—Particulars later.
No. 1645. Length, 728 ft. Price, £12 2s. 8d. net.

The Armchair—A Perfect Sticker.

A film that will hang wherever shown.
No. 1645. Length, 560 ft. Price, £9 6s. 8d. net.

The Effects of Bad Wine.

A realistic take-off of a quiet, respectable citizen who has a fill of cheap liquor.
No. 1642. Length 230 ft. Price, £3 16s. 8d. net.

Wipe your Feet.

A genuine "top liner" of the first order. "Wipe your feet" on other poor set-offs and stick to Elge productions.
No. 1647. Length, 395 ft. Price, £6 11s. 8d.

The Winking Woman

The extreme of mirth and drollery.
No. 1629. Length 520 ft. Price £8 17s. 4d. net.

Ma-in-law goes to the Fair

Comic and fun that can't be outdone.
No. 1627. Length 555 ft. Price £9 5s. 0d. net

A Humble Friend in Need

A Beautiful Drama.
No. 1632. Length 745 ft. Price £14 8s. 4d. net.

The Inlaid Floor Polisher

Must be seen to be appreciated.
No. 1649. Length 230 ft. Price £3 16s. 8d. net.

Mark Twain at the Oxford Pageant.

The latest of popular subjects; an event of wide public interest.
No. 600. Length, 65 ft. Price, £1 12s. 6d. net.

1600 YEARS OF ENGLISH HISTORY.

A great Feat. Unprecedented Success.

Results beyond Expectations.

The Educational, Industrial, Political and Social History of England produced in film.
The greatest thing ever attempted.
The greatest thing ever accomplished.

NOW PRODUCED.

The Oxford Historical Pageant

Oxford, ye ancient mother of men.
Mark Twain at the Oxford Pageant.

Bury St. Edmund's Pageant

Bury, so closely associated with our religious life.

Romsey Pageant

Romsey, around whom raged scenes of mediæval chivalry.
It was at Romsey that Charles I. last rested on his way to execution at Whitehall.

We have the SOLE RIGHTS for the

St. Alban's Pageant

so closely connected with the stirring wars of the middle centuries and modern social life.

"Good-Night" customers please note correct Price, 13s. 4d. net.

"CHRONO HOUSE,"

5 & 6, SHERWOOD ST., (Back of the County Fire Offices) **PICCADILLY CIRCUS,**

LONDON, W.

Telegrams—"Chronophone, London." Telephone—2430 Gerrard.

London, Paris, Berlin, Barcelona, Milan, Moscow, and Cleveland, Ohio, U.S.A

The Gaumont Company, often using their trade name of Elge at this time, was responsible for many pageant films.

referred to today, a highly inflammable film base made of cellulose nitrate. If the film stopped in the gate of the projector even momentarily, the heat from the light, (limelight often during the early years, which is a block of lime with a high intensity flame playing upon it, or later an arc light, which is a flame from an electrical arc burning between two carbon rods) the film would burst into flames. The fire might not stop there, as there might be several hundred feet of film either on the top spool or the bottom spool, or possibly both if it was a long film, and this material would burn quickly and fiercely. Film was often stored on the floor or table naked on the spools, so that if something hot from the light, or even a cigarette, fell on the film it would catch fire instantaneously.

One of the worst fires occurred early on in motion picture film history – at a show in Paris on May 4th 1897, when 121 people died when gases supplying the lime light illumination for the projector exploded, igniting the nitrate film. The wooden building soon burned, hot dripping tar from the roof fell on people, and panic set in. People were burned, others trampled underfoot. It was a horrific disaster.

The fire at Newmarket had similarities, but was not so severe, and only three died. The jury's verdict published in the Kinematograph and Lantern Weekly of September 19th 1907 states "The town surveyor said the seating capacity of the hall without the gallery was 400. Frank Simpson, captain of the Newmarket Town Fire Brigade, described his fight to reach the fire, and how he and his men soon extinguished the burning woodwork. The kinematograph he believed was erected exactly in front of the closed half of the exit doors. The fumes inside the hall was so bad that he feared collapse, and it was only by putting a water soaked handkerchief on his face and dropping on his knees to direct the water that he was able to stay. The kinematograph was not overturned. When he left the hall there was a rush towards the exits, and someone might have collided with the machine. Had it not been for the cry of 'Fire' the disaster probably would not have happened.

"Rohda Wollard, caretaker of the hall, stated that she arranged the seats, leaving two gangways. The exhibition manager filled up a gangway with

YACHTING ON THE
NORFOLK BROADS
-
HORNING REGATTA
ALDOUS

A record of Horning regatta filmed by Charles Aldous.

*From Charles Aldous's "**Horning Regatta**" of 1908.*

chairs. She stood ready to relight the gas at the interval, when the cry of 'Fire' was raised. She was swept away. At similar exhibitions an iron screen had been erected round the apparatus. Nothing guarded it on the occasion. Sergeant Gorham and Constable Wright saw a woman fall on the blazing hydrogen cylinder, and others in stepping over her, had their clothes ignited. They both assisted to widen the exit opening by forcing the closed portion of the door, and rescuing those who fell. The gas laden atmosphere and burning celluloid film rendered the place suffocating.

"Wilfred Black, an hotel hall porter said he saw the operator open the lantern door. A piece of white hot lime fell out, and either rolled or was kicked against some spools of celluloid film on the floor, and these ignited. The operator, Greenwood, attempted to extinguish the flames, and then a cry of 'Fire' was raised, and a rush followed for the exits.

"The operator said he had had experience of bioscope work for over nine years. The machine was fixed in the normal way. A fireproof box was used only when such was requested by the owners of the hall. The machine was fitted with every safeguard. The mishap was due to the terrible thud against the apparatus by persons leaving the hall. This smashed the lime igniting the films near. The panic following the cry of 'Fire' undoubtedly caused the deaths.

"The jury found that death was due to shock, caused by burns, occasioned by accidental outbreak of fire caused by a panic at the Town Hall, Newmarket on September 7th".

Another local person who shot the occasional film was Charles Aldous, a photographer who had a shop in White Lion Street in Norwich, and another in Wroxham called The Bridge Studio. The Wroxham shop was to take advantage of the

*The prize giving at the end of the day from Charles Aldous's "***Horning Regatta***" of 1908.*

rapidly growing Broads holiday business, which at this time was only about 25 years old. Aldous supplied photographs of the rivers and broads, and photographed yachting parties. In 1908 he filmed "**Horning Regatta**", a leisurely affair that year in light winds. He set his camera up on the bank near the Swan Inn and filmed anything interesting that happened, including an interlude when the pleasure steamer *Queen of the Broads* ploughed triumphantly through the proceedings, fully laden with Broads sightseers. At the end of the film Mr. Aldous recorded the prize giving, with the Edwardians very aware they were being filmed.

The East of England region today is recognised as a distinct area, made up of the counties of Bedfordshire, Cambridgeshire, Essex, Hertfordshire, Norfolk and Suffolk. In one corner lies St Albans – a place that deserves a mention in film making history, as it was here that a man set up what was the earliest film studio in the region.

Arthur Melbourne Cooper was born in 1874, the son of professional photographer in St Albans. Cooper learned photography from his father, and became adept at taking photographs and making glass lantern slides. He became an assistant to Birt Acres when Acres was experimenting with moving pictures, and progressed to camera assistant and cameraman. It was not long before Cooper was making films for himself, and in 1901 he formed his own company, the Alpha Cinematograph Company.

At this time, films were sold outright to exhibitors. Cooper set himself up as a supplier of ready made films to the trade, to the middle men in fact, who then sold the films to those that showed them. These middle men, we might call them distributors, bought copies of the completed film, but could easily put their own name on the title, even alter the title, or shorten the film, before selling it on. The eventual purchaser could do the same. For this reason the films from Alpha studios are difficult to trace. Cooper's first studio in St Albans was in Bedford Park, but in 1908 he moved to bigger premises in Alma Road. During the centenary year of British cinema in 1996, the British Film Institute put up a plaque stating "on this site stood the Alpha Cinematograph Works".

Cooper never pushed himself into the public eye, never put his own name on his films. He did produce a catalogue or two, so we know some films he made, but most come from careful research of Alpha announcements in the trade papers by such people as Denis Gifford ("The British Film Catalogue - Volume 1, Fiction Film" and "The British Film Catalogue - Volume Two, Non Fiction Film"), from surviving correspondence, and Cooper's own reminiscences recorded on tape before he died in 1961. Much dedicated research was carried out over a number of years by Cooper's daughter Audrey, and more recently by the Dutch historian Tjitte de Vries to piece together a list of the films Cooper made.

Cooper made actualities, industrial records, sport, drama, comedy and animated films. This extraordinarily varied output continued until 1911 from the studios in St Albans where sets were built out in the open, where processing and printing was done in the laboratory part, and where some of the first successful animated films were made.

Ruby Vivian and Eric Lavers in St Peter's Street, St Albans.

*The animated toys in "***A Dream of Toyland***".*

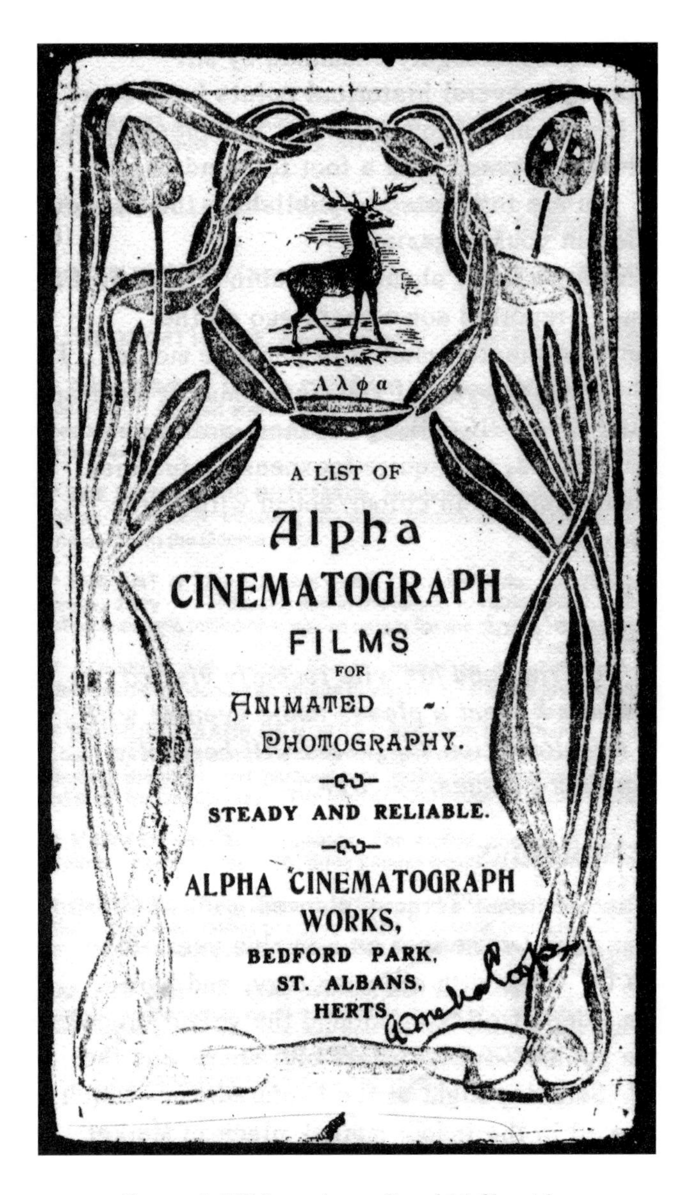

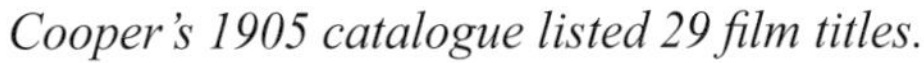
Cooper's 1905 catalogue listed 29 film titles.

Arthur Melbourne Cooper.

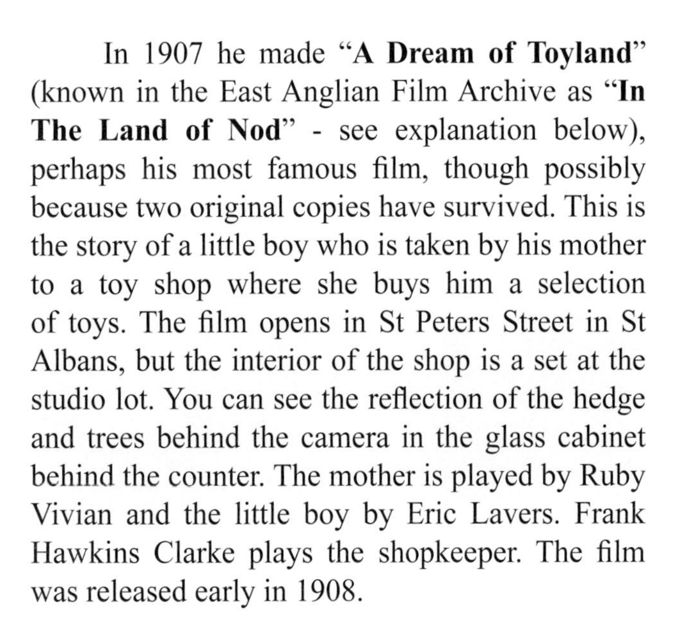

In 1907 he made "**A Dream of Toyland**" (known in the East Anglian Film Archive as "**In The Land of Nod**" - see explanation below), perhaps his most famous film, though possibly because two original copies have survived. This is the story of a little boy who is taken by his mother to a toy shop where she buys him a selection of toys. The film opens in St Peters Street in St Albans, but the interior of the shop is a set at the studio lot. You can see the reflection of the hedge and trees behind the camera in the glass cabinet behind the counter. The mother is played by Ruby Vivian and the little boy by Eric Lavers. Frank Hawkins Clarke plays the shopkeeper. The film was released early in 1908.

Directed by Cooper, the film then cuts to a bedroom scene, and the little boy is put to bed by his mother. This also is a set, with the sun shining and the wind blowing a picture on the wall about. Virtually all interiors were filmed out doors at this time – for there was plenty of light.

The picture fades as the boy sleeps, and the toys come to life. Again this is an outdoor set, with 'flats' painted as buildings and shops to form the background, and a stage in front where the toys are animated. The street scene comes to life as the toys walk and roam and the bus and the carts busily move around. Every toy had to be moved just an inch or less, and one or two frames of film were taken. Then they were carefully moved again, and

WALTURDAW'S

Latest Film Subject.

Dreams of Toyland.

An Ideal Subject for Juvenile Audiences,

Of brilliant photographic quality and very ingenious. Don't miss it or you will rob the youngsters of a treat and your programme of a draw.

Description.

Tommy is taken by his mother to the toyshop, where he is allowed to select a toy for himself. He chooses a Mechanical Motor Bus, a very fine model of the real thing. Tommy and his mother are now seen leaving the shop, the youngster showing evident delight with his present. Next, bedtime arrives and Tommy is put in his cot. He falls to sleep and soon dreams of Toyland. His vision is depicted in the next picture, which shows a public thoroughfare inhabited by toy men and women, animals, carts, motors and all kinds of vehicles, all of which move about like marionette figures in a grotesque but amusing manner. It is a veritable miniature world with the most lively scenes imaginable. Every toy operates by its own accord in a remarkable manner. At last Tommy's new toy, the Motor Bus, comes upon the scene, crashes into other vehicles and there is an explosion. To sleeping Tommy it seems a reality, and the moment the Motor Bus explodes he jumps in his sleep with such force as to throw himself out of bed upon the floor. This abrupt termination of his vision serves to awaken him ; and he is now seen sitting half dazed on the bedroom floor, rubbing his eyes. Mother enters and puts him back into bed again.

The subject has been produced at great cost, involving a great amount of apparatus to stage. It is thoroughly well worked out and forms the most fascinating spectacle it is possible to conceive for children.

— To avoid disappointment Order at Once. —

Length 350 feet. Price £8 15s. 0d.

The "Walturdaw" Co., Ltd.,

— 3, DANE STREET, HIGH HOLBORN, LONDON, W.C. —

Telegrams: "ALBERTYPE, LONDON." Telephone: 4707 Holborn.

Walturdaw's advertisement in The Kinematograph and Lantern Weekly, February 27th 1908.

*Title frame of "**Her First Pancake**", released February 1907.*

another frame or two taken – and so on. When sixteen frames or individual photographs – for that is what they are - have been taken, one second of screen time is in the can.

The film was completed in the autumn 1907. Cooper sold the film to The Walturdaw Co, who purchased a large number of prints. They put their own title on calling it "Dreams of Toyland", though on the model omnibus in the film can be seen 'Dream of Toyland' – Cooper's original title. There is a copy in the BFI and the East Anglian Film Archive with the title "**In The Land of Nod**", but this was added later. In fact this title belongs to another film Cooper made.

"**A Dream of Toyland**" was very successful, and it was sold worldwide by The Walturdaw Company. E. G. Turner of Walturdaw recalled taking copies to America in November 1907 when he sailed on the first voyage of the Cunard ship *Mauretania*. This five minute film was not the first animated film Cooper made, he had been making them on and off since 1899, but this was perhaps the most popular, and is still shown at festivals and film shows today.

The East Anglian Film Archive has an example of one of Cooper's dramas "**The Motor Pirate**", also known as "The Modern Pirates" and "The Raid of The Armoured Motor". Made in 1906, it featured armoured cars filmed in the country lanes around St Albans. Also in the Archive is a comedy made in 1907, "**Her First Pancake**", about a newly wed wife who cooks a pancake and accidentally makes her husband ill. In his delirious state he has a dream where the poor man imagines he is being cooked in a huge frying pan. He is revived back to normal with a good dousing of a bucket of water. These are just three examples of films that Cooper made, but over the years he made hundreds of fiction and non-fiction films, including animated films for which he will go down in history as one of the pioneers.

Film projectors at this time were hand turned or had an electric motor controlled by a rheostat. It was easy to make the projector go faster, producing speeded up motion on the screen. "**Her First Pancake**" was filmed about 14 frames per second, and should be shown at this speed to get the motion correct. During the 1920s cameras were turned faster, and projector rheostats were turned up by the projectionists so the machine ran at 18, 20, or even 22 frames per second.

Most of Cooper's work has been lost, though a few films exist in archives as mentioned above, as well as five in the Dutch Filmmuseum. Cooper's studio boasted the full range of film producing and print making facilities. He even had the ability to tint the prints on the premises, that is shots, titles or scenes dyed a colour. In 1908 Cooper opened one of the first cinemas, the Alpha Picture Palace in London Road, St Albans, complete with electric lamps, refreshment lounge, and a commissionaire in uniform. This was a success, so a year later he opened another in Letchworth. Like many of the pioneers, Cooper was exhilarated by the new art form, but the business side was not his strong point. A second fire at his Letchworth Picture Palace was the start of his financial problems, and in 1911 he sold up, and from then on worked for other producers.

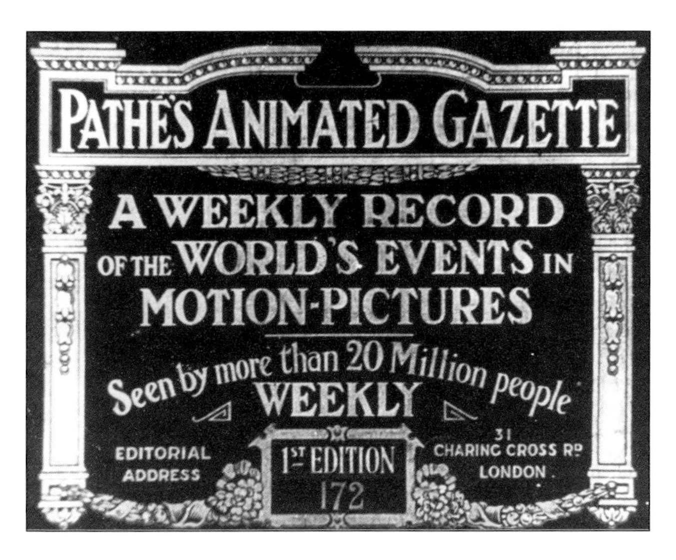

*"**Pathe's Animated Gazette**".of 1912 containing the sequence "**Famous Aviator Married**".*

*The King's procession in Upper King Street, Norwich, from "**Visit of King Edward VII**" 1909.*

Cooper was a friend and colleague of the early pioneers, and a letter in the Kine Weekly of 1947 by one of his former employees, Henry Maynard, states "I have seen many celebrities of stage and screen down in that basement watching him at work, including Charles Urban, [George Albert] Smith, [Robert] Paul, [Ernest] Moy, [Arthur] Newman and many others who have now passed over. The tricks I learnt from him stand me in stead today, even though we have advanced so wonderfully, and I think I can safely say that Melbourne Cooper was the pioneer of what we term today special effects".

Cooper filmed local events in St Albans while he was there, but most of these do not appear to have survived, but one very local newsreel made in Norwich by the family firm of Coes has.

On Monday October 25th 1909, King Edward VII visited Norwich "to review and to present guidons and colours to certain units of the Territorial Forces in Norfolk, and to lay the foundation stone of the extensions to the Norfolk and Norwich Hospital", as the official programme put it. A cameraman from A.E. Coe and Son, photographers and opticians of London Street, Norwich, covered the occasion, and the film was shown the next day at the Thatched Assembly Rooms, which stood on All Saints Green. Like so many films of the era Coe's film of the "**Visit of King Edward VII**" suffered from decomposition and all that survives is the King at Moushold Heath, travelling through Norwich, and at the Drill Hall in Chapel Field Road. After lunch, the King went to the Norfolk and Norwich Hospital in St Stephens Road to lay a foundation stone for a new extension. This section of the film is missing, but we do see the dignitaries and invited guests arriving at the hospital gates. It is a wonderful record of the Edwardians in all their best clothes excited about seeing the King.

Although regular newsreels had yet to arrive, news events were often covered, and issued as a distinct film in its own right. For instance in 1909 when Southend welcomed 'Admiral May and his Tars', as the banner hung on the pier states, a short film entitled "**Visit of The Fleet**" was produced by Charles Urban, a successful film businessman. This shows Southend streets with people, sailors, and a car or two, the pier, and a paddle steamer taking sightseers out to ships. Here they could board the vessels, look at the huge guns, or watch submarines passing by. In 1935 Gaumont British News covered another visit when "**The Mayor Pays an Official Visit to The Fleet off Southend**". At Sandringham an enterprising cameraman recorded brief scenes of the new King George V getting ready for a shoot to be included in the later film "**Episodes in The Gracious Life of King George V**".

It was in 1910 that the newsreels began on a regular basis. Charles Urban already issued topical events as single items but in 1910 he started the weekly Warwick Bioscope Chronicle on June 12th with a title that said "Pictorial Illustrations of

*George Beales of Boston with his winning catch from "***All England Angling Championship***".*

*"***The Royal Visit to Norwich***" King George V at the Royal Show in 1911.*

*From "***Famous Aviator Married***". The couple at Widford church 1912.*

The Worlds Happenings Day by Day". The "**All England Angling Championship**" at Ely filmed in 1912 does not exactly fall into the world events category, but it is a short record of the anglers quietly fishing on the banks of the Great Ouse beside the railway station with the Cathedral looking down on them. The catch is small, both in numbers and size, but Mr. George Beales of Boston is the winner, though he does not look excited by his achievement.

Pathe's Animated Gazette began in June 1910 with one issue per week. In 1912 two newsreels per week were issued, one for Monday Tuesday and Wednesday showing, then the second issue that week for Thursday Friday and Saturday. Of course these were for the first runs, for those exhibitors who could afford them. They would then cascade down to second runs and third runs and so on, getting cheaper as they became further out of date.

The Gaumont Graphic began four months after Pathe with the first issue on October 24th 1910.

Pathe covered "**The Royal Visit to Norwich**" in 1911 when the relatively new King, George V, visited the Royal Show on June 28th. In fact the cameraman did not film the King in Norwich at all, just scenes at the show including cattle parading around the grand ring, the Royal Pavilion, and the King inspecting the livestock from the comfort of his carriage. The Great Eastern Railway went to a lot of trouble building cattle pens at Crown Point by the side of the main line at Trowse, constructing a special station at Wensum Junction, laid temporary roads and built a bridge across the river Yare for some of the 121,000 people who attended the show over the five day period. The show was held at Crown Point, on 115 acres of land belonging to Mr. Russell Colman. Over 5000 farm implements were exhibited and the total number of livestock at the show was 2,943. No wonder the Great Eastern Railway had to build Crown Point sidings to cope with numerous trains bringing in horses, cattle, sheep and pigs.

Pathe also covered "**The Great Floods**" in Norwich on August 26th 1912. The cameraman arrived too late to see flood water, so shows us a chalked mark on a wall well above a plaque below which states the height of previous floods, a car going through some shallow water, and a bridge that was badly damaged at Coltishall, and the end of a cottage at Horstead also affected by the amount of water brought down the river following a deluge of six and a half inches of rain that fell in 12 hours. The newsreels at this time were quite international in their outlook, mainly because Pathe and Gaumont were both French in origin, though producing British versions in this country. The complete contents of a newsreel can be seen in an edition of "**Pathe's Animated Gazette**" issued at the very end of June 1912.

The contents consist of shots of two planes that had collided in a French military aviation disaster, students' revels in London, with shots of art students in the Botanical Gardens, the Battle of Flowers in Paris and, near Chelmsford the marriage of airman Claude Grahame-White and Miss Dorothy Chadwell Taylor. In London there is a sequence of the coaching marathon with four in hands, and at Windsor the Prince of Wales and the King review members of the St. John Ambulance Brigade.

Each item is short, the whole film running, at the correct speed, approximately five minutes.

Aviators were daring and glamorous people at this time, and the marriage of the 32 year old Graham White to Dorothy Chadwell Taylor was big news. The 1912 item, "**Famous Aviator Married**" only consists of three shots, the first showing a plane landing in Hylands Park, presumably Claude himself, as it is recorded he flew to his own wedding. Dorothy was staying with friends at the house in Hylands Park. The next shot shows an aeroplane circling over Widford church where the wedding took place. This was probably Benny Hucks, another famous aviator of the time, as he is recorded as circling the church as the choir sang, and then showering from the skies confetti on the happy couple as they emerged from the church – the final shot of the film.

Princess Beatrice was in Bury St Edmunds in 1912 at the ceremony of "**Presentation of Colours to the 3rd Battalion Suffolk Regiment**". She arrives by horse drawn carriage, and is presented with flowers. The new colours are presented and the troops give three cheers before the dignitaries depart. A military occasion of far bigger proportions was filmed by a cameraman for The Warwick Bioscope Chronicle in the autumn of 1912, when large scale military manoeuvres were held on the Cambridgeshire and Essex border. Thousands of soldiers were brought by train from Aldershot and Salisbury Plain to carry out a mock battle in the fields, one acting as the invading force, the other as a defence force blocking their way to London. One was the Red Army under Sir Douglas Haig and the other the Blue Army under General Sir James Grierson. On one of the days King George V attended, and watched for eleven hours as "Sir General Grierson's defending Blue Army counter attacked around Horseheath and Ashdon, and General Haig narrowly escaped capture by the defending cavalry. The operations were also watched by the military attaches of a number of foreign countries, who showed great interest in the progress of the fight". All this is seen in "**His Majesty's Manoeuvres**". By Horseheath church a plaque in the churchyard wall records the King's visit that day seeing his army at work.

Scenes of "**Bedford Regatta**" in 1912 were covered by a local cameraman, and shown at one of the town's new Picture Palaces, and at Ampthill a short record was made of an unusual private zoo owned by Anthony Wingfield who lived at Ampthill House. Mr. Wingfield is seen very briefly moving off the right of a shot at the beginning of the film of "**Ampthill Zoo**". There were a variety of animals in his menagerie, including 12 llamas, a Barbary Ram, and eleven ostriches. The zoo must have been quite extensive, as Mr. Wingfield employed seven keepers. The ostriches were not only for decorative reasons, for the sale of their wing plumes when made up into boas and fans brought in about £100 a year. Also the eggs were used in cooking – one egg equal it is said to 20 hen eggs! The other novelty was that the keepers were able to ride the ostriches, and this is seen in the film. In the 1920s the zoo was scaled down, and the animals transferred to Whipsnade Zoo when that opened. Sir Anthony Wingfield, as he became,

King Geoge V arrives to watch manoeuvres at Horseheath.

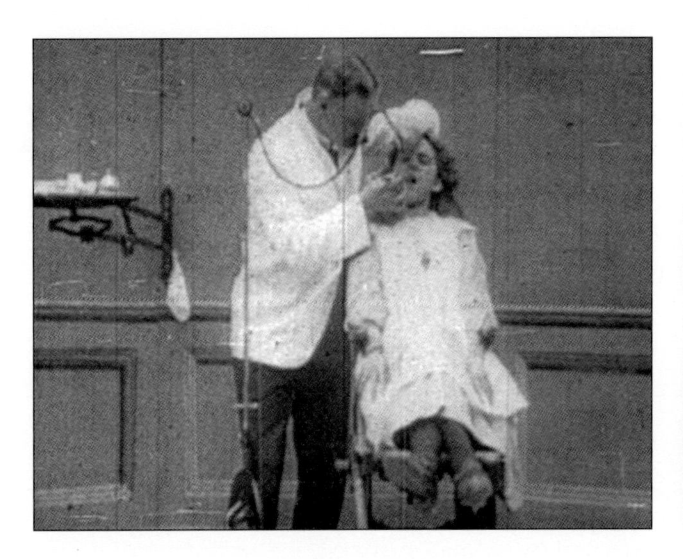

"Came the Dawn".

Abbey Gate Street, Bury St Edmunds. This shot was tinted blue.

died in 1952, and a year later Ampthill House was demolished and an estate built on the site.

In Cambridge at this time was a dentist, an unusual dentist by all accounts, for he was a pioneer of preventive dentistry, and founder of the Children's Dental League. This was Dr George Cunningham, who had a practice at No 2, Kings Parade, Cambridge. In 1912 he made a short 35mm film about how to look after your teeth. This begins by showing children going to the dentist (this was shot outdoors for light, and the wind blows the girls dress about as she sits in the dentist's chair), the importance of breast feeding, the wrong and right type of toothbrush to use, and an acted sequence of men being turned down for recruitment by an army officer because their teeth are bad. After examining four recruits the officer selects a person who has good teeth. There is also a sequence of scouts with a blackboard stating "Children's Dental League, Fit For Cambridgeshire Boy Scouts". Dr Cunningham gave lectures illustrated with lantern slides and his film, and founded a toothbrush school in Sweden. He died in 1919 just as he was about to depart for Germany to teach oral hygiene to the Army of Occupation of the Rhine. About 1960 the British Dental Association restored this film, put new titles on, and added a piano sound track. It is this version called "**Came The Dawn**" that exists today.

Censorship of films in this country was introduced at the end of 1912. Harold Brown, the National Film Archive's first Preservation Officer, states in his "Film Identification By Film Examination" compiled for the FIAF (Federation of International Film Archives) Congress in Berlin in 1967, that during 1913, the first year of the British Board of Film Censors, the President was Mr. G. A. Redford. Therefore if his name is on the certificate, then the film was released in 1913. From 1914 the President was Mr. T. P. O'Connor. From then on the only way of dating a film by the certificate is by the address of the organisation, as they changed locations several times. From 1913 to 1920 they were at 75-77 Shaftsbury Avenue, from 1920 – 1925, 167 Wardour Street, from 1925-1935, 80 Wardour Street, from 1935-1941, Carlisle House, from 1941-1945, 31 Soho Square, from 1945-1948, 113 Wardour Street, from 1948-1952 113 Oxford Street, and from 1952 at No 3, Soho Square.

A film entitled "**Bury St Edmunds**" has an original certificate at the beginning, and G. A. Redford's signature is there, so this dates the film as 1913. This film, possibly shot by Ronald Bates, has an Isle of Man symbol within the inter-titles which is the trade mark of the distributor. The film has various shots of the town, which shows wide streets virtually uninhabited by traffic. There is the occasional pedestrian, cyclists and horse drawn carts – and one car. The film shots are tinted. Tinting was common in the silent film days as it relieved the monotony of black and white. In fictional films tinting added to the emotional impact of the film, as well as highlighting particular scenes, such as blue or green seas, red fires and blue moonlight. At

*"**Pheasant Shooting**" 1913.*

*"**Meet of The Oakley Hunt**" at St Peters Green, Bedford.*

this time tinting was achieved by dipping the shots to be coloured into baths of dye, then joining the shots up in the right order to form the final print. In the film of Bury St Edmunds, tinting is used arbitrarily to colour individual shots. These shots include the Town Hall, the Butter Market, Moyses Hall, the Abbey Ruins, Abbey Bridge, Abbey Gate, Abbey Gate Street, and others. Although the film is only five minutes long, it is a record in static shots of a town in a different age. This 'travelogue' was available to any exhibitor to show, along with similar films of towns and cities in the kingdom listed in the film trade magazines of the time.

The national newsreels, Pathe, Gaumont, and the like, sometimes used to add a local story to their newsreel for showing in an area only. This would be spliced into the prints going to a town for instance. It is quite difficult to know if a story was shown thus, or actually shown nationwide. Several stories survive around 1913, including "**Ipswich Baby Show**", a sequence filmed on the steps of the Town Hall in Ipswich showing women proudly holding their babies. Look closely, and they are all twins!

"**Pheasant Shooting – Excellent sport at the opening of the season on a Norfolk Preserve**" gives us no idea where in the county this was filmed. The short film shows a shooting party on a big estate somewhere, with a lady shooting, then a man firing almost continuously, as his loader works feverishly to reload his other gun, and finally the 'bag' of pheasants laid out on the ground for all to see, with a line of dead birds that stretches beyond the view of the camera. At Felixstowe another short newsreel item showing country pursuits is titled "**Felixstowe Beagles**", and shows "an eventful day's sport after finding the scent an exciting run follows", but unfortunately the action is really too far away from the camera to tell us much, though we do see the beagles scurrying under a gate falling over one another in their excitement. At Bedford about this time comes another rural story, though this time it is in the town. "**Meet of The Oakley Hunt At St. Peters Green**" is just that, horses and hounds on the green next to the statue of John Bunyan, with many Bedfordians enjoying the excitement in their town, and also hoping to be filmed no doubt so they could see themselves on

*"**Ipswich Baby Show**" 1913.*

*One of the participants of the "**Ipswich Swimming Race**" is greeted by fellow members of the Ipswich Swimming Club.*

*The damaged house in Brooks Hall Road from "**Ipswich Air Raid – The Damage Caused by the Zeppelin Visit Over Ipswich**".*

the cinema screen, as this was a local newsreel for one of the town's cinemas.

In Ipswich a four-minute film of "**Ipswich Swimming Race**" in 1913 down the River Gipping at Ipswich, for the Bulstrode Cup, shows us members of the Ipswich Swimming Club demonstrating various styles of swimming, including the now obsolete trudgeon stroke. They swam from the West End Bathing Place, under Princes Street Bridge near the station, down the New Cut and past the docks, finishing at Stoke Bathing Place.

The Cinema Palace in Magdalen Street, Norwich, which was opened on October 31st 1912, arranged for a cameraman to record the "**Norwich City versus Leicester**" football match which took place on January 16th 1913. This away match was a second attempt following the first match on January 11th which had to be abandoned because of a severe snowstorm. Coverage was difficult with the heavy wooden hand-turned cameras on tripods, and what with the cold weather - there is snow lying on the pitch - the cameraman was lucky to record a goal. Norwich did well, winning 4:1. They were however knocked out of this F.A. Cup in the next round when they played Bristol Rovers. Seeing their local team on the big screen beating Leicester must have been very exciting for those Norwich supporters who did not make it to Leicester to witness the match.

At Colchester on October 3rd 1914 David Ager, the owner of the Vaudeville Cinema in Mersea Road, either filmed himself or got someone to do it for him, the children attending that day's matinee performance. Some children are lined up for the camera, with the commissionaires in their uniforms posing as well, others are seen as the camera pans along the queues which stretch towards St Botolphs.

The Vaudeville was opened in 1911, and was Colchester's first purpose built cinema. It was later called the Empire. It was managed by David Ager, who built up a circuit of cinemas including ones at Sudbury (The Gainsborough) and Woodbridge, as well as The Regal and The Headgate in Colchester. The Vaudeville closed in May 1959, and according to Stephen Peart in his book "The Picture House in East Anglia", it was used for a short while as a furniture store before being demolished in 1971 to make way for a new roundabout.

The film "**Children's Matinee**" was not shot just for David Ager's amusement, but as a sound commercial judgement. Filming dozens of children, so that you could see their faces, meant they would come to the cinema to see themselves on the big screen the next day or so when the film would have been shown, probably bringing their parents along as well. David Ager was anxious to get as many people as possible into his cinema, and this was a good way to do it. The film is a

*The queue for the "**Children's Matinee**" at the Vaudeville Picture Palace.*

record of people of the time, as well as of the cinema frontage, as we can see the film posters on the walls, including one advertising a newsreel about the Occupation of Louvain by the Germans – the beginnings of the First World War.

At first the war had little impact on those living in the East of England, but in January 1915 all that was to change. The Zeppelin airships were huge, over 500ft long, and moved slowly through the skies – even though they could travel at nearly 50 miles per hour. The first raid was on January 19th 1915, when Zeppelins L3 and L4 dropped incendiary bombs on Yarmouth, Sheringham and Kings Lynn. Four people were killed and sixteen injured. On April 30th a Zeppelin dropped incendiaries on Ipswich. One landed on a house in Brooks Hall Road, and set it alight. A Topical Budget (a screen newsreel company that had been going since 1911) cameraman soon came up to film, but the fire was out so all that is seen is the burnt remains of the houses. The film, "**Ipswich Air Raid – The Damage Caused by the Zeppelin Visit Over Ipswich**" shows a crowd gathered round No 60, 'Rosebery Villas', and Superintendent Galloway of the Fire Brigade holding up the remains of the incendiary bomb. This was a conical metal canister wound round with tarred rope. These were set alight and simply dropped over the side of the airship. The Zeppelin went on to bomb Bury St Edmunds, and a similar incident occurred at Colchester which was also filmed, though again well after the event.

In Hertfordshire a short newsreel film records "**Zeppelin Shot Down Over Cuffley**". More correctly an army Schutte-Lanz airship, this SL-11 airship, on her way to bomb London, was shot down on September 3rd 1916 by Lieutenant Leefe Robinson. Scenes show the mangled wreckage and soldiers clearing up the mess. On September 9th Topical Budget covered "**The Funeral of The Crew of The Zeppelin Shot Down Over Cuffley**" with scenes of officers of the RFC (Royal Flying Corps) carrying coffins in Potters Bar Cemetery. Six coffins are laid in one grave, and officers and men salute.

On September 24th 1916, at Little Wigborough, on the Essex coast by the Blackwater estuary, Zeppelin L33, following damage by anti aircraft shells, came down intact across the lane that led to the church. The crew set fire to the airship, and walked up the lane. There they were met by special constable Edgar Nichols on his bike. He arrested the men, and took them to Peldon Post Office. Sergeant Edwards of the Metropolitan Police, off duty at the time, took charge of the situation and marched the men through Peldon towards Mersea Island, where armed officers then took the men to West Mersea Church Hall. They were later taken to Colchester. Several of the men, it is said, were wearing the Iron Cross, and one knew his way around as he had once worked in Colchester. There is a story that as they were coming down the lane at Little Wigborough a local inhabitant quickly hid his home made wine, as he did not want that falling into enemy hands.

L33 was new, having been built in July that year. She was 680ft long, had four gondolas suspended underneath, six 240 horse power engines, could travel in favourable conditions at 60 miles per hour, and could carry sixty bombs. The remains of this once 50 ton airship were cut up, one piece of the lightweight aluminium alloy frame being kept for display in Little Wigborough Church –where it can still be seen. The full story of the Wigborough incident, and others of the time, is told, with many people who were there at the time, in a BBC Television East documentary entitled "**Zeppelins**" made by Douglas Salmon in 1972.

*Jumping from a window during practice of the "**Ladies Fire Brigade**".*

A variety of horse drawn conveyances take workers to Theydon Bois in 1916.

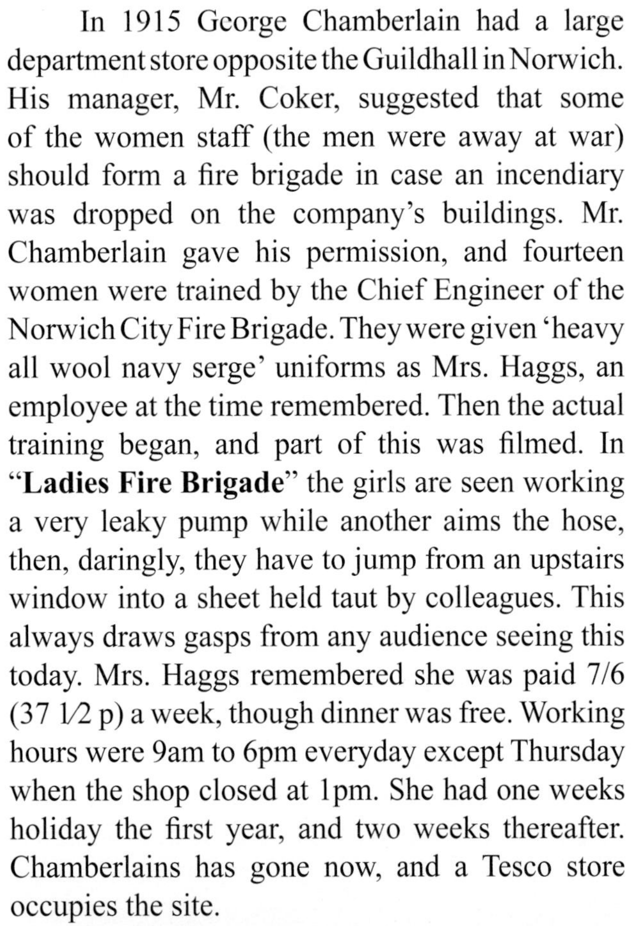

In 1915 George Chamberlain had a large department store opposite the Guildhall in Norwich. His manager, Mr. Coker, suggested that some of the women staff (the men were away at war) should form a fire brigade in case an incendiary was dropped on the company's buildings. Mr. Chamberlain gave his permission, and fourteen women were trained by the Chief Engineer of the Norwich City Fire Brigade. They were given 'heavy all wool navy serge' uniforms as Mrs. Haggs, an employee at the time remembered. Then the actual training began, and part of this was filmed. In "**Ladies Fire Brigade**" the girls are seen working a very leaky pump while another aims the hose, then, daringly, they have to jump from an upstairs window into a sheet held taut by colleagues. This always draws gasps from any audience seeing this today. Mrs. Haggs remembered she was paid 7/6 (37 1/2 p) a week, though dinner was free. Working hours were 9am to 6pm everyday except Thursday when the shop closed at 1pm. She had one weeks holiday the first year, and two weeks thereafter. Chamberlains has gone now, and a Tesco store occupies the site.

In the East End of London, where life was probably harder, it would have been a welcome treat when workers were taken on a day's outing to Epping Forest. Workers from Messrs F. Sunderland and J. Coulthard are seen travelling in a variety of horse drawn waggons for a day out at Theydon Bois and Epping Forest. Another part of "**Epping Outing**" of 1916 shows a train, also loaded with workers, leaving a station, followed by everyone having a wonderful time at one of the retreats in the forest. Here there are fairground rides, races, and an alarming contraption of people, mostly ladies, riding down a rope by gravity. A clergyman appears throughout the film, and is seen also in another film of 1916 where "**Children With Father Christmas**" are seen being given presents, so there is some connection between the two films. There is also "**East End Gramophone**", a third part of this early film collection all found in the attic of a house in Essex, which appears to be an unedited fiction film. Viewed together, these three films give an idea of what life was like and how people enjoyed themselves, and that some of the children appear to have no shoes.

These films are professionally made by cameramen who could be hired to shoot whatever you wanted. Gaumont offered this service, and were particularly busy with this type of work. An account says "Their price is reasonable, and it is well known that speed is one of their strong points, though quality is never forgotten. There are many exhibitors who do not yet realise the value of a local film, they would do well to try the experiment and entrust the work to Gaumont".

Perhaps Mr. J. A. Campbell saw this write up, for if so, it gave him an idea, a family film. Jack Campbell had opened the Picture House in Grantham in Lincolnshire on February 12th 1916. Three months later his daughter, June Mary was born. On her first birthday he wheeled her out

"The Golden Wedding of Mr. and Mrs. William Gamble of Runcton House".

"Women Hay Makers" at Warden's Hall Farm, Willingale.

into the garden of his home and had her filmed. "**Baby's Birthday Party**" is a record of the little girl's birthday, with her elder brother John giving her presents. This could be classed as a home movie, for he no doubt showed it to the family in the cinema, as the film was shot on 35mm. He might well have even included it in a show with a paying audience present. The interesting part of this story is that the little girl then became an actress – Judy Campbell. She used for her stage name Judy instead of June, and acted in plays by some of the greatest twentieth century playwrights such as George Bernard Shaw, Eugene O'Neill, Arthur Miller and Noel Coward, sang "A Nightingale Sang in Berkeley Square" in 'New Faces' revue, and starred in numerous films including "Convoy" with Clive Brook in 1940. She continued to work in the theatre and films, as well as television until 2003. In 1943 she married Lieutenant Commander David Birkin, and they had three children, one of whom became an actress – Jane Birkin. Judy Campbell died in June 2004.

The story does not end there, as Judy Campbell's grandfather was William Gamble (her father's name was really Jack Gamble, but he used the name Campbell instead) a livestock farmer and cattle dealer at Home Farm, North Runcton, near Kings Lynn. On July 1st 1919, William Gamble and his wife Anna celebrated their golden wedding at North Runcton, and their son Jack arranged for the occasion to be filmed. "**The Golden Wedding of Mr. and Mrs. William Gamble of Runcton House**" was made, and showed their extensive family including thirteen children (they had had sixteen in all), and thirty eight grand children. Sixty people attended altogether, and the Gambles received congratulations from King George V. The film, like many 35mm celluloid films, did not keep well, and most of it decomposed. However the first few scenes did survive, and have been preserved as a record of this occasion. Adults and children are seen around the garden at Runcton House, all dressed in their best clothes for the occasion. Judy must have been there as one of the thirty eight grandchildren, though she was only three at the time. William Gamble died aged 78 in 1921.

"**Women Hay Makers**" and "**Serving Their Country**" are two newsreel clips showing what was happening down on the farm, though more importantly, women helping the war effort. Filmed in June 1916 at Warden's Hall Farm, Willingale in Essex, the first shows women at work on the hay harvest, the second "The horse which was wounded in the battle of Loos, still doing his bit for the country, helping the women working on an Essex farm". This was not an organised land army of which we are familiar in the Second World War, but an initiative of the daughter-in-law of Field Marshal Sir Evelyn Wood.

It was in 1913 that the Admiralty said there were to be naval air stations on the east coast at Yarmouth and Felixstowe. Felixstowe Air Station as it became known, was constructed on the spit of land running out to Languard Fort and was

*An operational flying boat No 4434 believed to be a Felixstowe F.2A from the 1918 film "**Seaplanes**".*

*Newsreel shots of U-boats moored in the River Stour, from "**Q Ships**", made in 1928.*

codenamed Seaplanes Felixstowe. The base grew rapidly after 1914, and the sheltered waters of Harwich harbour were ideal for seaplane tests. In 1918 an official film was made, probably to show top brass in London what was happening at the Felixstowe base, showing "Short S.P. Seaworthiness Trials" and a PV5 seaplane manoeuvring amongst the sailing barges and larger ships, and taking off. A larger flying boat is brought out of a hanger, which also takes off. The wooden built planes seem flimsy and vulnerable, but played a big part during the 1914-18 war, particularly with the menace of the Zeppelins.

Another record of flying boats at "**Felixstowe Air Base**" was taken by an amateur cameraman in 1935, and is a useful guide to compare how things were developing at the base.

When the armistice was announced on November 10th 1918, there was great jubilation that evening, particularly in Harwich, where ships and boats sounded their sirens and hooters, and Verey lights and rockets lit up the sky. Ten days later the first of the German U-boat Fleet arrived off Harwich and surrendered to Admiral Tyrwhitt along with a German transport ship. It was a calm misty day when a newsreel cameraman filmed "**Surrender of U-boats - Admiral Tyrwhitt's cruiser squadron takes over the German pirate craft**"," for cinema audiences. There are shots of U-boats, an airship hovering overhead, nervous German crews on deck, and British sailors looking after them. Only a handful of U-boats arrived that day, but as part of the armistice agreement, all German submarines were to head to Harwich, and by the beginning of December 122 had been handed over. The U-boats were moored in the River Stour in what became known as 'U-Boat Avenue'. Over a period of time engines were taken out, and the boats dismantled for scrap. In 1928 a silent feature film called "**Q Ships**" was made telling the story of British warships disguised as merchant ships used in the war to combat U-boats. At the end of this film there is a summing up of the 1914-18 war, with scenes of the German U-boats moored in the River Stour.

George Swain was a young photographer working in Norwich alongside his father, also a photographer who had a photographic business in St Giles Street, Norwich. Both were busy on May 15th 1919 when the body of Edith Cavell was brought back to Norwich.

Edith Cavell (pronounced as in travel) was the daughter of the vicar of Swardeston, and was born in 1865. She worked as a governess before taking up nursing at the age of 30. She worked in the slums of London before moving to Belgium where she started a nursing school. At the time Belgium was overrun with Germans and in 1914 Edith Cavell was matron of a hospital in Brussels. She was offered the chance to leave and return to England, but refused, continuing to help wounded soldiers. She worked secretly to get Belgian, French and British soldiers out of occupied territory, knowing the possible consequences. She was arrested by the Germans, tried by court martial, and shot on October 12th 1915.

After the war her body was brought back to this country, travelling first to London where there was a service in Westminster Abbey, then on to Norwich. It is said people lined the railway track from London to Norwich in silent tribute. The young George Swain was charged with making a film that day of May 15th 1919 for showing in a Norwich cinema. "**Edith Cavell's Funeral**" has survived un-cut, that is it is just as George shot it. There is no title. It shows the coffin being removed from the gun carriage on which it had been conveyed from Norwich Thorpe Station and carried by soldiers, one of whom was Jessie Tunmore of the Norfolk Regiment, who had been with Edith Cavell at the Brussels clinic. In the background is a photographer at work. It is George's father. The procession following is of nurses, nuns, war wounded, the Lord Mayor, and dignitaries. As they emerge from a side door of Norwich Cathedral we see the huge number of people attending that day. Some have climbed trees and a lamp post to get a view as the procession makes its way to Life's Green, close to the south east side of the Cathedral. It is almost impossible to see the coffin at the grave for the dense crowd. In 1979 Douglas Salmon made a programme called "**Past Positive**" for BBC East in which George Swain remembers that day in 1919, and shows, by stopping the original film and zooming in, his father taking a photograph.

There was, even before the funeral, a memorial to Edith Cavell in Norwich on Tombland, just outside the Cathedral gate. It was on October 12th 1918, that Queen Alexandra visited Norwich to open the Cavell Memorial Nurses Home, and unveil this memorial which stood in front of the Maid's Head Hotel. This was filmed by a London newsreel company, is quite short and titled simply "**Queen Alexandra in Norwich**". The Eastern Daily Press was moved to write "For the sake of local and historical interest the film being shown at the Prince of Wales Palace, recording the visit of Queen Alexandra to Norwich ought to be preserved for as long a time as such things are capable of preserving. Presumably there is some authority charged with the duty of keeping historical films in hermetical safety. If not, there ought to be". Strangely this was the very time moves were afoot to set up an archive of film of the 1914-1918 war, which eventually became the Imperial War Museum's Film and Video Archive, though this film was not in it. It may be that this film, shown at the Prince of Wales Theatre was another local record, which has since become lost. The memorial on Tombland has since been moved from its position in the middle of a busy road to a site beside the Erpingham Gate. A regular annual duty for buglers from the Royal Norfolk Regiment depot at Britannia Barracks was to sound Last Post and Reveille at the memorial service at Edith Cavell's grave on Life's Green. This was often filmed and appears in a number of films such as "**A Fine City Norwich**".

After the conflict had ceased, as recognition of their contributions to the war effort, and as a memorial, some towns were given a tank brought back from France. "**Presentation of Tank**" to Chelmsford is a short film record made on Saturday November 8th 1919, and shows soldiers and a tank proceeding along a street in the town. Then members of the public inspect it. This film, commissioned by the manager, Mr. Starkey, of the Regent Theatre in Moulsham Street, Chelmsford, is the only reminder that this happened at all, for this tank, and others that were presented to towns across the country, were melted down in 1939 towards a new war effort. More moving is a film made up entirely of still photographs of those who died or were injured from the Braintree area. "**Roll of Honour**" was made for showing in the Palace Cinema in Fairfield

*Braintree Boys from "**Roll of Honour**" 1919.*

George Woods-Taylor experimented with ultra rapid cinematography producing slow motion films, colour films, and was official film maker during the Prince of Wales Tour of India in 1922.

Road in 1919, and lists each man's details. For those that did come home, new houses were built by the local firm of Crittalls. "**Homes Fit For Heroes**" shows these houses under construction in Cressing Road.

Amateur movies were yet to come, but in 1919 George Woods-Taylor made what was probably one of the first 'baby on the lawn' home movies. However, he knew what he was doing, as he was a professional film cameraman. George Woods-Taylor began as a press photographer on Fleet Street, then joined the Topical Film Company and was news editor and occasional cameraman from 1911. He took the first film of British troops arriving in France, and was 'Official Kinematographer War Office Experimental Department at Shoeburyness.

George Woods-Taylor met Lillian Oxley at a school in Bow, East London, where she was a teacher. He had permission from the LCC to take some still pictures of children in a class Lillian was taking where she was teaching them about the 1910 census. She was furious with this intrusion, and George made amends by making a large photograph of the census form to help in her teaching. They were married on March 1st 1919. Their wedding photograph is at the beginning of a film George made of their son also called George, but subsequently known as Bobbie, who was born in 1920. "**Bobbie Grows Up**" begins with a still picture of the new baby, then film of him having a bath at eight weeks old. He is filmed at intervals - twelve months, eighteen months and so on. Now Bobbie is walking and playing in the garden, and is filmed with his parents. Later a sister arrives, Betty, and over the next few years we see the two children and their parents having fun at the family home in Thorpe Bay, Southend.

Because George Woods-Taylor senior was a skilled cameraman and film maker, the film is well shot with inter-titles introducing each section. At the end of the film is a shot from the wedding of Phil Ross, a colleague in British Filmcraft, a company based at Walthamstow, and a scene from a period drama Woods-Taylor worked on. "Bobbie Grows Up" was shown on a hand turned projector at home, and luckily survived to be copied on to modern film stock, and preserved as an early example of what was to come – home movies.

*George, known as Bobbie, from "**Bobbie Grows Up**".*

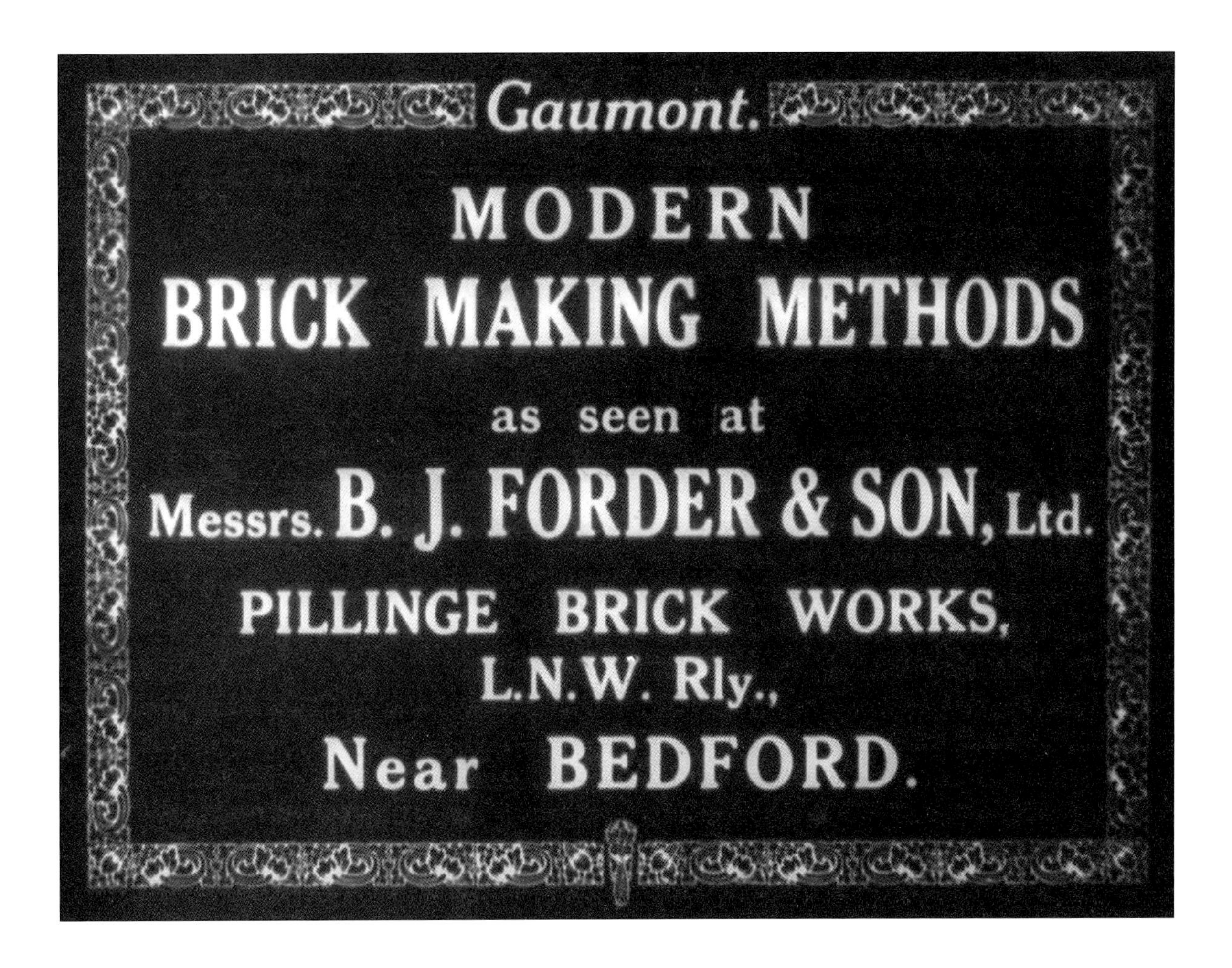

Industry

The eight minute advertising film "**Modern Brick Making Methods**" was made in 1921, and as the title says, was made at B. J. Forder and Son Ltd brickworks just outside Bedford. B. J. Harfield Forder opened the brickworks here about 1897, taking advantage of the rich belt of Oxford clay. Here they had an excavator working on the 50ft face of the shale in the clay pit. This giant machine had a 3 ton bucket which scooped the clay at a rate of 200,000 tons a year. The clay was loaded into trucks, which with an endless chain system, was conveyed back to the factory. The chain laid over the truck dragging it along. The bricks were made in automatic pressing machines, each of which turned out 22 bricks per minute. The 'green' bricks were loaded into the kiln and fired.

Although there are a lot of men seen in the film, the process was semi automatic. The battery of presses was powered by two 350BPH twin cylinder gas engines, which are seen in the film along with the process of making the bricks. The works had a canteen, and men are seen coming out of this strange brick structure. The bricks were sent away by train, as the works was next to the London and North West Railway, with one train of trucks a day holding about 250,000 bricks - enough to build fourteen houses. A caption at the end of the film states "Sixty million bricks were made at this works last year, sufficient to build over 3,000 houses".

Stewartby is a brick village in more ways than one. Here was a large village hall, social club, and sports institute, and of course houses, all built of brick by the London Brick Company. Stewartby was named after Sir Halley Stewart, a partner in Forders, and one of the businessmen involved in bringing together the various brick making companies in the area in the late 1920s. By 1936 they traded as the London Brick Company Ltd. The model village of Stewartby was the result of the success of the organisation, and had a population of 900 in 1938, nearly all of whom worked at the brick company's works close by. The film "**The Making of Bricks**" shows the full process at the site in 1938, from the huge walking draglines scraping the clay and feeding it to the works, the automatic brick making processes, the kilns, to the final bricks being taken by lorry to building sites.

"**The Making of Bricks**" was produced for the company on 16mm, unusual at the time as 16mm was not really considered a professional film making system until wartime. The gauge of film was more for amateurs and the distribution of cinema and other 35mm originated productions. As a contrast to the huge brickworks at Stewartby, the film shows a small brick and tile works at West Runton on the Norfolk coast. Here, at the works of Gunton and Sons, there was a small bottle shaped kiln. Most work was carried out in the open, everything being done by manual labour. This is a fine example of the working of a small local brick making works, which many a town and village had at one time.

"**Brick Making By Hand**" was made for use in Essex classrooms in the 1950s by Richard Pike. Hand made bricks are also shown being made at the works of W. H. Collier Ltd of Marks Tey in Essex. This short sequence shows the clay pit, the industrial small gauge railway hauling the clay to the works, the pug mill, and a brick maker at work using a mould which produced three bricks at a time. This was filmed in colour in 1981, and is incorporated in "**Industrial Archaeology in East Anglia**".

In 1920 the old established firm of Spicer Brothers had made the film "**Spicer Brothers Ltd, Paper Making at Sawston Mills**". It was in 1917 they bought a paper making business at Sawston, near Cambridge, to supplement their growing business. Spicers already had a factory at Eynsford in Kent, and had origins in paper making as far back as 1796 when the founder of the company, John Spicer, went into the paper making business at Alton Mill in Hampshire. According to Ian Ormes's 1997 book "From Rags To Roms: A History of Spicers", a new paper making machine was installed in the factory at Sawston, the site was quickly expanded with the purchase of more land from the Whittlesford estate, and stationery manufacturing was moved from a London works to the Cambridgeshire site. The 1920 film, though short, is a wonderful insight into factory conditions, though the smells and noise of machinery in the paper making process can only be guessed at. The film inter-titles tell of the processes involved in making paper from rags - 'Rag Sorting', 'Rag Cutting', 'Washing and Breaking The Pulp', 'Beating Machines', 'Waste Paper Pulper', 'Drying', 'Cutting Machines', and 'Sorting and Packing'. A small army of women,

*The endless chain drawing a truck of clay to the brick making works. From "**Modern Brick Making Methods**".*

*Boys working in the paper making factory at Sawston from "**Spicer Brothers Ltd, Paper Making at Sawston Mills**".*

*Making punnets in a Wisbech factory from "**Electrics, Local Pictures and The Mart**" 1926.*

*Workers coming out of Burrall Brothers, from "**Electrics, Local Pictures and The Mart**" 1926.*

many wearing large hats, are seen feverously at work, and young boys sit sorting paper at a large cutting machine. The film goes on to show 'Paper making by hand' at their Eynsford Mills factory in Kent, as well as envelope making.

In the 1960s and onwards, other films were used by the company, such as "**Winning Game**" and "**Paper**", and a number of selling and marketing films saved by Bob Rayner who worked for Spicers. Spicers is still there in the 21st century on the Sawston site, though owned by another company. They are the biggest wholesaler of general office products in Europe.

Paper making of a different sort is featured in a Pathe Pictorial item of 1967. "**Dunstable Paper Factory**" shows in colour the making of paper plates and table cloths at Headly and Company Ltd. factory in Southfields Road. Finally a couple are seen eating fish and chips off the paper plates.

There were three cinemas in Wisbech in the mid 1920s, the Electric, the Hippodrome Picture Palace, and The Alexandra Theatre, and one of them had a film made of local scenes in 1926. As the film is called "**Electrics, Local Pictures and The Mart**", it was probably made for showing in the Electric Theatre in Norfolk Street belonging to Mr. Frederick Cooper, who went on to command a chain of eleven cinemas in the region. The film shows the streets and shops of Wisbech, some taken from the back of a moving vehicle. Here is Wisbech life – cyclists, pedestrians, prams, handcarts, horse and carts, people shopping, a legless man on the pavement, a policeman, market traders, and the visiting fair. The interior of a factory, Burrall Brothers, makers of 'self fastening labels' is seen with hatted women at work. Outside the factory at knocking off time, the workers come out passing the cameraman, some reacting to the camera, some ignoring it completely. There are women walking, and men pushing bicycles. Finally there is a football match – believed to be Wisbech Town playing Lynn St Nicholas. There are two versions of this film, the best being the fine quality of the 35mm copy found by local historian Mr. Maxey.

"**Thomas Peatling and Son**", 'wine, spirit, ale and porter merchants', had a business at 9 Old Market, Wisbech, but it is a film of their bonded warehouse on Purfleet Quay at King's Lynn which features in a short advertising film of the late 1920s. Here is the wine and whiskey bottling plant, where bottles are filled manually (and slowly) by holding them close to the cask tap. An operator then works a simple machine to insert the cork. The bottles are then wrapped in paper. There is a close shot of one of their brands – 'Johncup' whiskey.

Thomas Peatling and Son were agents for Greene King ales, produced by that company at Bury St Edmunds. Greene King also had a film made of their works in 1929. Barley arrives by horse drawn waggon, huge sacks of hops are lifted easily by one man, large vats extrude steam, barrels are sealed, and bottles rattle along past women in the bottling plant. The variety of motor vehicles operated by Greene King drive past the camera,

*"**Thomas Peatling and Son**" of Kings Lynn.*

and the brewery's fire engine demonstrates its speed amongst a cloud of smoke. The film shows off the company's amenities – the cricket ground with what seem like two executives going out to play, and the swimming bath for employees.

Years ago there were many small breweries in the region, and one of these was at Ditchingham in Norfolk. "**Crowfoots Brewery**" is a short advertsing film made for use in local cinemas, and shows the interior of their premises with the bottling machine, and outside two motor lorries, one coming straight towards the camera. A crate of drink is delivered to a house, and the final caption says 'Crowfoot beers made from Norfolk malt and best Kent hops, in fact they are, without any doubt, 'the beers without a rival'. Well, there was a rival, Adnams Brewery, situated right in the middle of Southwold, seen briefly in 1981 before modernisation in "**Industrial Archaeology in East Anglia**", and the Adnams film collection consisting of "**A Local life – The Pub**", "**I Know What I Like**" and "**What'll You Have?**" exist in the East Anglian Film Archive.

Every town had its industries, and many companies had films made promoting or advertising their products or services. Films often had a short life – the products becoming out of date, or the company changing hands, being absorbed into larger organisations, or simply going bust. Some films have survived, some have not. Ipswich seems to have a remarkable number of companies whose film records have found their way into archives.

A scene of "**Cornhill**", the very centre of Ipswich, shows a busy thoroughfare in 1929, with trolley buses coming and going. From a high viewpoint the pedestrians, motor cars and bicycles weave in and out of the trolley bus traffic. In the middle of Cornhill is the Boer War memorial, which was later moved to Christchurch Park. The trolley buses collected their power from overhead wires, and the connecting pickup had to be manually positioned on to the wires by a man with

*East Anglian barley arrives at the Greene King brewery. From "**Green King's Brewery**" 1929.*

The bottling plant at the Greene King brewery in Bury St Edmunds in 1929.

Ipswich Cornhill, with trolley buses and the Boer War memorial.

A trolley bus in Tavern Street, Ipswich, in 1933.

a long insulated pole. There were two companies in Suffolk making these 'trackless vehicles' as they were known (there were no rails in the road like there were with trams) Garrett's of Leiston and Ransomes in Ipswich. "**Trolley Bus Advertising**" shows the manoeuvrability of Garrret's trolley buses on test in Doncaster about 1928, and "**The Construction of a Modern Electric Trolley Bus**" shows Ransomes versions being made in their works in Ipswich. This is a very detailed silent 16mm film with inter-titles explaining every aspect of construction. The frames are assembled, and the heavy pneumatic tyred wheels put on. Women wind coils, armatures are made and tested, insulators attached. The assembled trolley without a body is taken out of the factory and tested on the roads. At the works of Weyman Motor Bodies craftsmen build on the bodywork, and again the trolleys are tested.

"**Street Scenes**" in Ipswich in 1934 and 1935 show single deck trolley buses in Princes Street, Tavern Street, and Fore Street – where even at that time, there was a traffic jam, the trolleys trying to get past vehicles without the poles coming off the overhead wires. Ransomes trolley buses were sold all over the world (fifty went to Cape Town) and an adverting film shows "**Ransome Electric Trolley Buses in Leige**". Trolley buses ran in Ipswich for 40 years, ending in 1963. Anglia television made "**Last Trolley Bus Interview**" with reporter Chris Kelly talking to one of the drivers, and David Chappell made an 8mm record called "**End of an Era**". That is not the end of bus films in Ipswich, for there is "**The British Trolley Bus Scene**" made in 1960, and "**A Century of Transport**" which traces the history from the first horse drawn trams to the latest Atlantean motor buses of 1980. A humorous home movie made by the busmen themselves shows in speeded up motion how quickly you could get to Felixstowe in "**Its Quicker by Bus**", - in fact right into the sea!

But Ransomes was not all about trolley buses - agricultural equipment was the mainstay of this old established company. Robert Ransome set up a foundry in Old Foundry Road, then called St Margaret's Ditches, in 1789. Here he met the needs of the farmers with agricultural machinery. His most important discovery, in 1803, was that of the process of chilling cast iron plough shares, which hardened the underside of the share, making it last much longer, and at the same time making it self sharpening as the softer top part wore away as it went through the earth. In 1832 they introduced the first lawn mower, a diversification that was to be a winner with the company. Ransomes outgrew its premises, and in 1841 moved to a site close to the river, calling the factory Orwell Works. The expansion of the railways in the 1840s brought another lucrative side to their business, but agricultural equipment was still their main work. They were making threshing machines, steam engines, numerous small items of farm machinery, and over eighty different types of plough.

Known variously as partners came and went as Ransomes and May, Ransomes and Sims, and finally Ransome, Sims and Jeffries, there were always members of the Ransome family in there somewhere. In 1950 they had a film made of their plough department – "**Speed The Plough**". Men arrive at work, machines start up and the foundry begins pouring molten metal. The production lines for assembling ploughs, cultivators, disc harrows and potato lifters are seen in the Victorian atmosphere of Orwell Works. The construction of a heavy trailer plough is followed through in detail from the bending of the steel beam which forms the backbone of the plough to the paint shop, until the finished plough leaves the factory in gleaming condition.

Again the works was too small for the business, and by 1948 the company had another foundry and factory at Nacton, where amongst other things they made mounted reversible ploughs, a small tractor drawn combine, and the MG crawler tractor, so beloved by horticulturalist. In 1961 Don Chipperfield, their resident film maker, made "**Years of Achievement**", a 16mm colour sound film which not only traced to the company's history and its products, but explained that the company now employed over three thousand. The Nacton factory seen in the film is a hive of activity with noise from drop hammers, presses, casting, welding, grinding machines, and flame cutters. The film touches on the photographic and design departments, the apprenticeship schemes, and wood turning to make handles for lawn mowers, where women work alongside men on the factory floor.

Another film, "**All The Year Round**", shows the other end of all this work, the machinery in use. Cultivators, different types of ploughs, mole draining equipment, potato ridgers, and harrows – all working away in the fields of Great Britain. Made in 1962, this was updated in 1976 in a film called simply "**Ransomes**". Anglia Television made a half hour programme about the company in 1970 called "**Cast Iron Gamble**" which looks at the history and development of Ransomes, including the work done by the firm in the 1939 -1945 war when the factory made armaments.

"**The Big Spring Push**" is a short novelty cinema item of 1926, showing Ransome lawn mowers being assembled at the works and wheeled from the factory into the street. The final sequence shows a 'worms eye view' – a man's head looking out of the grass as a mower approaches. It was not just domestic mowers Ransomes made, but large motor driven gang mowers for parks, greens, golf courses and the like, for use all round the world. In 1959 "**East Anglian Coastline**" visited the many places where Ransome lawn mowers were at work on links, bowling greens, and sports grounds. "We begin our exploration of this sea-lashed coastline at King's Lynn on the Wash, where cockle gatherers are to be found busy in this vast area of sand and mud, over which the sea comes and goes for great distances. Along the coast road to Hunstanton, a seaside resort with miles of sand; gardens; golf courses and putting greens, and colourful chalk cliffs rising high above the Wash. It is not long before these cliffs give way to the wide beaches of North Norfolk. At Brancaster is one of the famous

All Ransomes films carried the Ransome logo. On the right is the variable density sound track of this 16mm colour film.

Don Chipperfield in his film editing room. He not only made advertising films for Ransomes, but also local record films .

golf courses, West Norfolk Club, its hazards laid out in the green grass….." and so it goes on - with lawn mowers at work. The seaside towns, their fishing activities and attractions are shown on this journey down to Harwich. Another film was made of a journey of a motorised lawn mower the length of England, as well as films like "**Keep On The Grass**". These were all made by Don Chipperfield for the company, including films covering other products, such as "**Electric Reach Trucks**", "**Crop Drier**", "**902 Combine**", "**Growing a Better Potato**", and "**Cropguard Sprayers**".

Don Chipperfield also made films for the social club of Ransomes, recording the sports and fun days. One of these, "**Ransomes Review No 2**" shows the employees taking part in events, with the fire brigade squirting water over everyone. Ransomes had their own fire engine at Orwell Works. In 1954 one of the regular exercises was filmed by Don. A fire is discovered in a corrugated iron shed. The alarm is raised and a succession of phone calls results in the workers leaving their workbenches, and rushing to get Ransomes own water tender out. They arrive at the scene (in the works on the other side of Duke Street in Ipswich) and reel out their hoses, connect up, and put the fire out. An inquest follows on the origin of the fire and a man brings out an oily rag. Everyone is satisfied this started the fire and back they go to their posts. A fun film with a message, "**Dial 369001**" was an early form of what we now know as a training video.

Don Chipperfield personally recorded changing Ipswich over a fifty year period. Anything interesting happening in the town, particularly the demolition of streets and buildings in the 1960s, was filmed in colour on 16mm. He seldom made them into complete films, but regularly showed the reels at evening meetings. The "**Don Chipperfield Collection**" is huge, with films covering a Salvation Army parade to the building of Civic Way, from the docks to trains, from the swimming baths to the building of the Orwell Bridge. Working wider afield, he recorded the excavation at West Stow in West Suffolk, where there was an Anglo Saxon village, and "**Wings for The Air Training Corps**" about gliding at Martlesham Heath airfield.

The demolition of Botwoods Garage in Ipswich. The Regent Theatre is on the right. A black and white still from a colour film in the Don Chipperfield collection of changing Ipswich.

In 1992 Don Chipperfield died. He bequeathed his film collection of personal films and his Ransomes productions to the East Anglian Film Archive. A year later a selection was taken from his films (and others) to make "**Don Chipperfield's Ipswich**", a compilation which was presented at the Ipswich Film Theatre for several showings to packed houses. Following this success, another compilation was presented by Bob Malster and David Cleveland in 1994. This included a trip down the River Orwell in the *Torbay Prince*, Ipswich airport, and the Wolsey Theatre under construction.

Don Chipperfield, in 1935, was a founder member of the Ipswich Film Society, which was among the first in the provinces. In 1956 he made for them a short funny recruiting film called "**Ipswich Film Society**", with the members acting out the comic scenes he devised. In 1977 Don Chipperfield was in charge of a number of local

Ransome and Rapier's colour sound film of their mobile crane. 1954.

*Testing the safety of a Rapier crane, from "**Rapier 6 & 7 Standard Mobile Cranes**".*

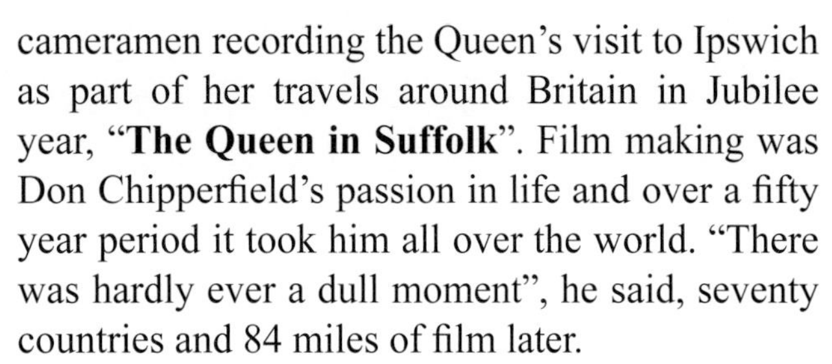

cameramen recording the Queen's visit to Ipswich as part of her travels around Britain in Jubilee year, "**The Queen in Suffolk**". Film making was Don Chipperfield's passion in life and over a fifty year period it took him all over the world. "There was hardly ever a dull moment", he said, seventy countries and 84 miles of film later.

Ransome and Rapier Ltd, another Ipswich firm with a history going back a long way, in this case to 1869, made heavy equipment for the railways, for water engineering schemes, and for earth excavation. The company was an offshoot of Ransomes, when J. A. Ransome, R. J. Ransome, R. C. Rapier, and A. A. Bennett left the company to establish Ransome and Rapier at Waterside Works on the opposite side of the river from the Orwell Works of Ransomes. In the 1950s Gilbert Hawker, at that time part of Boulton Hawker Films of Hadleigh in Suffolk, made a colour sound film of one of their products, the "**Rapier 6 & 7 Standard Mobile Cranes**". Shot in the works in 1954, this demonstrated the manoeuvrability and lifting power of Ransome and Rapiers mobile cranes which were selling well. "Rapier 6 & 7 Standard mobile cranes are to be found wherever large loads are to be handled. They have been supplied for industrial and public services in almost every country in the world. Many are to be found in goods yards, where they handle general merchandise quickly and easily including the largest fully loaded railway containers".

Shots of one of these diesel electric mobile cranes around the Ransome and Rapier Waterside Works show how it can lift a heavy load safely, how it can travel on uneven ground, and that "it is rather like driving a car, but simpler. There are no gears and no clutch" says the commentary. One test shows the stability of the crane if it is asked to lift a load that is too heavy. "The stability test shows the crane's inherent safety. An attempt to lift an excessive overload causes the driving wheels to leave the ground. The crane cannot be travelled, and the driver has ample time in which to stop hoisting". Another model is shown being driven around the streets of Ipswich. This is just one of a series of films that Gilbert Hawker made for the company over the years. Gilbert lived in Ipswich, and after leaving Boulton Hawker Films set up in business as a film maker. He made for Ransome and Rapier "**Rapier Truck Mixers**" in 1961. This is a lorry that constantly turns the load of concrete until it reaches the building site where the wet mixture is fed by pipe to the foundations of a building. Other films in the Ransome and Rapier collection include "**The Hydraulic Digger**", "**Walking Draglines**", "**Rapier Heavy Duty Fork Trucks**", "**Chains and Chain Driving**" and "**Couplings and Clutches**". They were agents for Koering cranes, and there are films of these in the collection.

Gilbert Hawker made a film of a different type of Ipswich industry in 1959, that of the printing of the '**Evening Star**" for the East Anglian Daily Times Co Ltd, at their works in Carr Street. This covers the physical process of producing a daily newspaper - collecting news and pictures, discussing advertisements with clients, selecting and preparing photographs, text being produced on the linotype machines, making the flong and castings, and loading into the rotary press. 35,000 copies are printed per hour, which then have to be bundled for distribution by vans and newspaper boys. This film shows the old 'hot metal' process of producing newspapers, a method that seems antiquated, demanding, labour intensive, and unhealthy by modern standards, but was the way of production for over a hundred years.

ER and F. Turner Ltd were 'milling and electrical engineers' with three sites in Ipswich – Greyfriars Works in Quadling Street, Foxhall Works in Foxhall Road, and St Peter's Iron Works in College Street. Yet another old Ipswich firm, being established in 1837, they specialised in flour milling machinery, grain silo equipment, grinding mills, and electric motors. An unknown film maker made a silent black and white 16mm record of their foundry in 1934, "**ER and F. Turner Flour Milling Engineers**", at their Foxhall Road works. Here they made parts for flour milling machinery, preparing the patterns, pouring molten metal, and testing the resulting castings for strength.

R and W Paul were maltsters with extensive buildings in Key Street, close to the quay. In the early 1960s they commissioned a film to be made not only to show their successful company, but also the way the handling of the malting process had changed over the years. In "**A Hundred Years of Malting**" all the manual labour of receiving barley in sacks, turning and raking the malt, and moving it around in large wheeled containers is depicted, alongside the more modern automated Van der Haufen malting system of the 1960s, where samples are taken throughout the process to insure consistency.

That is almost the end of filmed industries in Ipswich, except for one more – cigar manufacture. W. A. and A. C. Churchman, which was originally at Hyde Park Corner in London, expanded rapidly with the production of cigarettes which were rapidly becoming popular with the smoking public. New and larger premises were required, and the company took a long lease of a site at the junction of Portman Road and Princes Street and built a brand new factory in 1898. In 1902 the business was taken over by the Imperial Tobacco Company, but the Churchman brand remained. At the Ipswich works they made cigars, Grandee mini cigars, and cigarettes. Dennis Norden, comedy script writer and funny man, was employed in 1967 to write a script for a promotional film for Churchmans. He begins by noting that every where things were getting smaller – the 'mini' car, the Sinclair mini radio, a miniature television set, dogs, and mini skirts. At Churchmans in Ipswich he ditches his cigarette, and goes round the factory ogling the girls as he does so. The chief executive, a 'high churchman' as Norden calls him, Peter Eyres, dissects a large cigar, and explains all the intricacies and different types of products they make. The film is fun, with lots of jokes which are very much of the time – the late 1960s. The film, "**Revolutions For All**" won several awards, and was shown as a short in cinemas.

At Histon, near Cambridge, was the large factory of 'Chivers and Sons Ltd, Jam Manufactures'. In 1931 they had a sixty minute silent 35mm film made of their factory and products called "**From the Orchard to the Home**". At the time, the film was shown to invited audiences, with a representative of the firm talking by the side of the screen. It proudly showed off this famous and successful family firm and its products. Now it provides a valuable record of factory life and processes.

The Chivers family, fruit farmers in the middle of the 19th century, sent their produce to market as well as distributing it from their own

The title of an hour long 1931 film of Chivers jam factory at Histon in Cambridgeshire.

*The job of jam making begins at Chivers in 1931 in "**From the Orchard to the Home**".*

depot in Bradford. Finding that their best customers were jam makers, the Chivers decided to have a go at making their own jam, and the first boiling took place in a barn at Impington, Cambridgeshire, in 1873. The venture was so successful that Stephen Chivers and his sons were able to expand the business by buying an orchard close to Histon railway station and building the Victoria Works, opened in 1875. Ten years later a hundred and fifty people worked there, and by 1894 the workforce had increased to four hundred. Chivers introduced table jellies in 1888, followed by custard powder, lemon curd, mincemeat, Christmas puddings, and "Old English Marmalade". They renamed the works the Orchard Factory in 1910, and a year later received the Royal Warrant as purveyors of jams, jellies and canned English fruits.

The 1931 film opens with scenes at the Chivers farms, which covered almost eight thousand acres. We are shown, with informative captions, the orchards, the beehives –'necessary in fertilising the fruit blossom, also for honey for use in Orchard Factory', free-range chickens – 'for eggs for lemon curd and mayonnaise', two thousand pedigree pigs – 'fed on waste from factory and fallen fruit', and sheep, cows and Percheron horses which 'are used on all the Chivers farms'.

Because of its historical content it is worth examining the film more closely. The process of making jam is followed in detail - raspberries and strawberries are picked, weighed and taken to the Orchard Factory by horse-drawn waggons. The open boxes of fruit 'to be used either for jam, fruit canning or pressed to provide fruit juices for jellies' are unloaded at the factory by Chivers' employees, who seem extremely busy. Clean overalls, extra hands, often pretty girls, and the obvious presence of a supervisor or two all have to be looked for and taken into account when watching films made in factories and works. The boss or someone from 'public relations' as we would call them now, was often present when a film camera was at work, making sure that everything looked right and that employees were working hard.

The fruit for jam is tipped by hand into silver-lined boiling pans, and the correct amount of sugar is added automatically. Glass jars arriving at the unloading bay are individually inspected and washed before being put on a conveyor and filled automatically with jam. Rows of women nimbly put discs of waxed paper on top of the still-warm jam, the lids are put on by hand, and the jars of jam go through a sterilizer and vacuum chamber.

The Orchard Factory had an extensive tramline system carrying hand-pushed trolleys for conveying the jam to and from the huge cooling rooms. This transport system, complete with points and sidings, was used by the film maker for a tracking shot inside the store to show the smartly dressed women unloading and stacking the jars of jam for cooling. The tramline system, built into the original factory in 1875, continued in use until 1939.

In the labelling and packing department the jars of jam are seen being polished by hand, and then string is tied round the tops to secure the lids and a coding machine ensures that 'every individual jar can be traced throughout its career'. After the label is put on, the jars are wrapped in tissue paper, again by hand, and boxed. Chivers was the first to introduce transparent jelly in concentrated block form that could be made up at home. The process of making the jelly tablets is shown in detail in the film with shots of the fruit being pressed, the jelly being strained through muslin cloths and allowed to settle in trays. The cooled jelly is cut up by the cubing machine, wrapped neatly by hand and packed into cardboard boxes.

The final job was to wrap each jar in tissue paper.

Stringless beans, carrots, celery hearts, peas, spinach, new potatoes and tomatoes were just some of the canned vegetables and fruit marketed by Chivers under the Gold Standard, 'English Grown' label; all picked and packed the same day. In 1931 a new factory was opened at Huntingdon for canning only, and the pea canning section of "**From the Orchard to the Home**" was probably shot there. The process of canning is covered in detail, with sequences showing the peas being picked by hand and arriving in sacks at the factory by lorry. The pea canning is much more automated than any other operation seen in the film. The 'wonderful pea-shelling machines' are shown, as well as another piece of equipment which removes 'small, immature and large over-ripe peas'. Chivers were obviously proud of their canning machines which 'fill and seal 120 cans per minute!' but much of the work was still done by hand. The cans were placed by women into large metal baskets called crates, which were loaded by block and tackle into large retorts. After cooking and cooling the cans are seen being taken out of the crates by hand. 'The same care and cleanliness are predominant in the packing of all Chivers canned vegetables', says a caption that is followed by a wide shot of about a hundred women seated at trestles, each with a bowl, peeling and preparing vegetables for canning.

This 1931 film gives us a great deal of general information about Chivers and its products. Crates of jam and marmalade are rolled before the camera to show us the extent of Chivers trading - Hong Kong, Colombo, Montreal, Antwerp, New York, Jerusalem, Alexandria, Brussels, The Hague, Takoradi and Mombassa. The Histon laboratories in which the ingredients for Chivers products were tested are shown. In the kitchens, where foods are tried out, a young lady gingerly pokes a jelly to see how wobbly it is. At the railway sidings there is a

Everyone seems happy on Chivers farms.

great deal of activity loading boxes and crates into railway wagons, and we also see similar scenes of loading the Chivers fleet of vans and lorries.

At the height of the season about three thousand people were employed at the factory and on the farms at the time the film was made in 1931. It points out the canteen where staff could get food at cost price, the surgery, a girls' recreation ground, and Impington Hall, a sixteenth-century building where 'educational classes for all employees under eighteen years of age are held during working hours'. Chivers factory at Histon was taken over by Schweppes in 1959, and subsequent owners knocked down the old factory and built a new more automated business, as can be seen in the short film "**Chivers Hartley Factory**" of 1987. In 1959, a colour film was made of the factory called "**The Chivers Story**", from which the development of factory processes can be easily compared with the 1931 film. Incidentally, on the subject of peas, at Sawston, the other side of Cambridge, in the 1920s there was a quaint custom of the villagers being allowed once a year to pick free peas from a field. "**Everyone Should Have Enough Peas**" shows this event, with the locals gathering their free peas about 1925.

The first 'wireless' factory was opened in Hall Street, Chelmsford in 1899 – though this is not the wireless we associate with radio. That came in 1920 when Dame Nellie Melba sang in a 30 minute broadcast which was heard all over Europe. This was the first advertised broadcast from Marconi's factory at Chelmsford. An experiment a year earlier involved one of the Marconi engineers, W. T. Ditcham, broadcasting speech across the Atlantic. Ditcham appears briefly in "**Marconi Wireless Telegraph Company**", an amateur 16mm film made by one of the employees in 1934. The film shows large radio transmitter equipment being tested, scenes in the design offices, and people working in the factory assembling and testing wireless equipment. Mr. E. E. Triggs, a valve engineer, holds up a small valve in his hand, and compares it with a large earlier version standing on the floor. At the end of the working day the workers leave the factory, some walking, some on bicycles, and one or two in cars, and head into town.

Another major company in Chelmsford was Crompton Parkinson, electrical engineers. The firm was set up by Colonel Crompton and made electrical switchgear, alternators, generators and equipment for power stations. Their new factory just off the Writtle Road was built in 1885 and called Arc Works. In 1947 they had a couple of films made, one "**Colonel Crompton**", was the dramatised story of the man himself. In the advertising copy it is described as a 'record of his success in pioneering electric light and developing the dynamo, in constructing some of the first power stations, and in his work on instruments and electrical traction. With Ernest Thesiger in the title role and a cast of 60 supporting actors, the film achieves human interest of a high order, as well as providing an authentic scientific record'. This

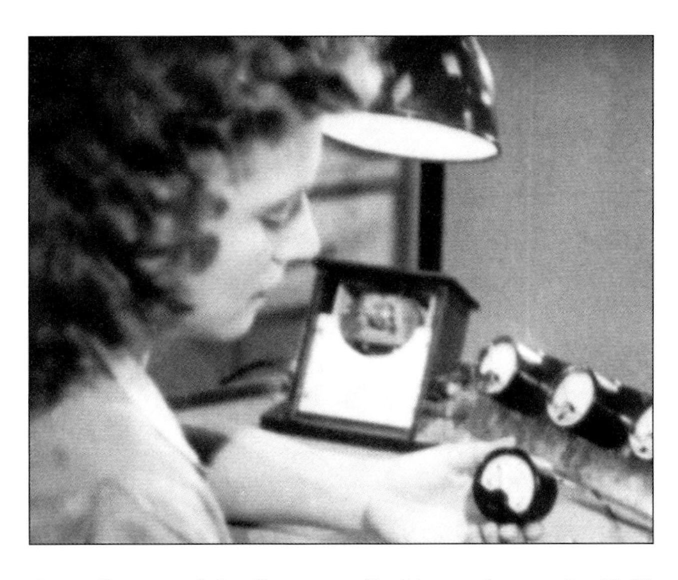

*A small part of the Crompton Parkinson factory in 1947. From "**Beyond The Pylons**".*

30 minute tribute was made on 35mm with 16mm prints available for free hire, and it is one of the 16mm prints that has survived thanks to a former employee, John Jay. The other film is a straight forward factual account of the company 'which takes the camera into the wonderland of modern electrical manufacture'. "**Beyond The Pylons**" was filmed mainly at the Chelmsford works, though mention is made of other Crompton Parkinson factories which by this time existed. At Chelmsford we see the works outside, and inside the machine shop where Ted Eave, the chief inspector in the machine shops speaks, as does T. H. Windebank, the works director. In the instrument shop there is a large workforce of women assembling and testing equipment. 'An intriguing sequence' says the film publicity 'is provided by an actual test to destruction at the switchgear short circuit test station'. The production of electrical motors, cables and bulbs is covered in this excellent film which has 'an orchestral accompaniment by the London Symphony Orchestra, which matches the high standard of the whole production'.

The Hoffman Manufacturing Company in Chelmsford took its name from Ernst Gustav Hoffman, an American who supplied the money to Geoffrey and Charles Barrett, who set up the company in New Street in 1898 to manufacture precision ball bearings. In 1969 the company became RHP (Ransome Hoffman and Pollard) and later had a colour film made called "**Bearings Round The World**" in 1976. This shows the many applications of their products in cars, planes, trains, tanks, combine harvester, lifts, etc. The high degree of manufacture is emphasised, and the distribution to international markets is shown. The Advanced Passenger Train, Concord, earth moving machinery – all used RHP's ball bearings.

The British Vitamin Company began life in 1948 in Chelmsford, changing its name to Britvic in 1971. Soft drinks was their line, and still is. A collection of advertising films for their products in the 1960s and 70s is a good example of the types of drinks popular at the time, as well as showing the people who bought them, and the pubs and other places they were available from. These, and film of factory quality control, and views of the works exist in the "**Britvic of Chelmsford Collection**". There is also a short sequence of interior shots of the factory in "**East Anglia Today**" made in 1984.

Not far from Chelmsford is Silver End, a new model village built between 1929 and 1932 to house the workers of Crittall's factory at Braintree. The film shows off the stylised houses, the shop, and the surrounding countryside, emphasising how up to date everything is, how clean and tidy "**Silver End**" is, where even the cows are vacuum cleaned! "**Braintree Crittall Windows**" gives a slight indication of this company's metal window frames business, and the "**Crittall Car Club**" of 1958 the more relaxed side of life.

Norwich was always a busy manufacturing place, with a variety of bewildering products. Wire netting was pioneered in Norwich by Barnards Ltd – 'inventors and original makers of galvanized wire netting'. "**Wire Netting Manufacture**" is a short

BOOK ONE OR BOTH OF THESE FILMS NOW ! !

Either or both of these films will be freely loaned to responsible bodies such as Engineering and Educational Societies, Technical Schools and Colleges, Industrial Organisations, Professional Associations, Electricity Supply Authorities and Exhibition Organisers, in fact any suitable group, large or small, to whom the films would appeal.

They are available in 35 mm. and 16 mm. sizes for sound projectors, the running times being as follows :

"Colonel Crompton" ... *approx.* 30 *minutes*
"Beyond the Pylons" ... *approx.* 50 *minutes*

By using the attached card, organisers can ensure that a copy of the film is booked for the date of their next show.

*Colmans factory in Norwich in 1935 from "**Family Scenes and Colmans Works**".*

*George Fenn "**Mill Stone Dressing**" in 1970.*

amateur film of Barnards, a company which held a Royal Warrant from 'His Majesty The King' in the 1930s. Boulton and Paul, mechanical engineers, were making, amongst other things, aeroplanes, and a shot in **"Norwich and District Film Review**", a local news and advertising film which is mainly devoted to the departmental store Bonds on All Saints Green, begins with a scene of canvas being sewn on to a Boulton and Paul biplane by women in 1922. This company was known for constructional steel work, and this side of their business is explained in the colour sound film "**Structural Steel at Your Fingertips**" in 1961.

One of the bigger employers in the city was Colmans, the mustard makers. In 1935 Mr. Bird went round the factory with his 16mm camera adding to his home movies shots of the Colmans works. "**Family Scenes and Colmans Works**" shows people arriving for work, the factory from the river and road, and the many forms of transport around about. There is a horse and cart, lorries and vans – one carrying an advertisement for Barley Water, boats on the river, motor cycles outside the works, Geoffrey Colman in a car, and the unusual rail locomotive in the works. This hauled wagons around the yard, and was fireless, for it was run on stored hot water from the works, so as to prevent smoke entering the factory.

Jeremiah Colman was making mustard as early as 1814 at Stoke Holy Cross, a village five miles south of Norwich. In 1823 he went into partnership with his adopted nephew James, and the firm became known as J. & J. Colman. In 1854 they started making mustard at the Carrow site, close to the railway line and the river Wensum. The company grew and grew, and in the 20th century acquired other brand names such as Robinsons Lemon Barley Water and Gales Honey. In 1938 the company merged with Reckitt and Sons of Hull. In 1973 the Mustard shop opened to celebrate 150 years of the company, and a museum of publicity and packaging was set up in Carrow Abbey with Reg Butcher as the archivist. The story of Colmans is told in a BBC East documentary made in colour in 1973 by Douglas Salmon called "**The Mustard Makers**". This covers the factory, mustard making and distribution, and the philanthropy and facilities provided by the Colman family for their employees over the years.

In 1970 BBC East made a short film of "**Mill Stone Dressing**" in the barley flour plant at Colmans factory. To make the stone ground flour in the traditional way, a half ton stone revolved slowly over a static bed stone, with the grain being fed into the slight gap between the two. The stones could last up to fifty years, but needed regular dressing, as the indentations or cracks that do the grinding wear away. The rather unscientific commentary explains simply how the work is done as George Fenn, mill stone dresser, demonstrates. "It takes three to four days to dress the stone, and it is done every nine months. The upper stone is lifted revealing the bed stone. George Fenn dresses the stone cutting new cracks in it. The art is to cut as many cracks to the inch as possible with the unwieldy bill. Twenty cracks to the inch provides a very fine grind, but barley flour grinding requires fewer cracks. George Fenn's stone will grind 1000 tons of the best barley flour before these new cracks grow dull".

At Norwich there was at one time an electricity generating station close by the river at Thorpe. In 1937 this was enlarged and the work was recorded in "**Extension to Thorpe Power Station**". The site had an overhead conveyor system for transporting coal from ships to the furnaces. This is seen briefly in "**Proud City**", a film made in 1955 to show off the work of Norwich City Council. "**Proud City**" covers several industrial sequences, including Reads Flour Mill, situated the other side of Carrow Road Bridge from Colmans, where many types of flour were produced. The packaging department was of interest to the film makers, as they recorded the bags of flour being shaken up and down and weighed – observed and measured by the city's weights and measures department. In 1993 the East Anglian Film Archive filmed inside "**Reads Flour Mill**" as it was shortly to close. The site was later re-developed for housing, though retaining some of the original structure.

North Heigham Cabinet Works Limited were manufacturers of furniture under the brand name of Norvayam. They had their works in Paddock Street, and in 1939 an 8mm film was made showing furniture from tree to delivery. Two men with axes cut down an oak tree, and at the yard it is sawn into planks. In the "**Norvayam Factory**" men and women worked on the furniture, and the final products produced by the staff were taken away in a Norvayam van.

The invitation to "**Come With Me To Norwich**" was put forward by Richard Dimbleby in this film made in 1952. Richard Dimbleby was at this time a radio and television personality, and therefore well known. The film is a mixture of travelogue and industry. It looks at Norwich as it was not long after the war, its shops, streets, old buildings and churches, and then examines the business of the Norwich Union, the making of mustard at Colmans, how shoes are made, and chocolate making at A. J. Caley and Son Ltd works in Chapelfield. Caleys became John Mackintosh and Sons in 1932, and after a further take over, eventually part of Nestles. In 1995, just before this factory closed, a colour film was made by Roger Hewins called "**Nestles Rowntree**" showing the staff at work and the processes involved in making chocolate bars of various sorts. On some days the smell of chocolate wafted through the streets, adding a glow of sweetenss to the air. Norwich was known for shoe making at one time, and this industry turns up in "**Norvic Shoes**", a colour silent film shot in the Norvic shoe factory in Colegate in 1981, and again briefly when Princess Elizabeth visited a shoe factory and a silk factory in "**Princess Visits Norwich**" in 1951.

"**Come With Me To Norwich**" shows Norwich not long after the war, when bomb sites were still in evidence, and old buildings were being replaced with new. What Norwich was like at this time is also visually evident in two amateur films. "**A Busman's Day**" demonstrates the importance of the local buses in the city when not everyone had a car. There was an extensive bus turn-around at Norwich Thorpe Station, now just known as Norwich Station. Here people arriving by train could get buses to any part of the city. The buses, with their metal destination boards with intermediate places listed, were prepared for the journey by the driver, clambering up the front of the engine to turn over the metal hinged plates bearing the bus number. Some of the conductors on the buses were women, as can be seen in this film made by one of the busmen, Geoffrey Campling.

In 1950 Sergeant Kemp drove Philip Armes through the streets of Norwich in a police car. Philip held a 16mm camera and recorded the "**Car Trip Through Norwich**" for his employers, Norwich City Council. They wanted to see the narrow streets and how congested they were for possible demolition of buildings so as to widen the roads. Phillip remembered filming on a Thursday afternoon, which was half day closing in those days and so there was not much traffic and not many people about. The camera films along St Stephens before it was widened, past Orford Place and along Castle Meadow, by Bank Plain,

*"**Car Trip Through Norwich**" filmed from the passenger seat of a police car 1950.*

*"**Labour and The New Society**" records the building of council estates in Norwich in 1950.*

Tombland, Fye Bridge Street, Magdalen Street, Duke Street, Exchange Street, Theatre Street etc. It is a remarkable record of the roads and streets in 1950, some almost unrecognisable today because of more recent changes.

"**Labour and The New Society**", also made in 1950 by Geoffrey Campling, shows Norwich in a run down state. Traffic and pedestrians are seen in the streets of the city, with shots of derelict and damaged buildings which need replacing. About 350 prefabs were put up after the war to house families while the council set about an ambitious programme of council house building. Geoffrey Campling's film shows the new estates going up at South Park Avenue, Tuckswood and Earlham. Within about fifteen years Norwich had built over 6,000 council houses. The city council made a film "**Construction of Houses by Direct Labour**", which shows in detail how these dwellings were built. Continuing with the upgrading of the infrastructure of the city during this expansion, "**City Engineers Work**" deals with preparing the ground at South Park housing estate for new drains, the sewage disposal plant at Whitlingham, resurfacing roads, and other improvements. "**Building a Sewer**" and "**Tunnel Works**" deal with the construction of the intercepting sewer from Hellesdon to Trowse pumping station. This served the north western part of the city as well as Upper and Lower Hellesdon. It involved building a two mile tunnel under the city to a maximum depth of 124 feet.

"**Proud City**", made in 1955, is a colour sound film made by the city council showing what was being achieved. The film covers a wide variety of services and schemes, from the dustmen collecting rubbish to take to the Harford Bridges land fill site ('where it is out of our consciousness' says the narrator, Bernard Story); gas and water pipes under the streets; resurfacing roads; the fire brigade; the police force; schools; the cattle market (then in the centre of the city, but soon to be removed to a new site at Harford); and the work of the weights and measures department, seeing if the pumps at the garages gave the right amount of petrol.

Laurence, Scott and Electromotors was a pioneer company in the field of electric motors, generators, and other electrical equipment. They employed a large number of people at Gothic works close to the railway and the river in Norwich. They ran an apprenticeship scheme for young men, and this is explained in "**I Want To Be An Engineer**", a film made by their resident film maker, Jack Farrant, in 1956.

Jack Farrant made publicity, training, and test films for the company, many of which survived and are in the "**Laurence, Scott and Electromotors**" collection. Their titles give an idea of the range of products. "**Heat Exchangers**", "**Variable Speed Arc Motors**", "**Design and Construction of The Scott Dynamic Winch**", "**Revon Control Systems for Cranes**", "**AC Contactors**", and "**City of Cape Town Electricity Department**".

Jack Farrant, the film maker of Laurence Scott and Electromotors of Norwich with his 16mm Bolex camera.

Two major industries in Colchester were the Colchester Lathe Company, machine tool makers, and Davey, Paxman and Company, diesel engine manufacturers. Founded in 1865 by James Paxman, the company's early products were mainly boilers and steam engines. In 1925 they started making diesel engines, becoming a leader in its specialist field of large high speed diesels. At its peak in the early 1960s, Paxman employed about 2,500 people making diesels at its Standard Road Works for generating sets, ships, trains, and excavators. Like many companies at this time they used publicity films to promote their products.

In 1957 British Railways ordered 22 Class 55 Deltic locomotives which were delivered between 1961 and 1962. "**The Deltic Story**" made about 1959 features the 18 cylinder Deltic engine, rated at 1650 bhp as installed in the Class 55. "**Triangle of Power**" made in the mid 1960s, is also about this engine, a unique two stroke engine which had three crankshafts and eighteen or nine cylinders, depending on the version. Each cylinder contained two opposed pistons. The engines were of aluminium construction to keep weight to a minimum. They were installed in fast naval patrol boats and mine sweepers as well as the Class 55 locomotives. The Deltic was designed by D. Napier and Son Ltd of Acton in London, which became part of English Electric, and the engines were originally built at their Liverpool factory. In 1966 Paxman was acquired by English Electric, which was taken over by GEC in 1968. As part of a GEC re-organisation, manufacture of the Deltic engine was transferred to Paxman in Colchester

A Deltic locomotive at Peterborough.

in 1970. They continued to repair and overhaul Deltics until 2002.

Another powerful engine used by British Railways was the "**Ventura**", introduced by Paxman's in 1960. Customers for this vee-form engine included the Royal Navy, and railways in Italy and Sri Lanka. The Ventura was followed by Paxman's Valenta engine introduced in 1972. This powered the High Speed Train (HST), better known as the "**Intercity 125**". To maintain the HST's top cruising speed of 125 miles per hour, two power cars were used, each with a 12 cylinder Valenta engine rated at 2,250 bhp, one at each end of the train. This not only spread the weight, but also had the advantage that in the event of an engine failure, the other could provide sufficient power for the train to continue its journey. The prototype HST broke the world speed record for diesel traction in July 1973 when it reached just over 143 miles per hour. Paxman's supplied more than 230 Valentas for the Intercity 125.

Also in the Paxman collection is "**Liquid Solid Separation**", about the company's filtration business which, among other things, made rotary vacuum filters for various industrial processes including water and sewage treatment, and "**Britannia Works**", a film showing the remains of the other Paxman factory close to Colchester Town railway station, which was badly damaged by incendiary bombs in February 1944.

The Colchester Lathe Company factory was built alongside the Elmstead Road (it is now part of the road to the University of Essex) in 1962, though the company itself was founded by John Cohen in 1887. They mainly produced heavy duty lathes, though in 1921 they introduced a small lathe suitable for workshops and garages. In 1961 their range of products was showcased in "**The World Turns**", a 16mm colour sound film. Between 1967 and 1975 they won the Queens Award to Industry several times, two of these being for their export business. The company ceased operations in Colchester in 1992 when production was moved to Yorkshire. There is one other company in Colchester that advertised their products with the use of film, Woods of Colchester. Maurice Woods formed a company in Colchester in 1909 to manufacture electric motors. Thirty years later the company was employing over 300 people. In 1945 a takeover began when GEC started investing heavily in the organisation. In 1962 a 16mm colour film called "**Fans Unlimited**" was made to explain Woods 'air movement' equipment that they were producing at the time in their factory overlooking Colchester railway yard. The site is now occupied by housing.

At Letchworth there was a steel foundry at Coburn Works called Kryn and Lahy, which in 1928 teamed up with T. C. Jones and Company to make cranes. Their first successful crane was put on the market in 1933. During the war they made over 1000 cranes, 180 of which were made in twenty five weeks for the D-Day landings. They went on to make many different types of mobile cranes over the next thirty years. "**Facts About Jones Cranes**", made in 1962 begins "One of the most widely used, and probably the most versatile mechanical handling machines, is the mobile crane. With suitable tackle there is virtually no article or material that it cannot handle with ease, speed, and safety. On any busy building site, at ports and inland waterways, in timber yards, coal depots, railway sidings, engineering works, and most any place where materials are being handled, you will find a mobile crane – probably a Jones"

The 10 minute sound colour film, "Produced for the George Cohen 600 Group Ltd by K and L Publicity Department", and with a commentary read by Richard Baker, shows many of the fifty types of cranes the company produced. The last

*"**Quality Engineering**" made by the Bedford engineering company W. H. Allen.*

sequence demonstrates the delicate handling of a heavy weight. "Watch this 6 ton load being lowered on to a wine glass without breaking it". The massive solid iron block is slowly lowered on to the wine glass, until the glass is just wedged under the weight. The shot which shows this also has the operator in the cab behind, and you can watch his face and his hand as he controls the lever that lowers the weight. He stops when the weight is on the glass, holding it tight without breaking it. "Every Jones driver has control like this at his fingertips". An impressive demonstration.

"**Quality Engineering**", is a 1976 film made by the Bedford engineering company W. H. Allen, at this time now known as APE-Allen – the APE standing for Amalgamated Power Engineering. These engineering films are often the only visual reminders of companies which at one time employed large workforces and produced well made, large scale equipment in the East of England region. The films often follow the same pattern, showing proudly their factories, workforce, and products, and the high quality of their design and manufacturing.

The commentary of Allens "**Quality Engineering**", is typical of the proudness and confidence of their business. "The long established APE Allen works at Bedford incorporates some of the most up-to-date advances in machine tools and supporting facilities for the manufacture of steam turbines, diesel engines, and pumping plant to the high standard which has come to be expected of Allens products. The design is carefully investigated for its suitability for the application. Wherever possible standard designs of certain components are used with other specially designed components to achieve maximum efficiency and optimum reliability for the special end use of the machinery. For these components which are to be cast, for instance turbine cylinders, diesel cylinders blocks, cylinder heads, pump casing and bell mouths, patterns are produced in the company's own pattern shops. This ensures that castings, be they in iron, steel, or brass, will be to the dimensions accurately required. After use the patterns are carefully stored in case of the need for a replacement in the future"

The colourful shots of the 16mm sound film show the work described being carried out, including the making of a pattern by a skilled craftsman out of wood. The factory in Bedford next to the railway line was built in 1894, after William Henry Allen was on a train going to Derby to look for a new site for a factory as the London premises could not cope with the expansion of the firm. The story goes that he looked out of the window when in Bedford, and saw a plot of land for sale. The train stopped in the station, he got out and examined the site, and bought 20 acres. Here grew up the Queens Engineering Works of W. H. Allen and Company.

The commentary for "**Quality Engineering**" goes on "Steam turbine rotors of integral design are received into the works as complete forgings, and the first stage in production is to accurately machine them. This lathe is a numerically controlled machine typical of the many up to date machine tools installed in a recent modernisation and expansion programme. The fitting shop is staffed with skilled fitters, many of whom received their specialist training with the company which operates one of the most advanced, comprehensive, and well respected training schemes in the industry. All these, and the up to date facilities and

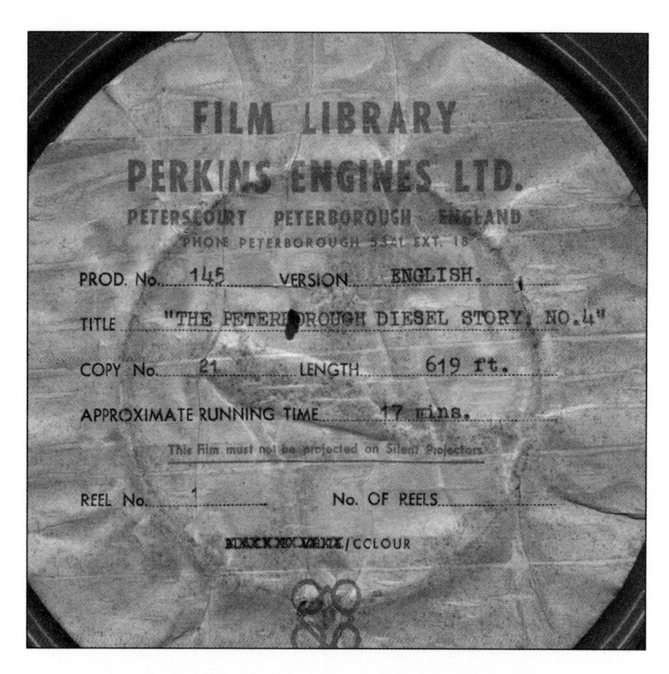

"The Peterborough Diesel Engine Story, No 4"
– this version was made in 1963.

techniques at the Bedford works of APE Allen Ltd add up to quality engineering providing reliable and efficient machinery for world industry".

"**Quality Engineering**" was produced by Allens own publicity department. Many of their films are now in the East Anglian Film Archive courtesy of Nigel Lutt of the Bedfordshire Record Office, including "**Marine Industrial Gas Turbine Engines**", "**Mechanical Advantage**", "**Wyfla Power Station**" and "**700 Miles of Oil**" - about the construction of a pipeline in 1961. Allens has gone in Bedford now, closing in 2000, but at Peterborough Perkins is still in existence.

This big engineering works specialised in diesel engines for transport, industry, agriculture, and marine applications. Frank Perkins, a Peterborough man, set up the company in 1932, and within five years had a range of successful diesel engines.

Perkins promoted their business in the 1950s with a 16mm colour sound film made by their own film unit. This film was updated from time to time, and "**The Peterborough Diesel Engine Story No 3**" was made in 1959 and runs for 25 minutes. The fourth version, released in 1963, runs for 17 minutes, but is basically the same as the earlier version except there are less shots of the countryside around Peterborough, and machines and vehicles powered by Perkins engines. "**The Peterborough Diesel Engine Story No 4**", begins with shots of the cathedral. "The cathedral city of Peterborough stands in its own administrative county of the Soke of Peterborough" states the commentary, as it goes on to show the streets and market. "On market days, when people converge here from the outlying towns and villages, the population of about 56,000 shoots up to a temporary 80,000 or more. The first stop by rail between London and the north, this ancient city is for its size, one of the most prominent industrial centres in Britain. Industry has brought great prosperity to the people of Peterborough. This is the modern works where nearly 7000 of them are employed. The manufacturing headquarters of the Perkins Group of companies, it covers more than 730,000 square feet. The administration block is the hub of the organisation. Spacious and air conditioned offices provide pleasant surroundings for the administrative staff. The main factory where the diesel engines developing up to 120hp are produced in large quantities is the most modern of its kind in the world".

The offices and factory floor are huge open spaces, with people busily working as far as the eye can see. The mechanics of making diesel engines is shown with examples of the finished machines at work in the field. These include road making equipment, cars, lorries, buses, delivery vans, a mobile library, refuse collecting vehicles, road sweepers, taxis, compressors, concrete mixers, diesel railway shunters, combine harvesters, and many more – all sporting the Perkins badge.

The film features the Perkins stand at the Peterborough Show, as well as other trade and dealer stands with machinery powered by Perkins diesel engines.

Perkins films were available on free loan to any club, society, or film show gathering that wanted to show them. An example of distribution can be gleaned from the records of the film "**Wherever The Waters**", a film about outboard motors, made in 1959. The following year the film was shown to 34 groups, including Bassingbourne Young Farmers Club, East Anglian Waterways Association at St Ives, Deeping Men's group, South Bedfordshire Sailing Club, Weymouth Yacht Club, Jay Ess Cruisers of Blackburn, Cameron and Campbell of Glasgow, Robert Craig and Sons of Belfast, and Modern Outboard Motors Ltd of London to name but a few. The film was also shown in Trinidad, and versions were made in different languages such as German, Swedish and French. Copies were sold outright to Arab Bros, of Lagos, Kemper En Van Twist of Holland, Messrs Holmes of Bermuda, and K. Pilakoutas and Sons of Nicosia amongst others.

Many of the films were in colour, which in itself was a draw, as all television was in black and white, and much cinema film also. People were happy to attend meetings with shows, and watch a wide range of films of an informative and instructive nature, as well as in many cases straight entertainment with little mention of the sponsor. An example here is the Perkins film "**The Years British Cars of 1955**". This is a film of the latest models being shown off at Goodwood for the overseas press, who had a chance to see the new British cars and drive them round the track. "This is the 8th motor show test day organised by the Guild of Motoring Writers" says the opening commentary. A wide variety of cars are on show, including a Morgan, MGA Sports Car, Austin Healey 100, Daimler Drop Head Sports Coupe, Aston Martin Hard Top, Bristol Type 405, Armstrong Siddeley Sapphire 234, Triumph TR3 Sports car, a Mark 3 Sunbeam, and a Humber Super Snipe – the only car out of 56 on show that is fitted with a Perkins diesel engine.

In the mid-1950s the Perkins Film Unit made a 30 minute film for the Red Poll Society. The advertising copy for "**The Red Poll Story**" explains: "Possibly the finest and most comprehensive film ever made of a single breed, it describes how in the 18th and early 19th centuries the old Suffolk Duns, polled and famed for their milk yield, were crossed with hardy Norfolk beef cattle. Their progeny were called Red Poll because of their distinctive chestnut colouring and natural hornlessness". The commentary points out that "during the past ten years Milk Marketing Board statistics show that on average Red Poll are the third best milking breed – the top two being purely dairy cattle. Red Poll cows have been known to give more than 20,000 lbs of milk per lactation, with high butterfat content. The film illustrates many advantages held by the Red Poll as a true dual purpose breed".

The Perkins Film Unit filmed on 35mm as well as 16mm and it seems to have been the practice to lend or hire the unit out to make films for other organisations. In the summer of 1959 they made "**Introduction to Anglia**" about the coming of Anglia Television, and in 1964 "**There Won't Be Time Tomorrow**", a film about the production of the Peterborough 'Evening Telegraph'.

The large collection of film from Perkins is an excellent resource for research of the 1950s and 1960s on vehicles of every type, employee education schemes, boats and ships, fishing, farming, engine history, industrial techniques, safety at work, and of course the products of this large Peterborough company. They also made a series called "**News Review**", which was aimed at the staff as well as being available for loan. No 5 in this series for example, made in July 1956, includes

*The Perkins Film Unit at work on the Sandringham Estate for "**The Red Poll Story**". The unit consists of cameraman Mr. R. Leatherbarrow with camera assistant Mr. L. Shipsides, and production supervisor Mr. K. Simms on the back of the car.*

diesel powered fishing boats at King's Lynn. No 6 includes extensions to the Perkins factory at Eastfield, one mile north east of Peterborough, and Mr. Frank Perkins, the company's Chairman and Managing Director, also High Sheriff of Cambridgeshire and Huntingdonshire, "seen leaving the University Arms Hotel in Cambridge to attend the opening of the winter assizes at the Guildhall".

The Perkins collection of motion picture films and some scripts and other related material was saved and deposited in the East Anglian Film Archive by David Boulton, who has done so much with colleagues to rescue and record the output of Perkins film unit.

Also in Peterborough, but unconnected with the above company, was Baker Perkins, a company established in 1920 by the merger of two independent firms making machinery for the bakery and confectionery industries. "**The Story of Baker Perkins**" is just one of 36 surviving films that the company used for publicity, training, and safety. This one traces the history of Baker Perkins, and begins in a Marks and Spencer store. "Any shop in any street is likely to sell goods which owe something to the company's skill and ingenuity. This applies particularly to the things we eat. For many years the organisation has maintained a leading position in the food industry". At the till a woman buys a swiss roll. "Probably this young lady is unaware of the story behind the manufacture of a swiss roll. But it is a fascinating one nevertheless. The swiss roll starts life as a batter.....". No doubt the woman has absolutely no idea about how the thing she is buying was made, but the film goes on to show us every stage in its production using equipment made by Baker Perkins. The company also made packaging machines for Persil, Brooke Bond Dividend Tea, Lucozade bottles, and, in the Norwich works of John Mackintosh and Sons, equipment for making chocolate.

"**Just The Job**" is a 1960s recruiting film for "A Future as a Craftsman in The Machine Shop". The film opens with David bicycling home from school. Arriving at his parents modern 1960s home, he rushes to the shed in the garden where he is making things on a small lathe. Next the film shows a coach arriving at the Baker Perkins factory. "David has always loved engineering. He has been looking forward to this afternoon ever since he heard his school had arranged a trip to a big engineering works. For most boys any excuse is good enough for an afternoon away from the classroom. But this could be one of the most important journeys of their lives, for they are going to take a look at some of the jobs they might do when they leave school. Now here is a real engineering works, a grown up version of the garden shed workshop".

The boys are shown round the machine shop to see the tools and the type of work carried out there. "This is a new world, but in many ways, it is like David's home workshop. Here is a lathe. It is turning out not schoolboy models, but a shaft 15 feet long for driving automatic machinery. Like all jobs in the machine shop, this is highly skilled. The shaft must be accurate to within a thousanth of an inch. Jobs in the machine shop are many and varied, for it is undoubtedly the hub of the whole works. These youngsters are working in one of the finest apprentice schools in the country, they are being taught by men who are themselves skilled machinists.

"It was several weeks ago that the school party visited the works. Some of the boys have been excited and interested by what they saw. One of them decided that a career in the machine shop was 'just the job'. After training he will join a group doing rewarding, interesting work in a modern machine shop. He will have become a modern craftsman".

The films were made by Baker Perkins own film unit, and include such films as "**Taps, Dies, and Reamers**", "**Fitters and Turners Work**", "**Manufacture of Chocolate**", "**Automatic Bread Making**" and "**Automatic Wafer Production**". Thirty years after these films were produced, several were made available to employee groups who wanted to see once again the place they worked, and the people they worked alongside – just one of the uses of archive films.

"**Eye To The Future**" was made in 1949, showing the making of Pye image Photicon broadcast television cameras. The ten minute black and white film appears to have been made for showing in North America, and some of the terms used are confusing.

The BBC Television Service was back on the air on June 7th 1946 after being closed throughout the war. All television was live, in fact it was considered cheating if a film was shown. The Pye Photicon camera (an early type of electronic

Pye of Cambridge used film to advertise their television production equipment.

television camera) was new in 1949, and involved many stages in its construction. This included producing the delicate glass tubes and inserting the various components within. They were hand built, and no two were quite the same. "It is true to say that in these Cambridge laboratories much of the research done into TV transmitters and receivers has passed into general practice. The image Photicon tube is a noteworthy example of Pye progress. It has sensitivity adequate for all normal lighting intensities, and particularly fine definition and tonal response". A selling point was that the image tube package could be easily slid into and out of the camera, useful for maintenance and replacement. The cameras had a four lens turret on the front so that the cameraman could change quickly to a wider or closer shot during the time another camera output was selected.

"It is significant that the British Broadcasting Corporation who were the world pioneers of telecasting, rely on Pye outside broadcast equipment for the coverage of all major news events. With this transmission unit, a producer is able to receive and edit on the spot vision from four cameras, and sound from eight sources, and to feed back to his transmitter a fully edited interesting programme. He is able to maintain contact with all operators and commentators, and give all necessary directions to all persons employed in transmitting and receiving the feature".

The film shows a BBC outside broadcast unit at work at the Royal Albert Hall in 1949, with a line of operators working the camera control units – the small monitors and electronic apparatus which could alter the brightness and contrast of the picture coming from each camera before it reached the vision mixing desk. It is also interesting to note that the producer of the programme was also the director.

In 1958 Pye released "**The Cambridge Story**". "Industry has played a vital part in the development of Cambridge, and it is a natural choice of home for a concern which deals with every aspect of the most modern of all sciences, the 20th century magic of electronics. There are several Pye factories in Cambridge producing everything from the tiny transistor to a complete TV station". This film covers remotely controlled closed circuit television systems for use in medical work (students watch an operation from a distance), in a railway marshalling yard, in a steelworks, and in a train carriage fitted out as a studio to supply passengers with programmes on their journey.

In September 1956, Pye showed off their portable camera which could be used in an aircraft. Portable is hardly the right word, as the camera and associated equipment had to be carried to and from the helicopter on a sort of stretcher by two men. However, Pye saw this equipment as an important step forward, with possibilities for military and civil defence applications, as well as for searches and traffic control. The "**Air To Ground Television**" system installed in the Bristol Sycamore helicopter, had a five mile range, and a special aerial to deal with rotor interference.

Other films in the Pye collection include "**Pye Magazine No 1**", "**Car Telephone Service**", a colour advertisement for "**Pye TV Ads**" with John Cleese, and a film called "**Colour TV Story**"- in black and white!

At Lowestoft Pye opened a factory making television sets in 1951. About 1967 a short film was made there mainly about the export side of the business. "**Pye TV Factory**" shows the semi automated production line, and the testing of the finished television sets with a test card on the screen. This factory was in the hands of Phillips in 1980 (they had bought it from Pye in 1976), when they announced its closure. Two years later Sanyo re-opened the factory, and at one time employed over 300 people turning out half a million TV sets a year. They stopped making televisions in 2006, concentrating on large public screens for shopping centres, airports and sports events. The factory closed completely in 2009.

"**The Photogravure of Printing Postage Stamps**" is just one of the films in the Del La Rue

*The Pye portable television camera being removed from a helicopter in 1956. From "**Air to Ground Television**".*

collection. The company goes back to the Harrison family whose works in High Wycombe specialised in printing postage stamps. In 1997 Harrison and Son was bought out by Del La Rue, an international company that printed bank notes. Del La Rue announced they would close the High Wycombe factory in 2002, transferring the work of printing vouchers to their factory at Dunstable, which was originally Waterlow and Sons Ltd. The Del La Rue collection of films cover the whole company, with several of the Harrison factory including "**Stamp On It**", the earliest film in the collection at 1937, "**Blue Peter Christmas Stamp**", and an uncut film of "**Diana Stamps**" of 1997. The future Queen paid a visit to the Harrison factory to see her coronation stamps being printed, and there exists about 600ft of 16mm film showing the "**Queen's Visit to Harrisons**" in 1952

A different form of printing was carried on at Richard Clay and Sons Chaucer Press in Bungay. In the late 1950s a television film was made here looking not just at the printing process, but the innovative ideas of the owner. Aidan Crawley, a reporter from the BBC, arrives in an Austin car outside the factory.

"Behind Bungay's dignified buildings, unseen from any of its main streets stands a modern printing works, a family concern, now in the hands of the fourth generation. Mr. Clay prints and binds books. It is a fascinating process. Beginning with the casting of type, which is here being done in single letters, then going through various stages to the printing press. This is a flat bed press, which can print as many as 64 pages of a book on one sheet, and as many as 1700 of those sheets in an hour.

"From the press to the bindery, where the sheets gradually take the shape of books, and may turn out to be anything from a paperback thriller to a treatise on higher mathematics. And it was here in the bindery that I found adventure – for although this business is thriving, Mr. Clay has called in a firm of industrial consultants deliberately to find fault with his methods and to put right what is wrong. Just watch the different processes as they are carried out. This is the first, a machine which folds the sheets into pages of whatever size the book is to be. After they have been folded, the pages are in sections, pages 1 – 64 on one sheet, and pages 65 – 128 from another sheet, and so on, and they have to be assembled, or gathered as it is called in the trade, in the right order so as to make a book. Now when the order is small, perhaps from two to three thousand copies, this is done by hand, and going at that speed I thought this woman was bound to make a mistake, and pull out two of the same sections at once, but she never did. Larger orders are gathered by machine, some of them may run to as many as 50,000 copies of a single book".

The film then shows the factory, with its ingenious equipment, and special sewing machines being used by women to sew the pages together. The owner, Mr. Clay, is asked about the improvements he has made in the factory, and he highlights the new pressing unit and the glueing of paperback books on a machine that can do 8000 books per hour. The interviewer asks "Why do you need the services of an industrial consultant?"

"Well, there are two reasons for that really. Between us here we probably know quite a lot about book binding. We probably know too much, and the un-biased mind from outside can contribute a lot, which we don't see the wood for the trees very often. The other point is that life just is not long enough to do it all yourself even if you had the special knowledge which is required. It is going to take over two years for three full time resident consultants to go through this factory, and it would take three generations of management fitting that in with their other jobs".

There are further shots of the factory, then the interviewer comes in again "I found the consultant in the composing room".
"What improvements have you actually made in this department?"
"The main improvements we have made in this department are one of handling. We have taken out the skilled man actually handling the form, and given it to a mechanical track".
"What is a form?"
"These are forms, underneath here, stored vertically. A form is a metal frame in which the pages of type are locked in order to go to the press".
"Well how used they to handle it?"
"They used to take the vertically stored form out of the rack. Two men lifting something over one hundred weight, and there are four forms to be taken out of the rack".
"What happens now?"
"The new method is the forms are stored horizontally on trays on rollers so they move easily. They are slid on to a trolley which is adjustable for height and moved along"
"And the trolley, is it hydraulic?"
"Yes, it's hydraulic".
"Has it actually saved anything in time or manpower?"
"In time it has saved 50%. In manpower, well, the skilled man does not have to lift the forms, he can slide them, that makes it that much quicker, and therefore spend more time on his skilled job".

"I would just like to have one word with the operative" says the interviewer.

"As a compositor, what do you think of the new methods they have introduced here?" "Well, I think it is definitely an improvement, there are some weak points about it, but they will be cleared up eventually. We have lessened the lifting – physical strain".
"Has it affected your earnings at all?"
"That hasn't at the present. We haven't reached down here, but taking on the majority of the rooms, they have benefited by that"
"So you expect to?"
"Oh yes, definitely expect to, if not we shan't think much of it"
"How long have you been in the printing trade yourself?"
"Roughly 29 to 30 years"
"What did you think when you first heard that outside consultants were coming in?"
"Well as a trade union member I was rather disturbed, and it is difficult to adapt oneself to modern conditions and modern trends. But I think that we all changed our mind now"
"Did you think they were going to come and teach you your job, and resent it?"
"Well, that was the impression we had in the first place, but that has been washed out"

The interviewer then asks Mr. Clarke, the trade union official, what he thought of consultants coming in.
"I viewed it with a lot of mistrust in the first place, I didn't like the idea of anybody coming round with a watch"
"What did the men and women themselves think?"
"At first a lot of mistrust, but some are coming round to the idea that it is definitely beneficial"
"And you yourself, what do you think?"
"Well the scientific studies we take and what we derive from these statistics, I am quite satisfied it is fair".
"Do you think the workers are going to get anything out of it?"
"Yes, I do. I feel the majority will get one third of their wages extra. The wastage of time will be cut out, the machines will be speeded up a certain amount and by different methods of disposing of the work, they will be able to give a bigger output each day"
"They produce more?"
"Yes definitely"
"Do you agree with that?"
"Well, in view of the fact that we are always asking for more wages, I have come to the conclusion we cannot go on asking for wages unless we do produce more"

The film concludes with the presenter sitting at a desk, facing the camera asking "Why does a successful businessman take this sort of decision. I think Mr. Clay's answer was the right one. He said 'I simply have not got the time to study all these details myself'. Now, not every employer will agree with that. But it took courage to take the decision, and I have a strong suspicion that the

*From "**To Make The Best**" 1961.*

results will justify it. And I cannot help adding if more of our executives had similar courage, we should be both happier and richer. Goodnight".

So ends this twenty-five minute film called "**Adventure in Industry**" as the credits appear – Film Cameraman Peter Sargent, Film Editor Harry Hastings, Producer Jack Ashley.

A film that has no indication in the title what it is about, and with shots of a food laboratory and a soup factory in the United States, may not at first indicate a film about a business at King's Lynn, but "**To Make The Best**" is in many ways local material. For here, in the kitchens at Campbell's factory, the staff prepare by hand vegetables for Campbell's canned products. Celery, growing in the Fens, is lifted by a small army of women, while other ingredients came from abroad. The factory had been making soup and other foods at their Hardwick Road factory since 1959, and the film about the company, made in 1961, was shown to visitors for over ten years before it became out of date. Now the whole factory is of the past, for it closed in 2007.

1959 seems to have been a good year for factories, for besides Campbell's new premises in Lynn, Hotpoint at Peterborough were building a brand new factory. Douglas Fisher's film "**Hotpoint at Peterborough**" is about the construction of this new building, which is fascinating to watch as the men go about their business before health and safety rules slowed work down. The film begins with shots of Peterborough itself, then shows workmen on the building site doing virtually everything by hand. Another Hotpoint film, this time aimed at salesmen, is "**Hotpoint Iced Diamond**", made by Neil Tuson. "The 1960 range of Hotpoint refrigerators is about to be shown for the very first time" says marketing manager John Parkin. "As you know, refrigerator manufacturers each year generally face lift and modify their models, but we in Hotpoint are not going to do this for 1960. Instead, what we have done is this". The curtains behind him swish open to reveal a fridge apparently hovering in mid-air above the shape of a diamond. "It's completely new. It has the most spanking good looks. It's the most lasting refrigerator. And the name? Hotpoint Iced Diamond". Elegantly dressed girls with furs dance round the refrigerator in an elaborately choreographed stage show.

Kitchen appliances are covered in several films from the 1950s, including "**The Electric Cooker**", which shows in very technical detail how an electric cooker works. The use of the oven with a meal cooking in it is shown, as well as full use of the hobs emphasising their quickness of heating various saucepans. This was a time when cooking with electricity was something fairly new. The film was promoted by the British Electrical Development Association, as was "**How To Sell Your Husband a Washing Machine**". This is a well made film with a big budget. The stars are a confident Jack Hulbert and his real life wife, and star in her own right, Cicely Courtneidge. Jack Hulbert was a very popular entertainer and film star in the 1930s and 40s. He was born at Ely in Cambridgeshire, and was an undergraduate at Cambridge.

Made in colour in 1956, this film begins with Jack Hulbert addressing an audience of women in a village hall. "I have been asked by the Electrical Development Association to tell you about the home laundry – the washing machine, the ironing, and the drying cabinet, and if you will pardon me for saying so, I happen to be an authority on all three. Women of Britain, I am addressing you...". At this point Cicely Courtneidge comes breezing in to say he is going about selling women washing machines the wrong way. She points to an ordinary woman in the audience, a Mrs. Brown, but Jack continues – with interruptions from Cicely:-

"Now women of Britain, I appeal to you, let me explain the advantages of a washing machine".
"Mrs. Brown knows the advantages, what she wants to know is how to get one out of her husband"
"Now consider your husband Mrs. Brown, consider the mechanical aids he has in his job - a telephone, a dictaphone, a typewriter, secretary – where would his office be without them?"
"Ah, but supposing Mr. Brown doesn't work in an office, he works in a garage"
"Fine, he works in a garage….."

The film moves to a garage set where a customer cannot get service from the uninterested owner. Cicely Courtneidge then plays the part of a garage owner to show how it should be done. She does everything to help the customer. The story then shows the uninterested garage owner as the 'wife' at home, doing the washing with a wash board and a packet of Omo on the table. The methods he uses are old fashioned and slow and the children play up while he gets on with the work.

In a showroom the latest washing machines are on display. "They not only wash the clothes, they are fitted with elements that heat the water as well" says the commentary. The camera pans along a line of gleaming machines, some with wringers. "This one dries the clothes not by wringing them, but by spinning them round very fast so all the water is extracted. And here's a machine that does everything. You have nothing to do except put the clothes in and switch it on. It really is automatic".

In the final sequence we see that Cicely has won Jack round, and he buys a washing machine, or should we say she buys it – as well as a drying cabinet - and he pays. This is a sophisticated advertsing film with first class acting. It sums up very much the time of the mid 1950s, particularly with what was happening in the home kitchen, and the availability of electrical equipment.

Hertfordshire was known for its supply of watercress, for in the 1930s there were eight watercress farms in the county, at Harpenden, Hoddeston, Hitchin, Watford, St Albans, Welwyn Garden City, and two at Hemel Hempstead. Herbert Paddick grew watercress at his premises in Burford Street, Hoddesdon. In "**Coronation Parade and Watercress Beds**", an 8mm home movie of 1953, there is a sequence of this industry, as well as the parade through the town. But it is in a 1945 cinema short, "**Queen of Hearts**", that the whole process is seen and described in detail.

*Using zippy brooms to beat lime into the cress at Croxley Hall Farm, near Rickmansworth in Hertfordshire. From "**Queen of Hearts**" 1945.*

Filmed on Charles Sansom and Sons Croxley Hall Farm, at Croxley Green, near Rickmansworth, where the clear spring water runs through Cassio Bridge, the film shows the large watercress beds, called creases, and the staff who lovingly look after them. The watercress is rolled, fertilised with lime which is then beaten in using long springy poles with a sort of bat on the end, called zippy brooms, pushed under water for a couple of days, then picked, trimmed and boxed ready to take back to the bunching sheds. Here it is washed again in clear running water, tied up in bundles, put into punnet type containers, and sent to market. "**Queen of Hearts**" shows these processes, accompanied by a slightly humorous commentary which contains references to the time (1945). "Fresh acres of the creases as they are called in the Domesday book are prepared, whilst crops are gathered on others. The spring fed clear water seemed just what the doctor ordered for a bumper crop. The beds are raised up, or drained down to an equal level. Care is taken that the crop should grow at a regular height. Deep holes in the beds can bring ruin to the harvest, for here troughs might linger and upset the even temperature in which the crop is so rigidly grown. The crop is treated as tenderly as a test match cricket pitch".

After shots of levelling the beds and rolling the cress with slatted wooden rolls, the fertiliser

*With a heavy load on both lorry and trailer, this Brooks lorry climbs from Mistley Quay on to the Harwich Road in 1933. From "**GB and KM Cow Cubes**".*

is applied. "Then the lime is beaten in by zippy brooms that any witch would give her high crown hat for. No longer tender, the men beat the crop in a way that makes a henpecked husband lick his lips with envy. Then it is pushed underwater, which also might give him a few ideas. There it stays for a couple of days to arrive thicker and greener than ever. The cress growing in these parts, amongst these Hertfordshire yeomen, is an hereditary craft, handed down from father to son, generation after generation.

"Gathering must be done strictly in rotation, thinning out to air the beds. The roots are trimmed and dropped back to root again, the foundation of the next crop. Old methods matched with new ideas. Dipped, trimmed, and packed – but only for transport back to the bunching sheds. Here it is unloaded again for more washing in spring fed water. As clean as a bachelor's bedtime story. Now the day's yield is all tied up. The exact amount in each bundle almost to a leaf, and about 800 bundles an hour. Then it is boxed and basketed ready for the market. A camouflage for a cold collation – spam to you – you'd pay 7/6 cover charge for at some restaurant tomorrow".

The firm of Brooks of Mistley, in Essex, had its origins in the middle of the 19th century. By 1859 William Brooks had acquired granaries that existed on Mistley Quay, near Manningtree, and in 1863 he set up the company of W. Brooks and Sons. Here there were mills and a private rail siding. The company was in the business of "merchanting of grain and agricultural produce and farming". Part of Brooks commercial activity was transferring cargoes from lighters that had come down the River Stour to sea going vessels - mostly sailing barges, which took the cargoes to London, bringing back horse manure from the capital's streets for farmers.

After the 1914 – 1918 war, Mr. Hilton Brooks, who had built up the firm in the late 19th century, and Mr. Charles Brooks, began more expansion, with the chief activities being malting, animal feed, fertilisers and agricultural seeds. In 1927 Charles Brooks died, and the company went through a reorganisation, and became known as Brooks (Mistley) Ltd. Brooks made foods in various forms for "cattle, pigs, horses, lambs and dogs". They were the pioneers in the 1920s and 1930s of feed cubes, which were made by mixing various ingredients with molasses and pressed through a die to a make a cube, or nut. Brooks became famous for their GB Cow Cubes, made to a recipe from a farmer from Mount Bures, Grosvenor Berry. Another well known cube was the KM, after Keith Miller. In the 1930s Cow Cubes were sold for £7 per ton. The company won many prizes for the fattened cattle fed on GB and KM Cow Cubes.

In 1933, Attfield Brooks made a 16mm film of the company, with shots of sailing barges by Mistley Quay, prize cattle fed on their cubes, and of course the making of the "**GB and KM Cow Cubes**". In 1977 Attfield Brooks, by now head of the company, passed his 16mm films to the East Anglian Film Archive. These included "**Yachting Scenes**" at Harwich in 1934 with the large J Class yachts, the "**Opening of The Drill Hall**" and "**Mistley and Manningtree Historical Pageant**" of 1937.

Mistley was known for its maltings. There were several on the quay with others in various parts of the village. In 1893 Robert Free of London, and William Hunter Rodwell of Holbrook, together with Robert E. Free, and E. N. Heneage, formed Free Rodwell and Company Ltd. Within ten years they had built seven maltings producing 10,000 tons of malt a year. These new buildings were of a revolutionary design as far as Mistley maltings was concerned, for they were several stories high.

Attfield Brooks donated his 16mm films to the East Anglian Film Archive in 1977. On the left is David Tilley from the University of Essex, and on the right David Cleveland.

The barley from East Anglian farms was taken to the top floor, where it was dried, cleaned, and stored. It was then led by gravity to be "steeped" in tanks of water, and then spread out on the large tiled working floors. Men pulled implements back and forth through the shallow grain (about 4-5 inches thick) which turned and ploughed the "piece of malt" to aerate and help the germinating process. A careful watch was kept on the temperature to make sure the germination continued at the right pace. After about four days the "green" malt, as it had now become, was put into a kiln to be dried, and to stop germination. This was a very hot and steamy job for the men, spreading the malt on the kiln floor. The floor was of wedge wire, which let the hot air from the furnace below penetrate through the green malt. Dressing and polishing followed to remove the rootlets, which had grown during the germinating period. It was then sacked and sent to the brewers. The whole process took about nine days to do one batch of about 30 tons. This labour intensive business continued in the seven maltings at Mistley until the late 1970s. In 1976 this process was recorded in "**Industrial Archaeology in East Anglia**", a film covering many past industries of the region. In 1957 Free Rodwell and Co. were taken over by Ind Coope, a company with extensive maltings at Burton upon

Trent. In 1969 this company became part of Allied Breweries. This new organisation planned to phase out the labour intensive maltings at Mistley, and on Thursday May 11th 1978, opened a brand new two and a half million pound automatic maltings behind Mistley railway station. This "**New Maltings**" was of a French design, and aimed to turn out 140 ton batches in six days. This was achieved by combining the germination and kiln work in one operation. Moving the grain and malt around is done by machinery, thus reducing the labour costs further. Concentrating on lager malt, the Mistley plant now turns out 27,000 metric tons per year. The old floor maltings were soon closed. Some were wholly or partly demolished within a few years, others turned into housing.

Most towns had maltings at one time, often primitive and small in appearance, and without any automation whatsoever, they were completely dependent on manual labour. A good example is that of "**Malting**" at Hadleigh in 1947. Filmed at T. W. Wilson and Sons Ltd maltings in the Ipswich Road, this was made by local film maker Peter Boulton in the early days of Boulton Hawker Films. This silent 16mm colour film is fully captioned to describe the malting process. A companion film made at the same time was "**Corn Harvest**", again filmed locally.

Peter Boulton also made in 1947 a film on coco matting in the Brett works of E. H. Price Ltd at Hadleigh. "**The Story of Co-Co Matting**" is in vivid Kodachrome, and begins with a little boy at home wondering where the mat on the floor comes from. His mother explains. After a shot of a ship on the Thames, the manufacturing and dying processes are covered in detail, with final shots of the finished product leaving by lorry. In the same year Peter Boulton filmed retired rope maker Ben Whiting demonstrating "**Rope Making By Hand**". Ben makes a short section of heavy rope using the rope walk principle, twisting strands together to make the final product. Boulton Hawker Films became quite successful in the educational films market. The early films were silent, though they used colour as much as they could. Films on agriculture, market gardening and geography were made, but some extra income for the business was obtained from distributing other people's films, both in this

*Forestry Commission sequence in "**East Anglia**" made in 1970. Made by Boulton Hawker Films of Hadleigh.*

country and abroad. The main income, however, came from the Educational Foundation for Visual Aids set up in 1948 to co-ordinate production and provide financial help for educational film makers in the form of a guaranteed final order for 12 copies of each film made with a teacher advisor appointed by them. This went on until the late 1970s when cuts in education rendered it impossible to continue.

Amongst the films Boulton Hawker made in 1949 are "**The Market Gardner**" at Layham, close to Hadleigh, and "**The Dairy Farmer**" at Wall Farm, Holbrook. Both these were in black and white. Not long after this Gilbert Hawker left to make films on his own in Ipswich, but the company continued to trade under the name Boulton Hawker Films at Hadleigh with Peter Boulton in charge.

The farming theme ran through many of their films. In 1975 they made "**A Farm in East Anglia**" at Elmsett, and five years previously, "**East Anglia**", which looked at many of the industries of the region including the work of the Forestry Commission.

Mr. A. J. Cannell, managing director of Cannell and Sons, farm and garden seed merchants, took 8mm film of the business at Chedgrave, near Loddon in the 1950s and 1960s. This was a well known firm that had been in business since G. W. Cannell founded the company in 1904. The "**Cannell Collection**" covers not only the preparation of seeds, but their stands at the Norfolk and Suffolk Shows, and the Sandringham Show in

1960. The collection contains the Cannell family films as well, so for the study of this family firm, the films have it all.

It is surprising how far back some of these companies go. In 1805 an Essex farmer, William Bentall, built new works to manufacture in quantity his Goldhanger plough which had proved so popular. He had built this plough to his own design for use on his own farm at Goldhanger, four miles north east of Maldon, but local farmers wanted to buy it, so William Bentall began making ploughs to sell. In 1795 he had to make the decision to give up farming and concentrate on making and selling his plough.

Business soon took off in the new premises he built in 1805 at Heybridge, close to Maldon, and he began making other agricultural products. They made threshing equipment, cultivators, root pulpers, chaff cutters, disc harrows, beet lifters, muck spreaders and so on. A few of their Super 8mm advertising films to show to farmers survived when the company went out of business in 1984. "**Bentalls Grain Drying Systems**", and "**Coffee Growing**", a 1975 film of the processing machines they built for use out in East Java, are two of the films which give us an idea of the range of products the company was producing a few years before they ceased trading.

The CAV factory at Sudbury, which made high pressure diesel injection systems, is recorded in "**A Market Town**", a film made by Nigel Rea in 1975 showing the economics and structure of a typical Suffolk town. There is a silk mill working, but many local people were employed at the CAV diesel injector factory, where much of the work was controlled by what appears now as a primitive computer system. "**Injectofact**", a promotional film by Lucas CAV of their Sudbury works, shows exactly how their computer system operated, and what it did to improve productivity in 1977.

Over at Stanton, nine miles north east of Bury St Edmunds, at Obel Warehousing Ltd, Jack Burrows opens up in the morning, and staff and lorries arrive for the day's work. This a warehousing and distribution centre. In the office John Oates deals manually with the paperwork. "**At Your Service**", made by David Orr, shows a day in the life of this busy company in the mid 1970s, and is a good example of how they organised their business before the days of modern computers.

When Harlow Town was new, one of the first industries there was the Key Glass Works. Here they made glass bottles and jars. The works had its own railway siding so that raw materials could be brought in by wagon. In the factory molten glass came from the furnace to the moulding machines, where compressed air pushed the glass into shape against the mould. "**Glass Bottles**", a film made in 1959, shows the complete process. The production line of the factory turns up again in "**The General Practitioner In Industry**", a film about doctors from Harlow Industrial Health Service who visit

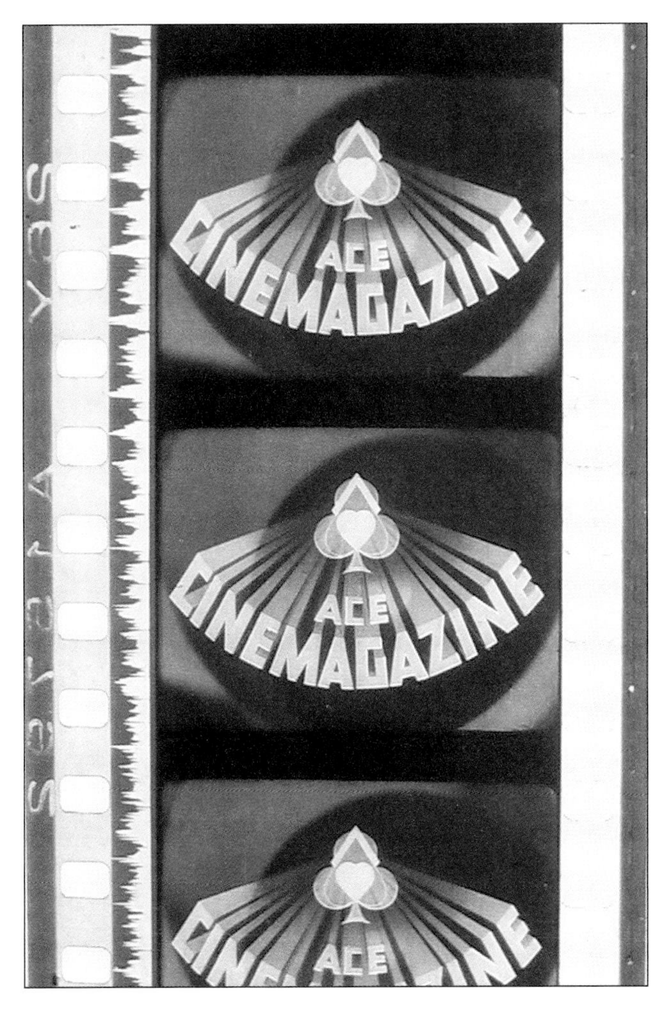

*Ace Cinemagazine. This series contained short 'interest' stories, such as "**Weaving Mill**" at Halstead in Suffolk.*

factories as part of a preventative health scheme, as well as to examine patients in factory clinics. The film points out the hazards encountered in modern industrial factories. The film also shows mothers bringing their babies to the health centres, people being x rayed, an ante-natal clinic, and first aid lectures.

In the 1960s there was expansion in and around Thetford. A home movie records new housing and industry in the 8mm film "**Thetford**". One of the new employers was Thermos, who made vacuum flasks in their new factory. In 1968 they were visited by the makers of the Pathe Pictorial. Photographed in colour on high quality 35mm film, the whole process of making a Thermos flask is seen from molten glass to finished flask. The workforce, mainly women, work the machines and carry out the repetitive and mundane jobs which were so much part of factory life at one time.

*The Palace cinema in Fairfield Road, Braintree. From "**The Opening of The New Town Hall**" 1928.*

Ace Cinemagazine was a similar cinema interest short which ran in the 1930s only. In 1936 there was an item in their edition called "Arty Egg Samples" about rayon, a silk substitute, being woven at Courtauld and Company's picturesque Halstead factory. The "**Weaving Mill**", an old watermill straddling the river, employed local girls to look after the machines, and wind threads with their nimble fingers. The Courtauld family had several businesses in and around Braintree, and in 1928 Mr. Courtauld himself attended "**The Opening of The New Town Hall**". This was such an important event in Braintree that the local cinema, The Palace in Fairfield Road, had a 35mm local film made. This showed the speeches (it is a silent film!) the sports that followed, and a shot of the cinema itself at the end.

The Birds Eye "**Frozen Pea Factory**" at Yarmouth was filmed in 1951 where they were using the latest quick freezing methods. Peas, gathered from the fields and processed in a viner, were transported to the factory, where they are seen being washed and graded, sorted on a conveyor belt by women picking out the black and damaged ones, then put into small cardboard boxes and frozen. This all took place, from field to freezing, in less than four hours. The factory began freezing peas in 1946, and it also played a major part in the development of fish fingers which were launched in 1955. Clarence Birdseye was an American scientist who realised the possibilities of freezing

*Horstead watermill in 1950 from "**White Wings**".*

*Horstead watermill inside in 1950 from "**White Wings**".*

food, and soon meat and vegetables appeared under the Birdseye name in Massachusetts about 1930.

The lavender oil harvest was one of the subjects of Pathe Pictorial No 217 issued in 1948. The lavender is harvested by women working along the rows of growing plants, and then loaded into a large still at Fring in North West Norfolk. After distilling, men pull the spent lavender out, and the film shows the result – some lavender oil in a small bottle. "**Lavender Harvest**" shows the original still at Fring which was moved to Heacham in the 1970s, where the lavender business is carried on at Caley Mill.

At West Newton, near Sandringham, there was a flax factory. The fibre of the flax plant can be made into thread and woven to make material. They began growing flax on the Royal Estate at Sandringham about 1931. Production increased during the 1939-45 war as the demand grew for such things as ship's canvas, parachute harnesses, and hose pipes. A factory was built by Norfolk Flax Ltd. and a silent 16mm film made called "**Linen Flax**". Flax was grown very much like corn, except that the sheaves were transported direct to the flax factory. Here it was sorted and arranged on a conveyor by women, followed by the complicated and dirty factory processes of retting and scutching. This involved soaking in a tank at a controlled temperature, drying out of doors, and separating in the scutching process the fibres from the rest of the plant.

Stramit, a company with bases at Stowmarket and the old Eye Airfield made compressed straw boards. "**Walls of Straw**" deals with 'Stramit as partitioning and wall linings for various forms of construction. Runs for 20 minutes in full colour' says their advertising leaflet for this 16mm film. "**Building With Straw**" illustrates the basic properties of this material for roof decking and partitioning, and "**Stramit Fire Test**" shows the resistance of these straw boards to fire under an 'Official Fire Test'.

At Horstead, near Coltishall in Norfolk, stood a watermill. This white, weather boarded watermill was filmed in 1950 for "**White Wings**", a film that was never completed about the Norfolk Broads. Victor Harrison, who ran many cinemas in East Anglia, was a keen sailor on the Broads, and owned the Chumley and Hawk boatyard at Horning. He decided he wanted a film made of his beloved Broads to show in his cinemas. He engaged Riccy Smith as director and cameraman, and over 1,000ft of 35mm film was shot; then for some reason the project came to an abrupt halt. The film was never completed and the nitrate rushes were left in a can for many years. A sequence of the mill at Horstead showed the exterior, and inside with the overhead power belts driving various machines. These mills in the 1950s were supplying mostly grist for cattle feed. They were noisy places, where you could hardly hear yourself speak.

In the cold winter of 1963, when the river Bure was frozen, a rat, it is said, gnawed through an electric cable, resulting in a fire. The white weatherboarded mill at Horstead built almost entirely of wood, soon burned, and machinery fell through the floors to the ground. The mill was a write-off.

The burnt out remains of Horstead Mill.

The next morning, at daylight, some 16mm colour film was taken of the iced up river and the smoking ruins, called "**Horstead Mill**". In 1973, exactly ten years after the fire, a compilation item was transmitted by Look East. "**Horstead Mill, Norfolk**" includes the 1950 archive film, the remains of the burnt out building, and an interview with Brian Read, the owner, talking about whether it could be rebuilt or not.

A type of plastic called celluloid was made at the British Xylonite Company works at Brantham, a village on the Essex Suffolk border near Manningtree. From the raw celluloid all manner of objects were produced - combs, pens, spectacle frames, dolls, bicycle pumps, beakers, candle sticks, rulers, and a host of trinkets. They also made tennis table balls out of this inflammable plastic.

The company was originally in the High Street in Homerton where they made the celluloid and various products from it. The site soon became too small, and following a number of explosions during the celluloid manufacturing process, it was decided to seek a new site away from this dense residential and industrial area of East London. The company found the ideal place at Brantham, close to the River Stour. The 130 acres of land had the main London to Norwich railway line running right through the site.

It was in 1887 that the British Xylonite factory moved to Brantham, with many of the original employees moving as well to live and work in the Suffolk countryside. The BXL business was a family one, run from 1877 to the late 1950s by the Merriam family. The company built a sea wall round their new site at Brantham, and began making celluloid and other plastic products. They built houses for their workers close to the site, and this developed into New Brantham, an extension of the main village.

Wardle Storey Ltd was the last owner of the plastics factory at Brantham, and celluloid was only occasionally manufactured in later years when an order came from the Ministry of Defence. They MOD required celluloid capsules to hold cordite in mortar guns. The celluloid burnt quickly and left very little ash. In 1992 a 16mm colour film was made called "**Wardle Storey's Factory**". This followed the complete process of the manufacture of this highly inflammable product, as well as showing other plastics produced at the factory. After a near fatal explosion when mixing celluloid ingredients in 2005, the factory ceased making the product and closed completely in 2007.

*Making celluloid at "**Wardle Storey's Factory**" plastics factory at Brantham.*

Northmet, the North Metropolitan Electric Power Supply Company, had a film unit just after the war, and in 1946 made "**Northmet Newsreel No 1**". This 16mm colour sound film was "the first in a series we hope to release from time to time in order to bring to the public notice some of the interesting public events in an area where over a million people rely on Northmet electricity service".

The film opens with the board of directors visiting the Brimsdown power station at Enfield, and then features a sequence of the 'Appliance Repair Service' at Watford. "New electrical appliances are still in short supply and likely to remain so for sometime yet. Consequently the repair and renovation of existing appliances is an important public service. Northmet's fully equipped factory is engaged in the repair of consumer's appliances where many thousands of items are handled each year". Over shots of a dilapidated boiler, a kettle, and a cooker, "these appliances are received in all sorts of condition, and after repair and testing they are returned to the consumer in first class order". The gleaming items are then seen being delivered to the consumer by a man in uniform travelling in a Northmet 500cwt van. He also delivers a vacuum cleaner "one of the 6000 – 7000 cleaners supplied to consumers by Northmet showrooms during the past fifteen months". The streets and traffic, the shops and pedestrians show in colour what life was like immediately after the war.

The film then shows the "first annual agricultural show of the newly amalgamated societies held at Cassiobury Park on July 17th". According to the commentary, 30,000 people attended to watch horses, cattle and dogs during this one day show which was visited by Princess Elizabeth. "**Northmet Newsreel No 1**" was shot on 16mm Kodachrome colour film, with a Kodachrome print made with an optical sound track. Part of the film runs at 16 frames per second, and part at 24 frames per second, so a change of speed is necessary when showing this film. The use of optical sound tracks on 16mm colour reversal prints was fairly new at this time. Camera film was expensive, and some film makers tried to cut corners by shooting at 16 frames per second, and then adding the sound. The quality of the sound however was not so good when reproduced at this slow linear speed of 16 frames per second, so they soon shot everything at the professional speed of 24 frames per second.

At Ipswich in 1950 the new generating station by the River Orwell was just about completed. "**Cliff Quay Generating Station**" is a 16mm colour sound film of the opening day. Dignitaries go round inspecting the works, their wives in their best clothes and hats looking somewhat bored. The power station lasted into the 1990s, with demolition taking place in 1994, when the high chimney was brought down in a controlled explosion. "**Cliff Quay Chimney Demolition**" shows this happening.

In the 1930s Southend hosted "**The Great Electricity Exhibition at the Kursaal**", and "**Southend Electricity Corporation Advertisements**" appeared in 1938 at a time when electricity was being employed more and more in the home. The "**Eastern Electricity Board Collection**" contains a large amount of films such as "**Electric Wave**", "**Electric Contacts**", "**Orford Cable Crossing**", "**Cook in Time**", and an advert called "**Piping Hot**".

W. G. Green lived at Wherstead, near Ipswich, which is where the headquarters was of Eastern Electricity. Mr. Green made 8mm colour

*Bacton gas terminal from "**East Anglia**" 1970.*

films from 1967 to about 2000, and his collection is a rich source of industry, work, events, and changing times in the Ipswich area. In the 1980s he filmed "**Alton Mill**", a watermill, moved from a site at Tattingstone, just south of Ipswich, to the East Anglian Rural Life Museum at Stowmarket. This was because a new reservoir was being built – which he also covered right up to the time it was completed. His "**Alton Reservoir – Boats Sailing**" culminates the story.

But perhaps the most fascinating film of building a reservoir is the 16mm colour sound film "**The Hanningfield Scheme**", made in 1957. This covers the whole business of making a reservoir in the days when traction engines and other old and basic equipment was all that was available. The film makes such a big undertaking seem so easy, and the shots are long enough for us to see how it was done. Perhaps it is the colour of the Kodachrome which makes these films seem to come from a different age – when the sun always shone, and everything got done with the minimum of problems. It is an illusion of course, but an evocative one at that.

The Essex Water Company was based in Chelmsford, and provided services beyond just water. Films were available for the public to see such as "**Trout Fishing at Hanningfield**", "**Bird Watching Hide at Abberton**", "**Essex Afforestation at Hanningfield**" and "**Your Water Supply**". They even made "**Christmas Party and Summer Outing**" in 1970, as well as "**Essex Water Supply and The Environment**" in 1975. A Mr. P. D. Hunt made a home movie on 16mm in 1938 just called "**Water**", about where your water came from, and in 1953 there was another gathering at Southend, this time for the "**Institute of Water Engineers**".

Considering that nearly every town had its own gas works before the days of North Sea gas, it is surprising there is little film dealing with this older form of heating, lighting and cooking. All that exists is "**The Gasman Cometh**", an 8mm film by Westcliff Cine Club at Southend, and "**Gas Naturally**". Bottled Calor gas is mentioned in "**Destination Felixstowe**", and "**North Sea Gas**" and "**Offshore Gas**" welcome us to the wonders of piped gas from Bacton. "**Gas Pipe Laying**" went on across the countryside in the 1960s to bring us North Sea gas – with every cooker being modified to burn this new supposedly everlasting wonder.

"Edgar Wymer of Hevingham", broom maker.

The smaller industries, perhaps they may be called crafts, flourished all over the region, and luckily many were recorded on film. At Little Whelnetham near Bury St Edmunds was the 'rake, handle and hurdle' works of John George and Sons. At one time 22 people were employed here. It was still functioning in 1984 when a sequence was filmed for "**East Anglia Today**". Noel Cullum was the only person left then, and he is seen making a wooden rake using some of the original belt driven machinery and basic tools. The atmosphere of this wonderful cobwebby factory comes over in this short sequence filmed in colour on 35mm film.

At South Ockendon, in Essex, Leslie Gillham made a 16mm colour film of "**Bill Eaton, Saddler**" in 1965. William Henry Eaton had been a saddler in Ockendon for over fifty years. He proudly shows off his tools to the camera, some so old and worn that they are almost past use. Bill demonstrates how he stitches the leather with waxed hemp cord. Marjorie Gillham records the commentary as he talks about his work and the things he makes.

Another craftsman was "**Edgar Wymer of Hevingham**", who demonstrated in 1988 how to make a broom. Working alone in his garden with all his materials and tools around him, he describes the process. At Stowmarket, within the East Anglian Museum of Rural Life, two craftsmen were filmed in the Boby building workshops as a record of how things were once done. John Wright from Onehouse, a village two miles west of Stowmarket, shows how he makes a potato basket in "**Basket Maker**", and "**Brian Palfrey, Cooper**" from Greene King's brewery at Bury St Edmunds, demonstrates how to construct a wooden barrel. In these two films made in colour in 1986, both men use traditional tools, and describe what they are doing as they go along.

Many a village had a blacksmith at one time. Harry Yaxley was one of these, and he is seen shoeing a horse outside his forge. Harry is recorded as being the village blacksmith at Worstead in Norfolk in the late 1920s, and he was still there 30 years later when Eric Owen filmed him for Harold Baim's short 1958 cinema film "**Royal County**". It is said Harry worked until his arms gave out. Then he stopped.

George Turner was a blacksmith at Brandon Creek, four miles north east of Littleport, and a sequence of his forge appears in a film of the Fens made in 1944 called "**Charted Waters**". Here, next to The Ship Inn, there were two blazing forges in the blacksmiths shop. In "**Essex Village**", a film shot at both Finchingfield and Great Bardfield, the local blacksmith is seen at work. Bernard

*Harry Yaxley, the Worstead blacksmith, who worked, it is said, until his arms gave out. From "**Royal County**" 1958.*

*George Edwards, Brandon flint knapper. From "**This Was England**" 1935.*

Polley of Colchester, a keen amateur film maker, shot a complete sequence of shoeing a horse at H. R. Griggs blacksmith forge at St Osyth, near Clacton, for his film "**Irons in The Fire**". At Ashwellthorpe, Norfolk, there is a huge pile of discarded horse shoes outside the "**Blacksmith**" shop; and in the "**Co-op Collection**" there is a film called "**Woman Blacksmith**". A mobile farrier at work at Overstrand Riding Stables appears in "**The Blacksmith**", a film made by Peter Hollingham for showing in Norfolk schools. This film admirably demonstrates the art of the master blacksmith, for the film is really about the work of Eric Stevenson, the well known Wroxham blacksmith. A group of school children visit his forge to see a demonstration of blacksmithing in this colour film of 1977. "**The Blacksmith**" shows Eric's expert work in creating village signs, church screens, and cathedral gates.

In 1942, the blacksmith in Water Street, Lavenham, was Frederick Huffey. He was filmed along with Henry Bullivant, the saddler in the High Street, for "**Lowland Village**", a film that shows the workings of a country village seemingly unaffected by the war. A wheelwright is also shown, and the commentary continues "Thus these trades, unchanging with the years, keep alive a tradition of the past, while serving the needs of the farmer today."

In 1935 Mary Field made a film for Gaumont British Instructional Films for classroom use

Flloyd Peecock hedge cutting. The brushwood will be used to make drains.

William Aldred broadcast sowing.

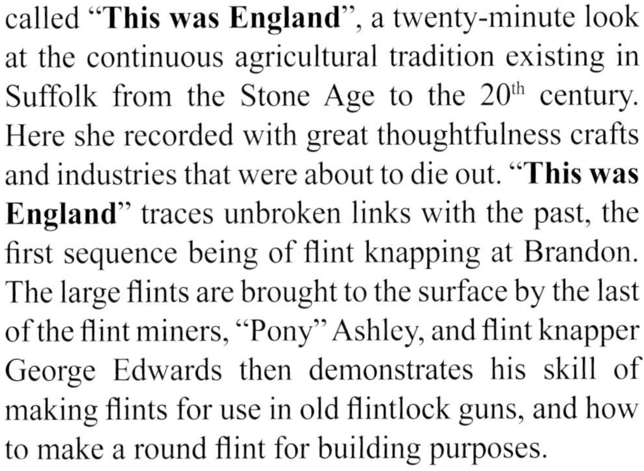

called "**This was England**", a twenty-minute look at the continuous agricultural tradition existing in Suffolk from the Stone Age to the 20th century. Here she recorded with great thoughtfulness crafts and industries that were about to die out. "**This was England**" traces unbroken links with the past, the first sequence being of flint knapping at Brandon. The large flints are brought to the surface by the last of the flint miners, "Pony" Ashley, and flint knapper George Edwards then demonstrates his skill of making flints for use in old flintlock guns, and how to make a round flint for building purposes.

The second sequence moves to Wood Farm, Peasenhall, Suffolk, where Flloyd Peecock farmed. "The Ancient Britons used to farm my farm, and like me they found this heavy land holds the wet, and needs draining. They drained the land in a very simple way, and I do it the same way because it's cheap and it works all right" says Flloyd Peecock, direct to the camera, in one of three sequences that start with the person involved telling us about their work. These sound shots were filmed in a studio with a background set to match the location surroundings. Flloyd Peecock is seen against a hedge which he turns to look at as he says "First of all we cut brushwood from the hedge", then the film cuts to a bush draining sequence – a method of draining going back to at least Roman times. Here is the laborious job of digging a network of trenches across the field, scraping out the bottom of these with the special tools, and the putting in of brushwood from the hedges. Finally we see water trickling through under the brushwood to show how the drain works. Another sequence shows the making of silage, with horses struggling with tumbrils up to the top of the heap to tip out the contents.

The Anglo-Saxon period deals with broadcast sowing, demonstrated by William Aldred of Poys Street, Sibton. His introduction gives an insight into the working life of a farm labourer living near the coast. In a warm Suffolk accent he says "In the olden times the Saxons used to broadcast all their corn and seed like this. In my young time I went to sea and was shipwrecked three times. Shipwrecked in the 'Sauce Pie' off Yarmouth - a quarter of a mile off Yarmouth. The skipper come on deck and said 'The mast and sails are over the side', he said, 'all hands on deck at once.' I've been a farming hand for forty years and I can sow seeds against anyone and I can sow ten acres of land with ten pints of seed." The first line he was probably told to say, though the bit about the shipwreck sounds like his own idea.

Hand sowing of seed had virtually died out by this time, the method only being used for headlands, and odd corners of fields, or for special small seeds or a top dressing of artificial manure. A tray of seed hung round the middle of the sower, and he walked along distributing the seed by picking a small

Brushey Whincop with some moles he has caught.

The sawpit at Walpole.

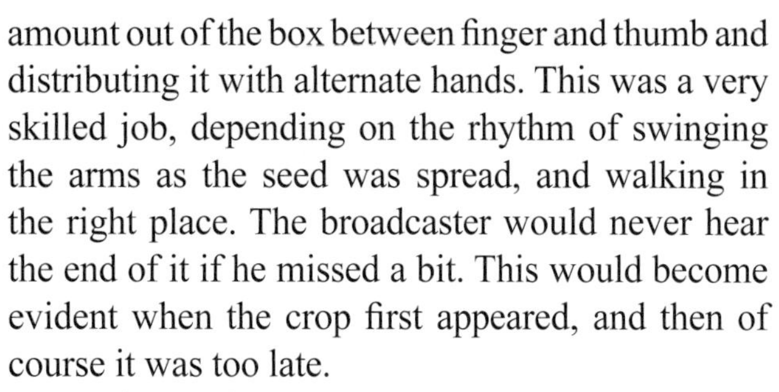

amount out of the box between finger and thumb and distributing it with alternate hands. This was a very skilled job, depending on the rhythm of swinging the arms as the seed was spread, and walking in the right place. The broadcaster would never hear the end of it if he missed a bit. This would become evident when the crop first appeared, and then of course it was too late.

The assistant gamekeeper on the Levett-Scrivener estate at Sibton Abbey, Brushey Whincop, shows how to catch moles. Moles can be a great nuisance by throwing up heaps which make meadows and pastures uneven. It was quite common at one time to see the results of the mole catcher's efforts hanging on a barbed wire fence, a row of bodies hung for all to see. Brushey Whincop demonstrates his art with self-springing traps made out of wood and wire. He also hangs his latest catch on the fence, and the camera pans along to show moles hanging on the wire almost as far as the eye can see.

Tudor England is associated with shipbuilding, and Mary Field shows us a Suffolk sawpit. This pit, at G. J. Aldridge's yard at Walpole, was in fact quite new. When George Aldridge moved his wheelwright, carpentry and undertaking business to the centre of Walpole, a new pit was dug in 1920. To demonstrate how a saw pit works George Aldridge, with assistant Billy Quinton, saw a tree trunk in half. The trunk is laid horizontally above the sawpit, enabling Mr. Quinton to go down underneath to pull the saw down while George Aldridge stands on top of the trunk pulling the saw up. The job completed, the two halves roll apart as soon as the "dogs" (irons which held the log in place) are knocked out. These halves would then be cut into planks. This was a slow business, and for the man in the pit under the log, a dusty dirty job. Before steam engines and circular saws, all timber was cut in this way. The pit at Walpole was filled in in 1947.

Ebenezer Joshua Rackham, straw and reed thatcher, introduces us to a cottage that is about to be thatched with straw. He says he helped his father to thatch this roof thirty-six years before. The sequence that follows shows Ebenezer and his sons working on the cottage at Cookley, a small village not far from Walpole. Straw as a thatch lasted about half the time of reed.

"The 19th century saw Suffolk farmers taking to machinery", says the commentary, and here is a threshing sequence, with thrashing drum and elevator driven by a portable steam engine. Finally we see what is described as a 20th century machine - a gyrotiller. At that time it was thought that these huge crawling machines with revolving tines which dug into the ground doing the work of cultivator and plough, would become common place. In fact they proved too cumbersome and expensive to run, and soon disappeared.

In the handbook which accompanied "**This Was England**", Mary Field wrote: "The development of communications and labour saving machinery during the last fifty years has

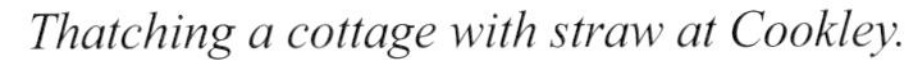

Thatching a cottage with straw at Cookley.

A gyrotiller at work.

speeded up the whole pace of everyday life and this film will more than fulfil the purpose evolved from a long tradition of individual skills for which it was made if it recaptures for those who see it, the natural and gentle pace of rural life adapted to the gradual changes of nature, and the careful and unhurried creation of individual work using simple hand tools and local materials. The Suffolk dialect, in which the men seen working explain how the various methods are used side by side, is rapidly disappearing and is therefore of special interest to the students of language".

Mary Field's use of sound is interesting. Sound films had been around for six years or so, but it was in 1935 that sound was beginning to be used to record ordinary people and what they had to say. Today we are used to interviews in the street or home, but in 1935 this technique was quite new. Mary Field was well informed about the advances in film making, and she used this direct to camera technique in "**This Was England**". Because of the lack of money, it was not possible to take the cumbersome recording equipment to remote parts of Suffolk. So Flloyd Peecock, William Aldred, and Ebenezer Rackham, went down to London and were filmed and recorded in a studio set. And it worked well. Mr. Peecock speaks easily without any kind of hesitation or self-consciousness. Seventy-seven-year-old William Aldred speeds through his lines, and at the end, almost before the last word is out, his eyes quickly move to one side, probably to Mary Field standing beside the camera, with a "was that all right?" look on his face. Ebenezer Rackham rests on a ladder, supposedly on the roof of the cottage at Cookley, which he is about to thatch. His piece to camera is a bit tense, and he appears to be putting on an exaggerated accent.

On Saturday September 7th 1935 "**This Was England**" was premiered at the Regent Cinema in Ipswich. Those who took part in the film, and family and friends, put on their best clothes and were taken by bus to the venue, about sixty in all. Undoubtedly the star of the occasion was William Aldred. 'A roar of applause', it is recorded, went up from the audience when they saw him on the screen. He had never been to the cinema in his life before, and when asked what he thought of it he replied "I liked it wonderful well."

*William Aldred on the left, Mary Field, and on the right Len Collins, manager of the Regent cinema where "**This Was England**" was first shown on September 7th 1935.*

An example of one of the many catalogues of films available for training and advertising.

*An early Fordson tractor seen in "**Boxted Hall Farm Scenes**" 1925.*

Farming

In Suffolk in 1900, there were 30,000 full time farm workers and 42,000 working horses. The acres of wheat grown in the county was 106,000. According to the Suffolk Agricultural Association these figures in 1950 were 22,000 full time workers, 12,000 horses, and 103,000 acres of wheat grown.

During the next fifty years things were to change a lot more as workers left the land, more machinery came into use, and yields increased. By 2000 there were 6,000 full time workers and only 10 horses, but the amount of wheat grown had gone up to 250,000 acres. These figures for Suffolk reflect what was happening to the East of England as a whole during the 20th century. The region fast became the most highly mechanised agricultural industry in the country.

But what was it like when labour was cheap, when nearly everything was done by horse and manual labour? Jack Leeder of Knapton on pulling sugar beet out of the ground: "That was hard work. Knock the mould off. Cut the top off, and then the team man and one or two other men would come with the horses and waggon and throw them on. Then used to cart them to the railway station. Believe you me, when you had finished at night you were tired"

Jack Leeder was a retired farm worker when he was interviewed for "**East Anglian Farming Scenes**", a film of 1974 of the then present methods compared with those of the past. "When I first started they had horses for everything. It was about 1914 when I saw the first tractor ploughing a field".

After the First World War mass produced tractors became available, but even in the 1920s they were few and far between. An early Fordson

*The men take their caps off in "**Boxted Hall Farm Scenes**" 1925.*

*A cinema newsreel item of "**The Farm Strike**" 1923.*

Some of the cycling pickets in the Norfolk countryside.

Another newsreel item of the farm workers strike of 1923.

tractor is seen in "**Boxted Hall Farm Scenes**", near Colchester, pulling a light harrow and a small cultivator. But the majority of work was still being done with horses. One is attached to a tumbril loaded with sacks of chaff, another pulls a water cart, two pull a drill across a field, and four struggle to move a waggon loaded with sacks of grain. One horse is lovingly attended by a horseman, before being put in the shafts of a tumbril. Filmed in 1925 by a member of the Blewitt family, this film shows a typical mixed farm of the time - arable and livestock. Drilling corn and threshing out, and shots of cows, pigs, and sheep - all feature in this amateur film, including the farm's milk delivery van. Attitudes are vividly portrayed by the farm workers at threshing time. Mr. Blewitt persuades the men to line up before the camera, and then asks them to take their caps off, and they all dutifully oblige.

Farm workers were amongst the very low paid. Their wages had already gone down since the 1914-1918 war, and in the early 1920s they were getting something like 28/- (28 shillings was £1.8.0 or in decimal £1.40) for a 54 hour week. In Norfolk farm workers were threatened with a reduction to 24/9 (approx £1.24). This worked out at about 5½d an hour. In March 1923 they decided to strike. The cinema newsreels picked up the story, and Topical Budget issued "**Farm Labourers Down Hoes**" showing George Edwards, the farm worker who became an MP, representing the men, and addressing them in Aylsham market place. Lord Kimberly, a sympathetic MP and local landowner, is also seen. "**The Farm Strike**", another cinema newsreel item, shows pickets on bicycles that went round the countryside persuading men to stop work. Both newsreel items have shots of work continuing on the land, regardless of the strike. It all ended on April 21st 1923, when really neither side won. Wages were fixed at 25/- (£1.25) for a 50 hour week.

In the early 1930s farm workers in Suffolk were getting 28/- a week (£1.40) and an extra £5 for getting the harvest in. They had Christmas Day, Boxing Day, Good Friday and Easter Monday off. By 1937 the weekly wage was about 35/- (£1 .75p) though it did vary from place to place. In that year John Ganderson made "**Men of The Land**" at Morley in Norfolk, which shows the day in the life of a farm worker. He bicycles to work and receives his money at the end of the day. Just a few pennies are left over it seems, enough to buy cigarettes and a pint or two. So in over ten years things had not got a lot better. In wartime wages went up. In 1942 it was announced that farm workers were to receive £3 per week, but as wages went up, so did the cost of things. More land needed to be brought into production. Charles Wharton, farming in East Norfolk, put his plans into practice of ploughing up some unused land in "**Crown of The Year**", and in "**Fuel and The Tractor**" a farmer explains to camera that fuel must be handled carefully and not wasted as every drop is needed to plough up the extra million acres the government wants put into food production. Machinery is a 'vital weapon' in wartime farming, and "**Welding Helps The Farmer**" is about how to keep equipment going. These are government information films of which hundreds were produced in wartime – though not many were made in the East of England, or if they were, the places are seldom identified. "**Clean Farming**" explains to the farmer the benefits of eradicating unwanted plants by removing root systems, burning weeds, and spraying. "**The**

Rabbit Pest" shows crops ruined by rabbits, and goes on to explain how to get rid of them by shooting and poisoning with cyanide gas, and "**Kill That Rat**" states that rats cost the country millions of pounds in lost food, and that 'Rats Do Hitler's Work – Kill Them Now'. In "**The Great Harvest**" (1942) the commentary asks people to work together, to forget their differences and help to get the harvest in.

But let's go back to the 1930s when little had changed to the regular routine dictated by the seasons. Basil Chaplin was a young farm worker then. "Gosh, I used to be up at half past four in the morning, and get up fourteen horses every other morning all by myself. Got to feed them, clean them, get them all right ready to start work at seven o'clock in the morning". Basil Chaplin, of Lawford in Essex, was interviewed in 1974 for inclusion in "**East Anglian Farming Scenes**", a film that compared farming in the 1970s with that of the 1930s.

"They used to have an interest in the work in those days. You'd see a horseman, he'd plough a field as straight as you could lay a line. A good horseman would draw a furrow across a field within an inch and a half. If you wanted them to come this way, you'd say 'cupiwee', and if you wanted them to go the other way you would say 'whee', and they knew exactly what you said".

Jack Leeder of Knapton continues "In Norfolk 'cupiwier' for left, and 'wheesh' for right. I've been all day and I have forgotten my reins, and I've turned my horses about all day with word of mouth. In the springtime you'd be ploughing, harrowing, drilling, and as spring advanced, you got early summer, you'd be drilling turnips, mangolds, horse hoeing and those sort of things. When I first started when you went drilling you had a man behind, that was the team man, the skilled man of the job. He was the man that fed the horses and groomed them. Then you'd have a man leading them, and a then a boy in front. You'd have three horses, but they soon done away with that, and had two horses do it".

The time Jack Leeder and Basil Chaplin are talking about is the mid 1930s. It so happens that the film maker Mary Field recorded these very activities in a series of films documenting the farming year. "**Farming in Spring**", "**Farming in Summer**", "**Farming in Autumn**" and "**Farming in Winter**", made for classroom use between 1935 and 1936, are now invaluable records of a way of working the land. They were filmed in Suffolk on two farms. One was Wood Farm at Sibton near Peasenhall, a heavy-land holding of about 120 acres, tenanted by Flloyd Peecock; and a combination of light-land farms near Leiston known as St. Mary's Abbey Farm, Lower Abbey Farm, and Upper Abbey Farm. The tenant here was Arthur Rope, then in his 85th year, although the day to day management of the 1,000 acres, farmed as a single unit, was in the hands of his son, Mr. G.A. Rope. Richard Rope, Arthur's grandson, was able to add information to scenes in the films and name many of the people.

"**Farming in Spring**" opens with the young cattle being let out of the yard and leaping for joy in a meadow with St. Mary's Abbey ruins in the back ground. Some of Abbey Farm's thirty men then get to work. Mr. Carey cleans out the yard, loading the manure into a tumbril which is taken to a field where individual heaps are made at regular intervals. The manure, or muck as it was generally known, is then spread by hand by Mr. Spall; and Charlie Websdale ploughs it in with a pair of horses pulling a Ransome's TCP plough.

Back at the farm, Lacey Smith and Jack Ford prepare food for the sheep. It is taken to the troughs and poured in by the head shepherd, Harry Self, and the sheep rush forward to eat. Will Walker is seen

Drilling with three men. The drill was made in the works of James Smyth of Peasenhall.

Pulling muck from the tumbril to make small heaps which will later be spread on the land by hand.

*Charlie Websdale ploughing with a pair of horses. From "**Farming in Spring**", 1936.*

doing some spring ploughing, while Eddie Clarke shows how a sheepfold should be made out of wheat straw and branches from a hedge.

A drill, made by James Smyth of Peasenhall, is filled with seed, and pulled by three horses and worked by three men, one to guide the drill by walking alongside operating the steering lever, one sitting on the seed box to look after the horses, and the third walking behind to make sure the grain was going down into the ground properly. Harrowing and rolling scenes follow, then a sequence of broadcast sowing by William Aldred as seen in "**This Was England**", released the previous year.

"**Farming in Summer**" shows some of the nineteen sows then kept at Upper Abbey Farm in a section dealing with the care of stock. Two old sheep shearers, the Palmer brothers of Kelsale, who were shearing contractors travelling around Suffolk, are seen at their trade, followed by a sequence of dipping ewes. A horse drawn hoe made by Garrett's of Leiston is seen working through the new sugar beet crop, followed by 'chopping out'. This manual job involved a man with a hand hoe slowly going along the rows of emerging beet plants, removing extra ones so that the remaining plants are regularly spaced with room to grow. This is also called singling, and was necessary as the seed was multi-germ before the days of the mono-germ beet seed accurately sown.

A thick crop of oats, tares and beans at Sibton is cut for making into silage, followed by Flloyd Peecock with tractor and mower cutting a rather thin crop of hay. The hay is left to dry, then turned with a swathe turner to dry some more. Finally the hay is made up into cocks as a precaution against rain.

"**Farming in Autumn**" contains the busy harvest period. Cutting maize, carting beans, the corn harvest, and lifting sugar beet. The wheat harvest sequence, filmed at Sibton, is particularly well covered. First two men scythe round the edge of the field to make way for the binder, and one of them ties the loose wheat with a straw bond, a length of straw wrapped round the sheave and neatly twisted to hold it together. The reaper binder, then goes round the outside of the field in the path

Harrowing the young crop in the spring.

The reaper binder at work. This cut the crop and tied it into sheaves which it deposited on the ground.

Someone came along after the binder and propped the sheaves up into stooks, shocks, or traves to dry.

*Loading sheaves to take to the stack yard to make a straw stack. From "**Farming in Autumn**", 1936.*

made by the scythers, and continues to cut the field in ever decreasing circles. The sheaves, laying on the ground in the wake of the binder, are stood up in shocks, stooks or traves, depending on what part of East Anglia you come from.

Jack Leeder, from Norfolk remembered in 1974 "After you had cut it you set it up in stooks, or shocks as we call it". Basil from Essex remembers it with a different term. "And you set it all up in traves, some people call them stooks, but we call them traves, and leave it there. And when it was properly dry you could cart it then. They used to say you can cut oats and leave them in the field until they had heard the church bells ring three times - that was three Sundays – then you could cart them".

After a suitable time, carting began. Jack continues "And then in come the horse and waggons, pitch it up on to the waggon, take it to the stack. Make it into a stack. It had a size bottom about – for a wheat stack – 13 yards by 5 yards. You'd put straw or dried grass on the bottom, keep the corn from getting damp, and you built your stack – which is a skilled job and hard work".

Basil remembers that "All stacks were thatched. There'd be a real thatcher. That was a skilled job, that was a trade years ago that was". Jack continues "I rather pride myself on my thatching. You want the know-how if you want to keep the water out. That's what you are up there for, to keep the water out. I'm afraid sometimes when we'd been a long harvest, we didn't be too particular and used to be getting home. Most people would look to find their rent out of that harvest. They got the noble sum of £7 at the end of about a month. £4 of that would go for the rent. The team man probably didn't have to pay any rent, he used to get house rent free".

Next in "**Farming in Autumn**" comes sugar beet. The beet are pulled up using a knife with a small hook on the end, and knocked together to get the earth off, and then the leaves are chopped off. These will be used for cattle feed. The beet are put into heaps, then heaved by hand into a horse-drawn tumbril which takes its load to a convenient point by a gate where the contents are tipped out and loaded by hand again into a large waggon to be taken to the railway station. Finally a bowler-hatted gentleman on a Fordson tractor ploughs a field – the only sign of a tractor in all these four seasons films.

"**Farming in Winter**" opens with threshing the stacks at Upper Abbey Farm. The tackle used, which belonged to the farm, consisted of a Garrett of Leiston portable steam engine and a 1917 Garrett threshing drum, with an elevator made by E.R. & F. Turner of Ipswich. The old-fashioned portable engine continued in use until the Second World War, and the threshing tackle on into the 1950s.

Next mangolds (mangelwurzel), or cattle-beet as they were known, are taken from a clamp, an open-air storage heap covered with earth, for slicing and feeding to cattle. The mangolds are fed by head stockman Lacey Smith into a root cutter driven by a Fairbanks Morse petrol engine. The roots and other ingredients are mixed together on the barn floor. Finally the bush draining sequence seen in "**This Was England**" is repeated in more detail. After the hedge is cut to provide the brushwood, a network of trenches is dug across

On the top of the threshing machine is the man cutting bonds (string round the sheave to hold it together) and then feeding the loose sheave into the drum for threshing.

A curved cupped tool for scraping a smooth channel in the bottom of the trench when making brushwood land drains.

the field to be drained, using specially shaped tools as the trenches get deeper. Each of these tools is shown, sometimes in close-up, so that we can see how it worked. The bottom of the trench is smoothed with a curved tool which is also cupped, forming a channel along which the water runs. The brush wood from the hedge is pressed into the trench just above the channel, preventing the earth from falling down and blocking the waterway when the trench is filled in. At the edge of the field, where the water runs into a ditch, two or three drainpipes are put in. Finally there is winter ploughing with a Ransomes YL horse-drawn plough.

Throughout these films equipment and tools are seen in the hands of men who used them. Today, they can only be seen hanging in museums or shown at events where traditional methods are demonstrated. The proper use of a cumbersome hay knife is seen when Flloyd Peecock cuts slices of silage out of a stack to feed the cattle. "The silage has now set into a thick, solid mass, like plug tobacco, brown and juicy. It smells extremely strong but the cattle love it", says the commentator, Mr. A.O.D. Claxton, who was deputy secretary for education in East Suffolk, an authority on the Suffolk dialect, and 'expert collaborator' for the films.

The farm worker lived close to his work, often in a tied cottage connected to the farm. He would have a garden to grow vegetables, and there would be a shop and pub within walking distance. Children would go to the local school, which might be in the next village, and many had to walk there, and home again before it got dark in the wintertime. Some of the luckier children had bicycles. Life in the countryside was organised. This is demonstrated in a film called "**Farm Factory**", released in November 1936. This compares a farm, Upper Abbey Farm, with that of a factory, by way of layout and organisation of the workforce. The management structure of the farm is shown, with G.A. Rope at the head, and his assistants Lacey Smith, head stockman; Will Walker, head fieldsman; and Harry Self, head shepherd, underneath. They in turn had field hands to help them. Growing different crops to keep the land in good order, and replenishing the earth with manure from livestock, was part of the cycle of keeping the land healthy.

Mary Field released eight films in the series. Besides the four seasons films, there was "**Wheatlands of East Anglia**" (explains why East Anglia is particularly suitable for growing cereals) which came first in 1934, followed by "**Town Settlement**" (looks at Saxmundham, and its place in the farming community) and "**This Was England**" in 1935. "**Farm Factory**" and the four seasons films were released at the end of 1936.

In 1983 the East Anglian Film Archive made a compilation film from this Mary Field material called "**To Plough To Sow**", assisted with a script by George Ewart Evans. This film included interviews with surviving farm workers of the Leiston farms - Jack Ford, Charlie Websdale, and Herbert Smith. Jack remembered vividly what the days were like. "The farmer used to come out in the morning, the foreman used to see him and get the orders for the day. Then the foreman used to come up to the yard where we were, and give us all the orders to carry out. Stockmen, horsemen or anyone used to have the day's orders. We used to do our best to carry out whatever he say."

"It was seven o'clock in the morning till about half past four at night with a little time off for dinnertime" adds Herbert Smith. Charlie Websdale recounts "We used to have to depend on the old bike to get round the farm. When I was a'ploughing I used to ride the horse there, get off, and get to work, then take him and ride home."

The films were photographed by George Pocknall and Frank Bundy, and directed by Mary Field for Gaumont British Instructional Films. Mary Field, with an M.A. from London University in Imperial History, became a film maker 'quite by chance' after taking an interest in films during her academic studies. In 1927 she joined Harry Bruce Woolfe at British Instructional Films, famous for its "Secrets of Nature" films which it began making in 1922. Short films of about ten minutes each, these were studies of plant and animal life for cinema distribution, specialising in micro-cinematography, speeded up and slowed down motion. British Instructional Films was eventually taken over by a feature film company, and Mary Field and Bruce Woolfe then joined a newly formed organisation - Gaumont British Instructional Films, in 1933. Their main output at GBI, as it was known, consisted of films on biology, geography, hygiene, physical education and science, together with a new series of nature films entitled "Secrets of Life". A sister company set up at the same time was Gaumont British Equipments, formed in July 1933 with the object of making 16mm and 35mm projectors available to educational institutions. "Suitable projection apparatus can be installed at shortest notice by means of the country-wide G.B.E. service organisation. Whether hired for the day, hire purchased, or kept for use to be shared between schools and classrooms, one of the various portable models will be suitable for all individual needs. The GeBescope 16mm projectors will show both sound and silent films at their correct speeds", said a Gaumont British Equipment advertisement of the time.

Mary Field's eight farming related films were made on 35mm, and prints were available on this gauge. 16mm reduction copies were made for schools that had one of the new 16mm sound projectors. Silent versions of the films with inter-titles were also available for those that could only afford a silent 16mm projector.

A film called simply "**The Fens**" in 1932 briefly shows, amongst other things, a reaper at work. Self delivery reapers came before the binder, and just cut the corn leaving it loose in the field. With their unwieldy revolving sails pushing the tall corn over the reaper knife, they made a strange site reminiscent of a Victorian photograph – for this is the age these machines really belonged. The reaper binder was a great advance, a machine that cut the corn, bunched it, and tied it automatically. They were the workhorse of harvest in the first half of the 20th century, and are seen in many films about the countryside. "**Major Gladdens Broads Film**" briefly shows rabbits laid out on the binder canvas after the field had been cut. Catching rabbits escaping from the cornfield was the pastime of many youngsters with sticks at the time, as well as farm workers with guns, but that did not mean

Flloyd Peecock using a hay knife to cut animal feed.

they could keep them if they caught one. The ritual was that all rabbits caught would be laid out on the binder canvas at the end of the day, and distributed according to the hierarchy of the men. The farmer would probably have first choice, then the tractor driver would have his pick, the man who rode on the binder had his also, then came others who made the stooks, right down to the local lads.

At Thaxted, in Essex, there is a harvest sequence in "**Ripe Earth**", a film made by John and Roy Boulting before their cinema feature film careers took off, and here men shoot rabbits as they escape from the corn. This is followed by a harvest supper in a barn. Combine harvesters, which did the work of the reaper binder and the threshing machine, appear for the first time in a 1933 film called "**Harvest**". This cinema short was filmed at a time when location sound was still being experimented with. Covering both scything corn, and cutting with a binder, the film goes on to show a large imported Massey Harris combine harvester at work somewhere in Suffolk. The sound was recorded at the time, with no attempt to add commentary. This works well, until a shot of a horse drawn waggon in a country lane is seen accompanied by noises of ducks, which are not seen. The microphone was placed somewhere near the view taken by the camera, but not exactly, so that it picks up sounds of people and animals not in the shot.

Rearing poultry was popular in the 1930s, with some farms almost totally devoted to this side of the business. The different breeds of poultry – Sussex, Rhode Island Reds, White Leghorns etc, and how to look after them is the subject of two films, "**The Story of a Norfolk Farm**" and "**Poultry Farming**". The first film was made by Triumph Substandard Films (meaning it was shot on 16mm and not the standard gauge of 35mm) and covers the hatching of eggs, the chicks taking their first steps, blood testing, and being fed in the yard. A breeding pen complete with a Light Sussex cockerel is shown, hens are weighed ready for market, and eggs are collected around the farm. There is some doubt that this film was shot in Norfolk, as various references throughout the film seem to suggest that it was Suffolk, and that the film makers did not know where they were. However, it was Felsted in Essex where "**Poultry Farming**" was filmed in 1939, and this film covers much the same ground, though there is a sequence on different types of chicken coops, the moving of these by horse, the mixing of chicken feed, and plucked birds ready for market. There are shots of free range chickens as well as an early form of battery house. The film maker obviously had a sense of humour, as there is an animated shot of a man spitting out a stream of eggs!

January 1940 began with intense frosts followed by much snow. William Newcome-Baker, of Wethereds Farm, Sedgeford, between Docking and Heacham in West Norfolk, was out filming with his 16mm camera the clearing of snow in the lanes with a snow plough. One tractor pulling farm machinery gets stuck and has to be dug out. This is the beginning of "**A Year on a Mechanised Farm**", a personal record by Mr. Newcome-Baker of his highly mechanised farm which is in sharp contrast to the farming films of the 1930s.

Winter work involved clearing tree stumps from land to be put under the plough. Drilling of spring crops begins followed by hoeing beet mechanically. Chopping out young beet still had to be done by hand. Women are at work hoeing in a potato field. Hay is cut and gathered in, followed by the grain harvest with two imported tanker (the grain was dealt with in bulk instead of sacks) combine harvesters pulled by crawler tractors. Rabbits run out of the standing corn and are chased. The grain is taken by lorry to a store, where there is a grain dryer. The stubble is ploughed up by crawler tractors pulling large ploughs. Sugar beet is lifted by machine, though subsequent handling is done by manual labour. The beet leaves the railway station for the nearest sugar beet factory. By now the roads are covered in snow again as the year ends.

This film, about twenty minutes long, is interesting for the amount and variety of machinery being used, and the ways of working on a farm with equipment that was becoming available to farmers a part of the war effort to grow more food. Here for instance a crawler tractor was being used to pull trailer ploughs on what appears to be quite light land. William Newcome-Baker was proud of his farm, and what he had achieved. A progressive farmer in a time of adventure, struggle, hard work and long hours. There are occasional glimpses of his children, but otherwise this is a remarkable record of farming in wartime.

At Newmarket, in 1943, they had a parade through the town of farm machinery, one of the many money raising schemes towards the war effort. "**Farm Sunday**" gives an excellent idea of what was being pressed into service. Equipment old and new, traction engines, horses, imported American tractors, etc. They parade through the main street, with the amateur cameraman filming sections when he thought the shot looked interesting.

Balaclava Farm lies on the wide open land between Terrington St Clement and the Wash. This was owned by Laurence Symington of West Winch. Sydney Gent was the farm bailiff on this 700 acre estate which the Symington family had bought in 1912. In the late 1940s Laurence Symington filmed the farm, his family, and their dog Buster. There are traditional shots of a binder cutting the corn, with scenes of threshing out, cutting kale, spinning out potatoes with women in the field collecting the crop, riddling potatoes in slow motion, and deep ploughing with a crawler tractor. There was a time when the thinking was that the deeper you ploughed the better. This might be true for burying plants and roots, but often this practice turned up new unwanted weeds.

An even bigger plough digging yet deeper is shown being hauled across a field by cable. Cable ploughing was originally done with the aid of a pair of steam ploughing engines at each side of the field. This is what appears to be happening here, except on closer inspection the steam ploughing engine has a replacement diesel engine on its chassis.

*The 'Spraycopter" of Pest Control at "**Balaclava Farm**".*

To continue the unusual aspects of Mr. Symington's 16mm farming film, there is a sequence of spraying by helicopter. A few American helicopters became available after the war, and one or two were bought by a company called Pest Control, founded by Dr. W. E. Ripper, a pioneer of aerial crop spraying. Dr Ripper, Managing Director of Pest Control, is seen amongst the farmers who have come to watch this demonstration of what he called his 'Spraycopter, which relies on the downwash from its rotors to force atomised spray droplets into the crop'. So "**Balaclava Farm**" gives us yet another unique sight into post war farming, where machinery was taking over from manual labour.

Rationing was still in place for some foods in the late 1940s, and more home food production was needed. The state of farming following the war can be seen in a 36 minute colour film called "**Britain Can Grow It**". John Birch, described as an agriculturalist, delivers the commentary. "The country is in the midst of a very severe financial storm that has arisen from the war. We just can't get sufficient food from outside and so we are on short rations". Over shots of people coming out of a factory in the Watford area of Hertfordshire, he says "Some 46 million people are looking for more home produced food. This fresh demand means that the farmer must produce one sixth more than he does at present". This film, made by Fisons, is about the use of fertilisers on the land to increase production. On an un-named farm the commentary continues "These farmers, who swear by farmyard manure, and are prejudiced against fertilisers, are often very hard to convince, but you would be surprised if you knew how much of their land I find deficient in lime and phosphates". After shots of cows and a field of grass which was sown after a potato crop, he continues "grassland such as this should be ploughed, limed, have fertiliser applied, and be put through a rotation of arable crops before we can expect it to reach maximum fertility".

John Birch goes round a farm with Herbert Read, a fictitious tenant farmer played by Herbert Chester, looking at the crops. A field of wheat which "is none too good" is shown with John Birch

Fisons film unit made a large number of films to advertise their products and inform the farmer.

*John Birch on the left and Herbert Read wander around a meadow in "**Britain Can Grow It**".*

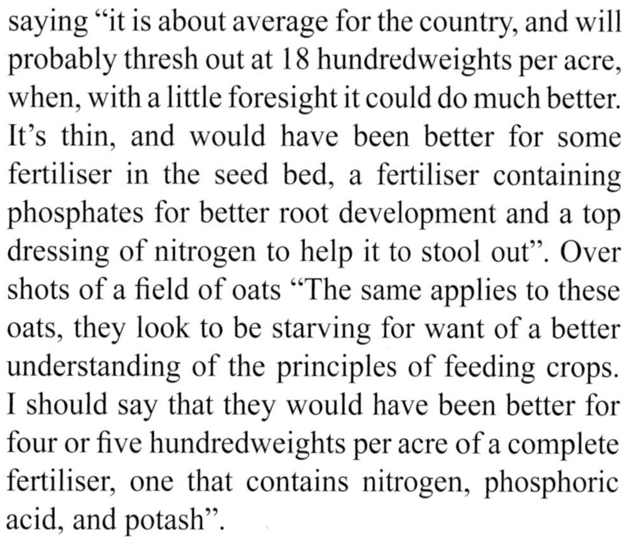

saying "it is about average for the country, and will probably thresh out at 18 hundredweights per acre, when, with a little foresight it could do much better. It's thin, and would have been better for some fertiliser in the seed bed, a fertiliser containing phosphates for better root development and a top dressing of nitrogen to help it to stool out". Over shots of a field of oats "The same applies to these oats, they look to be starving for want of a better understanding of the principles of feeding crops. I should say that they would have been better for four or five hundredweights per acre of a complete fertiliser, one that contains nitrogen, phosphoric acid, and potash".

Various root crops are shown; mangolds "a long way from making a good crop for stock after Christmas"; potatoes "this poor crop might produce 6 tons per acre whereas with a suitably balanced fertiliser considerable increase in weight can be gained during August and September"; and sugar beet "this crop is not as forward as it should be in July, and does not lift more than 6 to 7 tons per acre. It should be meeting in the rows, and no doubt would have been if there had been no lime deficiency, and it had been adequately supplied with plant food". Then, in a synchronised sound sequence with the two men chatting to one another, Herbert Read, still not convinced about artificial fertiliser, asks Mr. Birch "If you think I am putting too much faith in the value of muck, can you tell me how to measure its value".

John Birch replies "On a farm like yours, and yours is a typical stock farm, the amount of plant food supplied by the muck is about one third of the total amount required for high fertility and really profitable yields. The rest, some two thirds, must be made good by using fertilisers, and muck needs supplementing by at least 10 to 15 tons of fertiliser for every 100 acres of farm land".

"That means I must spend a fortune on fertilisers. How do I pay my rent?"

"Let me put it this way, for the first crop after mucking, the plant food value of a dressing of say 10 tons per acre of farmyard manure is about equal to that from three to four hundredweights per acre of fertiliser. Now maybe that's plenty for a corn crop or even grassland, but it is not nearly enough for some other crops such as sugar beet, mangolds, potatoes, swedes, and kale, and your know Herbert, you can't muck all your land at that rate each year. You may not believe it, but it is easier to get full crops without muck, and with the little you rely upon, provided of course you apply enough of the right kind of fertiliser".

"But surely, you don't really believe that you can keep on farming with fertilisers only, without ruining your land"

"Look, in the car I have a film which shows some other farmer's methods – some depend entirely on fertilisers, and others supplement muck with fertilisers, let me show it to you".

"I have got half an hour before milking, and I have heard about these no muck farmers, and I would like to see how they do it".

Mr. Birch sets up a 16mm silent Ampro projector, and shows Herbert a film called "Farming, Fertilisers, and Food".

"I find it very handy Herbert, to have a bit of film

to show you busy farmers, and bring out the point clearly without you having to go a long way to see it for yourselves. Of course this won't be a talkie, and so I will try to give you a running commentary, keeping in mind this far reaching topic of muck and fertilisers. You have your own views, but just see what other farmers have done by paying attention to drainage, liming, good cultivations, maintenance of organic matter, and adequate use of fertilisers, and by improving their methods".

The film shows farms and farmers in Staffordshire, Oxfordshire, Wiltshire, and Suffolk. The Suffolk farmer is Stanley Warth, of Manor Farm, Hintlesham. This is a mixed farm - livestock and arable.

"Mr. Warth's aim is making his farm as near self supporting in food for live stock as conditions will permit. Much of his revenue comes from milk and there are dairy cows here with yields that anyone would be proud of. He has found poultry quite profitable, and so realising that we can rarely ever meet the demands for eggs for the breakfast table, he has gone out to convert home grown grain into an article very much favoured by the housewife. Remember we have had to import millions of eggs, and we really cannot afford to do so. Great credit must go to Mr. Warth for his fine livestock performances. But what impresses me is that he sees to it that the whole farm is run on a properly balanced business footing".

Over shots of waving barley "as with stock, so with crops. He sees that they are supplied with sufficient quantities of food of the type best suited to their particular needs. Corn usually requires three to five hundredweights per acre of compound fertiliser, except when following a root crop that has been liberally manured. You are not likely to see many crops of this standard if the fertiliser application has been haphazard. When sowing barley with a combine drill, and using three hundredweight of a compound fertiliser per acre, he makes sure that his corn is not going to suffer for want of plant nutrients. You see, three hundredweights sown this way with a combine drill, gives a much higher yield than where it is broadcast before the seed is sown".

To emphasise the higher yield there are shots of many stacks of corn as a threshing tackle team are at work. "Mr. Warth will get a good deal of pleasure on looking at a well filled stack yard and the satisfaction of making a useful contribution to the food the country so urgently needs"

The film within the film ends, and Herbert Read says "Well John, you have done your best to show me that this fertiliser business is not just a racket. Mind you, I'm sticking to my muck, but after what I have seen, perhaps I will have a do with a bit more fertiliser. Of course I shall want your advice"

"I will give you all the help I can" says John Birch, emphasising the advisory service offered by Fisons.

This film, "dedicated to increasing food production through a better understanding of the use of fertilisers" is an ambitious one by Fisons. It was produced and directed by Reginald Broome,

*Herbert Read on the left and John Birch talking in a studio set up. From "**Britain Can Grow It**".*

John Birch laces up a film on an Ampro 16mm projector as Herbert Read looks on.

with Russell Holbrook as the cameraman. The film is in Kodachrome, and is well photographed. The two men, John Birch and Herbert Read, talk to one another in what must be an early attempt at 16mm synchronous filming. Lip sync sound for 35mm films was easy, as the equipment was available, even if it was large and cumbersome. But direct sound filming on 16mm had not really been developed yet, and as the set of the two men leaning on a gate has a background of the farm, it is probable that this was filmed in a London studio where sound recording equipment was available. But it is still an astonishing production for its time, with the use of an actor and a script writer also acting. The audiences of farmers who sat down to watch "**Britain Can Grow It**" must have been quite impressed at the professionalism of this and other Fisons films.

Like other big organisations, Fisons realised film was an ideal way to provide information. They first hired William Carson about 1946 to make films for them, and he produced "**Feeding Britain's Fields**" and "**Grassland Review**". William Carson wrote the scripts, shot the film, edited it, and read the commentary. Fisons, who now had extensive offices in Harvest House (the old Felix Hotel) in Felixstowe, decided that a full time film and photographic unit was needed, so they built a studio in the grounds and appointed Reginald Broome as producer and director and Russell Holbrook as photographer. Other staff were also employed to provide display and publicity material.

Fisons, like many other companies associated with agriculture, has a long history. James Fison, founder of the firm of James Fison and Son, owned White House Farm at Barningham in Suffolk, and traded as a miller in 1780. In 1808 he moved his business to Thetford. One of his sons, also a miller, married a Deborah Prentice. She had some nephews who had a company called Prentice Brothers in Stowmarket. One of James Fisons grandsons, Joseph, founded the firm of Joseph Fison and Company in Ipswich in 1847. About this time one Edward Packard was making history by his discoveries relating to the manufacture of superphosphate. He founded the firm of Edward Packard and Company in 1849 also in Ipswich. These companies, all with an interest in fertilisers, eventually became one in 1929 – Fison, Packard, and Prentice Ltd. Suffolk was the natural home of the fertiliser industry, for coprolites, the original source of phosphate in superphosphate, were first found on Suffolk farms. In 1934, a new works was built at Cliff Quay in Ipswich, where the raw materials could easily be delivered by ship. Here were the sulphuric acid and superphosphate departments, and later a granulating plant. This was something new, fertiliser in the form of granules, which were easier to handle than the previous powder, and would flow simply in seed drills and fertiliser spreaders. In 1942 the company changed its name to just Fisons Ltd.

"**Fisons Field**" sets the scene of the Fison group of companies, and the "**Royal Visit to Levington**" shows the Duke of Edinburgh opening the Fison research laboratory in 1956. "**Lord Netherthorpe, President of The National Farmers Union, Opens Fisons Nitrogen Factory**" at Standford-Le-Hope in Essex in 1959, shows exactly what the title says, and the film "**Opportunities With Fisons**" shows the many career possibilities with the company. These include trainee chemists, analysts, chemical plant operators, and soil chemists, as well as secretaries and calculating machine operators.

The studio made films for others parts of the group, such as the Garden Division at Bramford. "**Better Gardens**", "**A Compost For All Gardens**", "**A Garden For All Seasons**" to name just a few. But it was for the agrochemical part of Fisons that the majority of films were made. The large collection, which came to the East Anglian Film Archive after the studio closed, contained films such as "**Making Good Hay**", "**Facts About Fertiliser**", "**High Profit From Small Dairy Farm**", and "**The Search**", a film about the research involved in making better fertilisers. Reginald Broome retired in 1973, film slowly became less used, and the studio ceased in 1982.

Other filmmakers worked for Fisons from time to time. Gilbert Hawker made "**Nitro-top Spreads Like a Compound Fertiliser**", Athos Films made "**This is Fisons Pest Control**" at Fisons Research Centre at Chesterford, and Douglas Fisher made in 1973 "**Better Than a Lick**

*"**Making Good Hay**", a Fisons film shot mostly in Scotland.*

of Paint", a film about Gro-Bags. These were bags of compost which could be laid down, slit open, and seeds planted. The vegetables or flowers grew straight from the bag.

As 1950 loomed, there were still some things that had not yet been mechanised on the farm. In "**Mr. Starling's Farm Films**" the planting of celery is done by a man crawling across the field on his hands and knees putting each individual plant in by hand. With a person in front laying them out, he makes a hole with a dibble in his right hand, while his left hand picks up the plant and pushes it into the hole. This is done faster than it can be described. Celery plants were transplanted to the open field when they were about three or four inches tall. The earth around the plant was then pressed firmly, in the film seen done by a man walking slowly along in rubber boots compressing

FOR
McCORMICK INTERNATIONAL
FARM EQUIPMENT.
ASSENTOFT
GRAIN BINS.
BONNEL
ONE WAY PLOUGHS
and
SINGER CARS
contact
W. R. FORD & SON, LTD.
SALHOUSE. 'Phone 473.

the plants. This sequence, filmed by Claude Starling on his farm at Pymoor, near Ely, gives us an idea of the sheer physical effort once required of farm workers. Incidentally, a machine was developed to plant celery, and this can be seen in the 1961 film called "**The Fens**".

Claude Starling also shows off his Ferguson tractor. The Ferguson system was new, a small popular tractor with a three point hydraulic linkage system which brought tractor and plough together as one machine helping the tractor get a better grip on the land, and enabling implements to be lifted clean off the ground. Even the attachment of a two wheeled trailer (and a hydraulic tipping one at that) to the tractor was made simple with a one hook device instead of the cumbersome four wheeled swivel axle trailers and hitch pin hitherto in use.

The war had given a tremendous boost to mechanisation on the farm, and this trend continued in peacetime. Small companies sprang up making and repairing farm machinery. One such was that of W. R. Ford and Son, agricultural engineers of Salhouse in Norfolk, who were keen to show off their latest farm machinery to farmers at demonstrations. Mr. Ford made 8mm films of the farm equipment he sold and his engineering business in Salhouse, as well as films of his family, and these exist in the "**Ford Collection**". An enterprising businessman, he even sold cars!

But it was mainly farmers themselves who made these amateur films, as they wanted to record their latest tractors and implements, of which they were very proud. There were still a good number of people working on the land, but their roles tended to be overseeing the machines. Eric Barker filmed "**Farm Machinery**" in use on his father's farms in the Rickinghall area of North Suffolk in 1950. Here is their new Farmall tractor, and the latest baling

*Women tying bales on this baler from Eric Barker's film "**Farm Machinery**".*

A new Farmall tractor on Frederick Barker's farm, about 1950.

machine, with women seated on it attending to the tying of the straw bales. All these farming films by non professional film makers have been selected because they each have something unusual to show about agriculture and its development, and about working the land in the Eastern Counties.

The National Institute of Agricultural Engineers, NIAE for short, had a research station at Silsoe in Bedfordshire from 1947. In wartime their job had been to advise the government on tractors needed, servicing and training, mechanisation etc. After the war they concentrated on educational and research work. They made instructional films for the farmer and his staff. These were silent 16mm films with inter-titles to explain how to carry out a particular job like "**Cultivating**" or "**Tractor Ploughing**". Others explained how "**The Binder**" and "**The Combine Harvester**" worked, and how to go about "**Potato Cultivation**".

However something less formal was needed if the farm worker was to be able to hear about new machines, learn how they worked, and discuss the latest ideas of machines and farming techniques. This was solved with the formation in April 1946 of the Norfolk Farm Machinery Club. The aims of this organisation were; To encourage study of and contact with the latest types of machinery and plant; The giving of lectures and technical instruction to farm machinery operators; To hold demonstrations and competitions of farm machinery; and To help in the development and invention of machines and to make recommendations for improvements to the Institution of British Agricultural Engineers. The founding members were Mr. W. Parker, Mr. R. R. Wright, Mr. J. R. Ware, Mr. J. C. Mann, Mr. A. Garrod, Mr. S. Eglington, Mr. W. Newcome-Baker, Mr. N. Langridge, and Mr. Ben Burgess.

The first meeting was held in Norwich, and William Newcome-Baker showed his film "**A Year on a Mechanised Farm**". Twenty people joined. The next step was to put into practice the aims of the Club. This was a formidable task, and it was carried out by John Cleveland who was appointed honorary secretary. John Cleveland had been a poultry farmer at Horstead Cottage, near Coltishall since the late

NORFOLK FARM MACHINERY CLUB

A Programme of

SOUND FILMS

on

Fuels,

Tractor Maintenance and Grass Drying

(Speaker : N. F. A. MOORE, A.I.B.A.E.)
will be presented by the
ANGLO-AMERICAN OIL CO.
at the following Club Centres :

Monday, January 23rd — Town Hall, Attleborough
Tuesday, January 24th — Town Hall Annexe, Downham Market.
Wednesday, January 25th—The Council Room, Docking.
Thursday, January 26th—British Legion Hut, Blofield.
Friday, January 27th — Nelson Hall, Hempnall.

Commencing 7.30 p.m.

All members and their friends are cordially invited

1920s. He had three thousand birds on 56 acres of land. Just after the war he joined the Ministry of Agriculture Fisheries and Food (MAFF) as a National Agricultural Advisory Service machinery adviser for Norfolk. He continued this work whilst also running the Norfolk Farm Machinery Club for twenty years.

The first demonstration was organised at Gaywood, near King's Lynn, of rowcrop equipment – that is machines for hoeing out weeds between the rows of young plants. Farm machinery manufacturers submitted their latest designs for hoeing, and farmers brought along machines of their own making. One of these farmers was Dick Joice with his modified Cornish and Lloyd down the row hoe attached to an Allis B tractor. In order to make sure the farm worker was fully involved, a competition was included for the best tractor hoeing, irrespective of the owner of the machine. Eighteen men took part watched by a crowd of over 300. This demonstration was deemed a success, and the Club held many demonstrations each year from then on of all types of equipment used on the farm. In June 1948 the Club's first 'Newsletter' was produced, and this too was a success. John Cleveland wrote each monthly newsletter for the next 18 years.

Centres were established all over the county beginning with Norwich, Docking, Watton, Attleborough, North Walsham, Blofield, Hempnall, Downham Market, Dereham, Loddon, and Fakenham. There were regular demonstrations of one way ploughs, hedge cutting equipment, sugar beet harvesters, spraying and dusting machines, ditch cleaning and trenching equipment, forage crop machines for silage harvesting, muck loaders and spreaders, and tractor hoeing. Farmers willingly gave their fields over to these demonstrations which were held all over the county. There were ploughing matches, and the regular tractor driving competition at the Norfolk Show. The Club always had a tent at the show, where members could come in and chat and get refreshment. Talks, discussions, and competitions were held at the regular evening meetings in each centre. Film shows were a major part of theses winter evening meetings. 16mm films were available on free loan from such organisations as the Petroleum Films Bureau, as well as from individual companies such as Esso, Shell, Ford etc, and were shown on cine projectors borrowed from the MAFF base at Sprowston Hall. A few of the films found their way into the Archive, such as the colour film "**Adventure On**", a 1957 film by Tom Stobart about farming methods around the world, and an American film about safety on the farm – with a dramatic scene of a tractor overturning. These were donated along with others by Mr. Shorten of Norwich.

A few films were made in the 1960s of the Norfolk Farm Machinery Club demonstrations. "**Quick Haymaking**" is a record of the machines at the 'Quick Haymaking Technique and Equipment Demonstration' at Abbey Farm, Guestwick, on June 14th 1961. This included various models for cutting hay, tedding the hay (that is turning it over to dry on the ground) and baling the dried hay. These machines picked the loose hay from the ground and tied it into bales. These came out of the baler at the back

Machinery Club Film Shows

The Norfolk Farm Machinery Club has begun its winter programme this week with a series of well-attended film shows, arranged in conjunction with the Shell Mex-B.P. farm service, at Attleborough, Watton, Blofield, North Walsham and Hempnall. Programmes included a colour film dealing with grass drying and another on tractor maintenance.

Norfolk Farm Machinery Club film evenings in 1949. Most of the films were available free of charge.

A Norfolk Farm Machinery Club evening meeting, with films about to start.

to fall harmlessly on the ground – except for one, a New Holland machine which shot the bale at high speed out of the back of the baler into a following trailer. This never caught on!

There are two 16mm silent colour films of the annual rowcrop competition – "**Sixteenth Rowcrop Competition**" held on May 23rd 1962 on Mr. A Cargill's Hall Farm at Hindringham, and a year later "**Equipment For Spring Work in The Beet Crop**" at Hockering on May 29th on Gavin Alston's Heath Farm. These also show thinners and gapers, novel machines to thin the beet out so as to mechanise chopping out, that is removing unwanted beet so there was a standard gap between plants. These machines never really caught on, and anyway the mono-germ beet seed that produced just one plant was developed and sown at regular intervals. Chopping out became a thing of the past.

"**Demonstration of One Way Ploughs and Fertiliser Spreaders**" was held on seventy acres of stubble provided by Mr. E. F. Harrold on his farm at the old Oulton Aerodrome, near Aylsham on October 2nd 1962.The purpose was to show different makes of reversible ploughs at work in the same field, and to show the different types of fertiliser spreaders in operation. The correct spinning time of the spreader and other essentials were needed for the fertiliser to be distributed at the correct rate and evenly on the ground. The film is also important as this was the first time PVC bags were used to hold the fertiliser. Fisons supplied the fertiliser used in these new strong and waterproof bags that could be delivered direct to the field. The only problem was opening them, as this could only be done with a sharp knife, and not all operators had one with them. A demonstration of "**One Way Ploughs**" was held on Mr. F. H. Rockcliffe's Lanes Farm at South Runcton on January 23rd 1964. This was a day course of instruction on reversible ploughs, and the film goes on to show club member Mr. H. Wordingham of the Docking centre demonstrating how to set and use a one way plough.

The work of the club can be seen in "**Norfolk Farm Machinery Club**", compiled in 1964. This shows some of the demonstrations, a safety item depicting a tractor half fallen off a trailer, scenes at the Smithfield Agricultural Show at Earls Court,

Manufacturers showed off their equipment at the Norfolk Farm Machinery Club demonstrations, like these fertiliser spreaders, hoping farmers would be impressed.

and the Club's tractor driving competition at the Norfolk Show.

A highlight of 1961 for the farming community in East Anglia was the coming of the British National Ploughing Match to Norfolk. Ploughmen from all over the British Isles came to Keswick, just outside Norwich, to take part. Mr. A. J. Gurney placed over 300 acres at the disposal of the match at Keswick Hall Farm. Held over two days, the 8th and 9th of November, one hundred and forty eight entries were received, and much organisation was required to make sure the whole thing went smoothly. There were classes for high cut work for tractors and horses, general purpose tractor ploughing, one way ploughing, and semi-digger ploughing. The rules were rigorous. "Fifteen minutes after the start there will be a halt of 10 minutes during which the opening splits will be judged. A red rocket will indicate that all ploughing must cease for 10 minutes after which a second red rocket will indicate that ploughing may be resumed. The opening split must be completed in the first 15 minutes. Failure to do this entails loss of points".

The ploughmen, though slow, took remarkable care while ploughing their third of an acre plot in the four hours allowed, and this can be seen in the silent colour film "**British National Championship Ploughing Match**". The Norfolk Farm Machinery Club provided over twenty stewards, and was the local affiliated body. The only local success was that of Mr. Brown from Carleton Rode in the one way class. He came third.

The sugar beet campaign, that is lifting the beet and getting it to one of several factories in the region, began in early October, usually at the same time as the first frosts. A newsreel item, called "**Beet Crop Raises Sugar Hopes**", of the October 11th 1948, tells the story. "The first load of the season's crops of four million tons of sugar beet come rolling in" as shots of lorries loaded with beet arrive at the British Sugar Corporation factory at Felsted in Essex. "Around the factories the yards pile high with the hard parsnip like roots which nowadays provide the equivalent of the whole domestic sugar ration.

"With 400,000 acres of beet to be lifted, the new mechanical harvesters prove their worth. This year there are 550 of them in operation. Man power and time is being saved. Minus the tops, which feed the farmer's livestock, the roots are literally washed into the factory. They pass through a succession of cleaning processes, ending in great warm water tanks, where the roots are stirred mechanically. Samples are taken of each load to asses the sugar content. Despite a poor summer the yield is up to average. Two and half ounces to the average beet. Sliced into strips, the pulp goes through a defusing process, much like making tea, and the thin syrup flows away in a stream, which runs without stopping until mid January. Through evaporation, the syrup is whirled around to separate the molasses from the sugar. Pure and white, but still damp, it is sprayed out through the driers. By the end of the season there will be 500,000 tons of it. For Britain, it will be an achievement to be proud of".

Although there had been attempts at extracting juice in a concentrated form from sugar beet in the 19th century, with a small works at Lavenham in 1868, it was not until 1912 that the modern home grown sugar industry began. It was a Dutchman, Jerald van Rossum who realised that the soil and climate were similar to that of his native land, and that there was no reason why beet could not be grown here. The difficulty was not so much persuading farmers to grow the sugar beet, but getting investors to provide the capital to build factories. Rossum was head of the Central Sugar Company of Amsterdam, so he knew how to go about setting up factories and getting the money. He formed a company, the Anglo Netherland Sugar Corporation, and in 1912, at a site at Cantley in Norfolk, the first modern sugar beet factory to produce white sugar and sugar pulp was built. It was close the Norwich to Yarmouth railway line, and next to the River Yare, so excellent transport links. In the 1912-1913 season it sliced 21,000 tons of beet.

However, there were problems during the war years, and by 1916 the Cantley factory had shut down. Sugar beet was still being grown, so this had to be shipped to Holland for processing. By 1920 the factory was operating again, and the business came into profit in 1923. Two years later the government introduced the British Sugar Subsidy Act, and expansion followed quickly.

In 1925 the factory at Bury St Edmunds, drawing on over 8000 acres of beet grown locally, was opened, as was another at Ely, where the

*The marshalling yard at the "**British National Ploughing Match**" in 1961.*

*The horse section at the "**British National Ploughing Match**" – drawing a straight furrow.*

*A sugar beet harvester at work, with the beet being transferred direct to a trailer. From "**Beet Crop Raises Sugar Hopes**" 1948.*

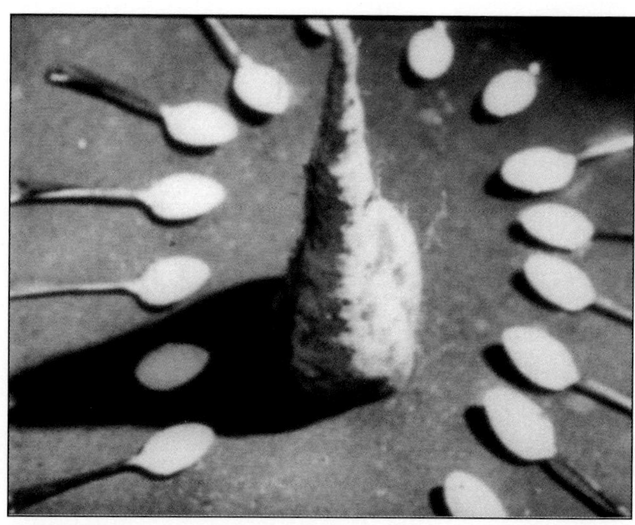

The ratio of teaspoons full of sugar to one beet - 15 spoons of white sugar.

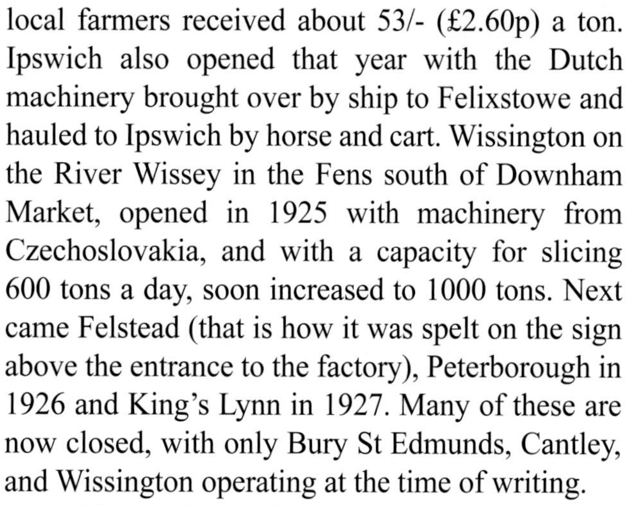

local farmers received about 53/- (£2.60p) a ton. Ipswich also opened that year with the Dutch machinery brought over by ship to Felixstowe and hauled to Ipswich by horse and cart. Wissington on the River Wissey in the Fens south of Downham Market, opened in 1925 with machinery from Czechoslovakia, and with a capacity for slicing 600 tons a day, soon increased to 1000 tons. Next came Felstead (that is how it was spelt on the sign above the entrance to the factory), Peterborough in 1926 and King's Lynn in 1927. Many of these are now closed, with only Bury St Edmunds, Cantley, and Wissington operating at the time of writing.

The whole sugar beet business was reorganised in 1936, and the British Sugar Corporation came into being overseeing all the seventeen factories throughout Britain. A number of films were made to show farmers the advantages of growing this crop, and how to deal with it, and these have survived thanks to Mr. Southwell who recognised their value. The "**British Sugar Corporation Collection**" contains films on drilling, hoeing, thinning, and harvesting sugar beet from 1938 onwards, as well as "**Sugar Beet Harvesting at Fakenham**" (1948), "**The Crop at Swaffham**" (1958), "**Sugar Beet as Energy**", (1960), "**Virus Yellows**" (1961), "**Cleaner Beet**" (1963), "**Sugar From Beet**" (1974), and "**Sugar in Your Kitchen**".

The Ministry of Information made "**Sugar Beet – Harvesting**" in 1946, newsreels picked up stories in the 1940s and 50s, and "**Beet Sugar**" was made for educational use in the 1950s. A 1961 film called simply "**The Fens**" shows the once familiar sight of heaps of beet by the roadside, waiting to be carted to the railway station or the local sugar beet factory.

Case and Steward, a company with bases in Norwich and Yarmouth, listed themselves as fertiliser and corn merchants, with Victoria Maltings in Southwell Road Norwich, and salt and kainit fertiliser works in South Denes Road in Yarmouth. About 1955 they made a series of films revolving around their supplies of fertilisers and animal feeds to farmers. "**Fertilisers in East Anglia**" begins with potash being unloaded from a ship, mixed, tested and bagged in Case and Steward's stores ready for delivery to the farmers. At "**Manor Farm**", Blofield, just outside Norwich, the company tested their fertilisers, showing the results with fields of potatoes and sugar beet. The company was also interested in the welfare of livestock. Pig and cattle husbandry is shown at their farm, and looked at in more detail in "**Dairy Farming – Three Norfolk Farms**". Friesian herds on the farms of Mr. Nash at Little Melton and Mr. Nicholson at Neatishead, and Major Allhusen's Ayrshire herd at Claxton Manor Farm, near Loddon are shown grazing, at milking, and with their calves.

These films were shot on 16mm Kodachrome (though there are some black and white sequences) at 16 frames per second, the normal speed for amateur films, and had a magnetic stripe added to the cut film for the commentary. Therefore a 16mm projector capable of playing back a magnetic stripe track was needed, but no doubt they had one of these. Magnetic stripe was fairly new at this time, the system becoming available from 1953. The films were shown to farmers as part of Case and Steward's promotion of their products. The fourth film in the series deals with free range and battery poultry. "**Systems of Poultry Keeping**" was shot on William Crawford's Wood Farm at Carbrooke and Mr. Daniels farm at Hingham, and discusses free range and battery keeping, the feeding of pellets and grain to the birds, and the business of egg packing and collection. Mr. Daniels battery houses hold 2000 birds. The keeping of turkeys is also featured, as it is in a "**Pathe Pictorial – Norfolk Turkeys at Catton**". This shows Broadlands Turkey Farm at Old Catton, just outside Norwich, where Mary Mussellwhite reared about 9,000 birds a year. Mary Mussellwhite was born into farming. She came from Boxted, near Colchester, married Eric Mussellwhite of Mistley in 1935, and ran a poultry farm in Cheshire during the war. In 1946 she began rearing turkeys at Old Catton. "I think it would be hard to find any section of British agriculture which had advanced with such rapidity, both scientifically and practically, as turkey rearing" she said in 1953. That year she was visited by Pathe News who filmed her farm at the beginning of October. The turkeys are outdoors, though Mary Mussellwhite said that "the less movement a bird has to put up with the quicker it makes flesh. Modern science in incubation has made hatching more reliable and today we have two large Dutch incubators which are capable of hatching about 2,500 eggs weekly. Testing the eggs for fertility is done by passing a strong electric light under them on the 24th day. By this method the operator can see quite clearly if the eggs are 'clear' or 'addled' and remove them from the tray".

Most of the film is shot outdoors, probably because it was too dark to film inside. One turkey is suffering from sinus trouble, and Mary and her assistant Betty Faulkner examine and clean the bird. "Turkey farming, especially in the Eastern Counties, is a coming industry" said Mary Mussellwhite in an article she wrote in 1953. "Housewives are fast beginning to realise that turkey is a nourishing meat which is just as delicious in the summer months as at Christmas. So far, we in England eat only roast turkey, but before long we shall find many other ways of cooking it. In the States one can buy roast turkey roll, tinned breast of turkey, and turkey cutlets". Mary Mussellwhite's enterprise must have seemed big business, but this was only small scale stuff compared to Bernard Mathews.

Acle market, on the Norwich to Yarmouth road, was where, according to legend, the Bernard Mathews story began. As a young man of 20, he bought some freshly laid turkey eggs for a shilling each (5p), and a paraffin incubator, and set about hatching them. The business had begun. Five years later, in 1955, he bought a large almost derelict mansion, Great Witchingham Hall, in Norfolk, and filled it with turkeys. He and his wife lived in a room close by.

Bernard Mathews himself talks about those early days to Hugh Barrett in "**Turkey Tycoon**", a television film made by Malcolm Freegard in 1966. "I am an agricultural industrialist" he says, denying he is a tycoon. He talks about his ventures into rabbit farming and rainbow trout business, neither of which came too anything. His wife Joyce, who is a board member, talks about renovating the Hall, selecting show birds, and entertaining visitors. Turkey chicks emerging from the shell are shown, then their living quarters - first in wire bottom drawers, and later in the large sheds situated on old airfields. Then the turkey factory is shown, where the birds are killed by electric stunning, processed and packed.

A few years earlier "**The Bernard Mathews Story**" was made. This does not contain any interviews, but does show in much more detail, and in colour, the young birds living out in the open in coops; de-beaking; the sheds where they spend

Turkeys on Mary Mussellwhite's farm in 1953.

*Bernard Mathews outside Great Witchingham Hall, as he appeared in "**Mathews Norfolk Farms Commercials**".*

Some of Bernard Mathews staff appeared in his television commercials in 1983.

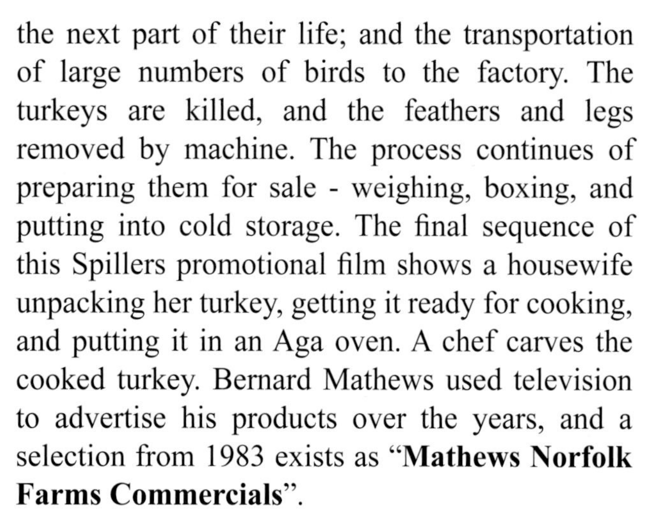

the next part of their life; and the transportation of large numbers of birds to the factory. The turkeys are killed, and the feathers and legs removed by machine. The process continues of preparing them for sale - weighing, boxing, and putting into cold storage. The final sequence of this Spillers promotional film shows a housewife unpacking her turkey, getting it ready for cooking, and putting it in an Aga oven. A chef carves the cooked turkey. Bernard Mathews used television to advertise his products over the years, and a selection from 1983 exists as "**Mathews Norfolk Farms Commercials**".

Bill and Devora Peake's fruit farm at Boxford in Suffolk was the subject of a short film in 1984 about Copella apple juice, the company she ran. The story behind this enterprise is interesting. The Peakes began fruit farming at Boxford in 1938, just selling fruit. Thirty years later they bought a press and began marketing juice, calling it Copella – the name made up from Cox's Orange Pippen and the last part of their youngest daughter's name, Carmella. Later they sold the business, only to buy it back again in 1991. "**Apple Juice**" shows the orchards, and the processes of washing, pressing and bottling the product. Devora Peake talks about the difficulties she had getting the company up and running, and Tamara Peake explains that apple juice is good for hangovers, and to prove this she had scientific tests carried out which apparently showed that apple juice does have sobering effects. One wonders how they went about this in the laboratory!

Fruit farming was also going on at Wickhambrook on the farm of Justin Brooke of Clopton Hall. Here was a dairy herd, a milk delivery service, and the production of soft fruit and apples. In a colour film made in the late 1950s, "**Fruit Production at Clopton Hall Farm**" shows men pruning the trees in wintertime, and then picking apples in the summer sun and placing them carefully into boxes. In a barn the apples are graded, weighed and packed ready for sale. Incidentally, a short black and white film was shot on the farm by Edith Brooke in 1935, when a large bonfire was built ready to celebrate the Jubilee of King George V. Cars and lorries arrive bringing people to the festivities, and a new delivery van is named *Jubilee*.

Mr. Whitwell of Pakenham had a 16mm cine camera, and recorded on Kodachrome film in 1961 his way of dealing with peas on the farm. "**The Pea Crop**" begins with bags of fertiliser being emptied into a tractor mounted spreader, which then does its work. Next a crawler tractor pulls a harrow across the field, then the pea drill is filled up, and the peas are sown, with a man and a boy riding on the back of the drill. The field is then rolled. The young crop is sprayed in the spring and scarecrows are put up to keep birds away.

The time comes when the peas are gathered, and they are placed on tripods by hand. A harvester comes along and the peas fed by hand into the machine from the cocks. Another method shown is that the peas lay on the ground in rows, and the harvester comes along and picks them up automatically. The threshed peas are taken away by lorry.

There were not many chances for relaxation throughout the farming year as there was always something to do on the farm. The agricultural shows were an exception. All the counties had their shows, but occasionally the Royal Show came to the region. This national agricultural event was held at Cambridge in 1961, and Mr. Whitwell went along with his 16mm camera to record some of his farm workers receiving long service medals from the Queen Mother. The men then pose for the camera. In those days farm workers often worked all their lives on the land for the same employer. However, this was a special occasion, for normally it was just the local Suffolk Show which everyone went to. These county shows had their origins in the Agricultural Associations of the 1830s and 40s. As far as is known, the first filmed Suffolk Show was that of 1927, when it was held in Christchurch Park, Ipswich, during the first week of June. The film was taken on June 2nd by a London cameraman named John Hutchins who was hired to make this local newsreel for an Ipswich cinema.

The shows travelled round at that time, to a different part of the county each year. In 1928 it was held at Bury St Edmunds, when 14,389 people attended. Other films depicting this annual event include "**Suffolk Show 1955**" by Eric Barker, and "**Royal Occasion**" in 1965 when the Queen Mother attended at the now permanent Ipswich showground.

"**The Royal Norfolk Show at Crown Point**" was filmed for a Norwich cinema in 1928. Prize cattle, a parade of horses, dog handling, and show jumping were filmed, and the Duke of Gloucester was in attendance. "**A Day at The Show**" was made in 1961 by Norwich Union film maker A. P. Cooper as a promotional film for the company in colour and sound. This begins with shots of Norwich cinemas and theatres as examples of other types of shows. At the Norfolk showground site cars arrive, and crowds watch the grand ring events and cattle judging, while others go round the trade stands.

The Peterborough Show is featured briefly in "**The Peterborough Diesel Engine Story No 4**" of 1963; the "**Essex Show**" turns up in the collections of Mrs. Tellwright and Norman Turner, both of Clacton, and in Hertfordshire there is the 1946 show in Cassiobury Park in "**Northmet Newsreel No 1**". In Bedfordshire there is a short sequence of the "**Bedfordshire Show**" in 1936, and almost thirty years later, in 1965, an excellent sound film also called "**Bedfordshire Show**". Here there was much to interest the town dweller, with parachute jumping (one lands almost on the cameraman) and the young farmers cavorting on a trailer. The "**Young Farmers Rally**" of 1961 held at the Norfolk showground was recorded in a 16mm colour silent film, and this shows the fun activities in the grand ring as well as tractor handling through a course of obstacles, cattle judging, and competitions between the various clubs.

*Parade of cattle at the Suffolk Show in Christchurch Park in 1927. From "**Suffolk Show**".*

*Parade of horses at the Suffolk Show at Bury St Edmunds in 1928. From "**Great Suffolk Show**".*

An event in the grand ring at the Norfolk Show.

The Peterborough Show.

Saturday was market day in most towns, and farmers and farm workers sometimes got the chance to go, though often it was work. In "**Town Settlement**", a film of Saxmundham in 1935, the farmer goes to market in his horse-drawn trap, while his wife walks into town. He looks at farm implements on sale and pigs, poultry and cattle. There is a lively sequence at the market when a pig escapes and everyone runs around trying to catch it. In "**Wheatlands of East Anglia**", 1934, there are shots of the cattle market in the centre of Norwich, and a good sequence in the Corn Hall in Exchange Street, where farmers offer up their little paper bags of samples of corn to the merchants, all trying to get the best price. One farmer is turned away, another gets a sale.

Bury St Edmunds had an extensive market for farmers which film makers found attractive. An unknown cameraman took shots of pigs, goats, cattle, and sheep at the livestock market in 1950, and in 1989 a sound film in colour was made of "**Bury St Edmunds Market**" and the farmers who went there. "**Simpson's Market**" is a film made in 1993 recording the last days of livestock auctioneers Simpsons and Sons, a company that was about to cease trading after 131 years. Several people are interviewed, one of whom has been visiting the market since he was 15 years old, and another remembering what it was like in the 1930s. Sheep arrive and are auctioned, and a bell would ring for the start of the cattle selling. Country life came to Bury on these occasions, with the noise and smells of farm animals, and the chatter of country characters, all of which is recorded in these films - before development swept it away.

Farm livestock is the subject of many films, some directly such as "**Suffolk Sheep**" made for the Suffolk Sheep Society in 1948, and "**Sheep Dip**", made by John Ganderson on a farm at Wreningham, near Wymondham, in 1937. The sheep were encouraged, often pushed, into the dip where they were supposed to be fully submersed in a solution against ticks. Sheep scab is due to the presence of a particular species of mites which burrow into the outermost layer of the animal which leads to the formation of scabs. At that time the treatment was to dip the sheep into a mixture containing such things as lime, sulphur, soap or carbolic acid.

A truly rural scene of calves being led by a cow-woman into a dilapidated barn appears in Margaret Wright's "**Village Peepshow**", filmed on a farm at Wheathampstead in Hertfordshire in 1948. Here they are fed from buckets, which they eagerly stick their heads into. A modern well laid out, though small farm, is seen in "**The Dairy Farmer**", made a year later. Here George Gall, the farmer at Wall Farm, Holbrook, in Suffolk, opens his bedroom window at six o'clock in the morning to look at his cows. They are beginning to walk towards the farm. He has a quick cup of tea, the other workers arrive, and milking begins. The udders are washed and the milking machines attached, as the cows contentedly eat at the other end. The milk is collected into a tank, where it pours down over corrugated panels to be cooled.

It goes into milk churns, which are loaded into a van and driven away. The milking parlour is then thoroughly washed. That is only the first part of the day for Mr. Gall and his staff. Next the chickens are fed which are all over the yard, and eggs collected in a basket. Food is mixed for calves and pigs, and straw bedding prepared. Throughout the day various jobs around the farm are done, including cutting hay. In the late afternoon the cows are wandering back to the farm for the evening milking session.

Churns were the way milk was transported to the bottling plants in the 1950s, when lorries travelled the country lanes collecting the milk churns from platforms by the road. When Nigel Rea made "**A Farm in East Anglia**" for Boulton Hawker Films in 1975, milk was transported in bulk, in this case by a Creamline road tanker. The film follows the activities during the farming year. The simple commentary of this classroom film states "The lorry takes the milk to a dairy in a town about 30 kilometres away. Other products leave the farm by lorry. This one has come to collect wheat. Like the milk tanker, this lorry carries its load in bulk. It's much quicker that way".

Like others with stock, the farmer where "**A Farm in East Anglia**" was made, shows off his prize bull at the Suffolk Show. It wins first prize. At the show the parade of cattle included Red Polls. "The red poll breeder, large or small, is generally a confirmed enthusiast for the kind of animal that occupies an increasingly prominent and popular position in Britain's livestock industry" runs the opening commentary in "**The Red Poll Story**". Made in 1955, and mentioned in the previous chapter as produced by the Perkins Film Unit, this colour sound film continues "It is the purpose of this film to illustrate the many advantages held by the red poll, the true dual purpose breed for any type of farmer who insists on economical management. The dominant physical characteristic of the breed is of course natural hornlessness or polling, along with a deep chestnut red colouring, hence the name red poll. Polled cattle take up less space than horned beef, and are far less likely to damage each other or their handlers. More polled stock can be kept in the yard at less expense. Whether passing through narrow farm gateways or being packed into transport, all the advantages are with the polled animal. By visiting the store rooms of the leading firm of curriers in Britain who specialise in the production of high quality leather goods, we can see the damaging effects after horning on cattle hides". The film shows hides with marks, as well as the company's products of "travel bags, bucket bags, and handbags".

Red Polls are shown in fields, many of them on the Sandringham estate where they were introduced by King George V in 1914. The theme of the versatility of the breed and long life of the animals is emphasised. "Today there are more red polls alive having had ten calves or more than any other breed. A long living dairy herd is cheaper to keep, and replacement costs are reduced".

"During the last ten years, Milk Marketing Board statistics show that on average red polls are the third best milking breed, inferior only to two breeds of purely dairy cattle. Remember that the red poll is a good bit smaller, and its food intake correspondingly less than several other milking breeds. The good milk yields of the red poll are easily achieved on the minimum of expensive concentrated food stuffs".

"Red poll breeders are constantly endeavouring to produce ever higher yields of better quality milk without losing the wonderful beefing ability for which the breed is famous".

A Dewhurst butchers shop sequence shows meat being cut up followed by a chef preparing joints for the oven. Prize cattle are shown and the commentary and pictures explain what to look for. "The cow's head should be fine and clean cut. The eyes bright and placid, and ears of medium size. The neck clean and blending smoothly into the shoulders, which should be sloping and full at the top for breathing and digestive freedom.

*Taking milk away in bulk. From "**A Farm in East Anglia**" 1975.*

Loading wheat in bulk. From the same film made by Boulton Hawker Films.

The body should be deep and of medium length, with the ribs well sprung and arching out from the back bone, providing a roomy barrel and ample heart space. The hind quarters should be long and well filled from hip to aitch bone, but not patchy at the rump ends. The buttocks deep and well fleshed down to the hocks. The hips evenly rounded and not prominent, the latter point indicating a good beef animal. The back should be level from the shoulder with a strong loin. A tail long and thin, and set on level with the back. The colour must be red, a solid chestnut red for preference".

The Red Poll Cattle Society had their offices at 32 Princes Street in Ipswich, where pedigree records were kept. It was they who commissioned this film. "Cattle are essential to maintain fertility in the land. A red poll herd, being ideal for yard and parlour method of farming, readily converts straw into manure, giving the complete cycle of fertility. Manure provides food for crops, to feed the red polls, to make meat, milk and more manure". Given all the qualities of the breed, why did they decline so? Farming has changed considerably since the 1950s. Mixed farms are not as abundant as they were then, artificial fertilisers have replaced muck to replenish the land, and other breeds now produce more milk than the Red Poll.

Other films with cattle as their subject are "**The Health of Dairy Cattle**", **Mastitis**", "**Contagious Abortion**", "**Winter Milk**", and the "**Cattle Breeding Centre**" at Beccles.

"**On The Farm, Winter and Spring**", made by Hugh Brandon-Cox on a farm near Fen Ditton, in Cambridgeshire, deals not only with calves, and the milking of cows, but lambs, sheep, horses, and pigs as well. In a wintry scene pigs root about in the snow in this colour classroom film made in 1966. Hugh Brandon-Cox also made "**Pig Farming**" in Cambridgeshire a couple of years before, which concentrates solely on this farm animal. The commentary explains that the pig's diet is important. The young piglets weigh about 3lbs at birth, and require feeding every two hours. The farmer has to cut their teeth to stop them biting their mother. After about three weeks they weigh around 15lbs. Their ears are stamped for identification. At three months they are examined by a vet, and some are sent to market as store pigs. The commentary explains they are clean animals, intelligent yet obstinate. Farm workers struggle to catch pigs that have to go to Cambridge cattle market.

An advertsing film for Tucks of Burston, the animal feed firm, was made in colour in 1971 about the Hylete pig. This was a hybrid animal from crossing pedigree Large Whites and Landrace pigs. "**The Hylete Pig – a Breeding and Feeding Success**" was filmed at the headquarters of Elite Hybrids at Colchester, with herds on farms belonging to Bernard Partridge at Weeley and Tony Doubleday at Stanway, in Essex, in Norfolk on James Laurie's farm at Carleton Rode, and in Suffolk on the farms of Captain Chute at Halesworth and the Redgrave estates unit at Botesdale. The young pigs were fed on a special diet that Tucks developed which allowed the baby pigs to be weaned from the sow at twenty one days. The system was sold throughout the UK and was exported to many European companies. At that time the government, through the British Export Council, encouraged companies like Tuck's and Hylete to attend European and World Agricultural Shows.

There are some specialised farming activities which are what one might call on the fringe of everyday agriculture. At Stuntney, near Ely, mustard was grown. Seeing a man cutting mustard with a sickle seems very old fashioned, but that is what was happening in 1960 in the film "**Harvesting Old Type Mustard**". The man has lengths of string tied to his belt which he uses to tie the bundles of mustard. John Hemingway took this 8mm film, and another called "**The Story of**

The Red Poll originated from the mating over a hundred year period of the old Norfolk and Suffolk Poll.

One of the Guernsey Herd on Bernard Cross's farm at Tasburgh.

Bernard Cross driving the tractor pulling his McCormick combine harvester.

Mustard" in 1969. He recorded a sound track on audio tape to go with the picture, with a commentary by Norfolk farmer David Richardson about the business of growing mustard. Over at Kelvedon, in Essex, Tony Bonner was growing plants for their seeds. This was even more specialised, as there was no machinery available to thrash out seeds from parsley, runner beans, marrows or tomatoes. "**Seed Specialist**" looks at the way Tony got round these problems with methods he developed himself. Tomatoes for instance. After women had picked the tomatoes by hand, they were pulped and sieved, and the result then steeped in hydrochloric acid for twenty minutes to clean the seed. This was a job Tony insisted on doing himself. Finally the seeds were washed and dried. Seeds from marrows were also recovered after they had been thoroughly mashed up. Some plants could be threshed, though not always by machine. In one case Tony resorts to the ancient method of threshing with a flail, beating the seeds out of the plants by hand. Another method was to lay the plants out on a large cloth on a concrete base, and run a tractor over them! The art comes in knowing when the seed is just right to be threshed out this way. "**Seed Specialist**" was made in 1978 by John Kenyon for the BBC Farming programme which used to go out on a Sunday. But Tony Bonner made his own films on 16mm Kodachrome as well of "**Tony Bonners Farm Films and Home Movies**", and a record of his own work in "**Tony Bonner Seed Specialist**" made between 1972 and 1977.

In the mid 1950s the average minimum weekly wage for agricultural workers was about £6.7.0 (£6.35p) per week. "**Farm Workers Wages**" went up in September 1960, and BBC East interviewed some men to see what they thought. They seemed happy and felt justice had been done. They talk about now not having to rely on overtime to earn a living wage. By 1962 it had gone up to £8.15.0 (£8.75p) for a 50 hour week. Wages for stockmen were slightly higher. According to "Mechanised Livestock Farming" by Ray Mortimer, published by Farming Press in 1964 "in recent years full time workers have been leaving the farms in Britain at the rate of around 20,000 per year".

Hall Farm, Tasburgh, near Norwich, was a small mixed farm run by Bernard Cross. Here was 150 acres of arable land farmed under the Norfolk four course system. This rotation of crops consisted of wheat the first year, a root crop the second year such as turnips or potatoes, barley or oats for the third, followed by a leguminous crop such as clover or beans. Then the process was repeated. On 45 acres of pasture land he had a fine herd of Guernseys, these supplying milk locally. He had a delivery van with 'The Hall Farm Golden Guernsey Milk from B. W. Cross' on the side. He was also very proud of winning the Supreme Championship at the Norfolk Show with a bull he bred himself. He proudly shows off his cattle in a sequence in "**East Anglian Farming Scenes**" made in 1974. He worked hard on his farm, and was able to buy in the 1960s a small tractor hauled McCormick combine harvester. This was small even by the standards of the 1960s, with its eight foot cut. It was driven by the power take-off from the tractor, and had a man riding on the combine

*Combining a field of barley at "**Lawford Hall**" farm.*

seeing to the bagging of the grain. The sacks were heavy and had to be carried to a trailer from the combine. A sack of wheat weighed 18 stone, and was known as a coombe.

In "**Lawford Hall**" made in 1983, Sid Hood is loading a drill with fertiliser as the farmer comes up to him to give him his envelope of wages. There were six farm workers on this farm at the time, and Francis Nichols goes round to see how they are getting on. They were Sid Hood "I'm the foreman about here when the governor is out", Harry Townes, Eddie Phillips, Kevin Hood, Stephen Noy, and Wynn Mander, the stockman.

On the film Francis describes how he became a farmer. "My father had the foresight to give me the farm and indeed the house when I was twenty one. But he made it entirely plain that he himself was going to continue to live in the house. This forced me to be interested in the farm, which at the age of twenty I had scarcely thought about. The whole property was 500 acres, of which a hundred was a mixture woodlands, and saltings which were effectively useless. That left 400 acres of which perhaps 250 were arable. We also rented a 150 acre farm called Woodhouse Farm four miles away, and with it got Sid Hood and his son Kevin. I have tried to run the two farms as one, growing barley, wheat, sugar beet, and potatoes. Potatoes were successful for a while, but I have now stopped growing them because I think you either have to grow a lot or none at all".

As he goes up to a tractor pulling a set of rolls at Woodhouse Farm, he asks Stephen "You made an early start?"

"I came over, I thought I might as well have a go at this, try and get this piece finished off".
"Gary did a bit last night did he?" (Gary, a casual worker)
"Yes he worked till dark".

At harvest time the Class combine works in a field of barley. "I think our old combine is going to give up after about eight years, and we have to think about finding a replacement". As Stephen then operates a large new John Deere combine "We got it for free for two days, but I don't think I can afford the enormous sum they are likely to ask for this green monster". The next sequence is of a harvest supper, where Francis thanks his men for all their hard work. The house is large, and Maureen Nichols describes what it is like to live in. "The problems with running this house are chiefly the cold. It is a lovely house to live in in the summer, and it is not that nice to live in in the winter, because a lot of your energy is simply devoted to keeping warm. We have done something now about the heating, we have a wood burning stove, but before that you did quite literally have to put your coat on if you left the kitchen. And going up to bed at night was really ghastly, and you always felt the children were too cold. I was always feeling their hands and their cheeks and they always felt absolutely freezing to me, and the dreadful moments in the morning when you get up and scrape the ice off the inside of the window".

The upkeep of the farm is not the only worry for a farmer, often the house needs expensive maintenance, as Francis discovered. "Last winter, when it was very cold, two of the valley gutters at the back froze, and the water came in, and we put two tin bathtubs up there, and the problem appeared to solve itself. But then in the summer we had to strip out the lead from the valleys and put in new flashing. They discovered the main chimney was dangerous, so they had to dismantle the main chimney completely, and rebuilt it straight upwards, where as before it had been angled".

There are also sheep on the farm. "A friend had a small flock of Jacob sheep. She said 'we might have to go back to South Africa, if we do, I don't know what to do with my 30 sheep'. Well send them over to us" Francis said without really thinking about it. "Eight months later that is exactly what she did. I got the telephone call saying the sheep were arriving. And indeed they did, and charming they were. But they were really good at escaping".

"My great grandfather bought the farm in 1868, and pulled down the old wooden farm buildings and designed new, and for those days, completely modern set of buildings at the bottom of the hill, and two cottages there. Both the buildings and the cottages have these extraordinary inscriptions like 'In Work is Joy' and 'Man Was Made To Be a Farmer'.

"I'm slightly embarrassed as a farmer, because I am of course owner occupier, and was not grown up doing every job that had to be done on the farm. I can do them, some of them rather badly, like ploughing, but I have now worked enough on the farm to understand exactly what is involved. My satisfaction comes from seeing that the jobs are done properly, and I hope in the next few years in having not only a well run farm, but also in trying to improve the layout of the estate. The roads are ruinous at the moment, a lot of the hedges are quite bad, and we are threatened with development from all sides. I would like to have a well run farming unit which will generate enough income to keep us going, certainly for the next five years, and hopefully for ever".

To complete on film a record of 20th century farming in the Eastern Counties, "**Norfolk Farming in The 1990s**" was made by Peter Hollingham for the East Anglian Film Archive in 1993. This was a time of further change, with new crops for the farmer, diversification, and set-aside. The film's commentary tells us all. "Cereals account for 6% of the country's needs, and are chiefly wheat and malting barley. Sophisticated combines are used to gather the harvest, with one man to drive the combine, and another to cart the grain to storage. Sometimes one man does the whole job. Before 1992, straw that was not required for other purposes was left to dry. On a windless day the straw was lit, and in a controlled blaze, was burnt off. After complaints of pollution, nuisance, and hazard from fire, the government banned straw burning. The farmer then had to purchase additional machinery to chop up the straw so that it could be ploughed into the land.

"Twenty-nine percent of all sugar beet grown in the country is grown in Norfolk. Every year a large number of farmers look to this crop to provide an important part of the year's income. Vegetables and fruit are important food crops, like these leeks grown in the fertile Fenlands. Blue linseed flower identifies a crop grown for oil. Farmers receive an EEC payment for this crop, and it is helpful as a part of crop rotation and has a good market and profit. Another oil bearing crop is rape, whose yellow flower in blossom is a wonderful sight during May. The oil from this crop is not so fine as linseed oil, but is a useful means of profit for the farmer.

"There has always been government control of what is grown, with subsidies used as the controlling factor. Today with a European market, British farmers must grow produce which fits into a market strategy. Owing to over production by European farmers, 15% of land must be set-aside – that is to grow no crops on an agreed acreage for a set period of time. The growth must be mown once a year, otherwise it is not cultivated.

"Animals are now being reared in more natural conditions than previously. The pigs are free range and are healthier and need less attention in consequence. Chickens are usually reared in batteries, but free range chickens are popular for the quality of their eggs.

"Conservation and preservation of the countryside is encouraged by the government and practised throughout the county. On Chris Skinner's farm just outside Norwich footpaths and rides have been cleared and properly signposted, so they can be used by many people who now have more leisure to walk or ride in the country. Hedges are being re-instated after they were removed some years ago to make larger fields. This hedge has been cut with a wide base to give additional cover for small animals. Woodland management is an important part of conservation. Contract foresters are clearing timber and brushwood on the Holkham Estate. The cut timber will be sold to help pay for the costs of maintaining the woodland.

"Government regulations, EEC directives, quality and quantity demands from supermarkets and other retail outlets, all affect the farmer. Dick Broughton, who is farm manager for Lord

Hastings, with an office at Swanton Novers, was told that the meat produced from his suckler herds had fat which looked muddy under fluorescent light. It was found that by changing the maize in the feed for wheat, the meat on display would look more attractive. The flavour was not changed in any way, but people would buy the meat more readily.

"These potatoes are specially grown for crisp production. They are all about the same size and shape for future processing. Casual labour is used in the harvesting and in the past upwards of twenty women would help in the fields. Now there are only two who are willing to undertake this work. The potatoes are left in the ground until late September when the skins are hardened. After harvest they are taken to temperature controlled storage where they are stacked in one tonne containers. They will not be sold until April or May the following year and so provide an income in what is normally a time of cash shortfall.

"In the past, work gangs would be a common part of the temporary labour available on the land. Today, labour regulations have reduced the number of people willing to undertake temporary work. This gang of local women, cutting cabbages near Kettlestone is a rare sight. The cabbages, loaded into containers, are ready for the wholesaler.

"This two acre glasshouse is owned by G. A. Bailey of Martham. Here and in other similar houses, are grown pot and cut chrysanthemums. The pots are filled by machine with a specially formulated compost. After planting they are packed in troughs which are watered, fertilised, and temperature controlled by computer. Over twelve hundred a week are planted, and in their ten week growth period they travel through the glasshouse, finally when fully grown, arriving at the packing area where they are prepared for sale. Flowers are produced continually during the year before being packed for sales outlets throughout the country.

"This tractor is collecting golf balls from the driving range. Alan Barnard leases the land from the Norfolk Show Committee for an 18 hole golf course run by golf professionals. Mr. Barnards's two sons run the family farm, and manage the golf course. This diversification uses land that is not often used after the yearly Norfolk Show.

"Security is an increasing problem with farmers. No farms are safe from theft, and those nearer the towns are most at risk. Sensors and lights cover all storage areas. Stolen cars are run over crops and then they are torched. Chris Skinner makes a final check in the late evening. After this, the alarm is switched on".

*Canvey Island, February 1st 1953, from "**Essex Floods**".*

The Coast

A tidal surge, like that of the 1953 flood along the East Coast, can occur after a small depression moves across from Scotland towards Denmark. "As it does so" Professor Keith Clayton of the School of Environmental Sciences at the University of East Anglia explained in "Floods of East Anglia", an East Anglian Film Archive DVD, "very strong winds blow northwards up the North Sea, pushing the water away from the southern part. Also the water rises under the 'low' as it moves across, because the low pressure doesn't push down the sea surface quite so much. It only rises a centimetre or so, but this is of course a very considerable volume across the whole of the North Sea. Then as the low moves away to the east, the very strong northerly winds on its western side come into play, and the water that had previously been pushed out of the North Sea is now pushed back into the southern part very quickly, not only by the wind, but also by the rising pressure as the low moves away.

"As a result, a rising wave of water, rather like the tide, moves around the North Sea in an anticlockwise direction, down the East Coast, down towards the Straits of Dover, and then northwards up the coast of Holland. Whenever this coincides with a high tide you have the combined effects of high tide and a surge, which can be as much as two or two and a half metres above the normal level of the North Sea".

This is what happened on January 31st 1953. The surge coincided with a high spring tide at the time of a full moon. Spring tides occur every fortnight or so, at new and full moons.

High tide in the Wash was supposed be about 7.30, but by 6.15 there was water in the streets of

King's Lynn, recorded in a film made by a Mr. Brown called "**King's Lynn Flood Scenes**". It was a cold, bitter night, and the surge came quickly, catching everyone by surprise. It was not until the next day that people realised how much damage had been done. Between Snettisham, Heacham, and Hunstanton bungalows, holiday chalets, and beach huts were badly damaged. Here American Airman Reis Leming rescued 27 people from bungalows single handed, but among the thirty or so who died along this coast, twelve were fellow Americans. Captain Leming went back the next day, and Ernest Swain filmed him wading in the water at one of the destroyed chalets. The Queen, proclaimed but not yet crowned, visited the coastline on the Monday and is seen in Ernest Swain's film "**East Coast Floods**".

Ernest Swain was a photographer at Hunstanton, specialising in photographing holidaymakers. In 1939 he took a picture of the pier on fire which made the papers, and with the proceeds he was able to open a photographic shop in the town. The day after the flood he was out with his 16mm camera filming the remains of the bungalows and chalets. The destruction gives some idea of the force of the sea along this part of the west coast of Norfolk. He filmed the railway line behind, the water cart which brought a supply of fresh water for the residents, and the royal party visiting the scene the next day.

The high tide at Yarmouth should have been about 10 pm, but by 9 pm water was already over the beach and the quay. At the Boys' Brigade Hall in Yarmouth, Bernard Bothams was giving a film show. Afterwards he was told "we can't get you home, the streets are full of water". He had to stay in a local hotel. The next morning he was able to get to his home in Gorleston, where he grabbed his 16mm camera and went out to film the flood water which remained in Gorleston. The main body of water had gone, and this is evident from the tide mark on the walls of houses, but much remained, and people were still being rescued. Cars were towed out of the water in Southtown Road, and a Jewsons' high-wheeled timber vehicle arrives with people to set down on dry land. A rowing boat comes into view loaded with rescued people who could not get out of their houses because of the remaining water, and a man wades out of his prefab along what was once his garden path. There is a lighter high and dry on Gorleston quay, and huge baulks of timber lying around on the roads where the water had receded.

Bernard Bothams, who was known as BB, ran a tobacconist's shop in Gorleston, and his hobby was making films on 16mm. His "**Gorleston 1953 Floods**" includes local coalmen delivering free coal from Lancashire which was distributed to residents to help dry out their houses. For this the coalmen got free beer from a local brewery, and they can be seen happily swigging from bottles. The prefabs were dried out using large hot air blowers supplied by the RAF. As soon as he could Mr. Bothams got over to Yarmouth to film in colour the clearing up operations on the sea front.

At Felixstowe the caravan park at the back of the town was severely swamped. It was the first place the water reached. Just before midnight an alert policeman realised something was wrong as water appeared, and he persuaded many people to leave their homes. In Langer Road to the south of the town a man got out of his prefab as water came flooding in. He swam down the road it is said, with his prefab following him. There are certainly shots in Mr. Whitwell's film "**Flood Disaster in Suffolk**" of a prefab deposited in the middle of the road after the water had gone. The tide line on some of the houses in the background gives an idea of the alarming height of the flood. The water can clearly be seen to have reached over the front doors. In all 39 people died in the Felixstowe area.

Mr. Whitwell of Pakenham was there soon after because his farm workers had been drafted into help with the clear-up operation. He also filmed them working along the coast near Aldeburgh making good the sea defences in "**Flood Damage Repairs**".

At Harwich there was four to five feet of water in the streets together with sewage from the drains. When the water got away, houses were left full of mud and filth, and were uninhabitable. Posters were stuck to houses saying "This Home is Dangerous, and must not be re-occupied without authority from the Medical Officer of Health". This is seen in shots taken by Richard Pike who had driven up from Southend. He had already filmed

*Frames from "**Essex Floods**" 1953.*

scenes at Canvey Island on the Sunday, after the flood had inundated the island at about 2 am in the morning. "People were awakened to find their houses surrounded by water in some cases many feet deep" runs the commentary of his film "**Essex Floods**". "It soon became apparent this was no ordinary flood, and that full scale emergency measures were required. To make absolutely certain that no people were left in danger, a house to house search was organised in every district". The film Richard Pike made so quickly is accompanied by scenes that the commentary describes.

This is the only film that shows the background to the flood, the homeless people with their few belongings waiting for transport to a warm safe place, of people preparing food, and of shoes and clothing for those that had nothing. The film was used throughout Essex schools, and was available from other educational libraries. The film continues "schools were requisitioned and rest centres and feeding centres were provided for this full scale emergency reminiscent of wartime years. Collections of clothing and footwear were made to help those who had lost most of their belongings. Babies and infants were given special care".

Over shots of water pouring through breaches, with men prodding with sticks to see where the sea walls ended, the commentary says "Engineers and surveyors of the River Boards were quickly on the scene to examine the damage and prepare a plan of action. When the tide had gone out it was possible to seal off the major breaches, but it was necessary to work both day and night under appalling weather conditions. Millions of sandbags were filled, and used to stem the rush of water. The inaccessible nature of the site prevented any extensive use of machinery, and manual labour alone had to accomplish the reconstruction. Even though the waters have returned to the sea, much still remains to be done, and many months of work are needed to ensure that a similar catastrophe shall not occur again".

More than 300 people died on the East Anglian coast as a result of this flood, and over 30,000 had to leave their homes. There was a loss of 46,000 cattle and sheep and other livestock, and 150,000 acres of farmland were flooded with sea water.

The clear-up operation went on for the rest of the year. At Burnham on Crouch an 8mm film has scenes of the aftermath of the "**Flood**" there, and "**The Purfleet Floods**" is a film record of

cleaning and getting Van den Bergh's margarine factory back into production. The "**The Great Gale**" is an advertising film showing how tractors, in particular the Ferguson tractor, not only helped rescue farmers and their equipment from Wallasea Island flood waters, but took part in reclaiming the salt covered farmland, and re-building damaged sea walls after the sea had gone.

The 1953 flood may seem to have been the most famous thing that has happened to the East Anglian coast, but all along are stories to tell of ships, boats and fishermen, of industries and local events, of towns and villages, and of course the sea itself. Film makers were never slow at picking up these stories and recording them on film.

"**The Northenders**" was a 1982 BBC East film about the pink shrimps in The Wash and the fishermen who went after them. The film begins with a history of fishing from Lynn, right back to the days when ships joined fleets from Russia and Norway to hunt the great herds of whales across the northern oceans. The Fisher Fleet, a small tidal creek that branches off from the River Ouse still has active fishing boats coming and going. The fishermen used to live close by in the northern end of the town, and were known as 'northenders'. Now only a museum at True's Yard housed in some of the original fishermen's cottages, remembers those days when the fishermen lived close to their work, seldom married outside the local families, and frequented the "The Retreat", "The Victoria", "The Bentinck", and "The Fishermen's Arms" when thirsty.

Frank Castleton was the last fisherman to catch shrimps under sail, and he demonstrates putting up a gaff rigged sail in his small fishing boat. In his seventies, he does not go to sea anymore, but spends his time catching eels close inshore and building wooden boats. David Howard has a modern fast boat to go miles out into deep water to catch pink shrimps. He goes out in LN 298 *Jean Howard*, trawls, and brings aboard a mixture of small fish and brown and pink shrimps. The catch is sorted, and the pink shrimps, which are known locally as Lynn prawns, are boiled in brine for a few minutes on board. The Eastern Sea Fisheries Committee fast launch "*Protector*" comes alongside and John Darlington, the skipper, and his crew, come aboard to measure the mesh to make sure the trawl net is legal. Though not always welcome they have a job to do just like the fishermen.

Back on shore Albert Balls, fisherman turned merchant, buys some of the shrimps. "it's a question of supply and demand" he says. "As soon as the supply exceeds the demands, then obviously the price falls. When the supply cannot fulfil the demand, then you get a high price, but of course you can only get the quantity you catch. To be a good fisherman you not only got to be able to catch a lot of fish, but catch a lot of fish when nobody else catches fish". Another merchant is Don Cole from Lowestoft who buys a considerable amount from the fishermen. These are packed and frozen in a modern plant, and distributed in France and Germany.

The Wash was the home of another breed of hardy men happy to go out when the weather was at its coldest. As one of "**The Punt Gunners**", actor James Robertson Justice delivers the opening commentary by some outbuildings, and declares he is a "man in a million" as one of only 55 left in Great Britain. Punt gunning is where the lone wildfowler paddles quietly towards a flock of duck at dawn or dusk, lying low in his punt, and firing a large gun into the unaware birds, killing as many as possible in one go. Punt gunning was first described by Colonel Peter Hawker in 1816, and the history of this sport is traced in the film. The preparation for a trip involves loading the gun with black powder and heavy shot, and setting off on an ebb tide. The worse the weather the better as the widgeon are slightly off guard. The wildfowler does not mind dodging the ice floes, or a squall of snow. When the wildfowler returns, the first thing to do is to brush the snow off the punt, and thoroughly clean the gun. Made by Roger Upton and friends for Ashley Manor Films, and featuring punt gunners Lawrence Thompson and Toby Bromley, the film is one of two records in the East Anglian Film Archive of this sport which in Victorian times was a way for many to make a living.

At Breydon Water, at the back of Yarmouth, the old time gunners went after anything all the year round. They used a muzzle loading gun with a measure of powder rammed down with about a pound of shot. The large guns, mounted on the bow of the low punt, were often antiques handed down from father to son. The old time Breydoners had fancy nicknames – such as 'Stork' Thacker, 'Silky' Watson, 'Punt' Palmer, and 'Pintail' Thomas. Thomas, like others, was after anything – duck, waders, even swan. He once shot hundreds of Dunlin in one go. The majority went to Norwich and London markets, though many it is said disappeared into his wife's pork butcher's shop in Yarmouth, and came out as pork sausages.

The 1880 Wild Birds Protection Act put in place a closed season – from March 1st to August 1st. Bill Gates, shooting on Breydon in the 1920s and 30s, remembers selling birds to Pettitt's of Reedham. They paid 9d (about 4p) for a Plover, 2/6 (12½ p) for a "big old black backed gull", and 30/- (£1.50) for a swan. These accounts are recorded in "**Master Guns and Master Gunners**", made in 1972, which not only looks at the old Breydon gunners, but goes on a punt gun shoot with Bill Aldiss. Bill demonstrates how to get close to, and shoot birds on the flooding tide early one morning at Stiffkey. Bill also shows the practical side of looking after the punt gun at his home at Hindringham, with special emphasis on cleaning for safety purposes.

To return to Lynn, at one time you could go "**From King's Lynn to Brussels**" from the docks, and the docks are seen in a 1927 amateur film called "**King's Lynn**", where timber is unloaded by manual labour. There are shots of a Roman Catholic procession through the town, and the annual fair. The opening of the fair is recorded in colour in "**Mirrors of Fun**", a film made by the Post office to celebrate a new set of stamps reflecting the fairs and the showmen who ran them. The commentary runs "During the 11th and 12th centuries, practically all our traditional fairs were granted charters by the crown. A charter gave the right to hold the fair, and the right to levy tax on the merchants who came to buy and sell. The church was already involved with both the trading and running of the fairs, and received many of the charters. When the travelling fairs open their season at King's Lynn Mart on the February 14th, it is still the custom for the church to give its blessing to the showmen and their families. This is followed by the reading of King John's Charter. "Oh Yea, Oh Yea, Oh Yea. Whereas by Royal Charter and Subscriptions, The Mayor and Councillors of the Borough of King's Lynn of North West Norfolk, Successors to The Mayor, Aldermen, and Burgesses of the Borough of King's Lynn, are empowered to have, and to hold in perpetuity, within the said borough, one mart or fair yearly on the 14th day of February, and for six days thenceforth next and immediately following…." The fair then continues with all its colour and fun. The designer looks at the decorated rides painted with "heroic gesture and exaggeration that takes place in order to build in excitement – lions, tigers, horses and things, are powerful, majestic, frightening beasts". Fred Powell is seen designing these evocative embellishments for the rides in this film which traces the history of fairs and fairgrounds. At Gaywood in 1966 in "**A Story of Steam**" some of the old showmen's engines as well as some farm and haulage traction engines are seen at a rally, with crowds fascinated by the gleaming machines.

"**The Port of King's Lynn By The Conservancy Board**" and the "**Opening of South**

*A punt and gun from "**Master Guns and Master Gunners**".*

Part of the catch after firing the punt gun.

Quay" are films that give an idea of the importance of Lynn to shipping after the Second World War. On April 26th 1954, The Mayor of Lynn, the Rt Hon. Lord Wise, took a trip on the motor launch *Robert Taylor* to the new quay. The film begins with King's Lynn's best known buildings – Southgate, Greyfriars Tower, Red Mount Chapel, The Guildhall of St George, St Nicholas Church, the Custom House, and the docks, where a freighter is unloading its cargo. The Mayor performs the opening ceremony, and the new quay is ready for business. The working port is emphasised in "**King's Lynn and West Norfolk**" and "**King's Lynn, Gateway to Opportunity**", two films promoting the area for the District Council. The local industries, factories, and business such as Campbell's soup factory, Bespack and Caithness Glass, and the importance of schools, shopping areas, and leisure activities are discussed. The busy Tuesday Market Place is seen, not only in these films, but in "**A Year's Journey – King's Lynn**" with ornithologist Eric Simms. Eric looks at the wildlife of the Wash and the history of the town, – once the third most important port in England.

Hunstanton is not a port, but it did have a railway station which brought holidaymakers to the town until the line closed in May 1969. John Betjeman famously took a ride on the train in 1961 from "**King's Lynn to Hunstanton**", a film mentioned in more detail in the chapter on transport. Out of the train window can be seen the chalets rebuilt after the flood. Many people came here to get away from it all, and "**Happy Days at Heacham**" is a typical home movie of fun holidays here. David Kenten took a film crew to Hunstanton in 1962 to record the "**Beach Donkeys**" on the sands for children to ride on, a quarter of a century after the first amateurs began using 9.5mm cine film to record their holidays here. As late as 1997 16mm film was being used to record the gleaming "**Motor Bikes**" parked on Hunstanton Green, as their owners enjoyed their visit to this North West Norfolk town.

In 1966 the "**National Schools Sailing Regatta**" was held at Brancaster over three days. The sailing became spectacular on the third day when the wind reached force 6, and some of the contestants had to be rescued. Dr Lincoln Ralphs, the Chief Education Officer for Norfolk presented prizes, along with a commemorative mug made in a local pottery to all who took part.

Amateur film maker Peter Scoles went out in one of the whelk boats off Brancaster with his 8mm cine camera, and came back with a nice little record of "**Out with the Whelk Fishers**" in 1958. This colour film shows the *Amethyst* LN62 leaving on the last of the tide, and heading for the whelk grounds ten or fifteen miles offshore. Here the men haul by hand the whelk pots, emptying the contents of whelks, crabs, star fish and other small creatures on to the floorboards where they are sorted, and the unwanted parts of the catch thrown back into the sea. It is hard work pulling the shank to which the pots are attached, and the whelkers haul two more lines of pots before heading home. At Wells at about this time there was a small fleet of boats going after whelks, which as soon as they were brought ashore were boiled in large vat like containers with a fire underneath. One could always tell when the whelkers were coming in as the chimneys of the whelk sheds at the east end emitted large amounts of black smoke. The boats, some of which were former lifeboats converted for the job, crept up on the first of the incoming tide. There is a sequence of whelk fishing at Wells in "**Norfolk Lifeboats**" with Tony Jordan out in the *Sally*, a specially built whelk boat on the lines of the Norfolk crab boats.

This part of the coast faces directly north, and it is difficult to imagine that many miles beyond the horizon fishermen worked for long stretches and often in severe conditions trawling for fish. "**Deep Sea Fisheries**" recorded the

Tony Jordan and the whelk boat Sally.

*The Gamecock fleet of trawlers at work in the North Sea from "**Deep Sea Fisheries**" 1925.*

practice of 'fleeting', a method of working the sea as the inter-titles of this 1925 film explain. "Two steam fishing fleets are permanently at work in the North Sea at distances varying from 150 to 300 miles from land. The fleet shown in these pictures is the Gamecock fleet alternately commanded by 'Admirals' W. Jackson and C. Dixon". They were part of the Kelsall Brothers and Beeching fleet, worked out of Hull, and spent up to eight weeks at sea. The admiral in charge gave orders when to shoot and when to haul. The catch from the trawlers was transferred in small strongly built rowing boats to the carrier, which took the catch to market as quickly as possible. "The Gamecock fleet consists of about fifty vessels, comprising 49 steam trawlers, six carriers and a hospital ship". The conditions were hard indeed, with the men rowing the small boats sometimes in mountainous seas, and transferring the boxes of fish to the carrier only when the sea lifted the small boat level with the gunwale of the carrier. "Another catch, the meagre result of trawling all night in a gale". It was cold hazardous work, more than once do members of the crew stop to flap their arms to keep warm, and injuries were common. "Many limbs are broken and lives lost in this desperately dangerous work". This is a short version of a much longer film called "Heroes of The North Sea", made when fleeting was just about a thing of the past. An unusual event affecting the fleet occurred in 1904, when the Gamecock trawlers were fishing on the Dogger Bank and the Russian Baltic fleet was on its way to the Far East to fight the Japanese. The Russians somehow mistook the fishing fleet for Japanese torpedo boats, and fired on them. One trawler was sunk, and two men died, a third being wounded, dying later. There is a memorial to the three men who died at Hull.

Another fishing activity, this time closer to the land, was "**Sprat Fishing in the Wash**". In the late 1950s and early 60s, the Leggatt brothers had their Faversham registered boats *Romulus* and *Remus* based at Wells-next-the-Sea, as well as *Cortina* (F2) and *Faustulus* (F21). A silent 16mm film was made about 1960 of two of these boats pair trawling for sprats off Wells. The process is shown in detail, a good record of how pair trawling was carried out at this time with two identical boats working as one. The catch, once aboard and stowed, was brought back to Wells on the incoming tide, unloaded by buckets hauled by block and tackle up on to the quay, where the fish were packed into boxes, and the boxes stacked ready for transport.

Strangely, another film was made about the same time of these boats at work, but for very different reasons. Perkins of Peterborough, manufacturers of diesel engines, produced promotional films showing the applications of their efficient and economical engines. Perkins Film Unit made on 35mm "**Why The Diesel No3 – The Boat Owner**". To show an example they picked the Leggatt brothers' sprat boats *Romulus* and *Remus* working out of Wells with a commentary more to do with engines than fishing. "The common need, whether they be fishermen, lifeboat men, bargees, or just pleasure seekers, is a reliable and economic

*"**Sprat Fishing in the Wash**".*

Faustulus *moored at Wells Quay.*

power unit. The need is more than fulfilled by the modern high speed diesel engine. But why the diesel? The fishermen who daily take their boats to the fishing grounds are perhaps the best qualified to supply the answer. The reliability of the diesel engine is one thing of which the skipper can be sure. It enables him to battle against the treacherous swift flowing tides and to negotiate the shifting sandbanks with safety and confidence. Engine failure in conditions like these could mean disaster. The diesel has no plugs, coils, magnetos, or carburettors, common causes of engine failure. The diesel, like the echo sounding gear, is one of the many advantages the modern fisherman enjoys today".

The commentary goes on to say, as the men stream the net, "The diesel also drives the winch as the wire with nets attached is carefully paid out, then reverts back to powering the boat, and the long arduous pair trawling begins. Pair trawling gets its name from the fact that two boats work together, towing the net between them". The nets are later hauled by the winch alongside the boat, and the net full of sprats is hauled aboard. "There are no guarantees of a catch like this. The uncertainty of the catch emphasises the need for maximum economy in operating costs. Of this at least, the fishermen who insist on diesel power, have some guarantee". This advertising film, part of the Perkins collection, goes on to show the advantages of diesel engines in hire craft on the Norfolk Broads, in boats and ships seen in docks, on inland waterways, speed boats, and RNLI lifeboats. "Diesel is cheaper than petrol and will give twice the running hours per gallon. The diesel operator can travel two hundred miles on less than 30/-"(£1.50). There is more about Perkins Film Unit and their films in the chapter on Industry.

Just west of Wells, at Holkham, the coaster *Dependance* came ashore in 1966 on falling tides, and was unable to be re-floated. A few hundred yards from Holkham gap, she proved a tourist attraction as she lay on a lump of sand surrounded by tractors and trailers removing her cargo of fertiliser. People were able to walk right round the ship, and watch the proceedings. Shots of the stranded *Dependence* are incorporated into "**Wells Lifeboat Station**", a film made to celebrate 100 years of the RNLI lifeboat station at Wells next the Sea.

The Dependance *ashore at Holkham about 1966 from "**Wells Lifeboat Station**".*

There had been an RNLI lifeboat station at Wells since 1869, and in 1969 Wells celebrated this fact with the issue of a special mug, and a film show by David Cleveland at the annual RNLI dinner with Lord Leicester present. The film charts the history of Wells lifeboats, and Frank Taylor, the harbour master at the time, talks about the old rowing and sailing lifeboats. The last rowing and sailing lifeboat on the East Coast was at Whitby, and a piece of film shows this boat being hauled off into the waves at Whitby in 1950. But to return to Wells, Frank Taylor also talks about the whelk industry which replaced the older oyster fisheries that were once so important to the town.

The first motor lifeboat to come to Wells was the *Royal Silver Jubilee* which arrived in 1936. This was followed by the *Cecil Paine* in 1945, and the last practice launch of this boat was filmed in 1965, the year a new lifeboat came to Wells, the *Ernest Tom Neathercoat*. This last boat was named by Princess Marina that year, when all of Wells seems to have come out to watch as can be seen in the film.

Colour film of the *Cecil Paine* and the *Ernest Tom Neathercoat* can be seen in "**Norfolk Lifeboats**" made in 1973. This also includes the whelk fishermen at sea hauling pots and the catch being landed and boiled. Both films mention the tragic capsize of the Wells lifeboat in 1880. The lifeboat *Eliza Adams* was trying to get to the *Silver Queen* in trouble off Holkham when she capsized.

A coaster arriving at Wells. Frank Taylor, the harbour master acted as pilot.

Eleven men died. There is a memorial on the quay at Wells not far from the original lifeboat shed.

In 1939 a short newsreel item "**Drawing The Line**" showed domestic scenes of life in the town, streets and houses, the allotments, and a woman drawing water from a communal pump. The cameraman could not resist, however, filming the whelk boats coming in on the tide, or a coaster arriving at the quay.

One of the harbour master's jobs was to act as pilot for ships coming and going into Wells. In "**The Pilot Service**" Frank Taylor goes out in the small pilot boat in 1977 to bring in *Mike 1*, a coaster waiting offshore. He scrambles aboard, and brings the ship through the deepest part of the narrow channel to the quay just before high water. A year later there were floods similar to the 1953 surge, though no lives were lost. In "**Wells and Wisbech Floods**" a ship is seen high and dry on the quay, lifted and left there by the extremely high tide. The harbour master tells of what happened with this flood of 1978, which was nearly as high as the 1953 surge. As the title suggests, this reached up the River Nene to Wisbech, where houses were flooded, much to the distress of the inhabitants who did not expect tide water to enter their homes several miles from the sea. People in wellingtons walk through water in the streets, and outside houses are ruined carpets, fridges, washing machines and televisions sets. One woman explains that she has lost everything in her house.

The winter of 1963 was a cold one. Snow fell in late December 1962 and lay on the ground until mid March. There were blizzards, cold east winds, and weeks of below zero temperatures. At Stiffkey the cold formed hanging shapes of ice in the marsh grass as the spring tides dropped, and the driving snow left artistic patterns on the sands. "**Stiffkey Marsh 1964**", a silent colour record of the 1963/4 year on the marsh, has Joe Jordan, the local Nature Conservancy warden, as the link. Joe was out on the marsh whatever the weather. In the film he buries a dead seal, and goes cockling after the famous Stewkey Blues, large cockles with a hint of blue on their shell, that lay just below the surface of the sand. At that time a peck of cockles fetched about 5/- (25p). He collects mussels from a creek where they have been left for a year or two to grow. A well wrapped up wildfowler comes ashore with a couple of duck.

It was not until March 4th that the temperatures began to rise, just getting above freezing, and the thaw began. Colourful flowers brighten the marsh in the spring, and the worm diggers begin their

The memorial on Wells quay to the eleven men who died when the lifeboat Eliza Adams *capsized in 1880.*

back-aching job digging for lugworms, which are about a foot below the surface of the sand. Joe collects winkles from the marsh and digs for a clam. The terns arrive and nest on the High Sand, a bank seldom covered by high spring tides. Here an RSPB official rings the young terns. At low tide, the creeks still have a foot or two of water in them, and here hiding in the sand are dabs and flounders. Joe and his son Laurence go after the fish with a butt fork, a long handled spear with barbs. The art is to spot the fish lying under the sand by tell tale arrow type marks leading to it and the small dots in the sand of the eyes just visible if the water is clear. The fish is speared and brought to the surface. It sounds easy, but in the expanse of water, and the way the fish keep ahead or dart rapidly away from the approaching fishermen means it is difficult sometimes to get a catch. When a film like this was made, during editing much film is discarded, but in retrospect, may be of use to the researcher. In this case the "**Stiffkey Winter Scenes**" of this film have been kept.

A further film of "**Stiffkey Marsh**" was made in 1970 showing the land and sands in all their moods. Joe Jordan talks about the marsh, Derek Cooper reads local poems, and Ted Ellis, the naturalist, talks about the birdlife.

There was at one time an army camp at Stiffkey close to the marsh, and Anthony Cooper from Cambridgeshire recorded this in his "**Stiffkey Annual Camp 1953**" with his 8mm movie camera. Anthony Cooper, commenting on his silent film, said that there had been anti-aircraft gun units in the area since the 1920s, first at Holme-next-the-Sea, and at Weybourne and Stiffkey, to practice shooting. "The gunners would shoot at a sleeve towed behind an aircraft. The aircraft operated from Langham airfield, just inland from Blakeney". The film shows the crew operating a gun close to Stiffkey marsh, and "A Sunday morning parade. The unit is parading regimental colours, those of the infantry battalion from which it originated, a common practice amongst anti-aircraft gun units at that time". The camps ceased in 1955 at Stiffkey, and all units then went to "**Weybourne Annual Camp**", which Mr. Cooper also recorded on film. Here is seen the firing point where the men are operating a gun. It was a common sight for people driving along the coast road to see the small bursts of black smoke from the shells in the sky around the target.

In 1937 Henry Williamson, author of "Tarka The Otter", bought the farm land which was originally attached to Stiffkey Old Hall. Williamson had served in the trenches in the First World War and worked briefly in Fleet Street before moving to Devon to write.

In the 1930s he decided he wanted to try something new, to become a farmer, so he set about rejuvenating the rundown farm at Stiffkey from Michaelmas that year. The 240 acres of land had been let go, and was a mixture of weeds and rubbish, and dilapidated buildings. It was a big job, and it took him two years before he broke even, let alone make a profit. The farm itself was old. One barn has 1683 in rough brickwork above the

Joe Jordan, local Nature Conservancy warden at Stiffkey.

Stiffkey creeks with the tide in.

entrance, another has a wrecked ship's mast as a beam, no doubt washed up locally. Part of the land was once farmed on the strip system. Strips of land were allocated to the people of the village and they farmed these to suit their own needs. Their names appear by their strips on an old map incorporated into the film "**East Anglian Farming Scenes**". Enclosure Acts of the 18th century did away with strip farming, and in 1793 these strips became part of the field that exists today. The fields, when Henry Williamson bought the farm, had wonderful and often sensible names such as Twenty One Acres, Fox Covert, Spong Breck, Hilly Piece and Lark's Bush Meadow. He employed a local lad on the farm, one Douglas Jordan.

To enable Williamson to survive the first few years, he wrote articles for papers and broadcast on the radio. His experiences of turning the derelict land and buildings into a useful state, learning to run a farm and get it to a modern profit making business is recorded in "The Story of a Norfolk Farm" published by Faber and Faber in 1940.

Henry Williamson worked hard for eight years, but in 1945 he gave up and eventually went back to Devon to write. In 1973 he returned to Stiffkey to re-visit the farm for the filming of "**Vanishing Hedgerows**", a film about his time there, and his feelings about modern agriculture and the countryside. He discusses the decline of the common partridge, and talks about the abundance of birdlife when he was there 35 years earlier with shots of marsh harriers, snipe, bittern, barn owls and sedge warblers. In those days it was mixed farming – cattle and corn -, and these are illustrated with shots of cattle feeding in the yard, muck heaps and ploughing and drilling with horses. Made by David Cobham, who lived at North Creake, the film was shown on BBC Television in 1973, with interviews with Williamson and Douglas Jordan. The farm a few years later can be seen at harvest time in "**Stiffkey Farming Scenes**", a colour silent amateur film of a holiday spent there in 1950 by Frank Pigram of Canewdon in Essex. Camping, helping get the harvest in, watching the thrashing, and children driving tractors were all part of a holiday on the farm at that time.

"**The Birds of Blakeney Point**" is just that, a film taken by Edward Charles Le Grice

Children helping get the harvest in at Old Hall Farm, Stiffkey in 1950, filmed by Frank Pigram.

of Norwich, a keen 16mm amateur film maker. He went there in the mid 1930s to film the terns and oyster catchers. The common terns winter in West Africa, and arrive here in the spring as the weather gets warmer. Ted Eales was the warden here from 1946 until 1980. He was to take over from his father, who died in 1939, but the war intervened, and Ted was called up and joined the Navy Reserve. Ted did quite a lot of filming for television of the Common, Sandwich, Lesser and Artic terns at Blakeney, but because the Roseate tern ceased coming after 1950, he had to go to the Farne Islands to film "**Terns**".

To get to Blakeney Point one has to go in a local boat from Morston. This is what the Countryside Club did in 1952 when they visited North Norfolk. In their film "**The Norfolk Coast**" they explored the Point, and filmed the birds and their nests before going to Blakeney itself. The village is recorded in a series of "**Local Scenes**" taken by Billy Bishop in the 1950s and early 60s. The annual regatta at that time included the greasy pole competition held just across the channel opposite the Blakeney Hotel. Contestants had to walk as far as they could without slipping off into the water. It was from here after the war that boats went out to deal with the wrecks offshore. Divers went down and fixed explosives to blow them up so as to reduce the hazard to shipping and fishermen.

At Blakeney, Stratton Long was owner of a chandlery called Stratton Long Marine and a boat builder. Before that he had done a number of things, as he explains to Denis Mitchell in "**Never and Always**" in 1977. "This is the type of boat we build, all fibreglass, mostly crab boats and that sort of stuff. First of all I started off cider making, and then I went into Norwich City Police Force. From there I had a fish shop. Then I met my wife and that changed the whole tempo altogether. You'll never believe it, but I was a ladies hairdresser, and what's more, I trained under one of the best men in the country at that time, a Frenchman who was the Queen's hairdresser. And then the war came to my rescue and I didn't have to do it, so I went to war after that. Of course I came home to almost nothing, so I had to start earning a living in the estuary, which I did.

"I am really worried about England, probably a bit too gloomy. I have got a young boy that works for me, if I ask him to work on a Saturday, he comes from Norwich, and I have to say to him - right, if you come from Norwich, come up to my house and have your dinner, I will give you some petrol to go back with out of my own pocket – and that's the only way that kid can come out level otherwise he loses by trying to do overtime. Well this is a sad state of affairs isn't it".

At Gresham School at Holt was teacher Dick Bagnall-Oakley. But he was more than a geography master, he was an ornithologist, film maker, and television personality, regularly appearing on BBC East. In 1966 he presented a programme for BBC 2 called "**The Norfolk Coastline**". In this he demonstrated on Cley marshes how he went about filming birds. He set up his 16mm camera on a sturdy tripod, focused the long lens, and filmed waders and oyster catchers. He discusses the vulnerability of this coast to the North Sea, and the work that has been done planting marram grass to bind the sand dunes together on parts of this coast, and cites a Dutchmen who was appalled that the English could build houses behind such slender defences such as at Sea Palling and Eccles.

*Stratton Long, Blakeney boat builder, from "**Never and Always**" 1977.*

On the stony beach at Cley every few months, twelve members of the coastguard and volunteers exercised, setting up and firing the rocket line throwing equipment known as the LSA (life saving apparatus). This enabled a line to be shot over a ship aground just offshore, and the crew rescued by hauling them ashore in a breeches buoy. The equipment, and smaller versions, were located at various points along the coast, and in 1967 an exercise was filmed and included in "**Manby**". George William Manby was born at Denver in 1765 and went to school at Downham at the same time as Nelson. He joined the Royal Military Academy at Woolwich, and later became master of the barracks at Yarmouth. In February 1807 he witnessed the drowning of sixty seven men and women from the gun brig *Snipe* after it was driven ashore close to Yarmouth beach. Manby realised that if a line could be fired over the ship, perhaps men could be rescued in such a situation. He devised a system whereby a mortar fired a light line attached to a grappling hook to the ship. This could then be used by the crew to haul aboard a heavy duty rope along which a travelling cradle, later a breeches buoy, could bring the crew ashore.

Manby had the chance to try out his idea when the dismasted ship *Elizabeth* came ashore almost exactly a year later. Manby's apparatus worked well, and seven men were brought ashore alive. A plaque on the back wall of his house in Southtown records the event. "In commemoration of the February 12th 1808, on which day directly eastward of this spot, the first life was saved from Shipwreck by means of a rope attached to a shot fired from a mortar over the stranded vessel, a method now universally adopted and to which at least 1000 sailors of different nations owe their preservation". His name has gone down in lifesaving history, and the film "**Manby**" recalls

George William Manby used a mortar to fire a line over a ship in trouble close to the shore.

Manby's mortar with grappling hook attached to the shot. Now housed in the Maritime Museum at Yarmouth.

*Loading the line carrying rocket at a practice on Cley beach in 1967 from "**Manby**".*

the life and work of this Norfolk man. His system was improved as time went on, and rockets replaced the mortar greatly increasing efficiency. The modern version as demonstrated at Cley in 1967 has a range of up to 500 yards.

"**Crab Fishing**" at Sheringham has been the principal catch here for the fishermen. For this, they have always used the locally made crab boats. In 1955, Brian Coe, who worked at Kodak, was given some 16mm Kodachrome colour cine film to try out. He decided to record "Scenes of the Fishing Industry and Lifeboat Service" at Sheringham. It is a comprehensive film, covering everything to do with the fishermen and the industry. This was a time when the "shanks" of pots were pulled in by hand – winches did not come for over a decade later. There are twenty pots to each shank, with a buoy at each end. One calm early summer's morning Brian Coe went with the fishermen, and filmed the pots being hauled, the catch removed, and the pots returned to the sea. The crabs are measured to make sure they are not undersize. Back on the beach the boats are hauled by cable, the catch boxed and taken by hand cart to a waiting van. Some are labelled for Billingsgate fish market. Some crabs go to local fishmongers, others are processed for crab paste which is displayed in West's shop window. Then comes the business of crab pot repairs, and maintenance of the boats. *Miss Britain* is a brand new crab boat just finished. It is hauled through the streets from Emery's boat building premises to the beach. The men are members of the lifeboat crew, and Brian Coe filmed a launching exercise of the *Foresters Centenary*, which was stationed at Sheringham from 1936 to 1961.

The next boat, *The Manchester Unity of Odd Fellows* was named by Princess Marina, and the ceremony and launch can be seen in "**Norfolk Lifeboats**".

Crab fishing took place from March to the end of September, or when-ever the crabbing fell away. In the winter months the fishermen tried for other fish. In "**Long Lining**" Henry 'Downtide' West goes out in a small boat with an outboard motor to see what is about. He was filmed for one of Malcolm Freegard's programmes, and speaks the commentary. "Really the whole town depends on crab and lobster fishing. Cause, the winter comes on, I have done really well sometimes catching the cod. I can remember some really good

*A crab boat at sea from Brian Coe's "**Crab Fishing**" 1955.*

The Sheringham lifeboat The Manchester Unity of Odd Fellows.

The crew of The Manchester Unity of Odd Fellows.

catches of herring, sprats. You don't know what to do in the winter, but you just try something. Cause winter fishing isn't everybody's idea, unless you like fishing. You wouldn't do it in the winter because it is so chancy from the fishing point, and you get some very nasty weather. You can be nice and comfortable one minute, hauling your lines easy, then down comes the fog, and within seconds you've got a job to find your lines, find your buoys. Sometimes it is pretty cold, but of course the more you work with your lines or nets the warmer you keep, although I have seen the mussels freeze on the line when we have been laying them. And when we have caught the fish sometimes I have seen the eyes freeze as we have laid them in the boat. One of the things we have to go by is the colour of the water, if there is fish in the water and food, the water gets coloured."

They haul some cod and flat fish into the boat, and with a shot of the other fisherman in the boat, "Downtide" goes on to say "Teddy Craske here he's the mechanic of the lifeboat. He has to keep fishing during the winter months, cause he can't take a job, he never knows when he's wanted, he has to be close at hand so he does a bit of winter fishing with me. This is one of the prettiest sights you'll ever see, go where you like, there is nothing or nicer as a bunch of sprats all in the net. After all, it's beautiful!"

Most of the fishermen lived close to the sea. Bennie West lived in a cottage built in the 1830s by his grandfather. The loft was made so that nets could be stored and repaired there. In 1983 Mr. West is seen doing just that for a film about traditional building methods called "**A Stone's Throw From The Beach**".

There are many amateur holiday films from 1933 through to a film showing the "**Sheringham Sea Defences**" in 1998. In the 1930s the Pennefather family had a thatched house above Sheringham overlooking the town and the sea. Claude Pennefather made 16mm films of the family, both in London at Sheringham. "**Pennefather Pictures Present Summer Holiday 1933**" has all the ingredients of a holiday film – family and friends in the garden, enjoying the beach, though one girl just reads a newspaper oblivious of the scene around her, or the cameraman. The latest plaything of the time is the lilo which they have fun with, and they play lacrosse in a field at Runton, and go out in a boat fishing for mackerel which they thread on string and hold up proudly. They also made in 1934 "**Rapturous Raspberries or The Purloining of Poppy**", a riotous escapade which includes dressing up and a rough and tumble happy fight in this acted out comedy melodrama. Just the sort of thing to do with the 16mm cine camera while on holiday. Great fun.

In 1934 "**Sheringham Regatta**" was filmed, when the preserved *Ramey Upcher* pulling and sailing lifeboat was launched as a special regatta day event. Four years later this was filmed again by Mr. Gowing on 8mm film, as well as many other items including a ship aground, Cromer Flag Day, an M& GN train, Fakenham Races, and on July 4th 1939, a mock air raid in Sheringham. Many holiday films have been made by visitors to this delightful North Norfolk town, particularly when something special was going on, like carnival time. In 1963 the pancake race through the streets of Sheringham was filmed with the winner, Miss Mary Wright, receiving the prize of a non stick frying pan. Miss Wright, later Mrs. Mary Home, recalled she gave it to her mother who "was delighted with it, having never had such a thing before!"

In 1961 Sheringham and District Chamber of Trade and Commerce commissioned a promotional film for the town. "**A Fine Resort**", a colour sound

*On the beach at Sheringham in 1933, from "**Pennefather Pictures Present Summer Holiday**".*

*Cromer pier from "**Cromer Lifeboat**" 1975.*

*From "**For Saving Lives**" with Henry Blogg in the middle.*

film, shows all the local beauty spots, and points out the fun one could have when on holiday at Sheringham. There are pony rides, golf, bowls, and of course the beach. Dick Graham delivers an eloquent commentary "There is enjoyment to be had on, beside, in, and near the water. Bathing is safe and level, below stretches of flint blue beach stones". Over shots of crab pots being made he describes the components as "strong slender, bendable hazelwood, and netted nowadays with nylon by cunning fingers in the craft". Over some final shots his commentary gets even more lyrical "Girls like goddesses shake loose their gilded hair as they walk up from the water while the sun goes down on a coast they will always remember". The End.

Cromer had a similar film made in 1958, though of not such high quality, for it was shot on Standard 8mm colour film with a magnetic stripe sound track. However "**Lets Go To Cromer**", made by Jack Bryant, does its job. The fishermen land their catch of crabs, there's the waiter's race through the town, Bernie Winters crowns the carnival queen, and the *Henry Blogg* lifeboat is launched down the slipway at the end of the pier. On board the lifeboat, the commentary says "At the wheel is Coxswain Henry Davies, known to all as 'Shrimp'. Tall, broad shouldered, lean and powerful, 'Shrimp' is a born leader and has already proved himself a worthy successor to his uncle, the world famous Henry Blogg, in whose memory this boat is named".

The story of lifeboats is an interesting one at Cromer, for they had a private boat here as far back as 1804 and subsequent boats were all launched from the beach until the lifeboat house was opened at the end of the pier on July 26th 1923, housing the motor lifeboat *H. F. Bailey*. This was a gift from Mr. Henry Francis Bailey of Brockenhurst in Hampshire. This was now the No 1 Station, there being another boat on the beach, No 2 Station. The *H. F. Bailey* proved unsuitable, and was replaced in 1924 by a slightly different boat also called the *H. F. Bailey*. In 1928 another boat came temporarily to Cromer, again called *H. F. Bailey*, and so it is not clear which boat is seen in the 1928 film "**For Saving Lives**" which shows the launch of one of the *H. F. Baileys*, as well as shots of Coxswain Henry Blogg and the crew.

The reason for two stations was that in rough weather, it was not possible to rehouse the No 1 boat, and she would have to go to Yarmouth to shelter until such time as the weather improved. Then the No 2 boat was on call, though there were occasions when both boats were out. The *Harriot Dixon*, the No 2 "**Cromer Lifeboat**" was filmed on 35mm for an unknown purpose in 1942 and is seen being launched from her carriage, and also in a dramatised sequence in the RNLI publicity film "**Gale Warning**", made in 1956, along with the now nine years retired Henry Blogg.

The No 2 lifeboat was replaced in 1964 by the *William Henry and Mary King*, and the launch of this is recorded in colour in "**Norfolk Lifeboats**" as is the new No 1 boat *The Ruby and Arthur Reed* being launched down the slipway at the end of the pier. In the mid 1960s, David Kenten filmed the "**Cromer Lifeboat Crew**" on a visit to the Anglia Television studios in Norwich, such was their fame.

The Ruby and Arthur Reed *just hitting the water from "**Norfolk Lifeboats**" 1973.*

The evening of Sunday November 14th 1993 is one that Cromer will not easily forget. There were storm force winds and high seas. A jack-up construction platform, the *Tayjack 1*, used by MacAlpine to build the outfall to Anglian Water's North Norfolk sewerage system scheme, broke loose and crashed into the pier. Frank Muirhead was there with his video camera to record the flashes of electricity that lit up the scene. The video was transferred to film, and incorporated into "**Cromer Pier**", a film taken by Robin Williams which followed the reconstruction. The repairs to the pier were completed by John Martin Construction by May 1994, and the end of the pier variety show at the Pavilion Theatre opened on time. Acts from a later show are included in the film.

In 1997 the lifeboat house at the end of the pier was found to be too small for the new type of craft, so it was removed and a new one built. The old one eventually found its way to Southwold to house the restored *Alfred Corry*, a rowing and sailing lifeboat of 1893.

It is impossible to say when crabs were first caught at Cromer, but it is a fishery which always seems to have been there. But like all things we think will continue for ever, often they do not. Motion picture film is an ideal way to keep a record to show in the future how things were done in the past. "**Cromer Crabs**" is just that, a factual record by Peter Hollingham, made for educational use in 1973. This shows the whole process in detail, not only the capture of crabs and lobsters at sea with Richard Davies, but the background to crab fishing as well. Everyone forgets that once caught, the creatures have to be graded by size, scrubbed, cleaned, cooked, and dressed before they sit on the shop counter ready for an appetising sale.

Colour film with shots of Cromer streets, the *Harriot Dixon* lifeboat standing ready on the beach, Henry Blogg, and a crab boat ready to take passengers on a trip on the briny, are part of a record of a holiday in Norfolk taken by Mr. Gamble from Merton Park in London. He obtained some of the new Dufaycolor 16mm film which became available in 1934. Mr. Gamble filmed the beach with bathers in colourful costumes, children playing in the sand, and youngsters with a lilo – the latest novelty at this time. "**Cromer 1934**" also includes the surrounding countryside in high summer, and a day spent on the Broads. With some black and white film for "**Cromer 1**" he took shots of the end of the pier show called 'Out of the Blue',

The gap in the pier with temporary bridge as reconstruction work begins.

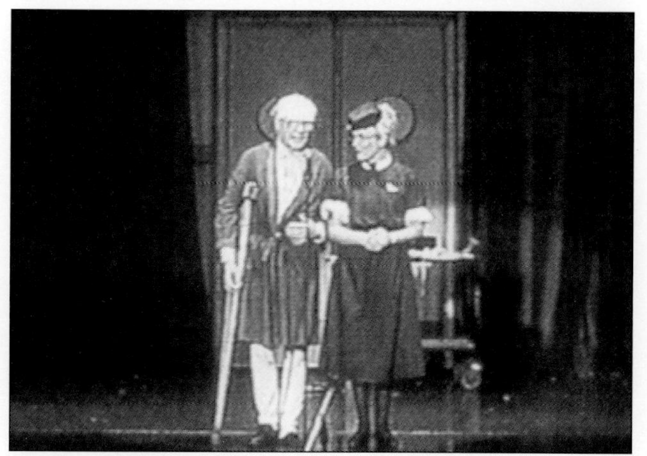

*One of the acts on stage in the Pavilion Theatre on the end of "**Cromer Pier**".*

*Outside Rusts shop in Cromer from "**Gowing Films**".*

with some of the artists performing for the crowd on the beach, the family having tea in a beach hut, Cromer streets, Rust's shop, the town crier, and the pier in wartime with a gap in the middle so that the enemy could not reach the mainland. Mr. Gamble's film runs from the 1930s to the 1950s, and includes outings to Blakeney Point and Walsingham Abbey, where a person drinks from a spring.

Arthur Gowing, a Cromer resident, filmed many local events in the late 1930s in the town on 8mm film, and the "**Gowing Films**" reach as far as Sheringham and Holt in content. There are shots of the building of the new police station in Cromer, and at Holt on May 29th 1938, "Francis Wortley, President of the Holt St. John Ambulance, asks the Lord Lieutenant for Norfolk, Russell Colman, to receive the new ambulance for service in the county". During the ceremony two of the ambulance men faint! At West Runton on July 14th 1939 the remains of a crashed plane was filmed, and there is a shot of the Gowing family business, a butchers shop in Station Road, Sheringham, from where you could also hire a 'drive yourself car' complete with a radio. The shop, which indicates they were also farmers, probably supplied Roys of Wroxham, as there are shots of the store there, with the title 'food arrives'.

In 1955 Robin Ridgeway made a short film of a day at Cromer, "**Cromer Excursion**". Beginning with a steam train pulling carriages into Cromer Beach station, there are carefully constructed shots of holidaymakers on the beach, boats, the town, shops and pedestrians, finishing with the 5.0pm train leaving for Norwich. This was an exercise in filming and editing, in fact Robin went on to be a film editor at BBC East in Norwich.

Trimingham lies between Overstrand and Mundesley. Here in 1932 a film maker on holiday from London filmed on the Gotts Brothers farm and on the beach where a crab boat comes ashore. The interesting thing here is that it is a traditional crab boat, without engine, propelled solely by oars placed through holes in the gunwale. Before motor driven boats were around, these lightweight and smaller crab boats were handled on the beach by inserting the oars through these 'orruck' holes as they were called, and the fishermen lifted the boat bodily up, and walked her up the beach. This is the only surviving movie example of this practice.

Colour shots taken at the back of Mundesley in 1937 introduce us to the driveway and gardens of "**Mundesley Sanatorium**". Founded by Frederick

*"**Cromer Excursion**", 1955, a short film by Robin Ridgeway.*

*Time to catch the 5.0pm home. From "**Cromer Excursion**" 1955 by Robin Ridgeway.*

William Burton-Fanning in 1899, this was the first specially designed TB sanatorium to be built in England. He devised a revolving open air shelter for the patients, as he was a strong advocate of the open air treatment of tuberculosis. According to Peter Lindsley of Ealing, the film was shot by Dr G. Day, resident physician at Mundesley Sanatorium. Peter was a patient there. "Put simply, Mundesley Sanatorium and Dr Day saved my life, and it is something I shall never forget". The film shows the day to day life of the hospital. A black and white section shows a patient undergoing an x ray, the chefs in the kitchen preparing food, and the distribution of meals to the patients by heated trolley. The recreational facilities include walking in the woods, golf, darts, acting, and skating on frozen Westwick Pond near North Walsham. In 1903 Burton-Fanning opened another sanatorium at Kelling, near Holt.

In 1944 an antibiotic was administered for the first time, and anti-TB drugs appeared over the next few years. The sanatoriums were no longer needed and the premises at Mundesley and Kelling became part of the National Health Service. The Friends of Kelling was formed in 1948 to provide special amenities to the hospital patients. From 1948-1965 Sergeant W. G. Kemp of the Norfolk Constabulary shot 16mm colour film of the work of the Friends. This included taking children to Cromer to be by the sea, providing books, radios and televisions, and a trolley telephone for use by patients in the wards. In 1965 David Cleveland took over the filming, recording the events and additions to the hospital the Friends made, such as a children's Christmas party, a new sun lounge, day rooms, and the building of a house in the grounds of Kelling Hospital where relations of patients could stay while visiting loved ones. In 1975 the silent films were compiled into one colour sound film called "**Friends of Kelling**" with commentary. The money was raised by the tireless efforts of the secretary of the Friends, Jack Thomas.

Mundesley is more than a village, it is a small town. It had its own fire brigade, and from 1938 the local doctor, Hugh Miller, filmed on 8mm the various activities and appliances of this unit. His "**Mundesley Fire Brigade**" covers the years to 1966. William Hugh Miller, who lived at 'Brannocks' in Mundesley, made many documentary films including "**Mundesley Past and Present**", which ranges from the station with a steam train, a washed up mine, a wrecked spitfire in a field, a pipe being laid on the beach, building sea defences, the last brick maker at work (Mr. Clark), to Mundesley inshore rescue boat, the beach café being rebuilt, and roads being dug up for the new gas main. This is good local material as well as excellent for showing family life. His "**Family Portraits**" shows them at home, making sand bags in the garden in 1939, having tea by the fire with the children, making a snowman, feeding chickens, cutting the lawn, playing with the dogs, and many other everyday things one takes for granted. Jean, aged about three, is having a bath and cleaning her teeth, and in the garden making a daisy chain. There is a sequence in Wales where the children were evacuated in the

Jean Fox, Dr Hugh Miller's daughter, demonstrates the separate sound system using a Tandberg tape recorder linked to a Syncrodeck which varied the speed of the Standard 8mm projector to keep the film in synchronisation with the separate sound track.

war. 1947 was a year of great snowfalls. January was mild, but on the 23rd it got colder and snow set in, and there were heavy snow falls until mid March. Hugh Miller filmed the clearing of snow from outside his home, and the blocked roads with gangs clearing a way through to Paston, and a bulldozer doing the job at Knapton. Coal had to be collected by sledge, which they then used for tobogganing on Mundesley golf links. In "**Welsh Holiday**" in 1948 they get a trunk ready for sending on the train, then, as there is no petrol - vividly demonstrated by Dr Miller, they take the train from Mundesley heading for South Wales.

Then there is "**Lets Make a Pantomime**" made in 1974 – complete with sound. This shows the preparations and rehearsals in Coronation Hall, costumes being made, building scenery, make up, tea making, and people buying tickets. Dr Miller made most of his films with sound tracks, normally complied during the editing stage. For the Standard 8mm films he used a separate reel to reel tape recorder running in synchronisation with the film. A Syncrodeck device kept the film and tape in synchronisation. The quarter inch audio tape looped out of the tape recorder, round a capstan on the Syncrodeck, and back to the tape recorder take up spool. A flexible Bowden cable from the projector also fed into the Syncrodeck. The projector speed was then automatically varied slightly by the Syncrodeck to keep the sound and picture in synchronisation. The picture on the projector, and sound on the tape, both had to have start marks, and the two machines started up simultaneously.

There are over seventy films in the "**Hugh Miller Collection**", including his 8mm projectors (a Kodascope De Luxe and Bolex), and scripts and papers. Dr Miller came to live at Mundesley in July 1930, and was in practice there from then until his retirement in 1974.

The sea made its presence felt at Mundesley on Saturday March 15th 1969 when a 250 ton coaster bound for Rotterdam ran aground right in front of the town. This was the *Jonet*, lost in the fog, ending up on a lump of sand on the beach and beaten by waves. A few shots were taken under the title "**Shipwreck**". These shots also appear in "**Norfolk Lifeboats**". Dr Hugh Miller

Dr Hugh Miller filming with his Standard 8mm Bolex cine camera.

also took some shots which appear in his film "**Local Events**". The *Jonet*, a forty-two year old Dutch freighter, was never refloated, but broken up on the beach, with a crane hoisting the sections on to the cliff. Another film maker at Mundesley was Barbara Simpson, a retired doctor's wife who came to live in the town for a short time in the late 1950s. She made "**Mundesley 1959**" and some other films as well. So Mundesley is well covered in moving images during the second half of the 20th century.

The first gas from the North Sea came ashore at Bacton in Norfolk in 1968, but like all new energy complexes, a lengthy "**Gas Terminal Public Enquiry**" took place first. It was held in Bacton Village Hall and filmed by Anglia Television news. There was considerable opposition locally, but the building of the terminal close to the cliff went ahead. "Look East" sent reporter Tony Scase

The coaster Jonet *aground at Mundesley in 1969. She was going from Boston to Rotterdam.*

along a year later to see how the construction was going and to interview local people. In "**Interviews Connected with Gas Terminal**" the local MP, Bert Hazel, and Councillor Charles Pitt-Steele, are asked for their views and the local vicar and residents give their opinions, but whatever people had to say, the terminal was going ahead, and the busy construction work is contrasted with rural scenes of farming and the church.

The drilling rigs, supply ships, and the pipeline coming ashore at Bacton are shown in "**Off Shore Gas**", a colour film made later tracing the history of North Sea gas and the development of the Bacton terminal. Here the gas was cleaned and refined before being pumped through the network of pipes which had been laid across the countryside. "**Gas Pipe Laying**" shows some of this work. Of course for the consumer all this meant little, until the time came for the conversion of domestic appliances in the home.

"February 13th 1938. A northerly gale, accompanied by abnormally high tides, resulted in the sea breaking through at Horsey and flooding an area of fifteen square miles" records Harold Jaffa in "Norfolk Events". The report goes on "At Cley houses were flooded to a depth of two or three feet, and at Walcott Gap the road was undermined". The cinema newsreels were quickly on the scene, and Pathe Gazette, in their "**Sea Invades Norfolk**", covered the story with shots of flooded fields, people wading trough water, closed roads and the isolated Horsey Post Office. They also took aerial shots to complete their 19 shot sequence for the newsreel.

This local flood was also recorded by Patrick Jackson of the GPO film unit, who made an eight minute film called "**Horsey Mail**" about the people who continued working regardless of the water. Claude Simmonds, the local postman, and Bob O'Brian, a Yarmouth post van driver, are the real stars of this film. The commentary informs us that Claude normally has a two mile daily delivery, but because of the flooded coast road he has to make a 15 mile detour. Bob O'Brian, brought into drive Claude to work, then takes over the commentary, and in a jolly Norfolk accent, comments on things they see as they drive along. When a submerged car is spotted with just its roof showing, Bob tells us that the owner spent 15 hours on top of it before being rescued, and that a submerged tractor in a field only recently cost the farmer "200 quid".

After emptying his boots of water, Claude falls into a boat and is rowed to a remote farm. Here he is given a cup of tea. "What, more tea? Old Claude must be half full of tea by now", says Bob. The film ends with a small army of labourers doing their best to repair the gap in the sand hills, and the final line of commentary tells us that "until the roads are clear again Claude has to row six miles every day to deliver the Horsey mail." There are two versions of this film, though the differences are hardly noticeable. It seems that perhaps the Norfolk accent could not be understood, so in the slightly shorter version some dialogue is altered. However, whether it is the 35mm copy that you look at, or the 16mm version, it is a gentle and amusing film, reminding us of one of those coastal incidents that are so often quickly forgotten.

*The Post Office takes to the boats in "**Horsey Mail**" 1938, directed by Pat Jackson for the GPO.*

*Claude Simmonds, the local postman, and Bob O'Brian, a Yarmouth post van driver, in "**Horsey Mail**" 1938.*

Sometimes an event sounds as though it has historical origins, but it is not always the case. Hemsby "**Longshore Herring Festival**", with its service of Blessing of the Herring is a relatively recent affair. A prayer is given by the vicar from a fishing boat, and people tuck into herring cooked on the beach in this film of 1992. The "**Fun Day**" part of this film shows the amusement arcades, side shows, fairground rides, fast food outlets, cafes, and the Sunday market with traders at their stalls. Once Hemsby was a much quieter place, where people came in the 1930s for a more rural seaside holiday as the Booker family did in 1936, bringing with them a cine camera to record their stay on small one minute rolls of 9.5mm movie film. Others came to Hemsby from far flung parts of the country to the holiday camp here. To get "**To Hemsby Holiday Camp**" one family in 1937 travelled from Cornwall as the first shot shows Saltash Station. The views out of the window, together with titles cut in, tell us the journey they took. After the train passes over the Tamar Bridge, it goes through the counties of Wiltshire, Berkshire, Buckinghamshire, Middlesex, London, Essex, Suffolk, Norfolk, eventually arriving by the Midland and Great Northern Railway at Hemsby station. Other people came by car, as there are cars parked in front of the chalets where the family stayed. They took part in organised games, such as running races and bobbing for apples, watched keep fit exercises and a beauty contest on the beach.

There had been a holiday camp, or "Socialist Camp" as it was called, at Caister since 1906, when people stayed in tents in a field close to the sea. The "Caister-On-Sea Holiday Camp Ltd" brochure of 1938 says campers can book a tent, instructing the potential visitor "early booking is most essential, especially if you require a hut". It goes on "if you have any gift for entertaining, or any musical instrument (which be sure and bring with you), your talent will be highly appreciated". Film of holidaymakers enjoying themselves can be seen in a series of short silent 16mm films in the "**Caister Holiday Camp Collection**".

The camp had changed considerably by the time comedian and broadcaster Roy Hudd visited Caister in 1972 to make a promotional film for

"Ladbrokes Holidays" 1972.

"**Ladbrokes Holidays**", the new owners. All the amenities on offer, including the swimming pool, the beach, the donkey derby, football, tennis and fancy dress parades are shown, as well as the entertainment, ranging from a magician to wrestling. The film is very seventies, with hot pants and rock and roll music. Roy Hudd spells it out in his commentary "lots of people to talk to, and they talk the same language, I made lots of mates there last year. Everybody was knocked out by the accommodation and all the amusements. The chalets are smashing, really well thought out. A number of them are self catering, and you won't have to worry about where you will buy the grub. It's all there, right on your doorstep. And there are the restaurants and snack bars guaranteed to give you plenty of variety. The mums were really pleased with what they found, I can tell you. Things like the nappy service and baby sitters, well it gives them a chance to go out in the evenings, and have a bit of fun themselves"

Seashore Caravan Camp with its "all electric" caravans is just down the road at Great Yarmouth, and at California, between Caister and Hemsby, is the Sunbeach Chalet Camp, and back at Caister is Silver Sands Caravan Camp. Here the caravans are ultra modern, even equipped with showers says the commentary. These promotional films made on 16mm were available on free loan to clubs and societies, sometimes shown at afternoon and evening events where a speaker might give a talk before or after the film.

Before we leave Caister, it is worth remembering this was also a fishing village, with the men working small boats off the sandy beach. In the late 1950s Philip Rumbelow made two 8mm films, "**Crab Fishing**", and "**Skipper on Lines**", the latter covering long lining. Philip Rumbelow lived in Napoleon Place, Yarmouth, and was a plumber by trade. He was an expert model boat builder, with examples of his work in Merseyside Maritime Museum and the Royal Scottish Museum. He was also a local historian. He made his 8mm films mainly as a record of what was happening at the time. On Sunday February 13th 1955, something was happening. The Boulogne trawler *St. Pierre Eglise* ran aground at 5.30am during a squall on Waxham beach. Some of the crew jumped overboard and swam to the shore, others were rescued by Winterton LSA rocket team by breeches buoy, and were taken to the Seaman's home at Yarmouth. Three days later, while a salvage crew were on board, the boat tilted on her side and 14 men had to be rescued again by Winterton LSA company. Eventually a couple of tugs got the *St. Pierre Eglise* off the sands, and towed her to Yarmouth, where she was repaired at Fellows Yard. The salvagers celebrated in the Star Hotel in Yarmouth in getting the vessel safely to Yarmouth. After repairs she left Yarmouth for France, the final shots being her leaving Yarmouth harbour. Philip Rumbelow filmed the ship on the beach, the attempts to refloat her, and the repairs at Yarmouth, naming his film "**Calling PISL**", a reference to the company which specialised in towage and salvage assistance. The film is fully titled throughout, and tells, and shows, in detail, the salvaging story of the *St. Pierre Eglise.*

The old RNLI lifeboat shed at Caister became the home of the Caister Volunteer Rescue Service.

He also filmed the "**Caister Lifeboat**" in 1957 when an RNLI boat was there. The RNLI closed the station in 1969, but local people re-established a station, first with a small 16ft dinghy with an outboard motor, and then with an ex RNLI boat. "**Norfolk Lifeboats**" made in 1973, takes a peep at this volunteer rescue service in its survey of lifeboats along the coast at the time. It also features coxswain Jack Bryant and the Gorleston boat *Kahmi,* a modern 44ft all steel boat built by Brooke Marine at Lowestoft in 1967

Although there were lifeboats on Yarmouth beach in the early days, after 1919 when the last station was closed, the Gorleston station was re-named Great Yarmouth and Gorleston, and assumed full lifesaving responsibility in the area. The Gorleston station had an energetic fundraiser Mrs. Dowding, a doctor's wife who filmed "**Lifeboat Affairs**" with her 8mm camera covering the years 1967 to 1979. The *Kahmi* arriving in 1967, a fund raising lunch, an Anglia Television outside broadcast van with camera crew and presenter David Jacobs, a baby party, Sir Alec Rose visit, the Sea Scouts band – these are just some of the varied ingredients in Thelma's film. She made many other films, including a film of the stalls and traders on "**Great Yarmouth Market**" in 1960, and in 1957 a film of her beloved pet, "**Sparta The Dog**".

It is 1953, and a publicity film for Great Yarmouth and Gorleston-on-Sea is released to encourage visitors to come here for their holiday. The film begins by saying that 500,000 people come to Yarmouth every year, for "the week, a fortnight, or three weeks". Franklin Engelman (of BBC radio's "Down Your Way" programme) delivers the commentary informing the holiday maker that "you are now on the drier side of Great Britain, the climate always seems to be a little better than at home on the sands of Great Yarmouth. You soon forget the old home town work-a-days, making meals and clearing meals away. These are happy days, and at long last father finds time to be with his children".

"**Great Yarmouth and Gorleston-on-Sea**", with the sub title of 'The Resorts That Have Everything', shows the crowded beach, holiday

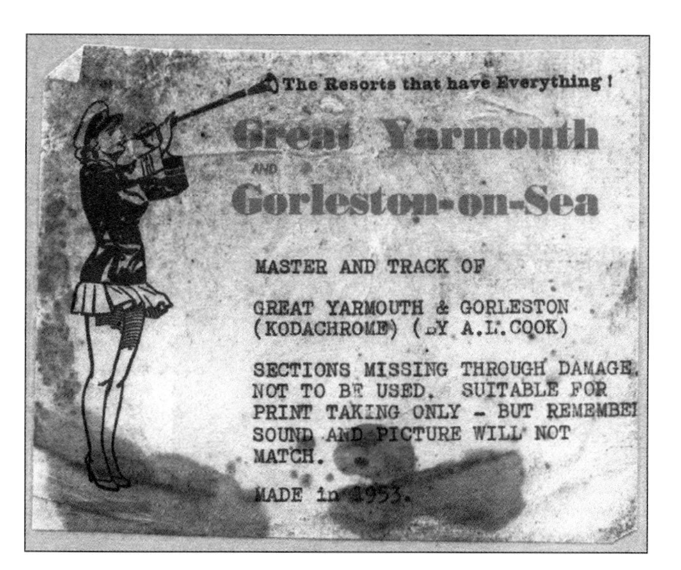

*The label from the master films of "**Great Yarmouth and Gorleston-on-Sea**", 1953.*

makers roller skating, in boats on the waterways, and diving and swimming in the swimming pools, with "daring men diving and graceful girls to charm our eyes". Yarmouth races are shown, the caravan site at North Denes, and Gorleston beach. "Gorleston is a quieter place than Great Yarmouth, and much favoured as a family resort". Children play on the beach and in "Children's Corner", while parents watch the regatta out at sea, and help when a boat comes ashore in a breeze.

"As the day lengthens, the sandman comes along, Punch and Judy give their last performance, the last pony cart gives its last trip, and evening takes the light from the sky. The beaches are almost deserted, and when the children are in bed and the evening meal over, then whoopee, a new life begins". Night shots of lights, amusements and theatres bring us to the end of the film – "Great Yarmouth and Gorleston are the resorts that have everything- definitely".

The film was updated from time to time, and was still being shown to potential holiday makers under the title "**The Resorts That Have Everything**" in 1963. Yarmouth had used film to advertise itself as far back as the 1920s with a silent film called "**Great Yarmouth for Health, Sunshine, and Pleasure**". The film begins with shots taken from the top of the revolving tower (the top platform ceased to revolve in 1915, but it was still known as the revolving tower), then concentrated on views of Marine Parade and children and adults in fancy dress, ready for the carnival, including an orientally dressed man selling "London roasted peanuts" from a barrow. The caption introducing him says "this seller of peanuts must have been 'sum knut from Pekin'!" Following scenes of the children's playground and the swimming pool, we are shown bags of salt being loaded on to a drifter at the quayside, and then a sequence taken from a Pathe Pictorial sub-titled "Sunday, A Yarmouth Study. The 7th day and stray boats of the great fishing fleet are returning to harbour". This section was obviously spliced in at a later date for it was not filmed until 1929.

In this sequence a Yarmouth drifter, YH 365, named *Oak Apple*, steams into harbour to join what seems to be an endless line of boats moored upriver. "On the quayside, the men whose toil combs the North Sea are resting - in their Sunday best", says a title as we are shown groups of fishermen standing around talking. These were probably the visiting Scottish fishermen who had followed the herring down the coast, for the Norfolk men had no reservations about fishing on a Sunday.

The final section of "**Great Yarmouth for Health, Sunshine, and Pleasure**" is in colour, and shows various postcard type views of the resort. There is the beach crowded with holidaymakers, the swimming pool, model boating lake, Nelson's Column, the harbour, Gorleston beach and Caister Castle, all awash in gentle colours added after the film had been made. Stencil colour, sometimes called Pathe colour, had been around since 1905

*The peanut seller from "**Great Yarmouth For Health, Sunshine and Pleasure**".*

as a method of colouring existing black and white films. The prints to be coloured were sent to the Pathe factory at Vincennes in France, where a small army of women was employed to make the stencils. Each frame of the film (there are sixteen frames to a foot of 35mm film, and in the silent days a foot of film lasted exactly one second) was inspected, and a pointer delicately moved around the area or areas to be coloured with one hue. The pointer activated a cutting mechanism that produced a hole in a separate blank piece of film in direct relation to the area scanned by the pointer. All parts of the frame for red were traced and cut, and then the process was repeated for blue areas and again for green and so on. The finished stencils would then be run on a special machine that brought the black and white prints in contact with the stencils, and aniline dyes would be applied to the film through the cut-out sections of the stencils. Trees with foliage were green all over, roofs were a red colour, and the sky blue. When stencil colour was used well, the results were very pleasing. If, however, it was done too quickly, and the colours were not accurately superimposed, the colour edges became unsteady. In a stencil colour film of "**Blickling Hall**", made in 1929, when this seventeenth century mansion was still a private home, in a long shot of the house and gardens the green colour does not cover the lawn adequately, but keeps hovering on the edge, leaving sometimes green grass, sometimes black and white grass. Many films were tinted at this time in the cinema, and "**Marine Parade**", filmed in 1924, was originally tinted orange. This film consists of a travelling shot of the busy front

*"**Marine Parade**". The marks –L after the word Kodak is a manufacturer's code for the date, 1924.*

*Yarmouth Races from "**Eastern Sunshine**".*

probably taken as part of a longer film which now does not exist.

About 1933 Yarmouth asked The National Progress Film Company to make a couple of sound advertising films about Great Yarmouth as a holiday resort. Albert Arch was sent down to photograph and direct "**Eastern Sunshine**" and "**Sunshine, Fun and Laughter**". These two films made out of the material he shot are very similar, except that Albert Arch had different personalities in each film. In "**Sunshine Fun and Laughter**" it was the actress Kathleen Daw, and in "**Eastern Sunshine**" it was two more from the entertainment world, Jack Hobbs and Dodo Watts.

In "**Eastern Sunshine**" Jack Hobbs arrives by aeroplane at Yarmouth where he meets Dodo Watts. The couple wander round the town, taking in the sights, strolling through gardens, having a go on the dodgems and looking at the boating lake, where a distracted oarsman rows straight into the bank. They visit the races and go dancing at the Wellington Pier Winter Gardens, while both of them keep up a continuous dialogue over shots of themselves and general views of places and activities. The film was shot silent and their commentary recorded later in the studio, with music mixed in. After riding in a speedboat and watching a concert party at the Wellington Pier, Jack Hobbs says, over shots of a firework display, "The wisest thing we have ever done is to come to Yarmouth". "It's the end of a perfect day", chips in Dodo. "It's the beginning of a perfect holiday", concludes Jack.

*Kathleen Daw aboard a speed boat in "**Sunshine, Fun and Laughter**".*

"**Sunshine, Fun and Laughter**" follows the same pattern, except that this time Kathleen Daw is the personality. Both films run for about ten minutes and, apart from the shots with the stars in, contain much the same material. In fact some shots have been duplicated and used in both films, while others have been cut in half with the beginning of a shot in one film and the second half in the other. Unlike "**Eastern Sunshine**", "**Sunshine, Fun and Laughter**" has a commentary spoken by Leonard Caplan, with occasional lines from Miss Daw. One sequence was shot from the top of the revolving tower (this 15Oft structure was demolished in 1941), with Kathleen Daw in the foreground and the Marine Parade and the sands below, with people moving around looking like ants. "Every inch of it a holidaymaker's paradise", says Leonard Caplan, and to this Miss Daw turns to the camera and replies in perfect synchronisation "marvellous". This would have been recorded in the studio as the silent picture was projected on the screen - a method known as post-synchronisation.

Albert Arch photographed and directed both films. His enthusiasm for using his best shots twice resulted in Kathleen Daw turning up unrecognised and unmentioned in "**Eastern Sunshine**"!

The 1958 advertising film for Yarmouth "**Having a Wonderful Time**" was shot in Eastman Colour, and has now faded somewhat as Eastman Colour prints are prone to do from this period. The film, made on 35mm for cinema showing as well, begins with a lengthy sequence of Somerleyton village and house before getting down to the treasures of Yarmouth and Gorleston. The old parts of Yarmouth are shown, including the towers and walls, and the house where, according to the sign "Mrs. M. Sewell, authoress of 'Mothers Lost Words' resided here. Her daughter Anna, of Black Beauty fame, was born here on the March 30th 1820. House restored 1932". Scroby sands, Gorleston and Yarmouth beaches, Yarmouth market, the river and quays, and a basket maker producing quarter cran baskets and swills for the fisheries make this a little more interesting than some of the publicity films of the time, even though it is general in its approach and style. The commentary by David Gell, a Canadian born disc jockey and radio compere, is typical of the time. At the beginning he says "They come by train, by air, and overland..." with shots of a steam train pulling into Vauxhall station, a light aeroplane at the grass airstrip, and

*Fun on the floating dodgems in "**Sunshine, Fun and Laughter**".*

the coach station. At the end of the film over shots of the Pleasure Beach and its rides and amusements he tells us "The development of the Pleasure Beach is symbolic of the demand for thrills and excitement in what we might call this restless age. Showman Alf Botton has catered for this demand in no small measure. He controls one of the finest pleasure grounds ever constructed".

But perhaps it is the shots of the theatres with their stars coming and going, like Tommy Cooper and Benny Hill, playing up to the camera, which make this so evocative of the time. At the Royal Aquarium Theatre - Vic Oliver, at the Brittania Pier – Joan Turner, at the Windmill Theatre – Derek Roy, at the Wellington – Ruby Murray and Tommy Cooper. "What an autograph hunter's paradise this is" runs the commentary as we also see Charlie Chester and Benny Hill, "Britain's greatest funny man".

An amateur record of a family going on holiday to Yarmouth shows the train leaving Huddersfield station in 1954. At Yarmouth they stay at the "**Central Hotel**", go on the beach, look at the piers, and let the children play in "Pixieland", a children's play area. The cameraman, probably dad, films fruit, vegetable and butchers stalls on the market, including one of Yarmouth's famous the chip stalls. There are street scenes, the quays, and a day out on the Broads. August Bank Holiday weekend in 1957 saw thousands of people in Yarmouth, some on holiday, and some out for the day. In "**August Bank Holiday Crowd**", filmed by Mr. Trimm, at Vauxhall train station people queue for tickets and board trains for home to places like Sheffield. Mr. Cooke of Long Stratton recorded "**Yarmouth in the 1950s**", and other amateur films exist in family collections, such as "**A Few Hours at The Pleasure Beach**" which shows us the beach and amusements.

"Lydia Eva Arrives at Yarmouth" shows the steam drifter coming back to Yarmouth in 1972 after years of dereliction following naval use for towing targets, and her subsequent preservation by the Maritime Trust and the Lydia Eva Trust as a tribute to the once great herring fishing industry. David Butcher, who has researched the history of the herring fleets, writes that in the heyday of the herring drifters before the 1914–18 war, about 1000 boats worked out of Yarmouth, and another 700 or so from Lowestoft. There were also a few at Southwold. The fleets consisted of local and Scottish boats, the latter out-numbering the East Anglian craft, especially in the port of Yarmouth.

At Yarmouth, in the 1913 season, there was a record catch of 824,213 crans (a cran is about 1000 fish) landed by 1,006 boats, of which 852 were steam driven, 58 motor powered, and 96 sailing craft. By 1930 the sailing drifters had gone. The herring swam in vast shoals past the East Anglian coast from late September to early December.

This was known as the Home Fishing. The Scottish connection with Yarmouth and Lowestoft

*Drifters at Hall Quay, Yarmouth. From "**When Do Bloaters Become Kippers**" 1930.*

*Gutting herring at Yarmouth from "**When Do Bloaters become Kippers**" 1930.*

went back a long way, to the 1860s and 1870s, with an ever-increasing number of craft coming down for the autumn voyage, especially from the Moray Firth area from ports such as Banff and Buckie, and also from Fraserburgh and Perterhead. Yarmouth was the world's premier herring port. Her quays, often both sides of the river, right up to Hall Quay by the Town Hall, were scenes of great activity.

About 30 miles north east of Yarmouth and Lowestoft was Smith's Knoll, the most productive of all the herring grounds, but other North Sea sandbanks and shoals also yielded large quantities of fish. There was keen competition to get out to the grounds first, and each skipper always kept his fishing secrets closely guarded. He would look at the water, and if it was thick and puddly-looking, he would shoot his nets. This would take about half an hour or so. As the first net went over the side someone might shout "over in the name of the Lord", a Biblical reference to the miraculous draught of fishes in St John's Gospel.

A herring net was 33 yards long and about 12 yards deep. Each boat shot about 80 or 90 of them, perhaps more, but it was always an odd number, never an even one. The net was buoyed with large canvas floats known as buffs, and the buoy and nets were kept down in the water by a continuous length of heavy rope, as thick as a man's wrist, known as the warp. Once all the nets were over the side, the boat stopped its engine, and drifted along with the tide hanging to the nets – hence, the term drifting.

The herring normally rose from the sea bed about dusk to swim to the upper levels, where they got caught in the net - although daytime swims also occurred. In the early hours of the next day, whenever the skipper gave the order, the nets were hauled in. Hauling could take as much as six or eight hours, depending on the weather conditions and whether it was a good 'shimmer', or catch. As the net was hauled in, it was shaken to release the fish - an activity called scudding. The warp was brought aboard with the help of a steam capstan, and stowed.

It was dangerous work out there in the North Sea, and there was the occasional tragedy. In October 1936 the Peterhead drifter *Olive Branch* capsized and her crew of ten men drowned. Her

The remains of the Olive Branch, *lost with all hands. From "**Sea Harvest**" 1936.*

broken remains on the beach can be seen in "**Sea Harvest**", an amateur film of fish quay scenes at Yarmouth in 1936.

As soon as the holds were filled, the boats would race to port to get a good price at market. The catch was lifted from the hold by quarter-cran baskets and swung ashore by a pulley wheel on the steam capstan. Each basket held seven stones of fish, and the buyers liked to see the baskets well topped up. At Yarmouth the fish were then tipped into large double-compartment wicker baskets known as swills. It was only at Yarmouth this type of basket was used for the herring, and any film featuring swills on the quay is Yarmouth. At Lowestoft, where there was much less room for the boats to land their catch, the quarter-cran baskets tipped their contents into wooden kits, and salt was sprinkled on prior to being taken to the pickling plots for gutting and packing.

Both at Yarmouth and Lowestoft, the fish were gutted by girls (these girls were aged anything between 14 and 70) working quickly at about a fish per second. The guts were sold to be processed into fishmeal and manure. The herring were sorted by size, and then packed into spruce-wood casks, with one layer of fish at right angles to another. These went to East European countries and Russia. The girls, who had travelled down from Scotland, worked in threes: two to gut and one to pack.

At Lowestoft there was a method of packing herrings for export called Klondyking, as it was invented in Lowestoft about the time of the gold rush in the 1890s on the river Klondyke in the

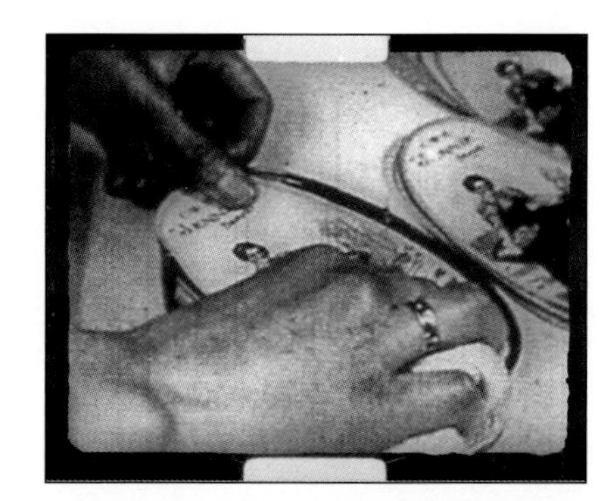

*Three frames from the 9.5mm copy of "**Herrings**" released in January 1935 for home projection. This included the "**CWS Canning Factory**" sequence of 1930.*

Yukon. The fish were packed in rectangular boxes with ice and salt and sent to Germany in German ships.

For the UK market there were kippers. The fish were steeped in brine, then split along the backbone and opened up, and hung in a smokehouse to be cured by the smoke from slow-burning piles of oak chips. This is seen in detail in a film made in the early 1950s called "**Herrings For Sale**". The latest methods of quick-freezing fish are also seen in this film, showing how the industry was coming into line with new trends. The bloater was a specialty of Yarmouth. This was smoked whole overnight, without any gutting. Red herrings were done the same way, but cured for longer, so they lasted longer – up to a month or more.

The Co-operative Wholesale Society had a cannery and "preserved food factory" in Waveney Drive, Lowestoft. In "**CWS Canning Factory**" in 1930 is seen the process of producing the Jennie brand of canned herring. The herring are cleaned and packed by hand in oval cans by an army of women. The lids are put on and the can sealed by machine. A small hole was then made in the can so that it did not explode when put into the steam oven for cooking. After this the hole was sealed up with solder to make the can airtight. Finally the label was stuck on – by hand.

Thirty years later another film was made at the CWS factory, but by then the herring were gone. "**It's In The Can**", a colour film of 1961 shows the range of products produced in the factory. Canned soups, bottled meat paste, cheese triangles, canned peas and carrots are just some of the lines in this detailed film showing how the processes were carried out. In the kitchens the products are tested. Again, women seem to do all the work in the factory. Labelling and packaging of the 'Waveney' products, the distribution by lorry, and the final display in a shop complete this advertising film for the Co-op.

Once a catch of 'silver darlings', as the herring were sometimes called, had been landed, it was off to sea again, pausing only to take on essential stores and bags of salt. Watching the boats coming and going in the autumn, and the activity on the quay, attracted many visitors with their 8mm, 9.5mm, and 16mm cine cameras, as well as professionals working with 35mm film. We have already seen that a cameraman was in Yarmouth in 1902 to film "**Fish Quay Scenes**", and a cameraman was here again in 1925 to shoot "**Herring Harvest Home**" for a Topical Budget newsreel item, and another called "**Harvest of The Sea**".

On October 21st 1930, when the new Haven Bridge at Yarmouth was opened by the Prince of Wales (later Duke of Windsor), Pathé brought a sound film unit down to record the event and film the quayside scenes. They not only recorded the natural sounds but also the Prince of Wales's short speech. The quality of this is not good by modern standards, as the microphone was too far away from His Royal Highness, but his words can just be heard. Both he and his brother, the Duke of York, later King George VI, were nervous speakers. At Yarmouth the Prince is seen speaking too quickly and unable to keep still, and in the film of "**Their Majesties in Norwich**", about the opening of Norwich City Hall in 1938, his brother, by then the King, had difficulty delivering his speech.

The rest of the Yarmouth film of the "**Haven Bridge Opening**", called "**When Do Bloaters**

Become Kippers", shows the Prince of Wales inspecting the fishing boats and touring the 'great yards' as the commentator calls them, where the fisher girls were at work gutting 'the harvest of herring'. The sound track carries the actual sound of the girls singing as they worked. A little commentary is sprinkled over this sequence, apparently done live at Yarmouth rather than recorded afterwards at the studio, as was normal practice later. This represents no more than a primitive attempt at sound, specially as there is a problem with the sound 'wowing' slightly because of insufficient dampening of the sound head rollers. But the unsteady recording of the cheering crowds and the triumphant blasts from the fishing boats' whistles overcome the inadequacies of the system. At this time silent and sound newsreels were running side by side, and there is a silent version of the Haven Bridge opening called "**The Prince at Yarmouth**", with almost identical scenes.

With the introduction in the mid 1930s of 16mm Kodachrome colour film, Victor Harrison, who owned several cinemas in Norfolk, filmed the boats bringing the herring in, and the "**Scotch Fisher Girls at Yarmouth**" at work gutting and packing the herring. The colour has faded slightly, as this early Kodachrome, introduced in July 1935, had a tendency to lose the blues and greens, leaving a pinkish image. Kodak, aware of the problem, solved this in 1938, and from then on Kodachrome retained its vibrant colours. Another colour system, Dufaycolor, was available in the late 1930s for the 9.5mm gauge. Short films exist of a Yarmouth "**Tug**", and "**Drifters in Dufaycolor**".

*The Prince of Wales delivering his speech at the opening of Haven Bridge in 1930. Note the microphones in the left hand corner of the picture, too far away from the Prince for us to hear properly. Note also the weak variable density sound track. From "**When Do Bloaters Become Kippers**" 1930.*

A drifter leaving harbour. This was filmed in 1938 in Dufaycolor.

Whether making a hat out of rope by an old Yarmouth fisherman was normal or not, we do not know, but a 1939 newsreel item called "**Fishnet Fashions**" certainly shows this novel headgear, and a woman trying it on! Another oddity is a cartoon film called "**A Fishy Subject**", informing us of the benefits of eating herrings. An animated herring points to a board which says they contain protein, fats, iodine, vitamin A and vitamin D. "Food For Children, Food For Women, Food for Men – We Are Food For Fitter Britons".

After the 1939-45 war, herring fishing was a greatly reduced business. The fish just weren't there in such quantity. At Yarmouth where there were once a 1000 boats, in the 1950s it was more like 100. The fisher girls were no longer girls, and the boats were mainly diesel-powered. "**Herring Moon Warms Yarmouth**" gives the impression in 1948 that everything is OK, as kippers are wrapped in cellophane and a steam train hauls away wagons of fish. Charles Scott of Norwich went in 1950 to Yarmouth to film "**Fish Quay Scenes**" in Kodachrome, and already the decline is evident, with not so young women gutting the herring. In Bernard Botham's "**That Little Fishing Village**" made in the early and mid 1950s along with his

The Yarmouth drifter Kernoozer *with Charlie Moll sixth from the left, from* ***"Here and There in East Anglia"***.

The Scottish drifter Maid of Thule *featured in* ***"Drifters"*** *1929.*

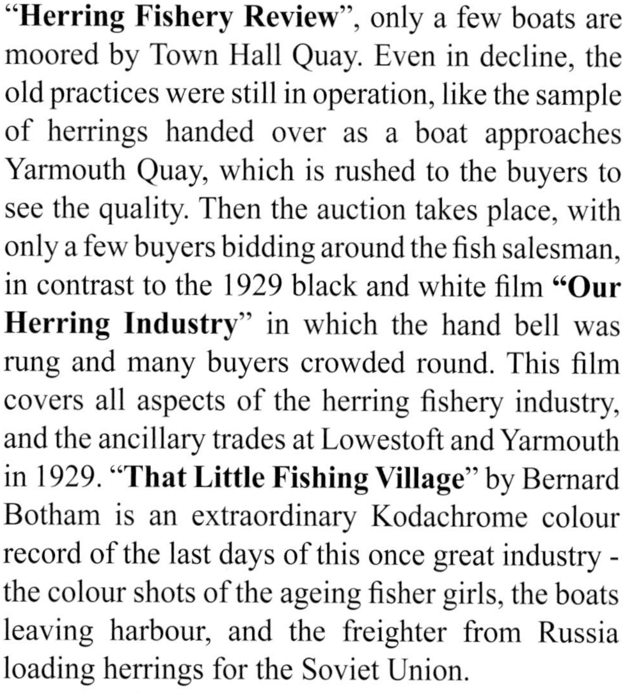

"**Herring Fishery Review**", only a few boats are moored by Town Hall Quay. Even in decline, the old practices were still in operation, like the sample of herrings handed over as a boat approaches Yarmouth Quay, which is rushed to the buyers to see the quality. Then the auction takes place, with only a few buyers bidding around the fish salesman, in contrast to the 1929 black and white film **"Our Herring Industry"** in which the hand bell was rung and many buyers crowded round. This film covers all aspects of the herring fishery industry, and the ancillary trades at Lowestoft and Yarmouth in 1929. "**That Little Fishing Village**" by Bernard Botham is an extraordinary Kodachrome colour record of the last days of this once great industry - the colour shots of the ageing fisher girls, the boats leaving harbour, and the freighter from Russia loading herrings for the Soviet Union.

So, the last steam drifter, the "**Lydia Eva**" is moored at Hall Quay at Yarmouth in 1991, a tangible reminder of Yarmouth's past. She was built in 1930 at King's Lynn for Harry Eastick, and named after his daughter, who is seen in the film explaining why. Jimmy May walks around the boat as he reminisces of the time he went to sea in her as a fireman, seeing to the boiler, working on deck hauling, and helping unload the fish at the quayside.

So where did all the herring go? Charlie Moll, from Winterton, was a fisherman in the drifter *Kernoozer* in 1905, and he puts forward his own ideas in "**Here and There in East Anglia**". Interviewed in 1970, he reckons it was because the spawning grounds were spoilt by trawling.

The humble herring could be said to have made a major impact on the film industry, for it was John Grierson's "**Drifters**", made in 1929, that began what is termed by some as the "documentary movement". In fact documentary films had been around since motion pictures began, but "**Drifters**" was different. It was not a straight factual film, but an impression of the hard labour involved, achieved through imaginative photography, cutting and pace. What is seldom realised is that most of the film was shot off the East Anglian coast, and at Great Yarmouth and Lowestoft.

In the spring of 1928, John Grierson joined the Empire Marketing Board as an assistant film officer. The aim of the government-financed board was the promotion of trade, and Grierson's first job was to make them a film. The board wanted a film on the herring fleets, so Grierson travelled to Lerwick in the Shetlands and started work with cameraman Basil Emmott, filming local scenes, some sea-birds and some shots aboard a local drifter, the *Maid of Thule*.

Attempts made in the Shetlands to film the actual catching of herrings were not successful, and Grierson and Emmott came down to East Anglia and went filming on the Lowestoft drifter *Renoulle*. "**Drifters**" opens with views of fishermen's cottages intercut with shots of gulls

*Herring in the nets, from "**North Sea Herring Harvest**" by Ford Jenkins 1930.*

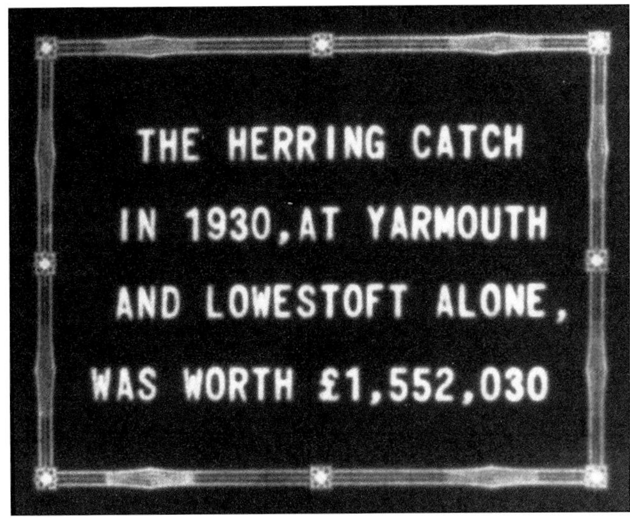

*From Ford Jenkins film "**North Sea Herring Harvest**" 1930.*

and seas breaking. There is much inter-cutting and quick editing in places done by Grierson himself. Some of the short shots taken in the Shetlands are mixed with the East Anglian material, though these soon become obvious.

At the fishing grounds the nets are shot and the crew go below. The interior shots of the crew's quarters were filmed on a specially constructed set while John Grierson and Basil Emmott were at Lerwick. What appear to be underwater scenes of herring swimming into the nets are faked. Not only were these sequences done in a tank at the marine laboratories at Plymouth, but apparently the fish are not herring at all, but roach. It seems that herring could not be caught and kept alive in a tank, so a substitute had to be found.

The crew turn out and the nets are hauled. The inter-cutting of hands on nets, ropes, and the throbbing engine, give the impression of long, hard work, and of the toil involved in catching herring. "Despite the help of the winch every foot has to be fought for". The returning boats head for Lowestoft and Yarmouth, where the catch is unloaded. Most of the sequences of landing herring were filmed at Yarmouth, for the swills (those double baskets peculiar to the town) give the location away. Next the catch is gutted by the fisher girls and then boxed and barrelled. Finally there is a sequence of railway fish trucks taking the herring away.

"**Drifters**" was released in 1929 to much acclaim. The original prints had a few tinted sequences, and a copy in the East Anglian Film Archive retains those tints. Another film was made for educational purposes constructed out of the material Grierson and Emmott shot called "**Our Herring Industry**" - a shorter, more straightforward and factual version of the herring story.

At Lowestoft, Ford Jenkins, a photographer in the town, made "**Herring Fisheries**" in 1930, a fifteen minute 16mm film very much like "**Drifters**". "**Herring Fisheries**", or to give it a subsequent title "**North Sea Herring Harvest**", follows the "**Drifters**" pattern. The boats leave harbour and the nets are cast. Numerous shots of hauling follow with some interesting camera angles and quick cutting. Back at Lowestoft the catch is landed and the fish gutted. There are shots of barrelling and boxing the herring, and finally we see crates for export being loaded into the hold of a steamer.

It is a well-made film with captions explaining the procedures and equipment, but like John Grierson, Ford Jenkins had trouble in obtaining the fishing shots he wanted. It was the practice of the herring drifters to go to sea one day and to return the next morning, but if the catch was poor they would stay at sea another night or so.

Armed with his 16mm camera and a supply of film, Ford Jenkins went to sea in a Lowestoft drifter one autumn afternoon. At seven the next morning the crew began hauling in the two miles of net. There was not a single fish in the meshes. The drifter stayed at sea. The next night a quantity of herrings were hauled in, but before there was any daylight to allow Ford to film. The drifter stayed at sea. The third morning produced a good catch, and Ford was able to capture some scenes as the last nets came aboard in early daylight. The drifter returned to Lowestoft, but Ford was not happy with the shots he had, so he went to sea again - this time obtaining the results he wanted in one go.

In 1931 Ford Jenkins took his finished film to London to show to Kodak. They were so impressed they put it in their Kodascope library of films for amateurs to hire, under the title "A Glimpse of the East Coast Herring Industry." A write-up of the film and a picture of Ford Jenkins appeared in the Cine Kodak and Kodascope Library News of August 1931. Another version of his film was put out by Home Movies and Home Talkies, a monthly magazine for cine enthusiasts of the time under the title "**North Sea Herring Harvest**".

In 1931 a short cinema film about "**How Kippers Leave Home**" was produced, showing how the herrings are turned into kippers in a local smoke house. There is still a smoke-house in Lowestoft, in Raglan Street, but the herrings now come mainly from Scotland and Norway - although some local 'longshores' can be purchased in the season. This smoke-house was filmed in 1982 for inclusion in "**Maritime East Anglia**", with Gordon Buckenham running it in a traditional way.

As one industry died, another rose to take its place. The production of gas and oil in the North Sea helped offset the unemployment caused by the herring fisheries collapse. "**Offshore Gas**", "**North Sea Gas**", and other films from companies like Shell record these new industries, but at Lowestoft they continued fishing - trawling for white fish. "**A Man's World**" made in 1973, encourages young men to come into the industry, by showing what trawling was all about, and the stress and attractions of the job. LT 979 leaves harbour for the trawling grounds, with shots on deck and below, intercut with budding fisherman learning how to read a weather chart and master navigation at The Navigation School, on Herring Fishery Score – an annex to the Lowestoft College of Further Education.

At sea the net is hauled aboard, the catch is released from the cod end, sorted, gutted and stowed. Back on dry land the students are shown how a trawl operates with the aid of a model, and learn about engines, electronics and lifeboat drill. On board the crew have tea in warm surroundings.

This can be compared with "**Trawl Fishing**", a silent 16mm film made about 1930 out of Lowestoft when conditions for the crew were much harsher. They had a steam winch to haul the net in, but the rest of the work was done in the open without much protection. The men work on deck sorting, gutting, and washing the catch on a trip lasting nine days. The film is unusual in that some of the shots are tinted a colour. The trawlers brought back cod and plaice mainly, with smaller quantities of roker, lemon sole, and dabs.

In 1921 a short local newsreel was made for showing in one of the Lowestoft cinemas of the "**School Sports**" on Crown Meadow, in Love Road. The obstacle race would be poorer if it were not for the spars, nets and barrels borrowed from the fishing industry for the contestants to climb over, crawl under, or dive through.

Before we leave the herring fisheries, we must mention Ted Frost, a Lowestoft resident who was apprenticed as a shipwright in 1916. His work and eye at Chambers Shipyard caught every detail of how a wooden steam fishing boat was built, from the timbers arriving to the finished craft. In later life, he took to technical drawing, recording

*"**A Mans World**", A British Trawlers Federation film of 1973.*

*Spars, nets, and barrels make up the obstacle course in "**School Sports**" on Crown meadow in 1921.*

what he remembered in a fascinating book "From Tree To Sea", published by Terence Dalton in 1985. Fortunately Ted Frost was filmed briefly in his flat in Lowestoft, putting the finishing touches to his pencil drawings for "**East Anglia Today**" in 1984. A wooden fishing boat being built at Lowestoft was filmed in colour by Don Chipperfield in 1952 for the educational film "**East Anglia**". This must have been one of the last wooden boats to be made there in the open air. The men are using the traditional adze to work the timbers. There were two main shipbuilders in Lowestoft, Richards of Horn Hill, and Brooke Marine, with an extensive inner harbour frontage at the bottom of Heath Road, Oulton Broad. The history of Richards is outlined in David Bucknole's three part 8mm film "**A Century of Ships**".

At Brooke Marine the *Cevic*, a brand new trawler, is launched down the slipway in 1959 in "**Where Broadland Meets The Sea**". This film also has a lengthy sequence of the old swing bridge at Lowestoft in action. "**The Royal Launch**" of the landing craft *Ardennes,* is typical of the small ships being built by Brooke Marine. Bill Hansford took the film in 1976 when Princess Alice launched the *Ardennes* in the traditional way with a champagne bottle breaking over the bow. The vessel is safely manoeuvered in the water by tugs, while the Royal party and guests attend the reception in a marquee. "**Up Anchor and Away**" made in 1968 is another film that looks at Lowestoft and the ship building business there.

At the beginning of the 20th century, Lowestoft had four coach and carriage builders, and two wheelwrights – though there were six more wheelwrights in the surrounding villages. It has been suggested that these trades may have influenced the building of omnibuses in the town. In Laundry Lane motor buses were made at the Eastern Coach Works Ltd. Mr. James, a local amateur film maker, made a Super 8mm documentary film in 1981 shortly before the works closed. Eastern Coach Works, or United Automobile Services as it was first known, began in a small way in 1912, the main factory being constructed 1919. "**All In A Day's Work**" shows in detail the construction of double-decker buses, from the draughtsman's drawing to the assembly of the parts. The work was manual throughout, and memorable shots include men carrying the whole side of a bus, and putting the roof in place in one go. Machinists, all women, work in the fabric shop stitching seat covers. The completed buses spend a week in the paint shop where they are painted by hand. Glaziers fit the windows, and fitters put the seats in. The buses are then filled with weights, the equivalent of passengers, for the tilt test. A bus had to be able to lean 28 degrees for it to receive its certificate of road-worthiness.

On a smaller scale is the wheelwright, Mr. S. W. Wright of Lowestoft. His passion was his car, a Morris 8, which he kept in immaculate condition. Although the car is a feature of the film "**Wheelwright**", it is the business of making a wooden wheel which Mr. Wright's son-in-law wanted to record in this 8mm film. Mr. Wright was over 80 when this film was made in 1978, but he is extremely agile as he nips round putting the iron tyre on. This is then cooled with water to make it contract tightly on to the wooden wheel.

Lowestoft was also a summer resort and like other East Anglian coastal towns, had a film made advertising its wares. "**Land of The Rising Sun**", made in 1938, shows off all the usual things, the beach, Kensington Gardens with its boating lake, Claremont Pier with the sign "Sailings to Ostend", and the South Pier where you could have "a merry time with Binnie Hale and Christopher Stone". There was the Commodore Grand Orchestra playing outside, roller skating, and circus acts

*Inside Eastern Coach Works in Mr. James's "**All in a Day's Work**", 1981.*

performed in a small ring in the open. This silent film has captions, one of which says "Why not come and live in Lowestoft, there are many attractive residential quarters", as the camera shows modern semi-detached houses in a tree lined avenue. The film emphasises the surrounding attractions, such as Nicholas Everitt Park; Sparrows Nest, with a display of women dancing, of the keep fit variety; and power boat racing on Oulton Broad. "For the Ladies, Lowestoft has excellent shopping centres" says a caption as we see the main street, and the cinemas The Playhouse, The Odeon, and The Palace. The film ends with a colour sequence of flowers and Lowestoft by night.

In the 1950s there were outings to Gorleston of the physically handicapped organised by the Norfolk Voluntary Association. "**Holiday Camp For The Physically Disabled**" is a record of one of these outings which shows the members arriving at Vauxhall Station in Yarmouth where they are helped into wheelchairs and invalid carriages and taken to Gorleston Super Holiday Camp. They go on outings to the Broads and Raveningham Hall, and have a trip in a light aircraft. The film ends with an exhibition set up by the Central Council for The Care of Cripples. A bit further along, at Hopton, there were several holiday camps. In 1946 an unknown filmmaker had what was probably his or her first holiday after the war. They travelled by train, as everyone seems to have done at that time, to "**Hopton Holiday Camp**" for their "**East Coast Holiday**" (the film is known under both titles) and filmed it all, including part of the train journey, in glorious Kodachrome.

The Beare family had a farm and nursery at Hopton, and a timber yard. Stanley Beare made a film of the yard and his family with his 16mm camera. This is a good amateur film, with one outstanding shot of the staff walking up to and past the camera, an excellent record of the men that worked there, their clothes and their faces.

The Workers Travel Association made a short film of what a camp holiday had to offer at "**Rogerson Hall**" at Corton. The chalets are well laid out, clean and tidy. There is a restaurant, lounges for sitting and chatting to other campers, areas to relax and write letters home, and games to play both indoors and out. The film ends with a slightly sinister torchlight parade and bonfire, though typical of the time of the late 1930s.

At Pakefield, just south of Lowestoft the sea is free from pollution but in the 1980s was the subject of much speculation concerning the toxic waste accumulating in what was known as Gisleham Pit. The waste deposited there over the years was seeping from the pit closer to the beach. In 1986 when a film was made called "**Come On In The Waters Fine**", Greenpeace were monitoring the situation. The uncertainty of the danger was causing great concern with the local residents, and they formed the Waveney Action Group. The film, made by Yorkshire Television, deals also with pollution at Yarmouth, and other parts of our coast.

Blow the wind to fill my sail,
Keep the water wet,
Give the fish good fin and tail,
To swim into my net.

This is said over shots of 'Worky' Upcraft hauling in his trawl off Southwold in the summer of 1954. It is a short sequence in "**East Anglian Holiday**", a British Tranport Film extolling the scenic delights of the Eastern Counties. In full Technicolor, even though the film was shot on 16mm Kodachrome, with Technicolor making 16mm release prints, we see 'Worky' going to sea and emptying out on the floor of his longshore boat plaice, soles and skate.

*'Worky' Upcraft, a Southwold fisherman, sets off to catch some fish. From "**East Anglian Holiday**" 1954.*

Around 1900 Frederick Jenkins came to Southwold and set up business as a photographer. In the 1920s, his shop in the High Street sold stationery, artist's materials, hand-made pottery, gramophones, wirelesses and photographic materials. Barrett Jenkins, his son, was then in his twenties, and worked in the shop. In 1928 a Kodak BB cine camera (a smaller version of the B) came into the shop, but it never had the chance of being bought by a customer, for Barrett took it from the shelves, and began to record local events.

On May 28th 1928, Whit Monday, Barrett filmed the races and prize giving of the "**Rural Sports**", held on the common. These sports had flourished before the First World War, and this was an attempt to revive them. Although on the film everyone seemed to be enjoying themselves, these Rural Sports were not held again. Barrett Jenkins was pleased with the results of his filming, and so continued. On the August 6th 1928, the beating of the bounds took place. This is described in Frederick Jenkins' book, "Story of Southwold" published in 1948, thus: "the beating or bumping was performed on the small boys who might reasonably be relied upon to accompany the party, with the purpose of impressing upon them by corporal experience the boundaries of their native town". Barrett's 16mm film shows the Mayor, Ernest Allen, and the vicar, Rev. Woodman Dowding, leaving the Town Hall, with the party equipped with the traditional willow canes, then walking along East Cliff to the beach. Here the party split in two, one set going north, the other south. Barrett filmed the party going south towards the harbour. They went along Gun Hill, passed some bathing machines on the beach, arriving at the harbour where they got into boats to go over to the Walberswick side. The Northern party and the Southern party eventually came together at the Harbour Inn for refreshments. "**Corporation Perambulates The Bounds**" was just one of many short films Barrett was to make over the next fifty years. He filmed the ladies' hockey team and the ladies 'Home Knit' team taking part in a Push-Ball match. This is where two teams try to score by rolling a huge inflatable ball into goal, a very popular game at the time sponsored by the Daily Mail. He filmed "St Edmunds Day" on November 29th 1929 when the Mayor, Andrew Critten, gave buns to children coming out of church; the laying of a foundation stone for the ex-servicemen's club in Hotson Road; the landing of large quantities of sprats by the fishermen on the beach in 1929; a Belle paddle steamer calling at the end of the pier; sea defence work; Frederick Jenkins taking a group photograph with a plate camera outside the Methodist Church; Trinity Fair; the opening of the hospital fete; a children's service on the beach complete with piano; dancing on the vicarage lawn by Gladys Cowell, whose parents ran the Crown Hotel; elephants arriving for the circus on the common; a cricket match; and the Jubilee celebrations on the common in 1935. The latter included Dorothy Hope, Southwold's first lady Mayor, watching an egg and spoon race, a backwards running race, and other fun sports.

These and other films are in the "**Barrett Jenkins Collection**", but one he made in 1929 was of the passing of the Southwold railway. "**Southwold Narrow Gauge Railway**" records the last days of this line which closed on April 11th 1929, fifty years after it opened. This was a narrow gauge line, only three feet, with stations at Walberswick, Blythburgh and Wenhaston, with the terminus at Halesworth in a separate station close to the London and North Eastern Railway line. There are scenes of the train travelling along, and the interior of a carriage where Peggy Jenkins and Howard Jenkins pose for the camera.

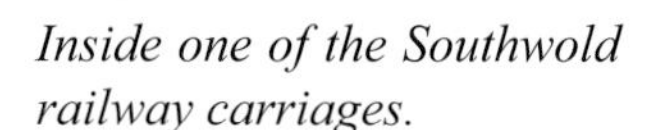

Inside one of the Southwold railway carriages.

The bus that met every train arriving at Southwold.

A clergyman, titling his film "Padre Pictorial", also filmed the "**Southwold Railway**", with shots of unloading goods, coaling the engine from a bucket, some shunting, and the local bus to convey passengers into Southwold. There was yet another film made about the railway, this time on 35mm for showing in cinemas, called "**A Railway Which is A Real Joke**". This refers to the uniqueness of the railway, its narrow gauge and its slowness, and the fact that the drivers were not allowed to go faster than 16 miles per hour. This is a good record of the line, and includes a signalman preparing for the coming train at the junction just outside the station.

In 1979, fifty years after the railway closed, a plaque was unveiled near the station site with Barrett Jenkins in shot, and he appears again when he was Mayor in 1965 carrying on the tradition of taking the first ride at Trinity Fair on the dodgems.

James Blythe who was manager of The Cinema in Southwold for 38 years.

Barrett Jenkins having the first ride on the dodgems when he was Mayor in 1965.

Photography ran in the Jenkins family. Henry Jenkins (1838-1921), was a photographer in Tunbridge Wells who had 14 children, six of whom became photographers. Of those six, Annie Jenkins went to Worthing, Ernest to Redhill and Polly to Cape Town. Samuel Jenkins stayed in Tunbridge Wells, Frederick Jenkins set up in business in Southwold and Harry in Lowestoft. Harry's son Ford Jenkins was well known for his photographs of the fishing fleets at Lowestoft.

Cinema films were being shown in the Assembly Rooms in York Road, Southwold in 1912. Three years later it is recorded that this was being run by a Mr. R. S. Ransome. In 1921 the cinema was bought by the Crick family, and Mrs. Crick's son by a former marriage, James Blythe, became manager. James Blythe acquired a 35mm hand-turned movie camera and began recording events in Southwold for showing in his cinema.

In 1925 he filmed Southwold's new "**Lifeboat**", the *Mary Scott*. This was the first motor lifeboat to be stationed at Southwold, and she was kept in the harbour, where James Blythe filmed her and the crew. This was a short local news item which would have been shown at the cinema as soon as it had been returned from the London film laboratories. He filmed other stories. On October 31st 1926, Henry Smith, mate of a Lowestoft drifter, jumped overboard fully clothed

The Southwold Cinema in York Road with a publicity float outside in 1927.

Henry Smith receiving the Freedom of The Borough in Southwold market place in 1927.

to rescue a colleague from drowning, and for his heroism Smith was awarded the Stanhope Gold Medal for the bravest deed of the year, and was made an honorary freeman of the Borough of Southwold. On April 28th 1927, a large crowd gathered to watch the "**Presentation of The Freedom of The Borough to H. E. Smith**", as the Mayor presented him with the medal and the scroll recording his admission to the freedom, the ceremony being filmed by James Blythe. At the end of this film is a panning shot in the market place of thc Kessingland lifeboat crew who came down for the occasion. The fun of this shot is a little boy held aloft by his proud parent, who runs along beating the panning camera so that the little boy regularly appears behind the lifeboatmen.

James Blythe filmed a steam paddle tug towing away the old Southwold to Walberswick "**Ferry**" and a new one named "Blyth" taking over, and a "**Shipwreck**" - the Lowestoft smack *Evela* which came ashore in thick fog on January 9th 1934. The crew were taken off by the Southwold lifeboat *Mary Scott*. James Blythe's film shows the *Evela* at low tide on the beach, from which she was eventually re-floated and, after repair, put back into service.

The highlight of the year at Southwold was, and still is to some extent, "**Trinity Fair**", opened at noon on Trinity Monday on South Green. The showmen were not allowed to set up the fair during the day before, so had to assemble outside the town, and wait until the evening service had finished at 8.0, then they were allowed in. For the 1928 fair James Blythe set up his camera on the flat roof which then existed at the side of the King's Head, and turned his camera as the procession rolled by. Horses and showmen's traction engines pulled the waggons. It was a long procession, so at one point James Blythe turned the camera handle slowly so that when shown the film speeded up the procession - always good for a laugh. Next he filmed the reading by the Town Clerk of the charter which has allowed Southwold to hold a fair since the time of Henry VII. The next bit of the ritual, the Mayor having the first ride on the roundabout, was at that time relatively new, having been introduced in 1922 when the then Mayor, Mr. A.J. Critten, accompanied by his officials, climbed on the gallopers. After the ride the fair was proclaimed open in two places, the Market Place and in front of The Crown Hotel. These local news stories were shown as soon as possible after the event, and brought out again on 'high days and holidays' at the Southwold Cinema.

James Blythe retired in 1959 after 38 years as manager, the cinema closing two years later. For some time it was used as a repository by Blythe Removals before being demolished in 1983. The 35mm nitrate films had been stored under the raked seating at the cinema for many years, and some decomposed. At closure the remaining films were rescued by Barrett Jenkins, and taken home. Storing 35mm nitrate films at home is risky, so he passed them to the East Anglian Film Archive

*Typical caption of the 1930s inserted in a home movie of a holiday at Southwold from the "**Harrison Collection**".*

This is father venturing in. Shown in the winter months on a 16mm projector at home, it brought back holiday memories.

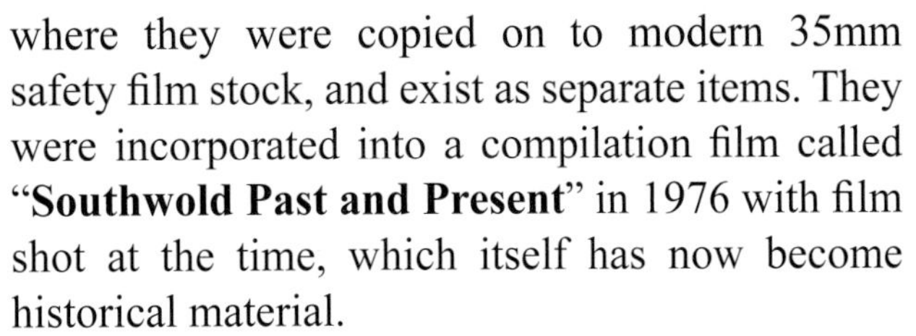

where they were copied on to modern 35mm safety film stock, and exist as separate items. They were incorporated into a compilation film called "**Southwold Past and Present**" in 1976 with film shot at the time, which itself has now become historical material.

Southwold has always attracted visitors, and they often brought their cine cameras with them. The Harrison family from Essex took 16mm films, including their holiday in 1935 at Southwold. They had inter-titles of their own words made by Kodak to splice into their home movie. What fun they must have had in the winter evenings watching these films of their summer holidays. The films were creatively captioned so that the film is amusing to watch, such as dad entering the sea after the caption "Father ventures in".

There are many more examples of amateur films made in and around Southwold in the 1930s including "**Family Film**", "**Hodge Compilation**", and "**Eversley School Sports**", through to "**Army Manoeuvres**" in 1958. Cinema newsreels often included shots of the "**Duke of York's Boys Camp**" held regularly on the Common between 1931 and 1938. Held in the week of the August bank holiday (then at the beginning of the month) about 400 youngsters were drawn from factories and public schools all over the country. They spent a week under canvas, and were well looked after. "The kitchen tent had white capped chefs presiding over a row of gleaming cooking stoves (the gas for which was conveyed by pipes across the Common). A table load of hundreds of lemons were being cut up for lemonade while, stacked conveniently near, were seen eighty seven 7lb jars of jam as part of the supplies" wrote Frederick Jenkins. The Duke of York (later King George VI) would come down and spend 24 hours at the camp, sleeping in one of the tents – in an iron bedstead! One of the films shows him looking through the viewfinder of a 35mm sound camera, there to record the fun, games and sport for the world to see.

Dunwich was once a large town, now gone beneath the waves. All that remains is a small village, and it is here that Sidney Manasseh discovered its history, and made a 16mm film trying to capture the past in "**City Under The Sea**" made around 1960. It is strange how this coast attracts non professional film makers; people come from other counties to film here. Sidney Manasseh came from Essex, and John Chear came from Hertfordshire to make "**A Suffolk Heath**" in the 1950s. Chear was fascinated by the stone curlew which nested here. A bird settles on her nest, waits 27 days for the eggs to hatch, and then the parent bird pecks away the shell and settles down on the chicks to keep them warm. Later the young birds leave the nest for the heather of Dunwich Heath. John Chear, a prolific film maker of wildlife films also made "**The Reed Marsh**" at Minsmere in the mid 1950s. His 16mm Kodachrome film shows the various birds there, and at Scolt Head in Norfolk. But again he dwells on one of the rarer birds at Minsmere, this time the Bittern.

"**Opportunity at Sizewell**" is a 1982 film that puts the case for Sizewell 'B', a second nuclear power station at the site. In the early 1980s this was a controversial subject. There had been a nuclear power station at Sizewell since 1966 but now Sizewell 'B' was proposed. There was a lengthy enquiry which took years and produced reams of paper - briefly seen in "**East Anglia Today**", made in 1984. This has a shot of a local boat just back on the beach with fish, then panning to the power station close by. It was not until 1990 that the new PWR nuclear power station was commissioned alongside Sizewell 'A', as the older one now became known. A couple of other films to do with emergencies and safety at these stations were made, and a record of the special train to Sizewell (actually Leiston) was filmed in 1991. This branch line ran from Saxmundham to Aldeburgh, with a 'halt' at Thorpeness, a "rapidly increasing garden village by the sea" said the directory of 1933. Once there was a small fishing village here, but just before and after the First World War, G. Stuart Ogilvie converted it into a model village, complete with the water tower disguised as a house, an 18 hole golf course, 'Ye Shoppes', and a 61 acre artificial lake called The Meare – opened in 1913. In 1934 a young man devoted to music, Tony Arnell, who went on to become a well known composer, came here on holiday. He made a 16mm film of his visit calling it "**Thorpeness Cuttings**". The film begins with a 16mm projector being switched on, followed by scenes of private roads and mock Tudor houses, and fishing boats on the beach. There is a treasure hunt with competitors running through the village and regatta day on the Meare. "**Thorpeness Railway**" shows the station or halt on the line before closure to passenger traffic in 1966. A16mm silent film was made showing the "**Last Train From Aldeburgh**" on September 12th that year.

A short quaint cinema film of 1932 shows an old boat called the *Ionia* converted into a house complete with windows anchored on the saltings at the back of Aldeburgh. "Originally a trawler, it is moored high and dry, and is used as a summer school" says a caption in this silent film of young ladies in bathing caps and swimsuits coming out to have a swim. The "**Girls in a Boat**" then play leap-frog before returning for a meal back on board. "Almost a life on the ocean wave – but the only waves are permanent ones".

Mrs. Basham, an Aldeburgh resident who lived in Crabbe Street, took films on her 9.5mm cine camera in the 1920s and 30s. Many of these films were saved by Keith Cable who lived in the town, and it is he who added a commentary to "**Aldeburgh Compilation**", a film put together in the 1970s of Mrs. Basham's films, showing fishing boats on the beach, the launch of one of the rowing lifeboats, a carnival, and fete. Another film of the lifeboat, made about the same time (1929) ,possibly by Mrs. Basham, shows the "**Aldeburgh Lifeboat**", a rowing and sailing craft, returning to the shore, where a team of people turn a capstan to haul the *Edward Z Dresden* back up the beach. In 1980, with a very different type of boat on the beach, and a tractor to do the heavy work, Derek Johnson took the 16mm "**Aldeburgh Lifeboat**" film of the activities involving the boat. This exists unedited as a record of the lifeboat there at that time.

The "**WI Sports**" was also covered by Mrs. Basham, who filmed the participants in the fancy dress race, the egg and spoon race, a slow bicycle race, a skipping race, and the sack race.

One of the most delightful scenes at Aldeburgh was to see Imogen Holst skipping down steps, and walking on the beach as she does in the 1966 film "**Gustav Holst Interviews**". She talks about Holst's life, and how important to him was the work of Ralph Vaughan Williams. This film was made to coincide with the opening of the Music Department at the University of East Anglia.

"Around Orfordness" was made by Leslie Gillham from Hornchurch in Essex. Leslie was a schoolmaster who made 16mm films as a hobby. He and his wife Marjorie made many films together all over the region. They built an editing room and a cinema in the attic at their home in Parkestone Avenue, Hornchurch, and took their film making very seriously. In **"Around Orfordness"** their sons Roger and Geoffrey helped with the film making, taking shots of Leslie setting up his 16mm Bolex cine camera and filming the village, the marshes, the birds, and Orford Castle. Like all the Gillham films, it is in colour and has a commentary, in this

Leslie Gillham filming at Orfordness in 1960.

case explaining the history of this quiet Suffolk coastal village.

A little further down the coast lived Sir Cuthbert Quilter at Bawdsey Manor. Lady Quilter ran a dairy, and in a short amateur film this is seen in operation. They had a large herd of cows on the estate, and a delivery van, driven by Arthur Jarvis, who is also seen in the film carrying a calf. "**Lady Quilter's Dairy**" is just a home movie, but it is one of those films that somehow just captures a small slice of rural life and work from a different age.

The River Deben slices into Suffolk here at Bawdsey. There has always been a ferry here, and in 1937 a Mr. Hudson, who worked for Ilford, which manufactured film and photographic materials, took some 16mm film of Felixstowe ferry in Dufaycolor. He had already filmed the Southwold ferry in Dufaycolor two years earlier. The "**Hudson Collection**" has a great variety of sequences ranging from Southend carnival in 1931, holidays at Covehithe in 1932, and an Essex aviation display at Hillmans Airfield near Brentwood. He also travelled widely, as there are sequences of Moray Firth and New York

Six miles up the Deben on the left hand side is Waldringfield, a great yachting place. In 1934 a family spent their holiday here messing about in boats while watching "**Waldringfield Regatta**" which took place on the Friday and Saturday of August 17th and 18th . With the tide in, there is a swimming race, a shovel race, and the greasy pole, with contestants trying to walk to the end without falling off - but most of them don't make it. Members of the cameraman's family climb in and out of boats, one being called *The Ranzo*, and having a picnic aboard the *Cornelia*.

At Woodbridge in 1969 the yacht *Sun Cloud* was lying in dry dock bedecked with flags waiting to be launched. The crew make last minute preparations, then a lady in a fur coat names the boat in the traditional way by smashing against it a bottle of champagne. "**Launch of Sun Cloud**" takes place and *Sun Cloud* is afloat against a background of Woodbridge tide mill.

Jim Desborough was the miller here in 1951 when a film unit recorded the working of the tide mill. There was a large accumulation of water behind the mill left when the tide went out. This provided the power for about four hours work. The rush of escaping water from the mill pond drove the paddle wheel, which was connected to a square oak shaft 22 inches in diameter. From this the stones were turned and the sack hoist operated. Jim is seen at work, feeling the fine flour the stones produced. This is a good record of the tide mill working as it had done for the previous 150 years. But it was not to last much longer for the main shaft broke in 1957, and the tide mill never worked for a living again. This unique Suffolk building was bought for preservation, which was completed in 1982, with further refurbishment work 20 years later. In the Shell series of 'Craftsmen' films, **"The Tide Miller**", records on film what is considered to be the last working tide mill in England.

At Felixstowe, an amateur film, this time of a family on holiday there in 1933, contains a brief shot of a shrimp boat. At one time shrimps were a popular teatime food, and both pink and brown shrimps were caught in the vicinity of Harwich harbour, and boiled in sea water on the boat, hence the name for these craft, Bawleys. Some of the catch was sold locally, but the majority went away to London by train. By the 1950s there was a serious decline of the shrimping fleet, but "**Felixstowe Holiday**" does show a Bawley still working, mixed in with the family's holiday footage.

Felixstowe had been a seaside resort even before the railway arrived in 1877, but it was not until 1898 that Felixstowe got a proper passenger station in the town. There is no film of the Great Eastern Railway station, though there is a brief view of the platforms with a tank engine manoeuvring in "**Pilot Engine**" filmed about 1953. But it is "**Felixstowe For Sun and Fun**" which gives us an idea what the town had to offer to the holidaymaker, who normally arrived by train. The main street, the sea front, the flowers, and the fishermen, all filmed by H. H. Whitley to persuade the viewer to visit Felixstowe, a place with a whiff of more sedate holidays, as we see quiet gardens, a pony and trap, and a girl riding a horse down the street. The pier in the background appears unrepaired after the war, and the paddle boats on the boating lake and the children's yacht pond are evocative of the early fifties, as is emphasised by a local harvest scene with a traction engine driving a threshing machine. Finally a steam train leaves the station, the end of 'Sun and Fun' at Felixstowe as it appeared in 1950.

At the other side of the town the quays facing Harwich harbour were about to expand. There had been a dock here for ships since 1886, but it was not until 1956 that it became a port handling large ships dealing with over 61,000 tons of dry goods and bulk liquids. In 1964 a new oil terminal jetty was built out into deep water, catering for ships of 25,000 tons, and drawing up to 33 feet of water. Roll on, roll off facilities were added, and later quays and handling areas for the new container freight. It is a story of continued expansion. "**Growth Port**", made in 1972, chronicles the development of Felixstowe docks, even including some archive film of the former flying boat base and Schneider Trophy high-speed seaplanes of the early 1930s. The directors of the Port of Felixstowe feature in an updated film made in 1975, "**Living Port**", as they discuss the day to day issues of running such a complex organisation. In September 1988, the millionth container passed through the port of Felixstowe.

In 1977 the Royal yacht *Britannia* was here to collect the Queen following her visit to Suffolk as part of her jubilee year celebrations. She had arrived by plane at Ipswich airport, and was driven through Ipswich to cheering crowds, and attended a performance at the Corn Exchange of "Welcome Ode" specially composed by Benjamin Britten for the occasion, and performed by Suffolk Schools Orchestra and Jubilee Choir. At Felixstowe docks Anglia Television covered her departure in the *Britannia*, and as evening descended, an army of small boats accompanied the Royal Yacht out of the harbour, ending a special day of "**The Queen in Suffolk**"

Bernard's was a naval outfitters at 63 Church Street, in Harwich. Charles Bernard had a 16mm camera in the 1930s and recorded not only his holidays, but events and happenings in Harwich and Dovercourt. The films were saved by Paul Amos of Dovercourt who put them together in 1985 with music to form the compilation "**Harwich and Dovercourt in Jubilee Year 1935**".

The film begins with Charles son Tom switching on a 16mm projector and showing the films. "The films my father took over a period of years in the 1930s, some taken on longer trips round the world. This is a trip to Norway in 1935, we had a Humber which that is [the car is seen being loaded on to a ship] we did a coastal trip on the ship, which ran like buses". The film continues with their holidays "crossing Canada by train through the Rockies took four days, ending up in Vancouver. The Canadian Pacific Railway I imagine, with two engines to cope with the mountainous conditions". "**Tom Bernard's Home Movies**" have other overseas trips, including a holiday in Egypt in the 1930s.

But back to the Bernard Bulletin, the next sequence is of cadets from HMS Ganges, the naval training school on the opposite side of the river at

*Dovercourt sea front from "**Harwich and Dovercourt in Jubilee Year. 1935**".*

Shotley, marching through the town "That is the band marching on to the Harwich Football ground, we used to go to the football matches down there". The film shows the match, watched by a big crowd, followed by the cup being presented "Looks like Harwich won the cup". There are sequences of the throwing of kitchels, those small torpedo shaped buns that were given to children once a year, from the roof of the Town Hall in Harwich (there is a 1963 sequence also of "**Kitchels**" in the Archive); the 1934 Guide and Scout Rally; swimming and diving in the open air pool; a carnival with lots of spectators watching floats, and the sports that followed. Flying boats are seen in Harwich harbour; *SS Vienna* steams out on her regular voyage to The Hook of Holland; the steel barque Archibald Russell, built in 1905, being towed in, and young Tom Bernard on board this four masted vessel, and the huge J class yachts that were so popular between the wars sailing off Dovercourt. These J class yachts were also filmed by Attfield Brooks in 1934-5 in "**Yachting Scenes**" and included the yacht *Britannia*, owned by the King.

Harwich harbour leads into the River Stour and the River Orwell. It is difficult to know where the coast begins and ends in these estuaries, but if we take it to be where the tide goes, then before 1970, the coast stretched as far up the Stour as Flatford Mill and Dedham, for in that year the sluices were built at Cattawade, stopping the tides flooding beyond, as can be seen in "**Here and There in East Anglia**". Just before Cattawade is Manningtree, where the local fishermen used to go after flat fish and eels, go punt gunning, sail their locally built punts, and take part in the annual regatta. "**Manningtree Regatta**" of 1973 shows all these things, as well as Joe Lucas talking about his work on the sailing barges. He describes the cargos, where he went, and how he used to get a sailing barge up to Greens Roller Mill at Brantham. "In 1943 I was asked to go to Lowestoft to join the *Thalatta*. We sailed to London, and our first cargo was 700 quarts of maize for Norwich. We carried wheat to Ipswich, cake to Mistley, maize to Pooles at Faversham, and wheat to Whitstable, and all round the coasts. Sometimes there were barges to take wheat up to Greens Mill at Brantham. But to do this they had to go up through the hump backed bridge at Cattawade. This was a bit of a problem. The old skippers used to moor up, so the nose was nearly under the bridge. The next tide, which might be one o'clock in the morning, as soon as ever the barge floated off the bottom they used to let go the ropes, then there was about three inches clearance for the barges stem to clear the bridge, and once they had got through, they had all the time in the world to get to the mill".

This canalised part of the River Stour was navigable at one time as far as Sudbury, and wooden barges were towed by horses walking along the river bank as described in the film. At Manningtree Peter Ainger takes us on an eel fishing trip early one morning. He lifts pipes laid in the bottom of the channel, and any eel hiding in the pipe is tipped out. One refuses to go into the bucket and escapes into the bottom of the punt, and is almost impossible to get out. In "**Peter Ainger of Manningtree**", made in 1982, Peter shows how to smoke eels in a small smokehouse he built himself. The oak chips burnt came from wood "acquired from the demolition of Manningtree church. Considering the church was built in about 1616, the oak I am using was probably grown at the time of the Spanish armada".

Next door to Manningtree is the village of Mistley, known for its twin towers, all that remains of a church designed by Robert Adam in the 1770s, and the quay. Mistley Quay has always been a busy place, with sea-going ships loading and unloading. In "**Manningtree Mechanics**", a film made in 1957 by schoolmaster Michael Barrett Brown, sacks of grain are lifted out of the hold of a ship, with some of the sacks leaking corn all over the place. Timber is unloaded at Baltic Quay (part of Mistley Quay) for Taylor and Butler, the Manningtree wood yard. Sailing barges come and go, and the little branch line down to the quay is busy as down trundles a steam locomotive with trucks. An amateur fisherman (David Cleveland) goes out into the Stour Estuary near Parkeston Quay in a small boat to go "**Shrimping**" in 1986. Using an 8ft beam trawl he hauls in a small catch of pink and brown shrimps. These are then boiled at home by Christine Cleveland.

As for the Orwell, the tide goes up to Ipswich, carrying anything from small pleasure boats to big commercial ships. The river and the docks at Ipswich can be seen amongst the large collection of films made over a 50 year period in the "**Don Chipperfield Collection**", a man who recorded on film changing Ipswich, as well as making industrial and advertising films for Ramsome, Sims, and Jeffries, the agricultural manufactures at Ipswich.

But it was Harwich's main harbour where all the shipping was, and still is. "**Parkeston Quay**", named after the Great Eastern Railway's first chairman, Charles Parkes is now called Harwich International. Derek Genzel of Harwich made two 8mm films covering the period 1970 to 1982. This is a detailed record of the port during those years, with many of the ships of the time being seen such as the *Koningen Juliana*, the *St George,* and the maiden visit of *Blenheim.* Other scenes include container cranes at work and pile driving for an improved passenger terminal, House of Holland warehouse destroyed by fire, and much quay and port reconstruction work

Trinity House has a main base at Harwich, from where, at one time, they serviced the manned lightships which marked the sandbanks and channels of the Thames estuary. These included light vessels named Cork, Sunk, Kentish Knock, Galloper, Shipwash and Outer Gabbard. In "**Lightships**", made in 1970, the tender *Vestal* from Harwich visited several of these lightships to change crews and top up with supplies. Each light vessel had a crew of seven, one of whom was the master. The main duty of the remaining six men was watch keeping, with two on watch at any one time. Each watch keeping period lasted for four hours, and in a 24 hour period, each man did two watches. The men also had specific duties, such as looking after the generators, and the light itself. Other jobs included general maintenance. A tender visited a lightship once a month to change the crew and bring fresh supplies of fuel oil, water, and coal. The relieved men then had a fortnight ashore.

At the time the film was made, no new lightships were to be built, for Trinity House was experimenting with a Large Automatic Navigation Buoy – Lanby for short. This was moored in Harwich harbour in 1970 on test. It had three diesel engines and three banks of light, each with one thousand watt output. If one light failed, the next lamp would automatically swing into place. Manned light vessels soon became a thing of the past. Charlie Moll, at one time a fisherman working out of Yarmouth after herring, joined Trinity House in 1920, and he talks on the sound track about life on a light vessel. "In those days there were no quarters like there are now. We all had to live and sleep in the foc'sle. We had a stove in the middle and a table at the side. At night we just used to sling up our hammock and get in, take it down again in the morning. Of course it was paraffin lamp in those days, and it used to be a job trimming the light sitting up in the lantern in a gale of wind. There were always plenty of jobs to do on board. Sometimes we used to have to clear up after the birds. They used to hit the lantern and grease

Light vessel No 71 on temporary station at the Kentish Knock. The tender Vestal *supplies oil and water.*

*The Cork light vessel five miles off Harwich from "**Lightships**", made with the help of Trinity House in 1970*

up the glass with blood. They used to make a hell of a mess, blood and shit everywhere".

In 1970 conditions on board were easier. There was a warm mess room, where the men off duty could relax and play cards. In the lantern it was all electric, with powerful reflectors enabling the light to be seen up to eleven miles away. The light flashed at various intervals, each light vessel having its own flashing sequence for easy identification.

Another Trinity House service was providing pilots to ships coming and going into and out of Harwich harbour. Local knowledge was important, and the pilots knew their way round. When a ship required to enter Harwich harbour, a Trinity House pilot was taken out in a small fast boat to the incoming commercial ship when it was a few miles off the coast. The ship did not stop, so the small boat had to come alongside at the same speed as the ship, and the pilot, at the right moment, grabbed a rope ladder and boarded her. He then guided it into the harbour and to its berth. Similarly when leaving, the pilot would take the ship out, being picked up just outside the harbour and brought back to Harwich by the small pilot boat.

For ships destined for the Thames, the Medway, and other small rivers, a reservoir of north channel pilots was kept on a cruising cutter stationed 15 miles east south east of Harwich, close to the Sunk light vessel. This was the cutter *Pathfinder*, and when there were only two or three pilots aboard, a muster would be arranged. A number of pilots would be called to congregate at Harwich to board the *Preceder*, which acted as a shuttle service, taking pilots out to the *Pathfinder*. The pilots waiting aboard the cutter did not know which ship they would be required to pilot until it was about three miles from the Sunk light vessel, when a small boat would take the next available pilot to the passing ship. The pilot would guide the ship to its destination, and often return home to Harwich by train. It might be they had a vessel which was leaving port, in which case they would pilot the ship out, being picked up by the small boat and returned to the cutter.

"**The Pilot Service**", made in 1977, shows how these pilotage systems worked. When a

A freighter passing the pilot cutter Pathfinder *from "**The Pilot Service**" 1977.*

A pilot scrambling aboard a ship on her way into Harwich.

pilot boarded an incoming ship, he usually gave the captain the day's newspaper to read, and then took over the job of piloting the ship safely into harbour, or wherever it was going. The captain was still technically in charge of his ship, but the pilot gave the orders as she entered the port. Two pilots, Phillip Vanner and Roland Jacques, describe their work, and demonstrate how they bring into Felixstowe one of the biggest container ships of the time, the *American Accord.*

In 1924 the train ferry service began at Harwich. Railway wagons ran directly on to three specially built vessels named *Train Ferry 1*, *Train Ferry 2*, and *Train Ferry 3*. The service was opened on April 24th 1924 by Prince George, and this is seen in "**Harwich Train Ferry**" made in 1985, not long before the service closed completely. Charlie Mudd worked on the *Cambridge* train ferry, and his voice is heard in parts of the film. "My name is Charlie Mudd and I am bosun on the *Cambridge* ferry, and I have been on this ferry since she came from the makers. When she goes, I will go".

The ferry, connected to the railway lines when docked at Harwich, worked between there and Zeebrugge, and as the captain explains "used to be run by British Rail Board, but has since been privatised, and taken over by Sealink Ferries Ltd, under charter to the B. R. Board. Dangerous goods are carried at the after end, in the open, so if there was any leakage of toxic fumes, they wouldn't be contained within the ship".

Charlie Mudd spent his time at sea checking and tightening the chains which held the wagons in place, particularly those at the open end at the stern. "I watch the cargo, and after one hour at sea, go down, check the chains. Always get several more turns, I always maintained to do that irrespective of anything". The *Cambridge* ferry docked at Zeebrugge, the wagons unloaded, new cargo brought aboard, and back she came.

In "Wreck and Rescue on The Essex Coast", published by Bradford Barton of Truro in 1968, Robert Malster writes "The men of the Walton lifeboat now carry a cine camera when they go on service, and films of their work have appeared on television". Some of these films are now in the East Anglian Film Archive with the title "**Walton-on-the-Naze Lifeboat**. They include various rescues in the 1970s, as well as a Christmas delivery of festive food to the crew of the Sunk light vessel. This was a regular occurrence to light vessels along the East Anglian coast by lifeboats and private craft. A boat from Bawdsey went out to the Cork light vessel five miles of Harwich every Christmas to hand over a turkey. A sequence of this appears in the film "**Lightships**".

The school at Walton-on-the-Naze had an enterprising teacher, Lew Broom, who made films. He made "**My School**" in 1949 showing the daily routine at Walton County Secondary School. The day begins with children arriving, and the register taken. The headmaster, Mr. Landsdowne, works in his office until it is time to address the school at the morning assembly. The children then get on with the day's work. First football training in the gym followed by a maths lesson. During the break the children drink milk, then attend an English composition class. The cooks prepare food in the

*Charlie Mudd being filmed by David Cleveland for "**Harwich Train Ferry**" in 1985.*

Recording a voiceover from the captain of the Cambridge *train ferry.*

kitchen and the children have lunch. The afternoon begins with a dancing class, then chemistry and biology lessons. There is a girl's 'home economic class' which includes washing, cooking, and baby handling, as well as embroidery and knitting. There are wood work, metal work, and gardening sessions, before the children are taken home by bus. The original film had a separate sound track on quarter inch audio tape which has been transferred to 16mm separate magnetic track for running in conjunction with the film.

There are many family films of outings and holidays to Walton and Frinton over the years, beginning with "**Walton-on-the-Naze, Essex, Family Films**" of 1929.

It was in 1928 that Kodak brought out a system for filming on 16mm in colour for the home movie enthusiast. This was called Kodacolor, and worked by using a tricolour lens and special embossed black and white film to record and recreate the colour. See information in the chapter "What's it all about?".

In 1935 Mr. Ratcliffe of Frinton took some Kodacolor film of the "**Walton Carnival**". To preserve this in the East Anglian Film Archive in full colour meant a complicated laboratory transfer carried out by film expert Paul De Burgh, who managed to print the apparently black and white film in colour. The film has the typical Kodak style titles. Mr. Ratcliffe used to send his whole film to Kodak for editing (they offered this service then when film making had a certain technical mystery about it), and with his supplied wording, Kodak shot and inserted titles. The second half of the film was in normal black and white.

The Ratcliffe Brothers had a motor garage in Connaught Avenue in Frinton, and here they experimented with a lorry with a detachable floor, so that it could be lowered at an angle to the ground for heavy equipment to be run up and down for easy loading and unloading. They made 16mm Kodachrome films of their invention as it developed over the years, though not a lot seems to have come of it. They called this piece of machinery either a "**Low Loader**" or in some of the films, the "**Pickaback Transporter Trailer**".

The Ratcliffe brothers also ran the Esplanade Hotel on the front at Frinton. It was a large hotel and, like other hotels in the area, used to close down for the winter months. It was in the late 1920s that the elder of the two brothers bought a 16mm cine

*"**Walton Carnival**" 1935 in Kodacolor.*

*"**Walton Carnival**", the second half in black and white.*

camera and made films of their holidays which they showed to the guests on summer evenings. "**Walton Carnival**" was no doubt one of these films the guests watched. They made "**Family Films**" as well, and a roll from the mid-thirties not only shows their own activities, but also includes shots of the Esplanade Hotel, their motor garage, a Boxing Day hunt, the 1934 Gymkhana, and Tendring Hundred Farmers Show – again probably shown to the hotel guests, whether they wanted to see them or not.

The brothers' niece, Joan, was married in 1941 to Ted Hammond, who took over the motor garage in Connaught Avenue, renaming it 'Hammonds'. The Esplanade Hotel had been sold and pulled down to make way for a block of flats. Joan Hammond writes "One day, in Clacton, several people decided it would be a good idea if a Cine Club could be formed. One of the main enthusiasts was Sidney Manasseh who was a good friend, and customer at the garage. Ted was fairly interested and was offered the loan of a camera from the local camera shop. I had two small children by then, and of course we had this film of them, and we just had to have the equipment to see it. My husband Ted went along to the inaugural meeting of the Clacton Cine Club and we both became founder members". The "**Joan Hammond Collection**" of family films is in the East Anglian Film Archive, as is "**Snowfall**" showing the children enjoying the heavy falls of the winter of 1958, and the intriguing "**Turkey Time**", where Christmas games include wrapping a person up in toilet paper.

The Clacton Cine Club was a thriving concern, the members working together to make a variety of films. Amongst the films they made were "**Full Circle**", "**The Witching Hour**", "**Nine Men and a Boat**", "**Anawotsit**" (a 1968 film about cinemascope!) and a film about the club itself in 1959 simply called "**Clacton Cine Club**". Clacton Urban District Council issued "**Back To The Sun**", a 16mm colour sound film advertising the town and beach as a seaside resort. The film, shot in the summer of 1961, was made by the Clacton Cine Club, and directed by Sidney Manasseh with the title borrowed from an earlier silent colour film made in 1952 by the Council. Sidney Manasseh's film shows off all the colourful amenities of Clacton, with the theatres and cinemas, the pier and the beach.

Clacton was for holidays 'beside the seaside', with people enjoying the beach and the pier with its fairground amusements. In 1927, a holidaymaker with a 9.5mm cine camera, could only afford one roll of film, enough for a minute's worth of filming. His or hers, because the origin of the film is unknown, "**Holiday at Clacton**" is obviously a very carefully constructed film so that the maximum amount of record is included in the one minute available. Probably filmed on a Pathe hand turned 9.5mm Baby camera, there is a title, a street scene, the family on the beach – all filmed with the camera on a tripod so the shots are steady and well composed.

*"**Introducing the Pickaback Self Loading and Unloading Machinery Transporter**", one of the Ratcliffe films.*

*"**Back to The Sun**" was available on 16mm, and later put out on Super 8mm by DCR Films Ltd.*

In the 1930s Frinton-on-Sea was a fashionable place, with the rich and famous, nannies and bright young things. It was Tatler country, where charabancs of trippers were turned away at the famous gates – the level crossing that protected Frinton from the outside world. The residents were well-to-do, living in large detached houses in the carefully laid out roads.

"**Cuttings From a Cinema Notebook**" is a 16mm family film made by Walter Lowther-Kemp who lived in Third Avenue, Frinton, and was chairman of Frinton Urban District Council in the 1930s. He was a great traveller, and also made "**Cinema Records No 2**" in 1929 of his travels through Europe, including delightful shots of streets and cars in Paris. But it is the family at Frinton that is the most interesting film. Described by the East Anglian Film Archive's cataloguer, Tanya Knighton, as "a delightful collection of films featuring the Kemp family doing family things", this shows walks in country lanes, at the tennis club, the children doing handstands and playing on the beach, picking daffodils, and riding horses. "The three dogs are the real stars" recorded Tanya.

Sidney Manasseh was a farmer at Thorpe-le-Soken, whose passion was films. He worked on 16mm, and had a spacious study at home laid out as a film cutting and sound dubbing room. He used professional equipment to produce a professional product, and looking at the films he made over the years, he should really have been a professional film maker. He experimented with sound, cutting images to music in "**Bottle Beano**" made in a Clacton bottling plant, and "**Crumpet Concerto**" filmed at Kenneth Race's bakery in Oxford Road where 'Essex Crumpets' were made and packed in cellophane. On these he worked with another talented non-professional film maker, Leslie Gillham from Hornchurch. Together, and with others, they were leading lights in the Institute of Amateur Cinematographers, the IAC as it is known. This is an organisation which brought together cine clubs and individuals across the country, encouraging their film making by holding film conferences, and offering help - one being the arrangement where amateurs could use copyright music with their films. Some of the IAC get-togethers took place at the Waverley Hotel in Clacton, where film competitions were held, and talks given by visiting speakers. One year a film was made of the event – "**At The Conference**".

There are over sixty films in the "**Sidney Manasseh Collection**" including "**Venture on The Wind**", a joint effort between Sidney and his wife Elspeth about an outing of cine enthusiasts on a Thames sailing barge on the Orwell, and "**To be a Farmer's Boy**", unusually for Sidney, an 8mm film, about a year on his Thorpe-le-Soken farm. The IAC national collection of films representing the amateur movement since the 1930s is now stored in the East Anglian Film Archive at Norwich, and Sidney Manasseh's films are held there as well.

Other film makers in the Clacton area included Laurie Stanton, who made many 8mm films about East Anglia, including "**Thorpe-le-Soken Market**" in 1968, "**Kessingland**" in 1972, "**Norwich Market**" in 1974, "**Sandringham**" in 1976, "**The Fens in Springtime**" in 1979, "**Parkeston Quay**" in 1980, "**Weeley**" in 1986, and other documentaries and record films as well as family films and weddings. Laurie Stanton was the owner of a clothing manufacturing company called 'Mascot' in Clacton. He was a member of the Clacton Cine Club, and had a small cinema in his attic where people were invited to see films.

There were many in the Clacton area who were active film makers, including Mr. Sterry who made a film about "**Little Clacton**", and Dick Moody who was the first president of the Clacton Cine Club. His collection of 8mm films is in the East Anglian Film Archive. He was a chemist in Clacton, with another shop which was rented to a Mr. Hildreth who ran it as a photographic business, where all the members of the cine club obtained their supplies.

In 1928 there were two cinemas in Clacton-on-Sea, the Tivoli in Rosemary Road and the Kinema Grand in West Avenue. One of these must have had an enterprising manager, as a couple of films were made of events for showing locally. On July 27th 1929 the "**Clacton-on-Sea Sports Meeting**" was held on the new 24 acre recreation ground. Alderman Brooks, Chairman of Essex County Council, opens the gates of the ground in Vista Road, and people pour in. The

*One of the Belle paddle boats at the end of Clacton pier in 1938. From "**Clacton Pier with Steamer**".*

new park was celebrated with sports events. These included a hurdles race, men and women's tug of war, various cycle races, a push ball match, and the Essex County Police relay race. At the end of the day the MP Sir John Pybus presents the prizes – a strange variety of horned gongs, clocks, model houses and a barometer. There are plenty of shots of people and the crowds, an essential part of local newsreels as the more people filmed, the more came to the cinema to watch. This also applies to the film "**Clacton Pier with Steamer**" shot in 1938 showing one of the Belle paddle steamers trying to call at the end of the pier in rough weather. The *Yarmouth Belle*, the *Southwold Belle*, and others, used to do daily excursions from Tower Pier calling at Clacton, Walton-on-the-Naze, Felixstowe, and Southwold during the summer season.

The film also shows a little play acted out on an open air stage in a gale of wind. The story, a woman discovered by her husband with another man, takes place in less than a minute, with different people from the audience playing the parts. The director plays the other man to start with to show how it should be done, then willing members of the audience come on stage to 'act'. The story also involves a third man hiding behind a chair which is never satisfactorily explained. This was the entertainment on the pier at the time, and of course the people filmed would flock to the cinema to see themselves up there on the big screen.

Butlins opened their camp at Clacton in early June 1938, and a year later K. O. King of Cambridge had a holiday there in August 1939. King was a garage owner in Cambridge, and a 16mm enthusiast, making home movies and semi-professional films to a high standard. His Kodachrome film "**Sunny Clacton**" really sums up what Butlins was all about, with communal activities such as the 'costume and figure' competition for the women, and knobbly knees for the men. The Clacton Hospital Carnival and the fairground are part of the attractions, and there is a man imitating Hitler, reminding us this was only a month before the outbreak of war.

Amateur acting on Clacton pier.

*"**Sunny Clacton**" 1939.*

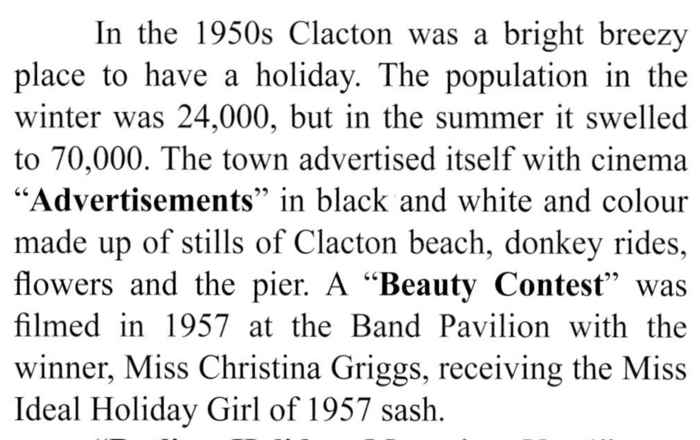

In the 1950s Clacton was a bright breezy place to have a holiday. The population in the winter was 24,000, but in the summer it swelled to 70,000. The town advertised itself with cinema "**Advertisements**" in black and white and colour made up of stills of Clacton beach, donkey rides, flowers and the pier. A "**Beauty Contest**" was filmed in 1957 at the Band Pavilion with the winner, Miss Christina Griggs, receiving the Miss Ideal Holiday Girl of 1957 sash.

"**Butlins Holiday Magazine No 1**" was filmed in 1960 with three stories. First band leader Eric Winston, who was musical director at Butlins at Clacton, showed off his collection of model stage coaches, and then holiday makers at Butlins took part in a pram race. This was typical of the entertainment provided by the red coats. An old pram, with one contestant sitting in it, was pushed by another around a course as fast as possible. The crowd watching loved it, and the contestants appear to as well. The last thing to do before winning was for the passenger to drink a bottle of milk. The final story was of limbo dancing, introduced it is said, into this country by Billy Butlin. Here a professional showed how to do it, then seemingly reluctant holidaymakers are pulled from the crowd to have a go. One looses his shorts, another falls on his bottom. All the fun of Butlins is here in this colourful entertainment. This is just one of a number of Butlins advertising films for their various camps around the country. They have titles which cover all questions, needs and destinations – "**People at Butlins**", "**All in Holiday**", "**From Coast to Coast**" and "**You'll Remember in December**".

Clacton-on-Sea is a new town in history and development terms. In William White's Directory of Essex published in 1848, there is only Great Clacton and Little Clacton. Great Clacton was "a large village on an eminence, about a mile from the sea beach". Little Clacton was "nearly two miles north of Great Clacton". All that existed near the sea was "Clacton Cliffs, on the seashore, where there are three Martello towers". Clacton-on-Sea appears in guide books from the 1880s. "The rapid growth of Clacton in size and favour has few rivals on this side of the Atlantic. It takes its name from the parish of Great Clacton in which it is situated, and dates from 1873, when the Royal Hotel was opened". Subsequent growth must have been due to the railway which arrived at Clacton in 1882. In 1971 local historian Terry Baker put on an exhibition telling the story of Clacton-on-Sea over a one hundred year period. "**Clacton Centenary**" contains an interview with Mr. Baker by John Myatt of BBC East, and potted histories of the pier, the Grand hotel, the lifeboat, the paddle steamers, and the beach.

In Pier Avenue in Clacton in the 1930s was Lewellen's ironmongery shop. This caught fire on Sunday June 4th 1939, with much destruction. Mr. Frank Allum took some shots with his 8mm camera of the fire, and these are in the Allum collection of "**Family Films**" together with other Clacton events. Frank Allum had a shop called Dot's in Beach Road, Jaywick, a new settlement three miles south-west of Clacton. Jaywick was the brainchild of Frank Steadman who purchased in 1928 some low lying meadow land close to the sea and set up Jaywick Sands Estate. Plots of land were sold off at prices starting at £30 for 20ft by 50ft site, with a chalet costing anywhere from £20 to £100. "The Estate Builder will be pleased to quote prices for any modification on these designs or any special plan a purchaser may prefer. Prices for extras such as leaded light windows, lining the huts with three-ply wood or insulating board, built in furniture, bunks, cupboards, etc. can be had on application". There was an office on the promenade at Clacton and local enquiries were dealt with at Dot's, where "high class confectionery, tobacco, cigarettes, stationery, postcards, and novels" could be obtained.

Jaywick was developed by Steadman, with new concrete roads, an artificial lake a mile long, and even a railway. This was a narrow gauge line, only 18 inches, and was opened on Saturday July 31st 1936. The miniature steam engines hauled three carriages which transported passengers from Crossways, close to the main road where the Clacton buses came every half hour, to Jaywick with a station close to the sea. Jaywick took off in the 1930s, with people acquiring sites and setting up small homes. Frank Allum filmed Jaywick as it grew, from 1935 to 1939. He took shots of Dot's Tuck Shop; of the roads; of the railway; of a chalet fire; of the beach and the carnival, and of course his family.

Just round the coastal corner from Jaywick is Brightlingsea, the river Colne going up to Colchester, and a network of tidal creeks around Mersea Island. In Pyefleet creek every September an oyster smack with the Mayor of Colchester on board celebrates the opening of the oyster season, with a dredge bringing up fresh oysters; a quaint ceremony of eating gingerbread and washing it down with gin, with the mayor swallowing an oyster. Nearly every year this ancient ceremony was filmed, in the silent film days – in 1920 "**Opening of The Oyster Season**"; in sound in 1934 "**A Moment in The Life of a Colchester Gentleman**"; and again in television days. Later the "**Oyster Feast**" was held in Colchester, where oysters were the main menu, and celebrities were usually invited. There are two examples – in 1930 and 1983. At Rowhedge was a shipbuilding yard, and an unknown film maker went there in 1962 to film "**Ship Launch**", as he called it correctly. Others were not so exact. At Colchester in 1937, a cinema magazine item of less than a minute, consisting of shots of the town and the quay, the sailing barges moored at the Hythe are referred to as black sailed trawlers in "**Lets Go**".

Mersea Island has a committed population, but visitors coming here for relaxation have to cross The Strood, that raised causeway which becomes impassable at high spring tides. In 1953 Leslie and Marjorie Gillham from Hornchurch came here with their two boys for their summer holiday. Leslie had a Landrover which pulled their small caravan. With his 16mm camera, loaded with Kodachrome, he filmed "**Holiday on the Saltings**", a bright colourful recording of the family just enjoying themselves by the creeks and marshes, swimming, having meals, looking at boats, and hunting for crabs on the beach. Admittedly Marjorie still has to peel the potatoes and provide lunch in the caravan, but she does have a chance to swim in the

A reluctant member of the crowd is persuaded to have a go at Butlins Holiday Camp.

*The holidaymaker trying limbo dancing, from "**Butlins Holiday Magazine No 1**" 1960.*

Butlins 16mm advertising films were available on free loan as can be seen in this 1953 advertisement.

*The Mayor swallowing the first oyster. From "**Opening of The Oyster Season**" 1920.*

creek, and take a couple of shots of her husband. The film shows the business end of West Mersea, where the boats are painted on the hard, and the quaint cottages by The Lane seem to be in another world.

In 1966 the Essex County Education Committee had a film made of the International Youth Camp here. A Hungarian girl arrives at Mersea, stays in a tent, has breakfast in a marquee, and then takes part in the many sports and activities on offer. She goes sailing and canoeing, is a member of the water polo team, and has a go at netball and archery. "**International Intent**" goes on to show the visitors in London and Cambridge, finishing with music, and couples dancing.

One of the creeks running past Mersea Island leads to "**Virley**", a small hamlet next to Salcott. About 1974 Jean Goodman came here to make a short film about these two villages, trying to find out about smuggling. Local inhabitant Eustace King shows the places the smugglers came to, including a pond with a false bottom where they hid their contraband.

On the other side of the Blackwater, at a point jutting out into the sea, is a lonely building, a church in fact, built by Bishop Cedd in the 7th century, known as St Peter's-on-the-Wall. It appears, with interior and exterior views in "**Britain's Historic Counties**", a film made about 1950 with sequences all over Essex, and again in colour in "**The Essex Coast**" made in 1976. A mile or two west is something more modern – a nuclear power station. "**Building Power Station**" shows this being constructed in 1958. It became operational in 1962, and four years later the Central Electricity Generating Board for the South Eastern Region had "**This is Bradwell**" made to explain why nuclear power stations were needed, and how they worked. "**Bradwell Says No**" takes another stance when it was suggested that a nuclear waste repository be sited in the village. Public meetings were held, Jonathon Porritt of Greenpeace talked to the press, and there were debates between the parties Nirex and Friends of The Earth on Radio Essex. This 1987 film was made by "World in Action", a series on ITV which took serious topical subjects and presented them factually to inform the public from both sides of the issue what was going on.

A bit further along the southern side of the Blackwater estuary is a quieter, more serene place, marked on the map as Ramsey Island, though it is not an island at all, and most sailing people know it as The Stone. Stone Point is a yachtsmen's starting and finishing place for the "**East Coast Old Gaffers Race**" of 1987. Any craft with a gaff rig is eligible for the Old Gaffers annual race, though many of the craft taking part are smacks – lovingly restored fishing boats peculiar to this part of the coast. Depending on the weather, the course is out of the estuary to the sea and back again, finishing with drinking and prize giving in a marquee. In 1960 a similar film, "**Pageant of Sail**", was made of the race on a quiet misty day. "Very little happens in this film, that its beauty" says Tanya Knighton, the East Anglian Film Archive cataloguer. The boats are just a delight to watch.

In the 1950s an unusual craft with an unusual cargo could be seen occasionally in the autumn months going along the Blackwater Estuary to Heybridge Basin. This was the *Helene*, a Dutch boat with a perforated hull to let the sea water in.

Her unusual cargo was live eels. She belonged to Hans Kuijten, and is featured in the silent film "**Eels All Alive-O**" made about 1950. I think it is best if we take Hans' commentary, specially recorded on video tape in the late 1990s, and let him explain. "This is Heybridge Basin. To this tiny port each autumn come live eels in their hundreds and thousands from places all over Europe. This is the vital link in the chain which begins in the Sargasso Sea, where the eels have spawned, and ends some 7 or 8 years later when the fully grown eels are delivered live to the cook.

"This grey November morning the Dutch motor ship *Helene* puts into Heybridge Basin. There are very few ships like the *Helene*. She has a perforated hull so that the water travels through her. Her bulkheads are perforated to divide the hull into compartments for a cargo of live eels. She carries 4000 gallons of Shell diesel oil, enough for 30 days continuous sailing, enough to take her to Ireland, to East and North Africa, where the eels are caught, and bring her back to Heybridge Basin without the need for refuelling.

"Now she brings a large cargo of 30 tons of eels caught in Lough Neagh in Northern Ireland. All eels start life in the Sargasso Sea. They travel with the gulf stream towards Europe, and reach the coast of the continent when they are about two years old and the size of a matchstick. In great numbers they assemble in rivers seeking the freshwater lakes. They remain in these lakes for some 4 or 5 years, then after the full moon in the autumn months, the spawning fever takes them. Now fully grown they begin their journey home to the Sargasso Sea. But in those few autumn nights, river fishermen are waiting with their nets, and the eels are caught by the ton.

"Here at Heybridge Basin the captured eels are given floating homes, Hans Kuijten's three large ones and 26 small barges. These are the home of half a million eels. They are unloaded quickly into these specially designed barges where they will be kept alive for as long as six months, with the help of diesel engines. These pump air through perforated tubing throughout the length of the barge, and also keep the water circulating briskly.

"Once a month the barges are towed out to the lock water estuary for a day's dosing of salt water, otherwise the eels would get rheumatism and loose their wiggle. From December until June live eels from Heybridge Basin are sent to Billingsgate at the rate of some 40,000 lbs a week. Some go in wooden boxes which were sprayed with water before leaving. The eels will arrive in the London markets alive and wriggling ready for the cook. Most of these eels will re-appear in jelly form at the seaside towns, and in London's East End. Some of the eels will go to Holland for smoking, and to Germany and Italy for the delicately flavoured eel pie. In fact live eels from this town in East Anglia have a market throughout Europe".

This was a Shell-Mex and BP (Eastern Division) Film, subtitled 'The story of a Unique Industry Carried On at Heybridge Basin'.

This is sailing barge country. Today these restored craft work for pleasure, but once they worked for a living. The *Centaur* was one of these working craft in 1954, when two young film makers made the film "**When the Wind Blows**" for cinema release. This featured the *Centaur* as she loaded sand at Fingringhoe ballast quay, and headed for London. Produced and directed by Nicolas Hardinge and filmed by Brian Everett, the 25 minute film was shot on 35mm Eastman colour film, a relatively new colour film system introduced by Kodak in 1951. Brian used two cameras, a British made Newman Sinclair, a clockwork 35mm camera holding 200ft of film, enough for two minutes of filming, and an Askania. This was a German camera captured just after D Day by a

*"**When The Wind Blows**" featured the Thames sailing barge* Centaur, *here seen alongside Fingringhoe ballast jetty about to load sand for North Woolwich in 1954.*

Captain D. Knight. He painted his name and home address on the camera case, and sent it back to the beach. Somehow or other it arrived at his home. He lent it to Brian Everett for the shooting of the sailing barges film.

Captain Fred Wilson of the *Centaur* set off from Fingringhoe with Nicolas and Brian on board for the trip to London. First the foresail is hoisted, then up goes the topsail, followed by the mainsail. "The main sheet block or pulley is hooked on to a ring which travels on a great spar called the main horse. The mainsail is hauled aft and made fast". This is how the informative commentary runs as written and spoken by A. P. Herbert, a humorous writer and lover of sailing barges. The method of setting sails depended very much on the wind and state of the tide, so there were many ways to begin the journey. The *Centaur* was built in 1895, and was capable of carrying up to 140 tons of cargo.

The film follows the *Centaur* on her journey until evening, when she anchors, puts up a riding light, and the captain and mate go below to fill up with sausages, peas, bread, and tea. In the morning the two man crew haul up the anchor. A. P. Herbert's commentary continues "The skipper is leaving the Swin channel to take a short cut over the Maplin sands". The mate heaves the lead to ascertain the depth of water. "Round the corner, and now there are 30 miles of river ahead". On arrival a grab lifts from the hold "the golden sands of Essex brought by water and the old fashioned sail to build some modern palace in the metropolis".

Other sequences in the film include the art of the sail maker, a sailing barge match, and how to colour the sails. "A mixture of cod oil, red ochre, horse fat and sea water. What a mixture. This has a smell all of its own. The dressing has the virtue of never drying completely, which keeps the sail both waterproof and supple, and so much easier to handle at sea".

At this time the production of numerous 35mm colour prints from Eastman colour cut

*Brian Everett filming for "**When the Wind Blows**" with the Newman Sinclair camera on board* Centaur *in 1954.*

Nicolas Hardinge on the left and Brian Everett on the right with the German Askania 35mm camera.

*Skipper Fred Wilson sailing the Centaur up the London River. From "**When the Wind Blows**" 1954.*

negatives was a difficult process, especially if there were 'opticals' in the film – that is fades, dissolves, superimposed titles etc. The opticals in "**When the Wind Blows**" were made separately by Technicolor, and cut into the original negatives, producing a sudden change of colour just before and after a dissolve or fade. These are quite apparent, though do not spoil the overall charm of this film. Prints were circulated to cinemas at a time when short films were part of the full supporting programme. One 35mm copy was kept, but like many 35mm Eastman colour prints, it has faded badly. The blues and greens have disappeared leaving the film pink. The original cut negatives had been kept by Nicolas Hardinge in his garage. Though they had suffered slightly over the years, it was possible to have a new 35mm colour print made by Film and Photo Film Laboratories in 1997. Now of course, the faded print can be restored to its original colours by digital restoration, but any of these processes are dependent on the original materials being carefully and securely kept.

A similar story of restoration revolves around another film about Thames sailing barges, "**Sailorman**", made on 16mm in 1975 by producers Ian Crafford and Trevor Underwood. This was also shot on Eastman colour negative film, and the sound colour print that survived had faded also. Then Jim Lawrence, a sail maker of Brightlingsea, who was also involved in the making of the film, found a 16mm print with perfect colour but minus the sound track. The Archive therefore made a new duplicate colour negative of the good picture, and with the sound re-recorded from the faded copy, produced a new colour sound print. This was the full version running over 50 minutes, and included interviews with Ephram Sharman, Bill Simpson, and that grand old man of racing barges, Chubb Horlock of Mistley in Essex. There are other sailing barge films. The 1966 film "**Blackwater Sailing Barge Regatta**" shows the *Venture* and other Thames sailing barges racing from Maldon, as does a newsreel item of the 1950s called "**Veteran of the River**".

A local newsreel film of 1924, no doubt for showing in the Electric Cinema in Burnham-on-Crouch, records the fun and frivolity of the "**Water Carnival**". There are rowing races, swimming races, a soot fight, and a tub and shovel race, where just staying upright was an achievement.

A little further round the Essex coast we come to Foulness Island, which in William White's directory of 1848, "is from 6 – 11 miles east north east of Rochford, forms a parish of 674 souls, and about 6000 acres of land jutting to a point in the ocean on the south side of the estuary of the river Crouch, and cut off from the main land by the river Broomhill, and the creeks encompassing the small islands of Potton, New England etc on the south". In 1931 the population was 414 according to Kelly's Directory. Perhaps this decline was because the area was used as an artillery range, and access was restricted. It still is today, as the area is under the control of the Ministry of Defence. In the 1960s it was difficult to get permission to go on to the island, but Frank Pigram obtained a pass so that he could make a film of the village and surrounding area. Frank made films on 16mm, often adding a sound track on to the magnetic stripe using his 16mm projector. His colour record of "**Foulness Island**" is one of the few films about this remote corner of Essex, a rural place with not many inhabitants and even fewer visitors. The Maplin sands lie off Foulness, a large area of sandbanks exposed at low tide. It was here that London's third airport was going to be built, and in 1973 there was an act of parliament authorising this, but it was soon withdrawn, and "**Stansted, The London Option**" was suggested instead.

Frank Pigram lived at Paglesham, the other side of the River Roach. "**Paglesham, Our Little World**", and "**Paglesham, Our Village**" are two 16mm films he made in the 1950s and 1960s about this village, a place with even less inhabitants than Foulness. Working the land was the main occupation, and Frank filmed "**Power Farming**" at Paglesham in 1966. Close by is Canewdon, where he recorded the "**Annual Ploughing Match**" in 1973. Frank's film making went back even further, to 1949, when he filmed in black and white "**Rolling Along**", the story of the new trains for Southend Pier.

The pier is one and one third miles long, with its own railway. There had been an electric railway since 1889 (there was a timber pier before that with a horse drawn tramway), but in 1949 a completely new set of rolling stock was purchased from A. C. Cars of Thames Ditton. The construction of these, and the transportation by road on low loaders, is covered in Frank Pigram's film, along with the manoeuvring of the rolling stock on to the rails. This silent film is amply provided with captions to explain what is going on. The Lord Mayor of London came down on April 13th 1949 to open the refurbished railway, consisting of four trains of seven coaches each, capable of carrying over 250 passengers per train. The old 'toast rack' carriages ran for the last time, as the Mayor enters one of the new gleaming trains, and drives it off through a ribbon, thus opening Southend's new pier railway.

The pier has had a chequered history, particularly as far as fires are concerned. An 8mm film was hurriedly shot of the 1976 fire at the end of the pier, and another 8mm film shows the maintenance of the pier in "**Winter Work**". Virtual every film about Southend has a shot or two of the pier, Southend's greatest asset. Many also include the Kursaal, that entertainment centre that existed at one time which is featured in "**Southend Kursaal**" in 1927, and again ten years later in a 16mm advertsing film made by the LMS railway called "**Southend on Sea**". This includes scenes of the Boulevard tramway, the Royal Eagle paddle steamer calling at the end of the pier, J class yachts in Southend's racing week, and a Yorkshire versus Essex cricket match at Chalkwell Park. The most famous cricket match here was between Australia and Essex in Southchurch Park in May 1948, when Australia, captained by Don Bradman, scored 721 all out in a day, the highest total scored in a day of six hours of first class cricket. There are two versions of the amateur 16mm film "**Cricket: Essex versus Australians**" in the East Anglian Film Archive, one fully titled, and another untitled. Both run about 10 minutes.

Ethel Wilson was the Carnival Queen in 1931, and received a medal, and a message from the King at Balmoral relayed by the Mayor – all filmed for "**Southend on Spree**", a cinema newsreel item showing the floats passing the camera, with actual sound recorded. Other cinema newsreels, made for showing in one of the town's cinemas, were "**Tiny Tots Parade**" and "**Faces and Places You Know**". The first, made in 1932, shows children taking part in a fancy dress parade, the second, filmed in 1937, shows business premises with the

Southend pier just after the new trains arrived in 1949.

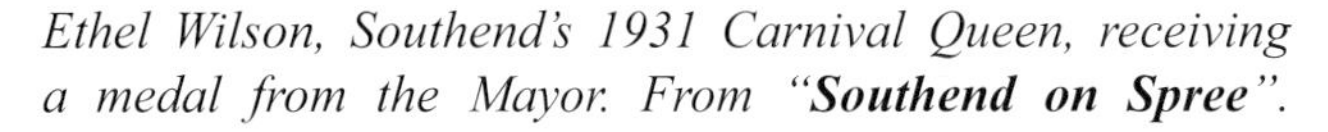

*Ethel Wilson, Southend's 1931 Carnival Queen, receiving a medal from the Mayor. From "**Southend on Spree**".*

*One of the floats from "**Southend on Spree**", a cinema newsreel item of 1931.*

proprietors and staff outside, Ledicott's bottling plant, Rossi's ice cream shop, the Kursaal, and street scenes around the town. Finally two very crowded pleasure steamers – *Prince of Wales* and *Southend Britannia* leave for the open sea.

The visitors that came to Southend were out for a good time, and this is evident from "**Wright and Cooper Outing to Southend**" in 1948. It was on the 30th May that the employees of this company piled into a coach, left the factory, but only got half-way before they stopped, got out, and had a beer and a dance. At Southend they ride on the amusements at the Kursaal, before heading home – again stopping for a knees up half-way. Who and what Wright and Cooper was still remains a mystery, but the film survives showing the workers' happy release of being let out of the factory for a day at the seaside. These and other Southend films of the past were shown in the early 1980s by Chris Taylor, who located many of these films in the first place, at the Cliff's Pavilion and Southend library. Of the show at the library Chris Taylor said "on the night a Bond film opened at the Odeon. We had a longer queue than they did". Such is the draw of nostalgia filled archive film.

"**The Best Place Under The Sun**" is how Southend was advertised in the early 1950s as a holiday resort. "Whether you choose to travel by road, rail, or sea, make sunny Southend-on-Sea your choice for a holiday resort" runs the opening commentary over shots of cars, trains and boats in a film made in 1953 by Richard Pike. "Southend-on-Sea caters for all ages of holiday maker, and all tastes in holidays". The film begins on the end of the pier, where an orchestra is playing as people relax in deck chairs in the sun. On the beach children play and paddle, the emphasis being on leisurely fun. There are sequences of the delights of Westcliff and Leigh, of sailing dinghies and carnivals, of a water ballet and cricket. The film then leaves the "hot sunny days" for the cool of the evening, when it becomes a "fairyland bestowed with light". "**The Best Place Under The Sun**" was made by Richard Pike, a businessman and film maker, for Southend Publicity Department.

Richard Pike was born in Southend, and inherited from his mother the business of Map and Sons, school uniform manufacturers in London Road, Leigh. Richard was their designer. But it was films that caught his imagination, and he not only made films himself, but helped others. In 1953, when the flood hit Canvey Island, he was out with his 16mm camera filming as much as he could which was edited into a ten minute film called "**Essex Floods**". This entered into the Essex Education Committee Film Library, and was seen by schoolchildren all over the county. In the 1950s he produced further films for the Committee, and assisted the Wansfell Cinematography Courses with technical help. The wide range of films included "**Essex River**", a film tracing the course of the River Chelmer from Chelmsford to Maldon, "**Litter Lout**" and "**Country Manners**", two films concerning countryside tidiness,

*From Richard Pike's "**Sunshine on Sea**" 1959 made for Southend's publicity department.*

Richard Pike filming for the Southend publicity films with a 16mm Bolex camera.

"**Country Dancing**" with children from Essex schools demonstrating particular routines, "**Milk Matters**", showing where the daily pint of milk came from and how it arrived on the housewife's doorstep, a film about how to go about making a brass rubbing called "**Witness in Brass**", and "**In Need of Care**", a fictional account showing a girl called Jenny who is taken into care and introduced to a children's home. There was a film about the Boy Scouts called "**Axemanship for Scouts**", "**Mind Your Bike**", a film for youngsters on how to maintain a bicycle, and "**Ingatestone Hall**" which looked at the 15th century building occupied by the Petre family.

*"**In Need of Care**", about the work of Essex Social Services in 1958.*

In 1959 Southend-on-Sea Publicity Department asked Richard Pike to make an updated film of the holiday resort. The result was "**Sunshine On Sea**". This followed roughly the same pattern as "**Best Place Under The Sun**", but included one or two extra sequences such as Southend Airport and the Kursaal. The film is brought to life by the witty commentary delivered by Johnny Morris. "At Southend, you can do just what you like" says Morris at the beginning of the film in that easy going way he had of seemingly talking direct to you, but at the same time talking to those in the picture. There is a sequence of the 'Miss Lovely' beauty contest where the girls walk past the camera in their bathing costumes. There is a cutaway shot of two boys watching, one clapping his hands vigorously "Hey, quiet, or I'll tell your mother" says Johnny. Over the end of the pier sequence where people are sitting in deckchairs he says "Out at sea on a ship that doesn't rock, basking and browning in the sun, dreaming in the breeze, lazily working up an appetite for lunch – lunch on the pier, what could be nicer". Over shots of some women at a table in the restaurant with a waitress standing by he delivers the imaginary conversation "Have we all decided what we are going to have? Fish? Certainly madam". The next shot is of some anglers reeling in a couple of plaice.

Richard Pike's daughter remembers Johnny Morris coming to the studio in the back garden to record the commentary along with other famous people who did voice overs for her father. She thought this was quite normal. Frank Phillips narrated "**The Best Place Under The Sun**", and Richard Baker came to read the commentary for a film on "**Watermark Disease of The Cricket Bat Willow**".

In the 1960s Richard Pike revised "**Sunshine on Sea**" using some newly shot footage to bring the film up to date; made a film called "**Southend on Sea Golden Jubilee 1914 – 1964**", and recorded the festivities on the opening day of the new "**Civic Centre**", a swish administrative building for Southend opened by the Queen Mother in 1967. There are a large number of films in the Pike collection, most being in black and white in the 1950s, with Kodachrome film being used for the publicity and later films. Nearly all the films were shot silent, with sound added in the studio. Here he had something that was unusual outside the London laboratories – equipment for recording sound direct to 16mm sound negative. This optical sound track could be synced up to the cut positive (after editing) and a 16mm combined or 'sound on film' print made ready for showing. Occasionally though he tried filming 'lip sync' films – that is recording picture and sound at the same time, then producing a 16mm print from the two masters – the optical sound track and the picture. He did this in 1956 with a film of the "**Syd Uren Trio**", a well known local group of musicians with Jan Coleman singing "Cry Me a River". This is more of a test film really, making sure the system works, as the film goes on to show Essex amateur film makers, including Marjorie Gillham, discussing making another film. About the same time, a sound film, again recorded 'live', is of Richard Pike's daughter Mary Ann at Christmas time. She remembers having to open the presents several times for the filming of "**Mary Christmas**". Her mother holds the microphone, and 'Dad' yells instructions from behind the camera. "**Merry Christmas**" as it is sometimes called, is an unusual home movie for the time, as there are sequences in the house and on the pavement outside, not only in colour, but with perfect 'lip sync' sound. It is difficult to date this film exactly, but Mary Ann Emma Pike, to give her her full name, was born in 1952, and in the film she is about 4 or 5. The neighbours are also in the film as, outside, the man who talks to her while riding her new bike was school teacher Bob Hepple who used to live at No 18, and the other little girl is Brigid Nightingale who lived at No 21 Kenilworth Gardens.

Richard Pike was a professional film maker, and the Pike collection contains over a hundred films. It is a rich resource of Southend and East Anglian life, and includes such diverse films as "**Loyal Greetings, the Royal Yacht Britannia**" in 1954 to "**Soil Stabilised Runways at Southend Airport**"; from "**Eggs for the Market**"; to a film about "**Stramit Boards of Stowmarket**".

Eric Kirkham Cole was a successful Southend businessman. With local partners he set up E. K. Cole in 1926 to make mains operated radio receivers. First they had a factory at Leigh on Sea, but this soon proved inadequate as the company expanded, so they built a large factory on a green field site (it was a cabbage field before they bought it) at Prittlewell. The all electric bakelite Ecko radio sets were a great success. By 1937 the company was employing over 4,000 people, and in 1938 they started making simple

*Introducing "Cry Me a River" by the "**Syd Uren Trio**". A well known group in the Southend area.*

Richard Pike of Kenilworth Gardens, Southend. In the background is his studio where he recorded the sound.

*Marjorie Gillham discussing making a film with a colleague from "**Syd Uren Trio**".*

television sets. With the coming of war Ecko diversified into specialist radar and military radio equipment, and in the late 1950s made nuclear instrumentation systems for atomic reactors. By now they were making films, and the titles show the range of work the company tackled. "**Looking Ahead with Ecko Radar**", "**Nucleonics in Quality Control**", "**Ecko Hits The Headlines**", and "**Ecko Airfield Aids**".

"**The Story of Old Leigh**" is just that, a 16mm colour film made by Frank Pigram showing the picturesque side of Leigh-on-Sea – the narrow street, the weather boarded cottages, the cockle boats, and the sea. Leigh was famous for its cockles. John Carr filmed the work of Messrs Osborne and Sons, whose boats brought back tons of cockles from the sands off Shoeburyness, where they had been raked from the sand by the fisherman. The cockle boats returned along the winding channel to Leigh, where the men unloaded their catch, walking on narrow planks between boat and shore. The cockles were steamed open, riddled, and the shells discarded. Next they were washed to ensure every particle of grit was removed so that they were ready for the London markets. "**Alive Alive-O**" was made in 1948, when everything was done with much manual labour. Thomas Osborne started the business in 1880 selling cockles from a shed in old Leigh, and the company is still in existence today. A film made in 1976 called "**The Essex Coast**" also features George Osborne's cockle boats, but this time the cockles are sucked up by vacuum pipe – mechanisation taking some of the back-breaking work out of cockle gathering.

One of the films in the Fison Fertiliser collection is of the "**Opening of Nitrogen Factory**" in 1959 at Stanford-Le-Hope, situated close to the Thames. Sir Clavering Fison meets Lord Netherthorpe who is to open the new works, which consists of a laboratory, workshops, compressors, and control rooms and a line of railway tankers specially designed for Fisons chemical products. Fisons was a large agrochemical company at the time, with bases all over the Anglia region. A bit further along is Tilbury. Here in "**Liner Departure**" is a busy scene in the 1930s, as dockers load trunks on to a large passenger liner, and deck hands stow them away. Two laden barges pass by as a steam tug gets ready with a hawser to assist the liner. Finally, in faded colour, we see passengers on deck watching the activity. Mr. Hudson, who worked for Ilford, the photographic company, filmed "**Tilbury Yard**" in 1932. These can be compared with scenes taken over forty years later, in 1976, in "**The Essex Coast**", which shows the then highly modernised container port.

"**River Scenes**" is a leisurely record of the Thames in the 1920s, with shipping coming and going and sailing barges tied up at moorings. There are views of the river scenery all the way down to Southend. In "**Royal Eagle Paddle Steamer**" we see just that, this famous boat near Tower Bridge, and "**River Pilot**" explains how the pilot's work moving ships up and down the river is done. "**Taming The Thames**" is about controlling the water, as is "**Thames Tidal Defences**", a film by David Williams about the massive flood prevention schemes along the Essex coast associated with the Thames Barrier.

***"Littleport War Weapons Week"** 1941.*

Wartime

"I want to speak to you tonight about the form of warfare which the Germans have been employing so extensively against Holland and Belgium – namely, the dropping of troops by parachute behind the main defence lines. Let me say at once the danger to us from this particular menace, although it undoubtedly exists, should not be exaggerated. We have made preparations to meet it already".

These are the words of the Secretary of State for War, Anthony Eden, broadcast on the BBC on the evening of May 14th 1940. This was to have an immediate effect on men of the Eastern Counties – and elsewhere in Britain. Anthony Eden goes on:- "In order to leave nothing to chance and to supplement, from sources as yet untapped, the means of defence already arranged, we are going to ask you to help us, in a manner which I know will be welcome to thousands of you. Since the war began the government have received countless enquiries from all over the Kingdom from men of all ages who are for one reason or another not at present engaged in military service, and who wish to do something for the defence of the country.

"Now is your opportunity. We want large numbers of men in Great Britain who are British subjects, between the ages of 17 and 65, to come forward now and offer their service in order to make assurance doubly sure. The name of the new force which is now to be raised will be the Local Defence Volunteers".

Immediately following the broadcast men queued at local police stations to register their names. At first there were no guns, and no uniforms, just an LDV arm band made in local shops. A few members already had shot guns and cartridges, which were considered legal weapons of war, but soon rifles began to arrive, most part of a consignment of one million given by the United States. It took a bit longer for the full battledress of the 'Home Guard' as it soon became known (the title was changed in the summer of 1940), to be issued. After organisation into battalions, and plenty of training, the Home Guard was ready as an army of home defence.

Charles Scott, a keen amateur film maker, was a member of the King's Lynn Home Guard at the time, and made a comprehensive film of the formation and activities of the Lynn Battalion. Charles, whose home was in Norwich, worked as a van driver for W. & R. Jacob, the biscuit makers. During the war when petrol became hard to find the biscuit companies formed a delivery pool, all the different companies, Huntley and Palmers, Peek Freans, Westons, Macfarlane Langs, Kemps and Jacobs combining their distribution. A depot was set up at King's Lynn, close to the railway station, and Charles Scott spent the war years there as manager.

One Sunday, with just 50 feet of film in his 16mm camera (two minutes' worth), he recorded uniformed members of the 7th Battalion on guard at the Cut Bridge over the Ouse near Lynn. When he showed the film to his comrades they were thrilled and wanted a longer film made. Cine film was hard to get in wartime, but an officer managed to obtain some rolls, with the proviso that it was used for an instructional film about the Home Guard. Charles Scott set to work. He recreated the formation of the Local Defence Volunteers following the broadcast on May 14th 1940. For a silent film the broadcast was ingeniously covered. First there is a title giving the date, then a shot of a clock coming up to 9 p.m. Next comes a shot of a radio, followed by pictures on the front covers of two magazines, one showing Anthony Eden, who delivered the message, the other a picture of Kitchener pointing (everyone knew the famous First World War poster of Lord Kitchener) out of the picture at the viewer saying "Your Country Needs You".

With long shots, close ups, and high and low angles, Charles Scott filmed volunteers being kitted out, attending lectures, and learning to dismantle and reassemble their guns. The men of Number Two Platoon, Three Company, 7th Battalion, Norfolk Home Guard co-operated fully with their filming colleague. In fact Charles Scott recorded their activities right up to the end in 1944, when they attended their last parade in the Tuesday Market Place at Lynn. "**Home Guard**" is a complete record of this unit, with scenes showing drill practice, stopping and checking people's identity cards, training around derelict buildings in the town, bayonet practice, mortar firing, grenade throwing instruction, and even helping out with the harvest on a local farm.

Home Guard units appear briefly in other films, such as the "**Wivenhoe 17 Platoon Essex Home Guard**" - seen training in a gravel pit in almost dense smoke somewhere just outside this north Essex village, and in "**Crown of The Year**",

*Members of the King's Lynn **"Home Guard"** operating a spigot mortar.*

*A tank in Haverhill from the **"Gurteen Family Films".***

a 1943 film reassuring the population that the harvest is being safely gathered in. East Norfolk farmer Charles Wharton not only supervises his farm workers during the day, but is their platoon commander in the evenings. The Home Guard was stood down on December 3rd 1944, and parades were held over all the country. A couple of these can be seen in the King's Lynn "**Home Guard**" film and "**Home Guard March Past**" in Luton.

Preparations for the possible coming of war began in the late 1930s. At Haverhill in Suffolk a tank is on exercise in the countryside. It then trundles down the main street and people stand and stare at this rare sight. This was filmed by Mr. Gurteen and is part of the "**Gurteen Family Films**". In the cinemas of the county, "**Suffolk Territorials**", a short recruiting film was being shown, which had overtones of the impending war with soldiers training with a Vickers machine gun and on a large calibre gun mounted inside a building, though eventually these heavy guns were placed on the coast at places like Clacton. Colonel Coburn, Chairman of the Suffolk Territorial Army Association, appeals for volunteers by referring to their sense of responsibility to the Empire.

A more local appeal for volunteers, both male and female, is given direct from the cinema screen to audiences in Norwich inviting people to come forward to join the ARP (Air Raid Precautions) by Alderman Riley. In this short film also made before the outbreak of war, preparations are more obvious with fire-fighters, ambulance personnel, policemen and others training. "**Alderman Riley Would Like a Word With You**" is about getting men and women to volunteer for these vital local services, and concludes with a direct appeal from Walter Riley asking, as he points his finger out of the screen in Kitchener fashion, "Will you help?"

George Swain by now had a 16mm camera, and in 1939, not long before hostilities broke out, filmed the ARP and the AFS (Auxiliary Fire Service) training in Norwich. Calling his film "**Dawn Raid**", it begins with planes flying overhead (supposedly enemy), a shot of a siren (these had been installed and tested earlier in the year), men and women leaving their homes in response to the air raid warning, and firemen rushing through the city to a fire in a 'fire engine' - actually a converted car with ladder on top towing a trailer water pump. The men stand half-in and half-out of the car just like a real fire engine of the time. The film shows vividly how the services worked, with scenes of setting up the equipment and fighting the fire in disused buildings given especially for this ARP and AFS exercise by the City Council. 'Casualties' are taken away in a converted lorry. The film then simulates a poison gas bomb attack, with members of the ARP testing for the gas, sprinkling bleach powder to render it safe, and then filling in the hole made by the bomb. Finally a man is seen vigorously ringing a hand bell to give the 'all clear'. At Sheringham in July 1939 the "**Gowing Family Films**" also show a mock air raid, and for this local volunteers had to lay on the road and pavements with labels on them stating what injuries they had, so that the officials knew what to do. A certain amount of giggling from those 'injured' laying on the ground added light relief to what was really a serious bit of training. An unknown amateur film maker in Luton made a short film which shows an ARP warden demonstrating to a housewife how to put on a gas mask, of which 38 million had been distributed.

From August 1939, London Transport began taking mothers and children from various parts of the metropolis by buses to Liverpool Street, Stratford, Hackney and other railway stations on the LNER network to board special evacuation trains heading for East Anglia. The number of people coming from a particular part of London was known to the LNER officials, so they were able to plan which train the evacuees went on – such as those from Hackney went to Cambridgeshire, and those from Liverpool Street went to Essex and Suffolk – and which town or village could accommodate them without becoming overloaded. Where possible families were kept together. In all the LNER ran eighty-two trains to the Eastern Counties from London, carrying over 101,500 passengers. There were to have been more trains, but quite a number of people opted to stay in their homes.

A gas mask in a cardboard box was carried by each child, along with a suitcase or other suitable holder containing clothes and other precious belongings. None of them knew where they were going to end up that night. Destinations on the

*The Smerdon family at home in Clacton from "**Town and Family Scenes**".*

Thumbs up from young Peter Smerdon as he leaves Clacton in 1940.

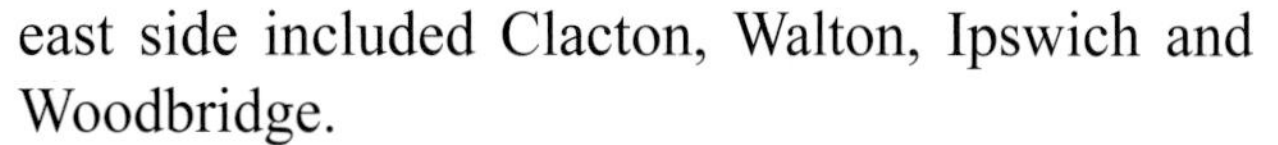

east side included Clacton, Walton, Ipswich and Woodbridge.

At Clacton lived the Smerdon family. Herbert Smerdon was a photographer with the local paper. He also had his own 9.5mm cine camera. In his "**Town and Family Scenes**" there are shots of evacuees arriving at Clacton station, where the bewildered children were selected by prospective foster parents. At Welwyn Garden City the "**Arrival of Evacuees**" shows a well organised line of cheerful uniformed school girls, as many schools made their own private arrangements of evacuation. In "**Boarded Out**" and "**Exodus**", two films by the Dr Barnardo organisation, children are seen settling in with families in rural East Anglia. There is an inspection by Barnardo's staff to make sure all was well.

Herbert Smerdon's film goes on to show life at home at 120 Dudley Road, Clacton, with blackout boards being put over a window, trying on tin hats, and the family having a traditional turkey lunch with the boys opening their presents at Christmas 1939.

By the summer of 1940 the authorities realised how exposed these eastern coastal towns were. It was decided to move the evacuees again, along with local children, to safer parts of England and Wales. Herbert filmed children from a local school, again clutching their gas masks, going to Clacton station, and getting on a train. Amongst them was his son Peter. Mrs. Smerdon wrote in her diary "They went in good heart, smiling quite bravely, the lasting photograph of little Peter's face at the carriage window with his thumbs up". In "**Town and Family Scenes**" there is that very shot Mrs. Smerdon described, of her son Peter at the window, followed by the steam train pulling out of Clacton station. He was evacuated to a farm at Droitwich, where later Mrs. Smerdon was able to visit him. She wrote "He was quite happy there with a little girl to play with. A pleasant family".

The Smerdons then had to leave their house in Clacton, as the town was virtually taken over by the army. Herbert filmed his own house, which was requisitioned by the army, with the removal van outside loading the family's belongings. With many people gone, Clacton became a bit of a ghost town, as Herbert shows with his shots of empty streets and boarded up shops.

At Huntingdon, "**Youngest Woman Billeting Officer**", twenty year old Barbara Meadows, is seen calling at a house persuading the occupant to take in bombed out evacuees. If the home owner was reluctant, then Barbara Meadows says she is "prepared to use compulsion in order to find homes for the homeless". Seventeen men had already failed at this job. Billetors received 10/6 (52½p) for each child, and 8/6 (42½p) for each subsequent child. Parents were asked to supply 2/- (10p) but many just could not manage this. Some children were evacuated with their mother, in which case the adult was allowed 5/- (25p) with 3/- (15p) for the child. This was less money, as the mother was supposed to do the cooking, so relieving the landlady of work.

Germany had invaded Poland on September 1st 1939, and two days later Britain was at war. There was an Emergency Powers Act which resulted (amongst other things) in all cinemas closing on September 4th. It was soon realised the importance of cinemas in keeping up morale, informing, and entertaining audiences. It was felt this outweighed the dangers of bombs falling on a building full of people, so within a week the cinemas were open again, and projectionists over 25 years old were excused war service. The newsreels often contained stories which reflected not only what was happening, but aimed to build confidence. For instance the Norfolk Broads and rivers were closed because of the possible threat of seaplanes landing on the large stretches of water. Old boats, barrels, anything that would float and pose a hazard to landing were moored in the middle of the broads. In addition armed speed boats raced up and down the rivers and in 1940 these were filmed for a newsreel calling the item "**Britain's Inland Water Patrol**".

With a shortage of raw materials for armaments, people were requested to give metals to the war effort. Anything made of iron, steel or aluminium was torn up, dismantled, rescued, and collected. Other everyday items were saved as well, even old bones which could be used to make oil and glue. "**Bring Out Your Bones**" a cinema short information film shows a dog not eating bones, but putting them into a bucket for collection.

At Billericay in Essex Frank Pigram, an amateur film maker using 16mm film, recorded

*"**Britain's Inland Water Patrol**" on the river near Wroxham in 1940.*

the activities of the ATC (Air Training Corps) for recruitment purposes. "**Youth Prepares**" begins with boys arriving on foot and on bicycles. There is a medical examination. Then they all take part in P.T. (Physical Training), have drill practice, and learn navigation. This is really only the start of their training, and Frank Pigram made a second film, "**Air Crusaders**", which shows the boys learning about electricity, radio, morse code, signalling and aircraft recognition. They are instructed into how a glider works. Soon they are qualified, and leave by train to join the RAF as Aircraftsmen.

At Ipswich another form of training was going on. In "**Orford Street Mobile Hospital**", a convoy of an assortment of vehicles from single deck buses to vans are seen arriving at a large garden in Ipswich where nurses and doctors set up a temporary hospital on the lawn. Filmed by Dr Leslie Moss, physician and surgeon of 433 Norwich Road, various simulated wounds are dressed. Probably shown to attract volunteers, as well as having instructional uses, this colour film shows how to deal with the casualties of a poison gas bomb, and the correct protective clothing required. Although poison gas was never used, the authorities were well prepared for the various types, blister gas, tear gas and lung irritant gas. A white bleach powder applied to the affected area neutralised the poison gas.

Towards the end of 1940 London suffered huge fires following raids by the enemy. "**The Great Fire of London**" is a newsreel story which is quite graphic, and it is surprising that the cameraman was able to get so close to blazing buildings which seem to be both sides of the streets and all round him. Looking at the film it is a wonder anything survived. The enemy were able to approach the outer area of the Thames estuary, lay magnetic and acoustic mines in the sea lanes, and head up the river to London where they caused tremendous casualties to life and property in the docklands and the City. It was decided that fully armed and manned structures were necessary in the Thames estuary between Harwich and Margate. Guy Maunsell, a young engineer, devised special naval forts which could be built quickly, towed to their site, and sunk into position so they stood erect above the waves. These forts were to be equipped with two heavy 3.7 inch guns and two Bofors guns, and have accommodation for one hundred men. On board there were to be provisions for three weeks in case of the weather restricting re-victualling.

The placing of the Roughs Fort off Harwich in 1942.

The forts, built at Gravesend in six weeks, had a base of concrete 170ft by 90ft, and 14ft high. The twin towers were a further 60ft high, and with a steel superstructure built on top in two weeks, the whole fort weighed 4000 tons. After commissioning the fort was to be towed to the site in the early morning. The first was to be situated eight miles east of Harwich, and was to be known as the Roughs Fort. Temporary wooden bulwarks 4ft high were constructed around the base in case of high waves during towing. These were to be dismantled before sinking. On the morning of February 11th 1942 at the site off Harwich, one side of the wooden bulwarks had already been taken off when the Naval Officer in Charge ordered immediate sinking as enemy planes were approaching. Water entered the hull and the fort rolled sideways alarmingly. John Posford filmed the sudden sinking, and this appears in his film "**Posford Duvivier**", the name of the company he and Guy Maunsell were to run after the war.

The base hit the bottom, and the fort righted itself much to the relief of all concerned. The Admiralty were so agitated by the near disaster that they ordered that those conversant with the fort should in future be in charge of the whole operation. John Posford then took control of the forts that followed at Sunk Head, fifteen miles

*Training and demonstrating during "**Littleport War Weapons Week**".*

south east of Harwich, and Tongue Sand seven miles north of Margate.

The Roughs Fort is still there today. It was abandoned in the 1950s, and in 1967 former Army Major Roy Bates occupied the fort and turned it into a kingdom called Sealand. It is often in the news as new schemes are put forward for the Second World War structure.

There were several ways money for the equipment of war could be raised – one being War Weapons Weeks. On Saturday March 8th 1941, Movietone News made a special short film in Cambridgeshire to help raise £30,000 during "**Littleport War Weapons Week**". With a population of approximately 5000, this works out at about £6 per inhabitant, but whether this target was achieved is not known. The film shows the people of Littleport and the men of the Auxiliary Fire Service exercising to stirring background music. The film was shown a few days later at Littleport's Regal Cinema, where it fortunately survived and was passed to the East Anglian Film Archive for preservation.

In 1941, at Aspley Guise in Bedfordshire, the "**War Weapons Week**" there was filmed by Alfred Sinfield using a mixture of black and white and colour 16mm film. Taking place from May 24th to May 31st, the film shows children in the Square posing for the camera and waving flags, a parade of vehicles belonging to the local area ARP and AFS units, sports events, and a parade of soldiers. The week raised £6188. At the end is a shot of Alfred Sinfield with the caption saying 'This is your cameraman saying cheerio'.

"**Wings For Victory**", another community way of raising money, this time for the RAF. In Alysham in Norfolk, in May 1943 there was a "**Wings For Victory**" parade through the town which included nurses and women from the WVS (Women's Voluntary Service) and Girl Guides.

*An inspection during Hitchin's "**Warship Week Parade**".*

*Unused graves from "**Captain Rowsell's Norwich**".*

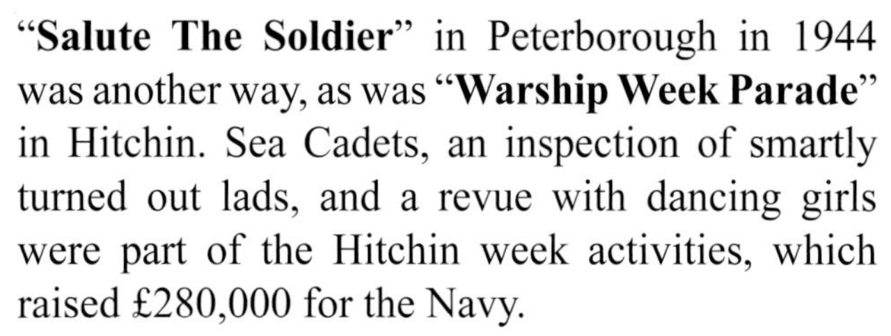

"**Salute The Soldier**" in Peterborough in 1944 was another way, as was "**Warship Week Parade**" in Hitchin. Sea Cadets, an inspection of smartly turned out lads, and a revue with dancing girls were part of the Hitchin week activities, which raised £280,000 for the Navy.

In the book "Norfolk Events" by Harold Jaffa compiled from Eastern Daily Press records, listed under April 1942 is the short statement "April 27th, Big air raid on Norwich. Fifty tons of bombs dropped. Six hundred casualties, including 162 killed". Norwich had suffered bombs before, but this was a severe attack indeed. The record goes on "April 29th. Second big air raid on Norwich. Forty-five tons of heavy bombs and many incendiaries dropped. Sixty nine people killed, eighty nine seriously injured". Ernest Croxton, a policeman who lived near Waterworks Road, went out the next day with his 9.5mm cine camera and recorded on film the damage to the houses. "**Day After Air Raids**" presents a sorry sight with residential properties with displaced or missing roofs, ruined houses, and debris littering the streets. In all, 1,200 people were made homeless.

In the colour film "**Captain Rowsell's Norwich**" made a couple of years later there are shots in Norwich cemetery of wooden crosses on the graves of those who died in April 1942. In one case a whole family was wiped out, mother and father and both children. A lengthy trench was dug ready for the casualties of future raids, and Captain Rowsell filmed this, a grim reminder of the seriousness of the situation, but luckily this second mass grave was never used.

A few family scenes in a garden of children playing, two women laughing together, boys riding bikes in the street, a woman hanging out the washing – just ordinary shots from a typical home movie one might think, but behind this is a story of war. Roger Last of Harwich recounted the story. The house is in Dovercourt, Essex, the home of the Last family, and one of the women is Mrs. Kapek, a refugee from Czechoslovakia. Mr. Kapek was a professional photographer and at one time Mayor of a town in Czechoslovakia. During the difficulties of that country, he and his wife, daughter, and mother-in-law escaped after being threatened with their lives. They fled on foot and any transport they could find across Europe to England, the mother-in-law being lost on the journey. They never saw her again or learnt what happened to her. They found a home with the Last family in Valley Road, Dovercourt. Mr. Kapek joined the Czech unit of the British Army. The short home movie film "**The Kapek Family in Valley Road**" of 1943 shows the families together, without a hint of the difficulties that lay behind. After the war the Kapeks returned to Czechoslovakia, but soon left for South Africa where they settled. There were other displaced persons, but what happened to a carriage-load of refugees that arrived at Norwich station, in "**Norwich Scenes 1938 – 1940**", with labels tied to their lapels, is not known, though they appear happy as they walk down the platform.

In Colchester in 1943 the "**National Fire Service**" held competitions for the quickest turn out of fire brigades. Although this was serious training in speed and getting the pumps working quickly, the film is fun for the competitors, for they start from their beds! At the word go, they leap out of bed, uncoil hoses, and get the pumps going. Exercises like these were going on all over the Eastern Counties, along with the Auxiliary Fire Service – small units in villages and towns made up of local volunteers.

James Wentworth Day, a prolific writer about the countryside, was filmed in 1942 as he set off on horseback on a tour of the Eastern Counties to see the present state of agriculture. In "**Bright and Early**", an item in a cinema magazine film, he is seen at West Mersea with Captain Bill Wyatt, a shipwright and local character, where Mr.Day downs an oyster. At Tollshunt D'Arcy Mr. Day has a 'stirrup cup' to help him on his way. The film suggests that the whole journey was to be on horseback, when in fact a car and horse box was in attendance, and when a certain place was reached, out of the box came the horse and Mr. Day continued his riding journey. The final part of this item is filmed at Hatfield in Hertfordshire, where giant eighteen-ton Caterpillar bulldozers belonging to Jack Olding, a farm machinery distributor, are seen levelling some uneven ground. The point being made is that derelict land can be made usable. The story of the expedition through the countryside is told in Wentworth Day's "Farming Adventure" published by George Harrap in April 1943.

The fertile fields of the Eastern Counties served as the nation's principal source of food production, a pre-war neglected industry now given major priority to cultivate every available acre, and help reduce the dependence on seaborne food supplies. Eventually 70% was home grown.

There was a photocall at Sandringham in August 1943 for a newsreel piece about the King giving up flower beds and a golf course for the growing of food. "**Harvest Time on a Royal Estate**" was covered by the papers as well, as the King and Queen and the princesses watched the gathering in of the harvest. The young princesses climb on a Massey Harris combine harvester, and with their father, ride their bicycles through the cornfields. The Queen however preferred a governess cart, and takes the reins from Mr. French, her groom. In the same year "**Crown of The Year**" was released, a film about getting the harvest in safely, and how hard the farmers were working to achieve this. Charles Wharton, a young farmer in his thirties in the Stokesby area of East Norfolk is featured in this film. Apparently Charles went to London to record the commentary, but on release another voice was on the sound track, as the

*Running hoses out, as part of a competion for firemen from "**National Fire Service**" 1943.*

*James Wentworth Day riding through the Eastern Counties in 1942 from "**Bright and Early**".*

producers thought his Norfolk accent would not be understood. Whether this is so I am not sure, but we do know two versions of this film were made, a short, and a longer version, the latter containing extra sequences of the day in the life of the farmer, such as rescuing a cow that had slid into a dyke by pulling her out by ropes, without, it seems, any harm to the animal.

The newsreels in the cinema gave audiences information about the war itself, and what was happening at home, even if the location was seldom divulged. Short morale boosting films were made like "**Crown of The Year**" for showing in cinema vans, with people standing watching a screen at the back, in village halls, and for community groups. Some were given British Board of Film Censors certificates and shown in the 'full supporting programme' at the cinema.

A bulletin on the BBC Home Service after war was declared in 1939 said "The Minister of Agriculture and Fisheries has appointed a War Agricultural Executive Committee for each county in England and Wales. Their immediate task is to see that additional land is brought under the plough with all speed". Cambridgeshire and Suffolk were set a target of 10,000 acres, Essex 15,000, and Norfolk 25,000.

The work of the War Agricultural Executive Committee in East Suffolk is recorded in "**Spring Offensive**", a film directed by Humphrey Jennings. Jennings was born in Walberswick, near Southwold in 1907, and learnt about film making when he joined the GPO Film Unit in 1934. At first he assisted on such films as 'Pett and Pott' as designer - and actor. He played the part of a grocer in this film promoting the use of the telephone. After a short spell elsewhere he came back to the GPO, and started work in 1939 on "**Spring Offensive**". The story is principally about the setting up of the 'War Ag' committee and how they went about their business of reclaiming land. Real farmers are included, some acting slightly awkwardly when filmed at a meeting to discuss their tactics. There is a sub-plot, if that is the word, about an evacuee, interwoven with sequences of ploughing, drilling, harvesting - in fact the full farming year. This is a record of Suffolk at work at the beginning of the war, with Suffolk people and Suffolk methods. Horse and hand labour go side by side with the latest machines such as the powerful gyrotiller. Land girls are seen helping in this twenty minute film released in 1940.

Reclamation was important in the Fens, where there were big stretches of age old marsh and scrub. Alan Bloom was a young farmer who had taken over Priory Farm and the adjoining fenland between Burwell and Wicken in Cambridgeshire in 1939. Here was Burwell Fen, which included Adventurers' Fen, a wilderness of soggy soil, dense reeds and thick bushes. It was decided that this un-productive land should be re-claimed, and brought into cultivation. Alan Bloom recalls in his "The Farm in The Fen" published in 1943: "The Executive Officer of the War Agricultural

Adventurers' Fen before reclamation.

Digging out a bog oak.

Committee gave me the task, with their blessing, of bringing Adventurers' Fen under the plough". Together with Bill Pledger, who had a 16mm camera, a black and white film record of the reclamation process was made.

It was in 1941 that work started. First excess water had to be got away, and this necessitated clearing drains and ditches, and making new ones. The reeds were burnt off, then the bushes cut down by hand and burnt, and the roots dug or pulled out by tractor. A Ransome Solotrac deep digger plough then tackled the rough land, turning a furrow twenty inches wide and twenty inches deep. It was hoped this would bury the mass of roots, but all it did was find the bog oaks that lay a foot or so below the surface. Bog oaks are the remains of a once ancient forest of oak trees which somehow or other fell or were blown down in some severe gale of the past. These had to be got out, and various methods were tried. Some were sawn in situ and lifted in small sections, some were hauled out whole by tractors, and other more stubborn oaks were blown up by the Royal Engineers. All this can be seen in Bloom and Pledger's film "**Fen Reclamation**". The bog oaks were piled high by the side of the field, the land then disc harrowed, then light tractors got to work to prepare for the first crop.

The land had been reclaimed, and crops of wheat, potatoes and sugar beet followed, with scenes of harvesting and lifting, threshing and loading into barges, and ploughing for the next years crops. Looking at the untamed wilderness as Alan Bloom himself does at the beginning of the film, one can hardly imagine it could be soon growing crops.

Alan left Wicken in 1946 and moved to Bressingham, where he went back to his first love of horticultural work, specialising in hardy plants. In the 1960s his sons took over the running of the nursery at Bressingham, leaving more time for Alan's love of steam and railways. Alan died in March 2005 at the age of 98.

An unusual wartime film about harvest and the feeding of the nation is "**The Harvest Shall Come**" released in October 1942. This is a dramatised documentary, looking at the plight of the farm worker at the time of the First World War, and through the dismal 1930s, to the so

"Fen Reclamation". *Ploughing begins with the Solotrac deep digger plough. The land was still littered with reed roots.*

called prosperity of the Second World War. John Slater plays the part of Tom Grimwood, a farm labourer, along with other actors and local people from the Needham Market area where the majority of the film was shot. We see Tom go through the various changes in farming economy. Some of his colleagues leave the land to work in towns for more money, but Tom stays loyal to his employer. He marries, and lives in a tied cottage until the farmer can no longer pay the higher wages that have been set. Tom is threatened with eviction, something that was not uncommon during the 1930s.

With the Second World War, when agriculture became another 'front', wages go up, and so do the prices, and Tom reflects on his larger pay packet, and the cost of food, cigarettes and a pint – which have also gone up. He is no better off.

" **The Harvest Shall Come**" is an odd film, as it states the history of the farm worker so far, but offers no conclusion. This thirty five minute film was made by the film making company Realist, but was paid for it seems by Imperial Chemical Industries and presented by ICI to the Ministry of Information. As the underlying message is that we are not looking after our farm workers, it is a wonder the MOI released it so liberally. It must have been popular as we do know that many 16mm copies were made available for non-theatric presentations, and the film was re-released on 35mm in 1944.

*Pre- title, main title, and scene with John Slater (left) from "**The Harvest Shall Come**" 1942.*

During the war more people were going to the cinema each week than ever before. According to Rachael Low in "Films of Comment and Persuasion" published in 1979, weekly cinema attendance in 1941 was about 21 million, more than two million more than an assessment made seven years earlier in 1934. Cinema programmes contained Government Official announcements, Food Flashes, Fuel Limericks, and other short snappy information films. Often only a few seconds long, they were straightforward in their approach, with messages such as "You will receive your new ration book soon, make sure the address on your ration book and on your identity card are the same" or more directly as a person is seen putting mouldy bread into a dustbin - "**Don't Waste Bread**".

"**Fuel Limerick No 2**" tells us that five inches of water in the bath is quite sufficient, and in "**The Battle For Fuel**" Commander Stephen King-Hall says directly to the audience "Have you seen your battle orders in the press, have you cut them out. This is a battle on the Home Front from which no one can stand aside. You use fuel, so you can save fuel".

East Anglia's other major part in the war effort was the air front, the RAF offensive against Nazi Germany, principally a bombing campaign aimed at limiting the enemy by destroying his war production, power sources, and communications. A fifty minute feature documentary called "Target For Tonight" was made in 1941 showing the work of RAF Bomber Command. A shorter version of this film, twenty minutes long, was also released called "**Air Operations**". Filmed at Mildenhall, the film shows crews being briefed, boarding their Wellington bombers, and preparing for take off as evening falls. The operation of this airfield seems quaintly simple compared with what was to come when the airfield building programme was fully under way. "F for Freddie" heads for Germany, dodging flak and releasing its bombs. The plane is hit and the wireless operator injured, but they manage to get back to Mildenhall where they land safely. The sad part is that "F for Freddie" and its crew who took part in the filming were lost a few weeks later.

The airfield building programme was a huge civil engineering project with each one costing over one million pounds. Each airfield had to have accommodation for, and to be able to feed, between two and three thousand men. What was termed Greater East Anglia by the Air Ministry embraced groupings of airfields in Essex, Suffolk, Norfolk, Cambridgeshire, Huntingdonshire, and the surrounding counties. There were 150 airfields in this area, 37 in Norfolk, and 30 in Suffolk alone. There were so many airfields that it took just a

*The Pilot Cinema in King's Lynn showing 'The Girls He Left Behind', a 1943 Technicolor film with Carmen Miranda. From Charles Scott's "**King's Lynn Town Scenes**" of 1944.*

twenty minute cycle ride between one and the next. Eighty of these airfields were eventually occupied by units of the United States Army Air Forces. One of these, established in the UK early in 1942, was the Eighth Air Force, which would include two thirds of the total USAAF combat strength.

The RAF flew mostly at night but the Americans operated in daylight. The main combat element of the Eighth Air Force was a heavy bomber group equipped with four-engined planes - Boeing B17 Fortresses and consolidated B24 Liberators. One of the bases for B17s was Thorpe Abbotts in Norfolk. John Schwarz had access to Kodachrome 16mm film, and he recorded in his "**Thorpe Abbotts 100th Bomb Group**" film scenes in the USA before arrival, Thorpe Abbotts still under construction, ground crews at work on aircraft in the open air, B17 formations, and shots of the crew in the aeroplanes. John Schwarz was a ground officer at the 100th Bomb Group from 1943 to the end of hostilities. He also recorded those off duty moments, with the G.I's looking at the Norfolk Broads, going to London to see Piccadilly Circus and the docks, and exploring the country lanes of Norfolk. Back to reality, and we see shots of planes taking off, enemy territory far below, damaged planes returning, and planes on fire.

"**USAAF Honington**", a black and white 16mm film taken by Robert Sturgess, is a similar record of an 'aerodrome' as they were often called then, but with a wider selection of aircraft. Honington, near Bury St Edmunds, was at first an RAF station flying Wellingtons, but in the summer of 1942 the United States Army Air Force took over, and the base was used as a repair and supply depot. Here in 1944 was the 364th Fighter Group which flew long range escort missions for B17s. Robert Sturgess was the Boeing representative, a civilian engineer at the Honington air depot from 1943 to 1945. He used out of date 16mm black and white film which had been brought in for use in the gun cameras fitted to aircraft to record mission attacks, and this accounts for some short sequences in his film. The footage includes the Pulham St Mary aircraft dump - a graveyard of damaged and derelict aeroplanes, Ixworth Street, and the road to Great Ashfield. On the runway at Honington is seen a B26 Marauder bomber aircraft. These

*A short version of this 1941 film was released called "**Air Operations**".*

were based at Matching, near Harlow in Essex, and a short 8mm amateur film "**Matching 391st Bombardment Group**" was made there in 1944.

The Americans were freely able to bring over cine film, including Kodachrome, and send it back for processing. Amos Golsch, a member of the 93rd Bomb Group, was stationed at Hardwick, near Pulham in Norfolk. In "**Hardwick USAAF Airfield**" he filmed briefly not only recreational activities such as golf, but also a scene from the air of the Norfolk countryside with a burning crashed plane below. At Seething, nine miles

*Taking off at Mildenhall from "**Air Operations**", 1941.*

*B17 taking off from "**Thorpe Abbotts 100th Bomb Group**".*

US airmen waiting for bombers to return from a mission.

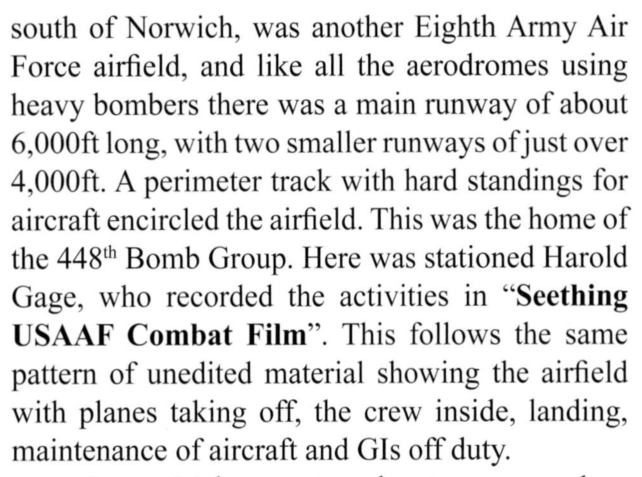

south of Norwich, was another Eighth Army Air Force airfield, and like all the aerodromes using heavy bombers there was a main runway of about 6,000ft long, with two smaller runways of just over 4,000ft. A perimeter track with hard standings for aircraft encircled the airfield. This was the home of the 448th Bomb Group. Here was stationed Harold Gage, who recorded the activities in "**Seething USAAF Combat Film**". This follows the same pattern of unedited material showing the airfield with planes taking off, the crew inside, landing, maintenance of aircraft and GIs off duty.

James Mahoney started out as a squadron commander with the 492nd Bomb Group at North Pickenham. He had a 16mm camera, and access to plenty of Kodachrome film. When the Group was disbanded he was moved to Rackheath just outside Norwich to become Deputy Commanding Officer of 467th Bomb Group. He shot some film at Pickenham, but the main part of the 16mm film in the "**Mahoney Collection**" is of Rackheath. Over 2000ft of film was shot, much of it donated to the East Anglian Film Archive by James Mahoney's son, Brian in 2001. Brian has also published his father's diaries of the time. The 467th flew B24 Liberators, which were distinguished by their twin fins and rudders.

There were also fifteen fighter stations to provide escort for the bombers, and these operated P38 Lightnings, P47 Thunderbolts, and P51 Mustangs. Mustangs are seen in the 8mm film made by Donald Kammer "**Raydon Airfield**" in 1944. Pilots check their parachutes, head to their aircraft, and prepare for take off. Some of the fighters are fitted with extra tanks for long range flights. Donald Kammer was a fighter pilot in the P51 Mustangs at Raydon, near Ipswich, during the winter of 1944 – 1945. His colour film of the 353rd Fighter Group escort fighters also shows RAF air sea rescue boats working out of Felixstowe. The group's last escort mission was on the 24th March 1945, followed by a five month period of winding down, and the trip home.

The airfield bases became little Americas in the English countryside. In "**If There Are Ghosts**", a BBC East film made by Christopher Lewis in 1979, the history of these bases is recounted with archive film taken from some of the above films. This was made possible by Roger Freeman, who as a boy grew up with bombers overhead, and went on to become the historian of the Eighth Air Force in this country. It was he who found many of these films on his frequent trips to the United States to visit those who flew from East Anglian bases. Their remaining memories were not so much of the dangers, but of the cold.

Perhaps the most vivid film of life in the UK for the American GI is "**Combat America**", a training film for gunners made in 1943. This colour film was shot on 16mm Kodachrome film by many servicemen and edited together to show back home what coming to England was really like. The customs and money of the country are explained, entertainment is emphasised with such people as Bob Hope and Tony Romano, along with relaxation in the English countryside and London

*Fighter plane at **"Raydon Airfield"** 1944.*

itself. The resulting 16mm footage was taken back to the States and 35mm black and white 'blow up' Technicolor separations made. From these, after editing, 35mm colour optical sound prints were produced, even 16mm prints for showing in non cinema locations. The result is not the best quality, but the content is riveting, particularly the battle at the end over enemy land – showing what really was expected. Clarke Gable gives the commentary. Gable came over with the new 351st Bomb Group to Polebrook in Northamptonshire, and set the story around gunners of the group during the summer of 1943.

Charles Rowsell was keen on amateur radio, and joined the local radio station as an announcer in Utah. He was also interested in aeroplanes, and joined the local Army Air Corps. In 1943 he came to England, and was at first stationed at Bungay. During an off duty moment he went to the Samson and Hercules, a popular dance hall on Tombland in Norwich. There he met Peggy Armes of 144 Bull Close Road in Norwich. Peggy worked in Henry Ash, a women's clothes shop in London Street, where she was trained in dress making. Lieutenant Rowsell invited her out to dinner a few times, took her to the cinema, and went to her home to meet her parents. They liked him a lot. Then he was sent to the USAAF bomber base at Molesworth in Huntingdonshire where he became a radar officer and a captain. After the war he was sent straight back to the United States, but soon returned to Peggy. They married in St Andrews Church in Norwich in June 1946. They flew back to the States where they set up home just outside Salt Lake City. Actually the home was built by Charles himself, after Peggy spotted a piece of land. The house was built of brick and wood, and was to be their home for the rest of his life. They had three children. Charles used his knowledge to set up the County Sheriff's communication system, and then went into the television retail business during the television boom years in North America. He was also heavily involved with a local airline – aeroplanes were always his first love.

Chuck Rowsell, as he was affectionately known to his colleagues in wartime, took 16mm colour film of Norwich in 1944, and it is this

'Chuck' Rowsell and Peggy Armes were married in June 1946 after meeting at the Samson and Hercules dance hall in Norwich in 1943.

film which tells us so much about the damage done in the 1942 air raids. "**Captain Rowsell's Norwich**" has panning shots of half demolished buildings which give little idea of locations as the destruction is so complete. Occasionally on the sky line can be spotted the City Hall clock tower or a church left standing. The cemetery shots already described are quite moving. There are also shots of Norwich carrying on as normal, with streets and vehicles, shops and factories, all going about their daily business. Peggy is seen, as is Chuck himself wearing a flying helmet, posing alongside some of his colleagues. There are scenes of soldiers at Thorpe railway station and around Norwich Cathedral, fire-fighters on exercise, inside Howlett and White's shoe factory in Colegate, and policemen outside the sandbagged City Hall Police Station. This is an 'off duty' film of Norwich, filmed with the love he found in the city.

Alfred Sinfield's film of "**Salute The Soldier**" covers a week of fund raising in the village of Aspley Guise, Bedfordshire between the 3rd and 10th of June in 1944. There is a parade of smartly turned out soldiers, firemen, nurses, scouts, guides, and voluntary organisations. The week continues with sports events, side stalls where games were played to help raise money, a fancy dress competition for children, and amusements such as a Punch and Judy show which Alfred filmed at length in colour.

Towards the end a piece of paper with the amount raised during the week is pasted on a board with a picture of a soldier whose arm raises to a saluting position. "Our Soldier Salutes and thanks you for raising £11,325" says a caption. This was well above the target of £8000, and a tremendous effort in a village with a population of not much more than one thousand.

At Watton in Norfolk in 1944, the Americans from the 3rd Strategic Air Depot put on a Christmas party for children from a local orphanage. The Americans were popular with children, as they had chocolate and chewing gum to give away. In "**Watton Christmas Party**" the children are given a good lunch of roast turkey at a time when food was short. The silent 16mm film was made by Eighth AF Combat Group Camera Unit which operated from London and took a variety of official

*"**Watton Christmas Party**" for orphans in 1944.*

film at various locations, mostly in black and white. As Watton was a photo reconnaissance base at the time, it would not be unusual for a Combat Camera Unit to be there.

The RAF had a royal day in early summer 1943 as seen in "**The King and Queen Visit Methwold**". In this 16mm film a line of airmen are inspected against a backdrop of aeroplanes. This is just before the two squadrons gave up the Lockheed Ventura which was unsuitable for operations over Europe. Also seen is a row of aircraft of 487 Squadron, a New Zealand unit, and those of 464 Squadron which was Australian. This film, taken in an official capacity by James Wright, was shot in colour, and exists in the Imperial War Museum Film and Video Archive. At Great Yarmouth a year later tests were being carried out on dropping lifeboats from the air. Richard Beard, who was based at Coltishall, was involved in the design of these airborne lifeboats which were released from a plane and dropped by parachute. Because of his involvement he was able to take along his 8mm camera and film the trials. Although the film, "**Air Sea Rescue**", is dark in places, the method is seen, as well as personnel, other craft at sea and in the harbour, and inflatable life rafts.

"Greetings Norwich from your boys of the well known Royal Norfolk Regiment in Burma" begins an unusual film in the "Calling Blighty" series. These were films of soldiers in different parts of the world sending home greetings to loved ones. The camera runs almost continuously as men come up in turn and say their bit for their

15 seconds of fame. The location of "**Calling Blighty from Burma**" is outdoors with a bridge in the background, and Captain Horner speaks first saying "I am sure the last thing you expected to see was me on a film. I am very fit and well as we all are, and we are going to keep that way. As you probably know the Regiment has been honoured and privileged of marching through the city with full honours, and we are all very proud of that. We've really got the Japs on the run this time, and we are going to keep it that way till we run them right out of Burma. Well cheerio, I'll being seeing you soon. Now here's Sid Page". Sid wanders into the picture "Hello everybody, as you can see I am looking fit and well, and I hope you are all keeping well. I hope to be seeing you soon. I haven't got much more to say, take care of yourselves and God bless you all. Now here's Ted Newstead. Hello….." and so on, as many more members of the regiment have their say. In "**Calling Blighty India**" the scene is in a café with a piano being played in the background by one of the members of the regiment. The first man comes on unannounced "Hello Mother, I bet you are surprised. I am in the pink as you can see, and I hope you are the same. Cheerio, thanks a lot", followed by a stream of others all saying roughly the same thing. The films must have had a great impact on worried relatives in Norwich who saw these films as part of invited audiences in a cinema in the city in 1944.

During March 1945 "**Preparation For The Rhine Crossing**" was under way, with men loading equipment into 1,348 gliders as part of Operation Varsity. This was for the airborne assault on the east bank of the Rhine, with over 21,000 troops being taken over in gliders, along with hundreds of transport planes. The film, taken at Great Dunmow airfield, shows the men loading the gliders with vehicles, a trailer full of equipment, motor bikes and even bicycles. The bicycles were of the fold up type, so as to take up little space in the glider. Obsolete Stirling bombers and other aircraft towed the gliders.

*Captain Horner sending a message home from Burma in "**Calling Blighty**".*

This was the last big push which led to the ending of the war. Hitler committed suicide on April 30th, and the surrender document was signed on May 7th 1945. Victory in Europe, or VE Day as it was known was celebrated on May 8th with people singing and dancing in the streets, searchlights illuminating buildings and displaying giant V signs in the sky, RAF and USAAF planes dropping coloured flares, and rather a lot of drinking. Nearly every village had hastily arranged parties. In Peterborough an unknown amateur filmed the street celebrations. This film includes the celebrations following the final end of fighting on August 15th, when Japan surrendered. This was Victory in Japan, known as VJ day, and both celebrations are on the same reel in "**Peterborough V E and V J Day**".

Alfred Sinfield's "**Salute The Soldier**" continues with "VE Day" showing in colour, tea being served at tables outdoors in the Square at Aspley Guise, and a bonfire ready with an effigy of Hitler on top. There are shots of "Mount Pleasant children at tea in the garden" and "The Rector and Mrs. Clothier pay a call", showing the Rev Harry Clothier and his wife. The evening celebrations, filmed in black and white, begin with dancing in the streets, an American in uniform being asked "Any gum chum?" followed by a shot of an old fashioned street light with the caption "The village lamp lit up again after five and a half years". Finally people dance around the bonfire.

In August 1945 Victory in Japan was celebrated over a couple of days in Aspley Guise with a tea party in Duke Street and a tea party outside Mrs. Tripp's tobacconists shop in the Square. A title introduces us to "Another tea party in San Remo Road". "May Peace Now Reign Forever" is the final title of this remarkable coverage by Alfred Sinfield of the efforts and celebrations of the people of Aspley Guise.

In May 1945 Major General William Kepner, Commanding General of the Eighth Air Force, was filmed in Norwich City Hall Council Chamber handing over a trust of £20,000 to the Lord Mayor, Mr. E. Williamson. This "**Norwich Memorial Ceremony**" was for the construction of a memorial room within the proposed new Central Library. The room was to be a "shrine that the families …of those gallant men can visit in years to come". It was eighteen years before the new library was completed in Bethel Street, and in June 1963 General Kepner came back to Norwich to dedicate the Memorial Room. The cinema newsreel item "**US Airmen Return**" shows a procession to the new Library building with Colonel Hurt carrying the Roll of Honour. At the library is the memorial fountain with fifty sculptured stones, one for each State. The Bishop of Norwich blessed the Roll of Honour, and dedicated the Memorial Room.

On August 1st 1994, a disastrous fire destroyed most of the Central Library in Norwich, including the Memorial Room. Scenes of that day were recorded in "**Norwich Library Fire**" by Robin Williams of the East Anglian Film Archive. The new Memorial Room is situated in the Forum, a modern building situated in the heart of Norwich next to the City Hall, and opened in 2003.

In September 1945 there was a Thanksgiving Week, which included a fly past by the RAF. In "**Many Salute The Few**", a newsreel item filmed partly at North Weald aerodrome in Essex, Lord Dowding meets officers of the RAF and Douglas Bader climbs into his Spitfire to head a fly past over London. The conflict was now truly over.

Douglas Salmon, a producer at BBC Television in Norwich, made a number of programmes about the Second World War, and some of those made on 16mm film exist, such as "**Finest Hour**". This colour programme of 1975 chronicles the first casualties of the war at Clacton-on-Sea, when a damaged Heinkel carrying a mine crashed on the house of Mr. and Mrs. Gill in Victoria Road, and exploded, killing six people on April 30th 1940. Other stories in the documentary are how Colonel Macrae of Bedford solved the problem of dissolving mine detonators, Derek Johnson of Clacton talking about dummy submarines at Wivenhoe, and Roger Weeley explaining the duties of 'Section D' – a highly secret force working all along the East Coast. Anglia Television also made documentaries of the time, including "**They Did Their Bit**", a film mentioned in the Television chapter, which was produced and directed by David Kenten featuring archive film and local television personality Dick Joice talking to former land girls at a gathering at the Norfolk Rural Life Museum located at Gressenhall in 1982.

VE Day was celebrated in Aspley Guise with this street party.

An Aspley Guise resident holds up a VE Day cake.

The Southwold Railway during the last week of working in 1929.

Transport

The Halesworth to Southwold railway closed to passenger traffic on April 11th 1929, and to goods just over a week later. This was not the first railway to close in the East of England, and it certainly wasn't the last. It was in 1928 that Southwold Corporation allowed passengers to be picked up in the town by motor bus, and the journey to Halesworth was much quicker than the train. "It has been known to complete the journey of nine miles in fifty minutes." says a caption in "**A Railway That is a Real Joke**", an item in a Gaumont Mirror silent cinemagazine of 1929 filmed during the last week of operation of the railway.

The film, already mentioned in the Coast chapter, shows the railway company's four engines, two in working order, *Wenhaston* and *Blyth*, and two laid up at the depot, *Halesworth* and *Southwold*, as they were named. The film's key sequences show a mixed train leaving Southwold station, a rural scene of the line with the train chugging along, an interior view of a crowded carriage with a ticket collector at work, and a slightly comic shot of a signalman pulling down a signal as the train approaches, as in the picture above. At Halesworth, or 'Hailsworth' as it is spelt on the film, passengers disembark, and one of the goods wagons is unloaded. These could not go on to the main line as the Southwold railway gauge was only three foot, so goods and mail bags had to be manually transferred to main line trains.

The Gaumont Mirror film was distributed to cinemas, but James Blyth of the Southwold cinema also filmed a sequence on 35mm of the last train, and attached this to his copy of "**A Railway That is a Real Joke**" to show in the cinema. Both versions exist in the East Anglian Film Archive on

35mm film. The amateur 16mm film "**Transport Scenes**" gives an idea of the amount of vehicles on the road outside Southwold station, for after each car or cart passes, the camera is stopped until another comes along.

Film makers often turned out to record a railway line, its stations and trains, when closure was announced. Of course it was in the 1960s when many small rural branch lines disappeared, and as soon as the notices went up saying "British Railways – Withdrawal of Passenger Services", cameras came out. Chib Thorp, an undertaker from Leigh on Sea, often went on a Saturday or Sunday in the summer months to a favourite branch line, either to travel on the train, or with his wife and dog Mickey in the car, to explore the countryside either side of the track. One line he covered was the Audley End – Saffron Walden – Bartlow line in 1963, a year before it closed. Chib took along his 8mm camera, a good supply of Kodachrome film, and a tape recorder, and made "**How Green Was My Valley**".

The amount of passengers had already decreased, with the result that often it was a single unit rail bus working the line. Chib filmed from the cab the single line ahead, the bridges, passing countryside, and coming into stations. When in his car he would get as near to the line as possible and film the track – usually as a train came along – and flowers, fields and farms. Sometimes he took shots of his wife sitting in the car waiting, or cleaning the car, or walking with the dog. At stations he would take shots of trains coming and going, signal boxes, platforms, and the staff of the railway. When the film was returned from Kodak, Chib would have a magnetic stripe added to the edited film, and on his Kodak projector, which had a recording facility, he would record his comments.

*A ticket collector on the Southwold railway from "**A Railway That is a Real Joke**".*

At Saffron Walden one day he filmed about eight people getting out of the rail bus. "It is a sad day today for driver Barnham, the train has broken down, but he worked wonders, and in no time at all he had hired a coach. But he couldn't understand why I refused to travel in it. I think he thought I was awkward or cracked, or both" says Chib on the sound track. The passengers get into a coach and it drives away. The driver then works on the broken-down unit, goes into the signal box to make a phone call, and then gets the train going again.

On another trip the train comes to Acrow Halt, opened in 1957. "They have their own private platform for employees called Acrow Halt" says Chib as he shows the platform and the factory of this agricultural engineering works. "Beautiful greenery everywhere round here". Then a brief shot from an embankment of his wife "a very patient lady in a deck chair down there". A train comes along "the 12.45 to Ashdon Halt to Saffron Walden". The camera then looks at vapour trails in the sky "somebody up there from the US Airforce base at Wethersfield. If I had known he was going to be in the vicinity, I would have got him to write in the sky 'it's safer by rail".

"On the left is Puddlewharf Farm, and here comes the twin set for Bartlow" as a diesel multiple unit passes by. When a train is filmed going along the line often Chib recorded the actual sound and put this into the final sound track. "Down the straight comes driver Barnham. Just round the bend is Ashdon Halt. What a lovely spot to live". The view is taken out of the front window of the train. Here is the little waiting room, a converted GER six wheel non-corridor railway carriage built in the 1880s. Cows wander down a road, and Frank Smith, a length-man, is seen working on the track. "He told me that for several years past they have gained an award for the well kept line. Coming up to the Bartlow fixed distance signal. Just round the corner is Bartlow Station and George Ogilvie should be there. There he is on the left – service with a smile, and Ron Cornell is helping the passengers in".

At Bartlow the track joined the line from Cambridge to Marks Tey and on to Colchester. A diesel locomotive hauling eight coaches comes through. "here comes the Clacton to Leicester train". Now comes another voice on the sound track. "Ron Cornell speaking. I suppose as a regular guard on the Saffron Walden railway I can claim to know almost everything of this picturesque line. We maintain a very reliable service and it is a strange thing, that if occasionally something does go wrong the producer of this film has a nasty knack of appearing on the scene with his camera. However, he has to watch his step otherwise we might eject him from the train in no uncertain manner. I might add he has not offered me any fee for delivering this brilliant piece of commentary".

"Here comes the Ramblers' Special from Clacton, quickly followed by the regular rail bus" says Chib as the film now comes to an end after 38 minutes. The "**Chib Thorp Collection**" contains many other films he made of rural lines in East Anglia which he used to show to rail enthusiasts groups. He was a friend of Joe Loss, the band leader, and most of Chib's films have Joe Loss background music throughout. In his study at home, lined with shelves of Phillips VCR video tapes (a now obsolete off air video recording system), Chib edited and worked on his 8mm films. The Kodak 8mm projector he used to run his films on and add the sound is now kept in the East Anglian Film Archive.

Over at Aspley Guise in Bedfordshire Alfred Sinfield, a builder, recorded with his 8mm cine camera "**Branch Lines of Yesteryear**", put together in 1962. Filmed in Kodachrome, this silent film looks first at the line from Hitchin to Bedford taken from a train showing stations at Southill and Cardington; then the line from Hatfield to Harpenden East with stations at Ayot and Wheathampstead; the Bedford to Northampton line going trough Turvey, Olney and Piddington; and finally the line from Bedford to Cambridge with shots from the train of stations at Blunham, Potton, Gamlingay, Old North Road, Lord's Bridge and Cambridge itself.

Other railway lines were filmed by enthusiasts. These include the "**Hatfield, Nast Hyde, and Smallford Railway**" that ran to St Albans; The "**Mid Suffolk Light Railway**" which closed in 1952; "**The Buntingford Railway Line**" in 1963; and Mr. Austin's "**Last Train From Narborough**" 1968.

Hemel Hempstead had two stations once, one of which was on what was known as "**The Nicky Line**", but was really the Harpenden and Hemel Hempstead Railway, which closed in 1947 to passengers, but continued to carry goods for many years. The line connected Hemel Hempstead, a few halts and a station at Redbourn, with the Bedford to London line at Harpenden. This short 8mm film was made in September 1958. The abandoned line is now partly a cycle and walking path, though the track bed at Hemel has long since disappeared under new buildings.

When there were mumblings about closing the Saxmundham to Aldeburgh branch from the East Suffolk line, Malcolm Freegard filmed for BBC East "**Railway Closure**", a film insert for a live television programme. A train in Leiston station is the backdrop to an interview by Ted Chamberlain asking what effect the closure will have. Mrs. Purdy raises the question of road safety with increased traffic, and Mr. Stornaway, a publican, points out that even though the early morning and evening trains are almost full, "most of the daytime trains are empty", while another says that the bus service offered in place of the train will take two hours to get to Ipswich where many Leiston people work and study. The Clerk of the Council, Stanley Bond, condemns the closure, and another person stresses that the railways are a nationalised industry offering a service to which the people of Leiston are entitled. The line closed anyway on September 12th 1966, and someone thoughtfully filmed the "**Last Train From Aldeburgh**".

Further along the East Suffolk line, at Beccles, there was a branch that connected to the Norwich to Liverpool Street main line at Tivetshall. This was the "**Waveney Valley Line**". It opened in 1881, but did not last a century. But before it closed to passengers on January 5th 1953, Mr. Knights of Harleston filmed the journey to Beccles with his 8mm camera. The film begins with shots of Harleston streets, Mr. Knight's garage, and the

*The Southend tramway from the LMS publicity film "**Southend on Sea**" 1937.*

The pier railway from the same film showing the old 'toast rack' trains in service in 1937.

railway station and signal box. There is snow on the ground as the train travels through Bungay, Ditchingham and Geldeston to Beccles.

Before 1959 there was a line from Beccles to Yarmouth, and just outside Beccles was a swing bridge over the river Waveney. Trains crawled across this at walking speed with the aid of a pilot man on the locomotive. In 1927 this crossing was updated with the latest swing bridge. A short cinema news item called "**The Swinger**" begins with the sub-title "Nothing to do with clubs, it's a new electrically operated bridge at Beccles, near Lowestoft. Crossing the river Waveney, the bridge is 140ft in length. Just a touch of a few levers and it swings its 300 tons across the river as lightly as a feather". And this is seen in the film, with the signalman pulling a lever, the bridge closing across the river to let a steam hauled train through at fast speed – or at least faster than when the old bridge was there.

In 1934 the London Midland and Scottish (LMS) railway showed its staff a newsreel of its famous locomotive *Royal Scot*. This proved so popular, according to John Reed in his "Moving Images" published in 1990 by Capital Transport, that the company formed a film unit and showed films in a cinema carriage they constructed which travelled around LMS lines. Perhaps it came to Southend in 1937 to show the LMS publicity film "**Southend on Sea**". The LMS line from Fenchurch Street to Southend, which the company had acquired in 1912, was six miles shorter than the LNER route via Shenfield. But this was a time of competition between the two big companies, and the film was made to attract visitors to Southend using Fenchurch Street. 'Southend on Sea for Health and Pleasure' was the subtitle for this film, which showed the beach, boating trips, and the amusements - including a water chute, at the Kursaal. A Yorkshire versus Essex cricket match takes place in Chalkwell Park, the Mayor meets the carnival queen, J class yachts sail at sea, and the *Royal Eagle* paddle steamer waits at the end of the pier. The Boulevard tramway and the old pier trains were popular forms of local and fun transport, along with boats on the lake and speed boats at sea – all giving the impression that Southend was indeed the place to have a holiday or a day out.

*A weaver in Norwich from "**LNER Presents East Anglia**" 1937.*

The London and North Eastern Railway (LNER) was also busy attracting visitors to the region, with a publicity film of 1937 titled "**LNER Presents East Anglia**". This shows picture postcard type views from all over Norfolk and Suffolk, with some interesting working scenes, such as Lowestoft fish market, and a thatcher demonstrating his craft. There are the Bede women of Castle Rising coming out for the camera in their traditional cloaks and high hats, and in Elm Hill in Norwich, one of the last of the weavers, Mr. Taylor, working a bobbin winder and Jacquard loom.

During the 1930s the LNER organised exhibitions of locomotives, rolling stock, and associated railway equipment which travelled round to various locations. In May 1939 it came to Norwich, and over the two days, 14,000 people attended. Local amateur film maker Edward le Grice made a short 16mm film "**LNER Railway Exhibition**". The company's biggest, brightest and best locomotives were on show, and those wandering round the exhibits could have a ride in a wheeless truck which was hoisted up in the air by a steam crane, see a demonstration of cutting rails, or watch a diver from Lowestoft harbour go into a huge tank of water. Finally, there is a shot of a normal passenger service leaving Norwich hauled by the steam locomotive *Dominion of Canada*.

On January 1st 1948 all four main companies, the London and North Eastern Railway; the London, Midland and Scottish Railway; the Great Western Railway; and the Southern Railway, were absorbed into British Railways. A year later British Transport Films was set up to make films for showing to customers, for staff training, and for information and transport issues. In 1951 they filmed the "**Whitemoor Marshalling Yard**" at March in Cambridgeshire. Here radio communication was being used in sorting laden wagons for distribution. A railman's voice-over tells how it worked. "A train

London & North Eastern Railway

In Aid of the Norfolk & Norwich Hospital
and Railway Charities

EXHIBITION

AT NORWICH

Saturday & Sunday, May 6th & 7th
1939

AT THORPE STATION GOODS YARD

Which will be specially arranged for the occasion

comes in with say, eighty wagons, all for different destinations. Our job is to shunt all the wagons for the same destination on to the same road, up to a limit of forty thousand a week or so, and we've got some up to the minute equipment to do it with. But the first job is to record the destination of every wagon, and pass it to the controller. He can preset the automatic points to divert the wagons into the correct roads.

"Radio control saves hours a day of expensive engine time, from then on the most difficult thing about gravity shunting is getting the speeds right. The diesel propels the wagons up a hump at a mile an hour or so. Once they reach the summit gravity takes over, the wagons roll off at say fifteen miles an hour, and according to the distance they have to travel, they can be slowed by the retarder. Operating the retarder demands experience and concentration. The weight and speed of every wagon is different and it must be slowed up just enough to bring it to a halt in its proper road. There's no let up once a train's on the move, a wagon every few seconds, and the automatic points sorting them one by one. Delicate loads get special attention. It's important they shouldn't run too fast, but speed can be critical here in lots of ways".

The use of radio for communication between controller and train driver at Whitemoor was not new, for a cinema newsreel item issued in April 1949 explained how it worked. In "**The Wheels Go Round by Radio**" the signalman gives an order and the driver replies – all done without seeing their lips, as the sequence was filmed silent and the sound post synchronised afterwards. The microphones covered most of the men's faces in the shots.

In 1954 British Transport Films made "**East Anglian Holiday**", a colourful travelogue of the Eastern Counties with little reference to railways. The commentary is delivered in a slow deliberate way. "Breckland, fens, and beaches, rivers, and rich countryside, fresh winds, and Broadland reaches, with sky and landscape stretching wide. Explore the features. You will find more curious histories behind.

"The flattest part of this land lies round the Wash, the place of the Fens. Here on top of layers of chalk and clay, came centuries of fine silt, the ages of marsh, swamp, the layers of deadwood and decayed leaves. All these to make this rich black soil – these Fenlands. Where the labour of man could produce the full grain, the plump root, the sweet tasting flesh. Where the skill of man might flower in the fields, and the earth yield its delicate bloom". Trays of strawberries in the bright sunlight and roses growing are the images here, filmed around Upwell according to a signpost by the road. Over this is stirring music by composer Doreen Carwithen, which helps lift the beauty of the landscape.

"The people of this land had no mountains, so they built their own hills to make a foothold for their minds, an Everest to climb into the vault of heaven. They built one in Cambridgeshire, on an island surrounded by marsh, where eels swam and birds nested in the reeds, and they called their mountain Ely". Paul Le Saux, the in-house writer at British Transport Films, wrote the poetic commentary. The film goes on to show Kings Lynn, Yarmouth, Lowestoft fish market, a Southwold fisherman, Norwich market, Flatford, Kersey, Lavenham, the Broads and Breckland – "a place where the trains bringing visitors to Norfolk pass through wild heath and newly planted forests".

"**East Anglian Holiday**" was photographed by Robert Paynter on 16mm Kodachrome, and the film edited by John Legard. The discarded rushes still exist. Technicolor produced 35mm prints and numerous 16mm copies were shown by British Railway staff at clubs, societies, and public meetings, as well as the film being available on loan. Paul Le Saux also wrote the commentary for "**Diesel Train Ride**", a 1959 film about the new diesel multiple units which were spreading across East Anglia.

It was in the autumn of 1955 that the new two coach diesel multiple units arrived for use on branch lines. These had under-slung diesel engines and mechanical transmission. With a one man engine crew, quick turn round times, and little time out of service compared with steam locomotives, these units cut journey times and made train travel attractive – particularly as passengers could see out the front. They were first used on lines from Norwich to Wells and Kings Lynn, but soon appeared on the Norwich to Lowestoft line via Reedham, and

*Leaving King's Lynn. From "**John Betjeman Goes by Train**".*

On the way to Wolferton on the diesel multiple unit (DMU).

the East Suffolk line. "**Diesel Train Ride**" showed how clean and convenient these trains were for passengers. The line from Lowestoft to Ipswich was chosen to film these new diesels multiple units in action, with passengers enjoying comfy seating and unrestricted views out of the windows. On the double line a steam train passes, and near Ipswich there is a shot of a steam train picking up water. The final part of the film, after a slow tracking shot of a gang working on rails at a junction, moves to North Wales, where there is a contrast of scenery from the train window. The film was shot by David Watkin in Eastman Colour, and the 35mm print is stunning even today.

The railway line from King's Lynn to Hunstanton became famous when John Betjeman travelled on a Diesel Multiple Unit from one station to another to make the film "**John Betjeman Goes by Train**". This ten minute film was made as an insert into the BBC East programme "All Along The Line" transmitted on April 17th 1961. The producer, Malcolm Freegard, asked British Railways for permission, which was given on the understanding they could have the film after transmission for promotional purposes. In return, it was agreed that British Transport Films would provide a film crew, thus helping Malcolm's small budget for the programme.

"We're leaving the London line do you see, from King's Lynn to Hunstanton, we're travelling to the sea" says John Betjeman over the opening shots. "I've always wanted to do this on a train, be able to go on one of these country lines just looking at the scenery far better than you could ever see it by car, and point out the things to left and right of us".

View from the cab as the DMU arrives at Wolferton station.

John Betjeman describes the building at Wolferton station.

On arrival at the first station Betjeman says "as soon as you step onto the platform at Wolferton Station you realise that it was built in the time of the railways when no expense was spared. Look at this carstone from a local quarry, a lovely brown colour, little bits of it there, big bits of it there, careful pattern, and a red brick here to contrast". Looking through an arch he spies a "station lantern in Queen Victoria's grandest manner with a crown on top. There are station lanterns like that all over this station. There are no posters on Wolferton station. You will notice the signal box is made to fit in with the cottage to which it's attached". Betjeman crosses the line and goes into the waiting room which has "leaded windows, framed pictures of prizes and things round the walls, a pelargonia on the round table, a patterned carpet, a fireplace – its just like home, and all clean and shining".

The next station is Snettisham where he sits down and admires the country station so different from the last. He notes the hedge with Snettisham cut into it, the seat with GER for Great Eastern Railway in the casting, and a poster saying "Come to Bavaria".

The gleaming diesel multiple unit carries him along, as he comments on the land between the line and the sea "long level land below the North Sea". From the cab Hunstanton station comes into view. "here we are, straight as a die, heading for the terminus. If the diesel goes too fast we shall go right through the barrier, out through the hotel and into the sea". The train brakes screech as it glides into the platform, and Betjeman and passengers get off and go through the barrier. "There's the Green at Hunstanton, just outside the station. A nice outline, except for that concrete lamp standard, and here, the sea. I am glad that there were children on the train; that was right. The train brought the children home from school to the sea, and it has brought me to this bracing, wide, Norfolk coast".

Wolferton Station has had its share of sadness, for it was from here that special trains departed carrying the bodies of King George V in 1936 and King George VI in 1952, funeral trains that are recorded on film in "**Kings Funerals**".

Electrification of the line from Liverpool Street was first envisaged in the 1930s, in fact work began in 1937, but the war put a halt to further work. After 1945 the task of preparing the overhead gantries and wires resumed over the 20¼ miles to Shenfield. This was an extensive undertaking, and it had to be done without interruption to rail traffic. At Romford 2,500 tons of steel supports were hand-cleaned and painted by a small army of men, and loaded on to railway wagons by steam crane. Hollow concrete foundations were prepared, and a travelling crane dropped the steel girders into the holes. The gantries crossing the tracks from one support to another were now put in place, and the catenary and contact wires put up by men working on top of a moving train. The cables then had to be adjusted so that they were in the right place, and this was done by men working aloft amongst the wires. When a train goes underneath, the men get engulfed in smoke.

*John Betjeman arrives at Hunstanton in 1961. From "**John Betjeman Goes By Train**".*

All this work is shown in great detail in "**Overhead Traction Equipment for Railway Electrification**", a film made by the contractors BICC (British Insulated Callendar's Cables) in 1949. This is a remarkable record of the railways at the time, and how they went about the project. Everything was done in such a way that the overhead equipment would last almost forever. Nearly all the work was done by manual labour. Health and safety obviously seemed adequate at the time, but now looks alarming. In one sequence an overhead girder has twisted slightly, and needed replacing. The commentary tells us, as we see it happening, that there is only a half-hour gap between services to do the job. A crane lifts the old gantry away, and swings in a replacement girder. The job is just finished in time before an express thunders through.

The film opens with shots of Liverpool Street station, where steam trains and electric trains are working side by side (filmed after the switch on) with huge amounts of smoke drifting across the platforms. The film goes through each individual process thoroughly of erecting the overhead equipment, and goes on to show insulation gaps, the welding of earth wires to the track, and the checking of the cables with a pantograph. It was on September 26th 1949 when the new suburban electrified services began running from Liverpool Street to Shenfield.

The new electric trains were maintained at Ilford Car Sheds. Brakes were checked regularly, and new brake shoes fitted. These only lasted about a month. Also wheels and doors were examined, cables checked, and axles greased. Every four years a major overhaul took place, when the whole body of the carriage was lifted. The pantograph was removed, compressors checked, and the wheels turned on a large lathe. This is seen in "**Safety Line**", a 1956 film made by students on the Wansfell film course.

The work of electrifying other parts of the network proceeded slowly, and not always in order. In 1956 electrification reached Chelmsford, and wires were put up from Shenfield to Southend. This section of the line, through Billericay, Wickford, Rayleigh, Hockley, and on to Southend Victoria, was opened at the end of 1956. British Transport Films made "**Service for Southend**", a film of the practical work of electrifying the line. Towards the end of the film the commentary states "On the last Friday in 1956, a special steam train stood at Southend-on-Sea Victoria. It had brought distinguished visitors to inaugurate the first electric service between Southend-on-Sea and Liverpool Street. In front of a battery of newsreel cameras the Mayor of Southend welcomed the officials. Newspaper reporters interviewed the driver of the steam locomotive on duty for the last time. Railway staff watched the excitement thinking about new routines and day to day working. And now the service begins. The driver thinks electric trains are easier to handle than steam, simple controls and no fire box. The passengers enjoy the comfort that awaits the businessman and holiday makers in these specially designed all steel coaches". The following Monday, December 31st, 1956, the full electric service through to Liverpool Street began.

The next to have electric trains was the line between Colchester and Walton-on-Naze and Clacton in 1959. Three years later the gap between Chelmsford and Colchester was electrified. Nothing much more happened on the main line until the 1980s, when the rest of the line to Norwich was done. The work involved adjusting the track, rebuilding bridges, laying slab track in Ipswich tunnel, and erecting hundreds of masts and miles of overhead cable. This work was filmed for "**Anglia Electrification**", which included the official opening in 1987 by the Queen Mother who named a reconditioned locomotive *Royal Anglian Regiment*. Actually the Queen Mother said 'Royal Anglican Regiment', but no one seemed to notice.

An unusual film in the East Anglian Film Archive is "**Crash**", a reconstruction of a train disaster on the Norwich to Yarmouth line in 1874. The line, opened in 1844, was single track, and had stations at Brundall, Buckenham, Cantley, Reedham, and Berney Arms. It was the first railway to be constructed in Norfolk, and was also the first to use Cooke and Wheatstone's electric telegraph block working system. "The telegraphing of train progress was in advance of any system in vogue at the time on any other line" said G. P. Neale, in his "Railway Reminiscences". So it is surprising that

*This engraving was published after the head on railway crash near Norwich in 1874. From "**Crash**" 1969.*

AWFUL RAILWAY ACCIDENT

Between Norwich and Brundall, Norfolk.

24 PERSONS KILLED & 70 WOUNDED.

On Thursday, September 10th, one of the most fearful disasters that have happened on any railway in the kingdom for many years occurred on the Great Eastern Railway, at a spot situate between Norwich and Brundall. The sacrifice of life and the amount of bodily suffering caused by it have been very great. By some unaccountable error the down express train from Norwich was allowed to leave that town while the mail train from Great Yarmouth was permitted to come on from Brundall. The trains met at Thorpe, with a terrific crash, and seemed to leap upright against one another, and the carriages were, with the persons in them, smashed up all of a heap.

there was much confusion on Thursday September 10th, 1874, when a mail train waiting at Brundall for Norwich was given the all clear to proceed at 9.25pm. The train standing at Norwich was given permission to leave for Yarmouth a few minutes later. Once the orders were given the trains were on their way towards each other on the single track, and there was nothing anyone could do to stop them. The head-on collision occurred near the rail bridge over the river at Thorpe.

The events that led up to the despatch of the two trains is told in "**Crash**", with the aid of stills, the stations and line in 1968, and two current steam hauled trains. One was filmed on the Bluebell Line in Sussex, the other being the *Flying Scotsman* which visited Norwich during the year the film was made. The trains are used to illustrate how the accident occurred. John Huntley, the film historian, condemned the use of these two locomotives to represent the steam trains of 1874, but the hybrid nature of the representation does help to build up the drama of this terrible accident. The result of the crash is shown with contemporary engravings, with the final shots being a gravestone in Lakenham cemetery.

To see the railways hard at work "**Scottish Express**" gives an idea what was involved running a train from London to Edinburgh. Paul Barralet made this film as a cinema short in 1946. The preparation that the passenger does not see is shown before the train backs into the platform at King's Cross.

The smoke box of the locomotive is swept out, and wheels, rods and bodywork are cleaned by women. The fire is lit with the aid of firelighters; a man comes along to tap the wheels as 'the ring of the hammer conveys the soundness of the wheel'; and the brake mechanism is tested. Tom and Fred, driver and fireman, sign on and look for any notices about the journey. The carriages are washed and polished outside, and vacuum cleaned inside. A shunting engine moves the carriages into the platform, and the main locomotive backed on and attached. At 10.0am the train leaves.

The commentary then asks the question "Does the driver enjoy the journey". Tom, in a voice-over, answers. "Yes, I suppose I do. It's my life. I still remember the great feeling I got when I brought my first express to speed over these tracks and felt the sway of the engine. Passengers don't feel that as one does up here. I did fifteen years hard slogging on local lines before I got my job on a passenger express. So that first run meant a lot to me.

"I remember how I welcomed the sight of Welwyn viaduct, feeling that the uphill drag was over, and we could get down to making up lost time. We were making 70mph average speed. Schedules were still pretty tight, one had to clip seconds off on straight runs. This opening haul up to speed fairly eats the steam. About time we picked up our first re-fill of water. At regular intervals down the line there are water troughs from which we suck up fresh supplies. Along we come, 70 mph, picking up 5,000 gallons in a few seconds hardly losing a drop. Back on the train the attendants are setting up the tables in the dining car. Passengers expect their meals on time just as if they were at home. We take ours from a Billy can. The chefs are busy in the all electric kitchen. Wouldn't my Missus like that cooking outfit?

"We're nearing Peterborough now. I can always tell it by the sharp smell of burnt clay from the brickfields. It is odd how one recognises places by the smell. I could tell some of the places on the line if I was blindfolded. York, Newcastle, they all put something of their own into the air. The passengers don't notice that sort of thing, only the kids who poke their noses out of the window. Fred gets down to a bit of firing. Only a little at a time, that is his motto. Coal in the tender is always kept wet to make it burn longer. Seven tons has to do the trip, and it keeps the dust down and prevents it blowing into our eyes".

Several train lines along the coast were affected by the 1953 floods. The branch line from Wivenhoe to Brightlingsea was closed after flood water washed away part of the track near Brightlingsea itself, and for ten months the town was without its railway. Many people thought that this would be the end of the line, and that it would never re-open again. But it did, and the first train to leave Brightlingsea was filmed by a Colchester enthusiast on December 7th 1953. "**Brightlingsea Railway**" was back in business, as steam locomotive number 46468 left with the head board '*Brightlingsea Thunderbolt*' after the film '*The Titfield Thunderbolt*' which was released in March that year. The footplate crew and station staff are seen, with schoolchildren running around looking at the engine. There is much waving from the windows as the train leaves for Wivenhoe.

The line remained open for another ten years, then on June 15th 1964, it closed for ever. But just before it closed Ken Pilgrim of Brightlingsea went out with his 8mm camera and made a film of a run from Wivenhoe, filming from the cab of a diesel multiple unit. He also shot the unit going over Arlesford Bridge which crossed a tidal creek. Ken called his film "**Sentimental Journey**", and it is a good colour record of the line, as is Michael Gate's film of the "**Cambridge to Mildenhall Railway**". This was filmed in 1959, three years before the line which ran across the Fens through Quy, Bottisham and Fordham and on to Mildenhall, ceased a passenger service.

There once was a line from Great Chesterford to Newmarket, but this closed as early as 1851. The original station building at Newmarket, now demolished and the site covered with houses, stood not far from the present line, and was used until the 1960s as a goods depot, and Mr. Cummings filmed "**Newmarket Railway**" here with his 8mm camera under the title "**British Railways**". Here was one of the last places where horses were used to move goods wagons about, and both Anglia Television and BBC East filmed here just before the horses were retired in 1966.

A line that ran from Yarmouth across Norfolk and through Lincolnshire to Bourne and on to

*The "**Scottish Express**" crosses Welwyn viaduct in Hertfordshire in 1946.*

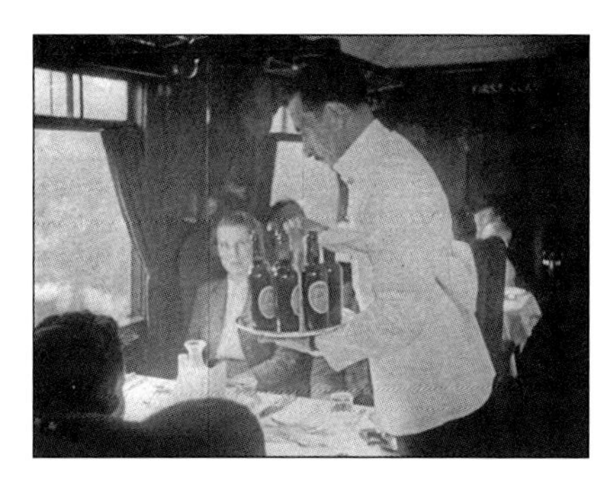

*Passengers on the "**Scottish Express**" are well looked after.*

*On the footplate of "**Scottish Express**" in 1946.*

Melton Mowbray and Leicester closed more or less all at the same time in 1959. This was the Midland and Great Northern Joint Railway (M&GN). A few surviving fragments show this line at work, though very little compared with other railways. An amateur holiday film of 1929 includes "**M&GN Railway**" locomotive shots, and a few turn up in "**Village Scenes**" at Worstead, near North Walsham in 1946. At Sheringham about 1950 someone took scenes of "**M&GN Railway**" locomotives in the station (by now British Railways), and another filmed the "**Last Goods Train From Sheringham**" in 1964. Anglia Television made a programme in 1972 telling the story, mostly with stills and interviews, of the M&GN railway called the "**Muddle and Get Nowhere**", and an amateur film called "**Sheringham Station**" shows the change from working station of British Railways to the preserved line of the North Norfolk Railway.

It wasn't long before the tracks of the M&GN were taken up. John Watson of Lingwood, near Norwich, was an enthusiastic 9.5mm film maker and collector, and he filmed in 1959 the rails being removed near Ormesby, calling his film "**Beware of Trains**". This shows how the contractors went about dismantling the single line track with the aid of a steam locomotive pulling the rails complete with sleepers along to be loaded on a special low wagon – all the time working backwards along the existing track.

In 1959 the Great Eastern Line had 22 *Britannia* class steam locomotives. One of these is seen coming into Chelmsford station in Michael Ham's "**Britannia at Chelmsford**" shot in 1961. Michael was to go on to make dramatic films during the next five years, but this is a sort of apprentice piece, as he tries to weave a story into the train arriving, taking on water, then departing for London.

Eleven miles west of Chelmsford is Chipping Ongar, generally known as just Ongar. The railway first arrived here in 1865, and steam trains continued to run on the line until the late 1950s, when it became electrified as part of London's tube system. Trains ran no faster than 20 miles per hour because of the insufficient electricity supply (no substation built, the power just continued from the main Central line at Epping) and the weathered condition of the track, to the terminus at Ongar. The service was reduced to just morning and evening trains towards the end of its life. There is a brief shot of one of the trains leaving the station early one morning in "**Chipping Ongar**", filmed in July 1994, two months before the line closed down. An earlier film of the line is just called "**8.45 Central to Ongar**", and was filmed on 9.5mm by a train enthusiast.

Some stations on rural branch lines lost not only their staff, but also their buildings. Not so at Reedham on the Norwich to Yarmouth and Lowestoft line. In 1969 the station was converted into an "**Old People's Day Centre**". For some reason this made the national newsreels, and cinemagoers saw the occupants playing cards and having a nice cup of tea. This was an initiative of the Norfolk Old People's Welfare Committee,

Sheringham station closed to passengers in 1964. British Railways provided a terminus on the other side of the road.

*The old M&GN track being taken up near Ormesby in East Norfolk. From "**Beware of Trains**" 1959.*

*Michael Ham's "**Britannia at Chelmsford**", 1961.*

with volunteers providing the help needed. After tea, some participants catch a train home, waving at the camera as they go. Reedham was on the line that was built in 1844 from Norwich to Yarmouth, the first railway in Norfolk. One hundred and fifty years later, in 1994, there was a simple ceremony at Reedham to acknowledge the longevity of the line, and a short film was made called "**150th Railway Celebration**".

The daily life of a station and its staff is recorded in "**Manningtree Station**", a 16mm colour film made in 1979. Manningtree is half-way along the Norwich to London line, where there is a branch to Harwich. There was a signal box with 67 levers to operate the various signals and points, and a level crossing with gates to open and close. The box was manned around the clock by three signalmen working shifts – Danny Holland, John Donnelly and John Crane. During daylight hours there was an additional box lad working from 6.40am to 2.0pm, then another lad working from 2.0pm to 9.40pm. When there were two on duty in the box, one would open and close the level crossing gates - normally the lad. When one person only was on duty, then one of the station staff would deal with the gates.

It was a busy box with lots of train movements as Danny Holland says in the film. "Quite a few pass this box during the day. Trains from London to Norwich, Norwich to London, you've got your Harwich branch trains, boat continentals, goods traffic, freightliners, un-fitted goods, fitted goods, parcel trains, and any light engines that happen to be floating around, and shunting engines as we do shunting in the yard and at Brantham".

At Brantham was Wardle Storey's plastic factory (mentioned in the Industry chapter) where they had their own siding. Dick Polley, one of the shunters at Manningtree, regularly worked trains to and from these sidings. Dick says "Over the past thirty years I have done much of the shunting work at Manningtree, which involves two trips a day to the plastics factory". As he and his colleagues crowd into the cab of diesel shunting engine 08256 and head for the siding he says "It is a matter of shunting the empty wagons out and bringing these back, and placing the loaded coal wagons. Also tanks which contain various types of acids. During that time I must have handled thousands of wagons which the contents must have been hundreds of thousands of tons. I do all the yard shunting at Manningtree, that involves marshalling the wagons up for various stations".

Back at the station Russell Parker describes his daily work. "After the early morning rush is over at 9.30, we go on cleaning duties and then signal lamps. We do ten on a Monday, ten on a Tuesday, eleven on Wednesday, and at Ardleigh there are nine, and at Parsons Heath there is only four. They are paraffin lamps which burn for eight days". The sequence shows the men climbing the semaphore signals and changing over the lamps.

At the time the film was made in 1979 there was a gang permanently based at Manningtree. "At Manningtree we have a mobile gang, which covers an area between Colchester and Bentley, and also a piece down the Harwich branch as far as Mistley. We are chiefly concerned with track maintenance, ditching, embankment work, and some renewal work. We have a gang of twelve men. This morning we are going to adjust rails on the down road, the joints are closed up, the breathing switches are closed up, and we have got to put them back in order to maintain a degree of safety".

Railways continued to attract film makers, whether it be a preserved line, a narrow gauge railway, a special steam run, or the everyday sight of trains at work. Someone filmed the Nene Valley Railway calling their film "**Out and Back**", and another the "**Cardington Miniature Railway**" behind the King's Arms pub. Tony Hare filmed

The mobile gang at Manningtree working on the rails in 1979 between trains.

the "**Cromer Train**", Robin Williams took shots of the opening of the "**Wroxham and Aylsham Bure Valley Railway**", and Christopher Lewis of BBC East got together as many film cameramen as possible in 1978 to man the line from Yarmouth to Liverpool Street for his "**Seven Twelve – Ex Yarmouth**". They filmed this normal early morning daily service at various points along the line, and there was crew on board as well. The completed film was transmitted on October 17th 1978.

Shots in the 1930s of rail and road traffic appear in "**Great Northern Railway and Great North Road**", filmed near Stevenage. The fast trains contrast with the slow moving road vehicles, some of which are steam traction. There are a surprising number of motor buses using the road, as well as cars. The amateur film is taken from one position, possibly an upstairs window, and the camera started whenever something passed. In one shot a train rushes along in the background while two cars use the road in the foreground. One complete shot, that is without the camera stopping, shows three motor lorries, three cars, and a horse and cart. Another shows a steam lorry and trailer, and a light van. The next shot shows a traction engine towing a cultivator, and then, after a camera stop, a road repair team consisting of a steam traction engine, the driver's overnight van, and behind that a water cart, all of which is overtaken by a motor bus while a cyclist travels on the other side of the road. One shot shows a double-decker bus which stops, a man with a limp gets off, is greeted by a dog, and comes to the house where the film maker is. A woman comes out of the house and waves at the camera. This is probably the reason the shots of the traffic were taken – waiting for a friend to arrive by bus.

There was a huge increase in the number of cars on the road in the early 1930s, and many deaths and injuries also. Manufacturers were already aware of the dangers. The safe construction of a Vauxhall car is demonstrated at Luton in July 1928 in the cinema news item "**Fit For Roughest Roads**". The 20hp car is driven to the top of a hill, and deliberately pushed down. It rolls over several times before landing at the bottom the right way up. A man gets in and drives it off. A good advert for the car.

On July, 6th 1929 the poor children of Ipswich were taken out in cars to Glemham Park. This was first organised by the Ipswich and District Motor Cycle Club in 1923, when about four hundred children were given a day out. By 1929, when this annual event was filmed, attendance had increased to 2,400 children, and was said to be the largest of its kind in the country. The youngsters, for whom this was a once a year treat, were taken from the Alderman Road recreation ground to Glemham Park. The 1929 "**Poor Children's Outing**" is a short film showing the decorated cars and children standing beside them waiting to go. It was taken by Harry West who worked for Bostock cinemas, one of his jobs being to operate a clockwork 35mm cine camera which held 100ft of film, about a minute and a half of screen time. He filmed lots of faces, hoping they would come to the cinema to see themselves. The film would have been shown in one of Bostock's cinemas, probably the Lyceum. The "**Poor Children's Outing To Glemham Park**" of 1930 is a very different film, possibly shot by someone else. It is much longer, and we are not restricted just to children at the Ipswich end. Here we see the cars going up the A12, and the festivities in Glemham Park on July 12th. It is said that the convoy included a van filled with lemonade – enough to supply two glasses to every child. The children take part in sports events, including a tug of war and three legged race.

The Lyceum was in Carr Street, Ipswich, and was originally a theatre of over 1000 seats.

*The "**Poor Children's Outing to Glemham Park**" in 1930.*

The front of the building is seen in "**Lyceum Theatre**" with people coming and going, and a woman pushing a pram along the pavement. On Cornhill a man sweeps the road by a van advertising "Remembrance" – the film showing at the Lyceum.

In 1928 Harry West filmed a variety of cars and motor bikes emerging from a gateway in "**Motor Rally**", but because there is no title on the film, the event is unknown. This may well have been one of the events organised by the Ipswich and District Motor Cycle Club. They held speed trials in Shrublands Park, near Barham, in 1928, and Harry West went along with his 35mm cine camera. In "**Shrublands Fete**" the trials take place over a measured quarter mile distance of the main drive. Both motor cars and bikes take part, and speed up the drive amidst clouds of dust.

In Cambridge there was another sort of outing, that of the staff of Eaden Lilley, the big department store. They advertised themselves as 'general linen and woollen drapers, ladies and children's outfitters, silk mercers, costumiers and milliners, carpet warehouse and complete house furnishers, grocers, oil and colour men, hardware and travelling goods merchants'. They had several premises, the main ones being Market Street and Market Passage, and in Sidney Street and Mill Lane. "**Eaden Lilley Staff Outing**" shows the employees leaving for a day trip to Felixstowe. There is a fleet of Varsity buses, and the drivers pose for the camera resplendent in their white coats. This local newsreel was made on 35mm, and probably shown in one of the cinemas in Cambridge.

Another well known Cambridge company was King and Harper. They were 'automobile engineers, and agents and accessories dealers in 6 & 7 Bridge Street, cycle agents at 3a Bridge Street; Thompson's Lane, Milton Road, & Hills Road'. So they could quite easily call themselves "**The Leading Motor Engineers**", and that is exactly what they did on a 1932 advertsing film they had made for showing in local cinemas. This shows

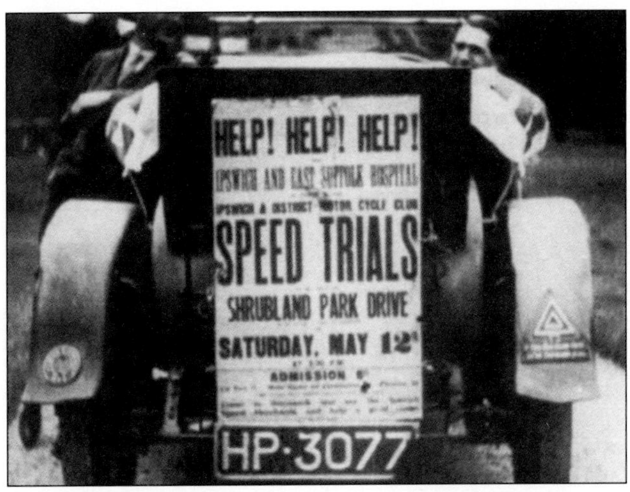

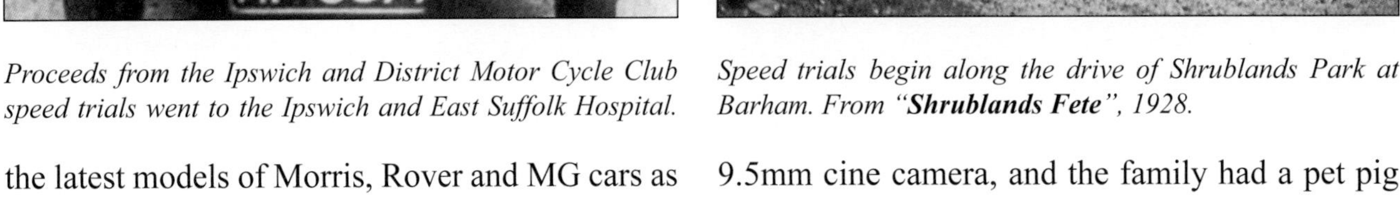

Proceeds from the Ipswich and District Motor Cycle Club speed trials went to the Ipswich and East Suffolk Hospital.

*Speed trials begin along the drive of Shrublands Park at Barham. From "**Shrublands Fete**", 1928.*

the latest models of Morris, Rover and MG cars as well as the motor cycle showroom and a selection of bicycles. After a procession of cars leave the showroom, a woman inspects the latest model, and looks under the bonnet. A man sits in an open MG, and a woman sits in the driver's seat of a Standard car – price £205. A broken down lorry is towed into the garage, and in the workshop men are repairing, welding, and spraying cars.

In 1935 an unknown film maker took "**London Scenes in Dufaycolor**". The traffic consists of buses, motor cycles, and expensive looking cars, all in wonderful colour. This is the year Belisha beacons were put up in Norwich (they were introduced the previous year along with the 30 mile-an-hour speed limit), the LNER ceased using horses for the delivery of goods around the city, and the trams in Norwich were replaced with motor buses. From an upstairs window near Merton Road, Edward Le Grice filmed trams going along Dereham Road. In his "**Jubilee Scenes**" the trams appear to race along the track (the 16mm camera must have been running slow) against a background of newly completed houses and gardens. The jubilee parade through the city shows lots of floats on various vehicles, and one of Norwich's fire engines. Mr. Le Grice also filmed the parade in Dufaycolor in "**Jubilee Parade and Alan Cobham's Air Display**".

In 1934 young Master Copperwheat was eight years old. He was living at 106 Dunstable Street, Ampthill, in Bedfordshire. His father had a 9.5mm cine camera, and the family had a pet pig called Andy. The final necessary item was a small cart. So everything was in place for the young boy to be conveyed by "**Pig Power**". This is the subject of this short but riveting film – a little boy being pulled along in his cart by a pig.

The advertising of cars was becoming big business, especially when they began to market them towards women in the 1930s. Ursula Bloom was a writer, possibly most widely known for her articles in magazines and papers. She is said to have written her first book at seven years old. Ursula Bloom was born in Essex in 1892, moving to St Albans in Hertfordshire just before the First World War. To make some money she played the piano to silent films in a local cinema. She got 30/- (£1.50) for a sixty hour week. She recounted in "Rosemary For Frinton" published in 1970, of how her hands ached playing all day and into the night, thinking 'this can't go on for ever' and longing for the end when she could play the national anthem – 'the most welcome music of the whole day'. She was playing in the cinema when the war began, though soon moved to Walton-on-The-Naze in Essex with her mother who was not well and needed sea air.

In 1916 she married and moved to Frinton, where she ran a house with ten bedrooms complete with a butler and two maids. Her husband died in 1919, and she re-married in 1925. She had always loved reading and writing, and her first book was published in 1924. She went on to write almost 500, some written under pseudonyms.

One of King and Harper's garages in Cambridge.

Working on cars in the garage of King and Harper.

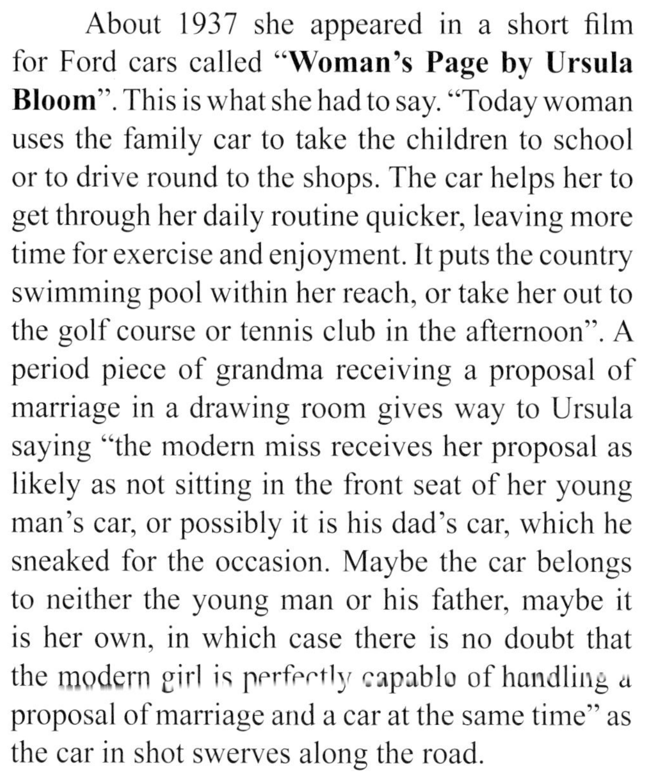

About 1937 she appeared in a short film for Ford cars called "**Woman's Page by Ursula Bloom**". This is what she had to say. "Today woman uses the family car to take the children to school or to drive round to the shops. The car helps her to get through her daily routine quicker, leaving more time for exercise and enjoyment. It puts the country swimming pool within her reach, or take her out to the golf course or tennis club in the afternoon". A period piece of grandma receiving a proposal of marriage in a drawing room gives way to Ursula saying "the modern miss receives her proposal as likely as not sitting in the front seat of her young man's car, or possibly it is his dad's car, which he sneaked for the occasion. Maybe the car belongs to neither the young man or his father, maybe it is her own, in which case there is no doubt that the modern girl is perfectly capable of handling a proposal of marriage and a car at the same time" as the car in shot swerves along the road.

"But since the modern girl has come to spend so much of her young life in a car, a big change has taken place in her outlook. Clothes, hair, dresses, beauty treatment, and personal accessories have all been influenced by the motor car. Styles of hair dressing for instance – windswept, streamlined, this style and that style, all suggest speed in the open air. And yet if your coiffeur is unsuitable for high speed, you can at least have all the air you want in your car if you see that your car is fitted with draughtless ventilation. This is how Ford does it", as the window is wound down to let the cigarette smoke out.

Following another period piece of a woman in a long dress getting into a horse drawn coach, "Present day motoring suggests simpler clothes. It has done more, it has even suggested ideas for pattern design". Beside the new Ford car a woman twirls in a button dress with a V pattern design.

"Most cars today are designed so that women can drive in comfort. See how Ford caters for woman, with foot comfort (a shot of her foot on the brake pedal), ease of control (light handling of the steering wheel), driving comfort (seat adjustment), and lightness of steering" (sharp turning of the steering wheel).

"Motor car manufactures are alive to the fact that woman today has a big share, not only in driving, but also in choosing the car. While man listens to the engine, woman is looking at the appearance, the upholstery, the colour scheme, and all those refinements which delight her in a car. Not forgetting the wide doors which permit

Messrs. Eaden Lilley & Co's employees start from Cambridge for a day out at Felixstowe.

of a graceful exit and entrance. And now let's look at some of the additional accessories you can obtain for your Ford car. Seat covers for filling the craving of the feminine heart for something that can be readily cleaned. A pair of suitcases that fit snugly into the luggage compartment of your Ten. A combined sun visor and vanity mirror so handy either for powdering your nose or keeping it from getting sunburnt. No need to disturb your handbag or exacerbate your husband by using the car mirror. Ash trays, in good looking Bakelite that can be attached to the door or instrument panel of your V8 and emptied in a second. And since it takes a woman to recognise how really important appearance can be, you might like to have a set of these attractive hubcaps and wheel trims, or better still, a pair of really luxurious looking rear mudguard shields for your V8.

"I have been keeping my most precious car possession to the last. Here it is. A radio set, which to while away long waits in traffic jams or to relieve the monotony of a long drive. See how nicely it fits into the instrument panel of the Ford V8 in place of the ash tray. Neat isn't it".

The dangers of cycling without due thought are shown in a 1930s amateur story film "**Approaching Wisbech**". Cycling without thinking what was coming up behind, cycling two or three abreast, or just weaving all over the road, can have disastrous results. This is demonstrated as a party of cyclists are knocked down by a car and lie in the road. Two St John members arrive on the scene. They summon help, and numerous more arrive, and tend to the injured. There is a certain amount of calming and cooling of the injured done by flapping handkerchiefs in front of their faces. The local policeman arrives on his bicycle. A telephone call is put through and the exchange contacts the ambulance. This arrives and one of the injured is stretchered into the ambulance. This is all to show how quickly and efficiently members of the St John Ambulance cope with casualties. The film ends with a 'sheet day', when a large cloth is held up at the side of the road for passing motorists to throw coins into. A flag day in Wisbech completes the film.

In the early years of the war some roads were guarded and some were out of bounds. Others might be busy with convoys of jeeps, trucks, lorries, or tracked vehicles. The government obviously wanted to keep the roads clear for the services, as can be seen in "**Keep The Roads Clear**". This very short cinema information film showed a motor cyclist coming towards the camera. The commentary ran "Today almost every road in Great Britain is vital for war traffic. The approaching despatch rider is carrying an important message – the order for a convoy to move, or final instructions to a unit ready for action. Everything is scheduled to the minute. The despatch must be delivered on time.......". The motor cycle rushes past the camera and there is a loud crash. The camera slowly pans round to reveal the wrecked bike and the rider lying on the road. "But this despatch will not be delivered on time. And what is the result – not only tyres which are vital war material, but men's lives are endangered and the success of an action. And all because of a piece of glass". The camera then shows us a broken bottle, and "Keep The Roads Clear" flashes on the screen to strong music.

In 1946 at the Ford factory at Dagenham the millionth car rolled off the production line, an 8hp Anglia. The cinema newsreels were there to record the occasion and "**Newsreel, 1946**" shows the company chairman, Lord Perry, looking at a long line of cars outside the factory. The commentary emphasises the importance of the export market for these vehicles.

The Cambridge Accident Prevention Council was very active in trying to reduce the number of injuries on the roads. They produced a light hearted film with a serious message in 1947 called "**Wise and Otherwise**", running for 33 minutes. The film begins with Donald Beves and Diana Crutchely playing the parts of husband and wife having a conversation about road safety. Mr. Beves says "Five hundred people are killed on the roads every month. Most accidents are due to carelessness and not taking care for others".

"I bet the most careless ones are mostly men"
"No, I won't have that, don't you forget darling, the female of the species is more deadly than the male"
"Maybe, but not on the roads"
"All right, I take it all back. As a matter of fact I have a theory that carefulness and carelessness runs in families, something like prominent ears or hammer toes. I remember near my old home, there were two families living next door to one another. They were the best of friends but what a contrast they were. There were the Wrights, a very happy family. Very kind and conscientious in the home and out on the roads. There was Mr. Wright, one of those quietly efficient people. His wife to, delightful woman, combined charm and underlying firmness necessary to running a family. I expect that is why their children turned out so sensible and easy to get on with. They took ordinary care and precaution and avoided accidents.

"But the others, what a contrast. Well the kindest thing you could say about Mr. Rong was that he meant well. He might have found life a little more happy if he had got more help from his wife. But she seemed to have a more untidy mind and habits than her husband. And of course the two of them set such an awful example that it was no wonder their children turned out to be a problem. I remember one particular day....."

With Ralph Brown and Gwen Pauley playing Mr. and Mrs. Rong, and Nelson Litchfield and May Wells playing Mr. and Mrs. Wright, the story unfolds of the two families and how they go about their day. The Rongs have trouble getting up in the morning, have a dirty bathroom and untidy kitchen, narrowly miss injury after a razor blade is left stuck to the soap, their son has holes in his socks, and their daughter tumbles down stairs. The Wrights are organised. They meet the postman when he arrives with the letters, they have a neatly laid out breakfast table, and their daughter carefully goes to work on her bicycle. On Mr. Rong's way to work he nearly runs over some pedestrians, drives dangerously, and parks in a No Waiting area.

During the day Mrs. Rong goes shopping with her youngest daughter in Eaden Lilley's department store, and causes mayhem by running out of the shop after her daughter, while Mrs. Wright and her son have afternoon tea upstairs. Mrs. Wright's other daughter attends a lecture on road safety, where on the board are the statistics for 1946. 'Children injured – 41; careless walking – 16; cycling – 19'.

On the way home Miss Rong senior has a lift on the cross bar of her brother's bicycle. Between a car and a bus they fall over and Miss Rong is injured. An ambulance takes her to hospital. Mr. Rong drives hurriedly to the hospital but has an accident on the way. An anxious time for the family as they wait for news of their daughter. "An operation is necessary, and there is nothing they can do but await the result, but the time passes slowly. The Rongs begin to realise that each of them deserves a share of the blame for the accident". The telephone rings, she is going to be all right. The film was directed by K. O. King, and was shot along the roads of Cambridge with some excellent street and traffic scenes that include all forms of vehicles.

Another film produced a year or two later, though running only nine minutes, is in colour. "**Horse Sense**" also shows the streets of Cambridge, with a story about a horse that has run away, a road hog who ignores road safety, and an absent minded professor who walks across the road without thinking. The film shows children all over the place outside the Tivoli cinema in Chesterton Road. K. O. King compares them with sheep, and the picture dissolves from children to a flock of sheep in the road! The point made here is that a dog rounds up sheep, and that a policeman shepherds children across the road. Both films end with the Highway Code booklet. "Study the Highway Code before it is too late"

Road safety films were made and distributed in the 1960s and 1970s by each county. In Suffolk "**How To Cross The Road**", "**It Could be You**", "**Whose Fault Is It Anyway**", "**Skidding**", "**In Dense Traffic**", "**Driving at Night**", and "**Alcohol**" are just a few. Some of these films were bought in, others made locally by film makers such as Boulton Hawker Films of Hadleigh.

At Snetterton, in Norfolk, is a race track converted in 1951 from a wartime airfield.

A racing car at Snetterton in 1967, filmed on 8mm by Bernard Polley for his " ***Guards One Hundred****".*

Bernard Polley of Colchester filmed the European Formula Two Championship at Snetterton on March 24th 1967, calling his film "**Guards One Hundred**". Graham Hill, Dennis Hulme, Bruce McLaren and Jack Brabham took part. Mechanics work on cars, drivers mix with the crowd, and Graham Hill checks his tyres. The race takes place, and the winner signs autographs.

One of the early users of the track was the Eastern Counties Motor Club which was formed the previous year. During the 1950 – 1951 season, Dr. A. Sherlock of Felixstowe made "**E.C.M.C.**", one of many films around the Club. About the same time N. K. Daykin filmed "**Bentwaters Spirit**". The "**Eastern Counties Motor Club**" collection contains 8mm colour films taken by members over the years. Many show regular rallies at Felixstowe, races in the 1960s at Snetterton, and driving tests in Reedham chalk pits.

In the amateur film "**Elm Motor Cycle Races and Garage Business**" motor bikes are seen racing, thought to be at Snetterton, followed by another race meeting at Cadwell Park in Lincolnshire. Here 250cc, 350cc, and 500cc, and sidecar races took place, but the main part of the film is of the garage business of Stan Parsons at Elm near Wisbech. Stan raced a Manx International Norton motor cycle, and in the film his mechanic, Ken Rowe, works on the machine. Stan Parsons' racing career never reached exotic heights, although he was a successful motor cycle dealer and garage owner. The film, taken by Stan and his wife, ends with a shot of the Wisbech and Upwell Tramway, a light railway serving the agricultural community of this part of the Fens. The railway closed to passengers on the last day of December 1927, and goods on May 20th 1966.

Various collections of films include motor cycle events and scrambling. George Bryant of "**Bryant Motor Cycles**" of Biggleswade took films of motor cycle events in the 1930s, and "**Don Harris of Ipswich**" did the same with his 9.5mm camera in the 1950s. The "**Napier Collection**" includes motor cycle films of Bedfordshire, and "**Pathe Pictorial – Motor Cycle Scramble**" shows in colour in 1962 two young boys from Romford being trained by their father to ride round a course at Grays in Essex. The boys are aged eleven and twelve, and wear matching pullovers as they ride round the bumpy course.

"**The Tortoise and the Hare**" shows how to cross the road, filmed in Beckenham, Kent.

'You've all heard the tale
Of the tortoise and the hare,
The tortoise took his time,
But he got there'.

Set to a catchy tune, two boys demonstrate kerb drill. They look right, left and right again, then, when the road is clear, proceed. The final sequence is animated, showing the tortoise taking his time, while a hare rushes across the road and gets squashed!

In the Suffolk County Council Road Safety Films collection there is "**Safe on a Moped**", made in 1976. Scooters had been around since the 1920s, but it was in 1946 that the first Vespa scooter was made. It was a low cost product designed to be comfortable with a certain amount of protection for the driver. In Italian Vespa means 'wasp'.

*The "**The Vespa Club**" meet at Romford Stadium in Essex in 1956.*

*Making last minute adjustments. From "**The Vespa Club**" 1956.*

In Bethnal Green's Oxford House Community Centre in 1956, a group formed a Vespa Club. There was also the South East Essex Vespa Club, and these and others joined in the first 'British National Rally' on May 6th 1956, held at Romford Stadium. Mr. E. R. Howard filmed the occasion with his 8mm camera using Kodachrome film, and produced an interesting record of these machines and their riders in "**The Vespa Club**". This event was organised by the South Essex Branch, which was number 12 of the 76 Vespa Clubs in the British Isles. The scooters arrive, owners lovingly polish their machines, and then the races begin. First there is an obstacle race, with a ramp they have to run up. One scooter falls over and the St John medics are called. Then there is a balloon bursting competition, where the pillion rider equipped with a stick with a pin on the end has to burst a towed balloon. There is an egg and spoon race; a wheel race (the driver has to stop and change a wheel half way through); a lemonade and biscuit race; followed by braking and acceleration tests. The Mayor of Romford is there, watching the goings on.

There were many car clubs whose members enjoyed showing off their prize possessions, and driving or riding them through the East Anglian countryside. One of the oldest was the "**Bugatti Owners Club**" which was formed in 1929. In the 1940s they held a rally at Cambridge. For cyclists there was the Norwich based "**East Anglian Cycling Club**" which had been going since 1921. They organised rides, time trials, and races. One of their members filmed their activities in the 1950s on 8mm colour film. Francis Jacobi filmed his "**Cycle Shop**" in the Norwich Road in Ipswich, Essex Education Committee made "**Mind Your Bike**" in 1953 to show how to look after the machine and ride it in the streets, and "**Car and Cycle Test Crashes**" depicts what can happen when things go wrong.

In "**The Cambridge Story**" made in 1958, Pye claim this was the first place radio taxis were used. As a smart taxi driver, complete with peaked cap, gets into his car and switches on the radio, the commentary says this is "one of the ways in which Pye have affected the life of Cambridge itself, the now familiar radio taxis. This service owes its existence to the ingenuity and foresight of Pye engineers. Now of course radio taxis are becoming commonplace on the streets of many large cities. But they were launched in Cambridge by Pye. What would Erasmus or Herschel or Newton have said of this strange device. Their enquiring minds would have been delighted. They would have noted with satisfaction that Cambridge was still a place where new ideas were thought up, tried out, and made to work".

The residents of Plumberow Avenue in Hockley in Essex set about surfacing their road after the council declined to have anything to do with it. This story made the cinema newsreels in 1965. The women, including 71 year old Mrs. Tibbles, set about shovelling loose material while the men did the cooking and looking after the baby. "It does a woman good to get out of the home" says the commentator in "**Wives Make Road**".

The British Travel Association had "**Light on East Anglia**" made in 1966, a colourful film of picture postcard scenes throughout the region. This was to encourage visitors whether by car or train to places like Newmarket to see horses on the Gallops, to Cambridge to see the colleges and students on bicycles, to Reedham Ferry where cars cross the River Yare, and to Aldeburgh through the Suffolk countryside to see the sea.

In the 1970s Mr. Haggar of Saffron Walden had an 8mm cine camera and filmed things around his town. When the hotel in the Market Place caught fire he recorded scenes in his "**Rose and Crown Fire and Cars**" film. The cars bit refers to his habit of changing his vehicle regularly, and filming the new one as it sat outside his house. A variety of films featuring transport include "**Light Van Operator**", "**Dial-a-Bus**", and "**I am a Mobile Librarian**" from Hertfordshire, and from Bedfordshire "**Dunstable Looks Towards 2000**", which examines the history of the roads around the town, and what needs to be done to cope with the increase of traffic expected in the year 2000. This was made by Cambridge photographer and film maker Mr. Mason Smith. "**Cambridge Planning Film**" shows the streets with cars and bicycles as it was in 1951, a wonderful record of life at the time. Traffic in towns was increasing fast, and towns were becoming congested. In Chelmsford "**Traffic Shots**" were taken at a speeded up rate to assess the amount of vehicles going through the town, and how they behaved, and in Norwich an ambitious road widening scheme of St Stephens, one of the main entries into the city, began. "**Road and Bridge Building Scenes**" includes the Mayor officially opening the redevelopment scheme in 1962. In 1970 "**Streets For Walking**" shows the busy roads in Southend, along with the pollution from exhaust.

We have already seen that road safety films were being made, such as "**Oliver's Lucky Escape**", "**Tyres and Wheels**", and "**Daily Checks**", but a different sort of safety, this time for van drivers, is demonstrated in "**Tale of a Driver**", made by the Road Transport Industry Training Board. Filmed at National Carriers depot at Watford in 1975, this film shows how not to go about your job - by using a fictional character called Fred.

"This is the tale of a driver who worked for a carrying firm – we can't really say worked, for the driver shirked his responsibilities. Fred couldn't get his wife out of bed in the mornings, so he went to work without breakfast. He couldn't be bothered to check his vehicles tyres, oil and water, but failure to do so.....". The van breaks down in a cloud of smoke. The commentary continues in rhyme "The other drivers are ordinary chaps, who do their work without mishaps. Their uniforms are clean and smart, but Fred as usual stands apart"

The film looks at the wrong way to go about delivery and documentation. Fred drives off with

*"**Wives Make Road**" at Hockley in 1965.*

*A petrol station at Cromer, from "**East Anglia Today**", made in 1984.*

*A slip road on the newly opened Ipswich bypass. From "**East Anglia Today**".*

the back open, and at traffic lights while stopped, boys steal parcels from the back of the open lorry. He gets lost and has to reverse at a junction, tries to lift a very heavy parcel, drops the contents of another, and gets in a muddle when the number of parcels does not tie up with his delivery sheets. A number of points are made in a humorous way, which are then emphasised towards the end of the film with captions – Smart Driver, Clean Vehicle, Security of Goods, Handle Carefully, Safe Lifting, Delivery Sheets Signed, Safe Driving, Breakdown Drill, Report Vehicle Defects, and Learn the System. The film ends with "All characters in this film are fictitious and any similarity between 'Fred' and any driver…..is entirely his own fault".

On October 8th 1880, horse drawn trams began running in Ipswich. There is no movie film of these, but the story of transport in Ipswich over a 100 year period is told in "**A Century of Transport – From Horse Bus to Atlantean**". The horse trams ran until 1903, then the 'electric cars' or trams took over. Next came the trolley buses, already described in the Industry chapter. The first trolley buses were one man operated, with passengers paying as they entered. In "**A Century of Transport**" exactly the same thing was happening on Ipswich buses in 1980, with people dropping their coins into a container as they got on.

In 1983 Anglia Television's "**Anglia Reports – Vauxhall Motors**" looked at the state of the car industry with emphasis on the Cavalier being manufactured at Luton. "The success of the new Vauxhall Cavalier, launched in 1981, has brought a new mood of optimism to Vauxhall Motors. Last year it was the fifth highest selling car in Britain, and it became the first of Vauxhall cars to sell more than 100,000 in a year. This year, the Cavalier is selling better than last, and Vauxhall is now capturing between 15% and 17% of the British car market. Yet, it is just four years ago there was a real possibility that the whole operation would fold up. The last four years have been hard times for Vauxhall. In 1979 17,600 people were employed here at Luton, but by this year it has fallen to 11,200. But now, with the dramatic upturn in the sales of Vauxhall Cavaliers, a nightshift is to be reinstated at the Luton plant from August 15th, and that has meant the creation of 400 new jobs. It is the first boom at Vauxhall since the heady days of the 1960s, when the car workers at Luton were held up as being some of the most prosperous blue collar employees in the country"

Sequences of making cars in the factory, aerodynamic smoke tests, and cars on a new motorway are followed by an interview with a dealer who sells them. "We are selling and supplying so many times more cars than we ever dreamt of before, but it seems almost that however many extra cars Vauxhall managed to put on, it only increases demand even further".

In 1984 petrol was £1.80 a gallon, a bypass was being built round Ipswich for the traffic working to and from Felixstowe as seen in "**East Anglia Today**", and the Orwell Bridge was already completed and opened – and filmed by Don Chipperfield. Ten years later it was the

Robin Williams filming bridge construction in 1992 on the Norwich southern bypass.

turn of Norwich to have a southern "**Norwich Bypass**" and Robin Williams of the East Anglian Film Archive filmed this work over a period of time. One section shows the construction of the foundations of the roadway, with the build-up of layers of supporting material for the road surface itself. The film exists un-edited, though one section was made into a finished product. That was "**Building Postwick Viaduct**" across the River Yare. This shows the earthworks necessary and the building of the buttresses either side of the river, the bringing of the bridge sections by barge to the site, and the hydraulic method of lifting the huge spans into place. The film then shows the bridge being completed.

The viaduct, although high, really ended Norwich as a port. In 1982 the small coaster "**Palbro Pride**", though not the last ship to come up here, made its way from Yarmouth to Norwich navigating the winding and at times shallow river. The skipper was Harry Westley, who started life in sailing barges in 1944. The *Palbro Pride*, which was typical of the type of ship which came up to Norwich, had a three man crew. "This ship is owned by J. T. Palmer of Gravesend, and the Sully Freight manager whose main office in Norwich gets the cargoes" says Harry as he negotiates the River Yare. "The reason it takes so long, five and a half hours, is you can't go full speed because you are close to the ground. In the summer there is a lot of pleasure traffic, you have to have your wits about you. And perhaps you may have to wait for the Thorpe Railway Bridge, or the other, Carrow Bridge. You have a time – 1 pm to 2 pm for the road traffic – so it is no good getting there before 2 pm at least". The ship, which had come from Holland has "two hundred and fifty tons of soya bean meal for cattle feed". It turned round in the widest part of the Wensum just short of Foundry Bridge in the city, and tied up opposite the riverside works of Boulton and Paul. This was the quay where ships came and went on a regular basis at one time, and scenes of commercial shipping appear briefly in "**Autumn Fashions**" and "**A Fine City Norwich**".

Shipping has really been dealt with in the Coast chapter, but some vessels went inland to some extent. At "**Sutton Bridge**" on the River Nene the coaster *Chartsman* negotiates the swing bridge on its way to Wisbech in 1966. In both "**Charted Waters**" and "**Draining The Fens**" barges are used to move bank building materials around the Fens, and in Hertfordshire narrow boats and commercial barges work along a canal in "**Queen of Hearts**", made in 1945. At Ware there was a corn merchant's premises where grain was sacked ready for transport by canal to flour mills. A horse called 'Basket' plods along the tow path hauling a barge. His handler, Timothy, walks by his side. The light commentary goes like this. "The barges go on to their next port of call, and we meet up again with Basket. Timothy's job is pulling his load easily along the tow path whilst his mate steers the heavy craft along the twisting water road. The old canal winds its way through the Queen's county to London, a modern roadway with all the charm of an old setting".

At a lock the bargee attends to opening the gates as the horse nibbles some grass. "As picturesque as the language of the men that travel it, they can, and do, become fluently poetic at the lock gates if another bargee happens to leave one open that ought to be closed. Basket has his elevenses, then the barge comes through. Motor or horse drawn, all the carts cover more or less the same amount of miles each day. Unlike the highroads, all the drivers are matey. The canal is long but mostly narrow, so there is no cutting in, which maybe be just as well, since each can give as good as he gets, and two bargees annoyed with each other sounds very basic English to me, with the accent on the base".

At a horizontal swing bridge across the canal a woman jumps from a narrow boat to open it. "No, the water gypsies are a friendly people. The women doing as much work as the men, rushing ahead to clear the way for their own particular craft. Sometimes the canal flows through the road instead of under it, so the bridge must be swung aside. Undeterred by faster methods, the inland tug pulls steadily through, and the bridge swings to again to link the road". The bridge connects the road up again and a car goes across. A horse munches contentedly in a nose bag. A narrow boat slides into the evening light. "One lonely craft winds her way. Then all is serene and still in the Queen's own county of Herts". Other films about canals are "**Canal Boats**", "**Canal Locks**", and in the "**Thornicroft Collection**" of canal films, "**The Narrow Boatmen**" and the 1945 feature film "**Painted Boats**".

"**Hot Air**" is a film about ballooning, but it begins at Felixstowe where an N. de Groot International lorry arrives and is checked by Brian Ribbons. "A Scania unit and trailer comes off the cross channel ferry at Felixstowe dock. It stops near the depot, just long enough for the driver to hand transit papers to Brian Ribbons. Brian is the UK director of N. De Groot, the international hauliers. A busy man, the transport business is a fast moving one with no time to hang around. So the fellow fits the pattern. He goes like a dynamo. A phone call from Birmingham about an export load, a message from Hull that a shipment is late, a teleprinter message to Rotterdam about

*A Scania lorry belonging to N. de Groot International, at Felixstowe in 1977. From "**Hot Air**".*

tomorrow's movements from Felixstowe. Now he is with a maintenance fitter, inspecting part of the company's fleet of trailers. How does a man like this unwind when not at work? Well, this chap is the owner and pilot of a hot air balloon named 'Contrary Mary', and he takes every opportunity to get airborne".

This 16mm colour sound film is a record of the 'First East Anglian Balloon Meet at Shrubland Park', at Barham, in Suffolk. Made in 1977 by Nigel Lister, the film shows the briefing room where the balloonists get the latest details of weather, navigation hazards, sunset time, and all the necessary information vital for the evenings flight. The balloon's air is heated by propane gas from lightweight bottles that are carried in the basket. The flight endurance is governed by the quantity of gas on board. The bottles are prepared and the balloon is laid out and filled.

*Inflating a balloon, from "**Hot Air**" 1977.*

A balloon lifts off into the Suffolk sky.

*From "**Norwich and District Film Review**" 1922.*

Finishing off a P15 aeroplane in Boulton and Paul's works.

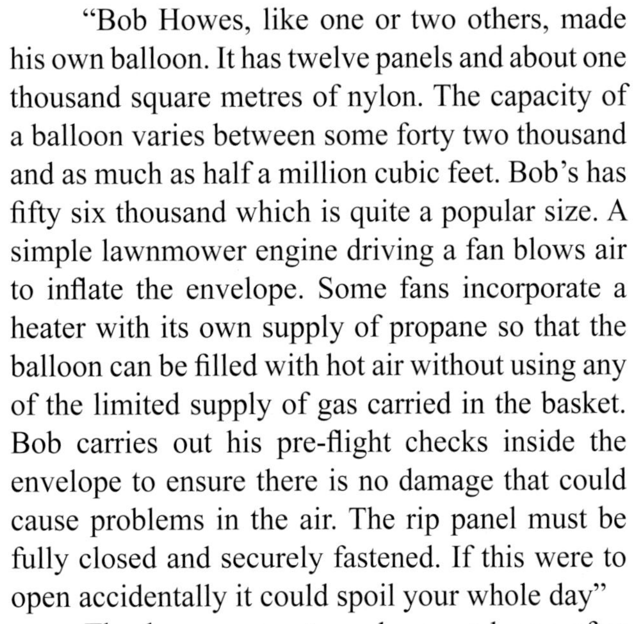

"Bob Howes, like one or two others, made his own balloon. It has twelve panels and about one thousand square metres of nylon. The capacity of a balloon varies between some forty two thousand and as much as half a million cubic feet. Bob's has fifty six thousand which is quite a popular size. A simple lawnmower engine driving a fan blows air to inflate the envelope. Some fans incorporate a heater with its own supply of propane so that the balloon can be filled with hot air without using any of the limited supply of gas carried in the basket. Bob carries out his pre-flight checks inside the envelope to ensure there is no damage that could cause problems in the air. The rip panel must be fully closed and securely fastened. If this were to open accidentally it could spoil your whole day"

The burners are turned on, and one after another the hot air balloons rise into the sky. "As we climb away, we see the others awaiting their turn. Eight are inflated, with two still laid out. One by one they get away, drifting off on a light wind into the setting sun. The balloons sit in the air without any lateral motion of their own, so they go where the wind goes – in other words, they go with the wind"

In late 1922 the Thatched Cinema on All Saints Green in Norwich showed an advertsing film called "**The Norwich and District Film Review**". This began with a shot of a tram descending Guildhall Hill, then women sewing canvas on a Boulton P15 aeroplane in Boulton and Paul's works, followed by a shot of the test pilot, Frank Courtney, standing in front of the machine. This aeroplane was designed to be a bomber, and had a frame of steel. It never went into production, though it was test flown in November 1922.

On February 25th, 1927, the Norfolk and Norwich Aero Club was formed following a flying demonstration at Mousehold Heath, just outside the city. This is where Boulton and Paul had been testing their aircraft since 1915, and it was here in 1927 that the Mayor of Norwich, H. E. Witard, was fitted with flying gear with his chain of office round his neck, a flying hat, and goggles for a flight in a biplane. He climbs into a Boulton and Paul machine, and takes off. "**Norwich – An Airport**?" also shows a variety of aeroplanes taking off and flying, and "**Norwich Airport**" shows the Club's buildings two or three years later, as well as the Club's De Havilland Moth plane taking to the skies. The airfield was officially opened as a municipal airport by the Prince of Wales in June 1933. The Club went on to train pilots and provide flights for the inquisitive. Flying had seized the public's imagination, aviators were household names, and the latest aeroplanes were always an attraction. The world's only three-engine, all metal bomber, the Beardmore Inflexible, flew up from Martlesham Heath in Suffolk to make an appearance at the Aero Club's open day in May 1929. "**The World's Largest Monoplane**" was huge, weighing 15 tons, with 150ft wing span, and people looked small beside the large wheels. It was not a success, and a year later it was dismantled.

The Suffolk Aero Club operated from an airfield at Hadleigh, and in 1928 their "**Easter**

Air Display" was filmed as a local newsreel for showing probably in one of Bostock's cinemas in Ipswich, more than likely the Lyceum. According to the reports more than 5000 people went along on the Monday to see the various aeroplanes displayed; a handicap race with five planes; have a ride in a De Havilland Moth; and watch Miss Sylvia Edwards arrive at the field towing one of the club's Blackburn Bluebird planes. Miss Edwards then unfolded the wings which appear to click into place, and flew off. The club had three Blackburn Bluebirds, the first British side-by-side two seater to go into production.

In 1932 "**Alan Cobham's Flying Circus**" visited an airfield near Brentwood. These aviation days devised by Sir Alan Cobham brought display flying and pleasure flights to the masses for the first time. Between 1932 and 1935 his Flying Circus visited at least twenty four places in East Anglia, often going back again the following year. This particular film was taken at Maylands Aerodrome, which belonged to Hillmans Airways and was situated alongside the A12 towards Harold Wood. The field was officially opened on September 24th 1932, with the 'Great Essex Air Pageant' attended by the Lord Mayor of London and many civic dignitaries. There was a fly past of planes from No 54 Squadron and No 600 Squadron, both based at nearby RAF Hornchurch. There then followed a display with aerobatics and stunt flying with planes swooping low over the crowds. In the sky some are in formation, one loops the loop, and another drops a parachutist. Roger Brighton kindly identified many of the planes in this film. "The three engined biplane was the Air-Speed 'Ferry' named 'Youth of Britain' which the circus took on charge on May 4th 1932. A second plane was delivered in June that year. The stunt plane was an Avro 404K, and the man standing on the wings was Martin Hearn. The De Havilland Tiger Moth was flown by Flight Lieutenant Turner-Hughes. The high winged monoplane was a Comper 'Swift', which was equipped with a radio whereby members of the public would talk to the pilot and request certain aerobatics. The pilot was H. Johnston. The Hillman Airways plane is a De Havilland Puss Moth, of which the company had two".

Alan Cobham's Flying Circus visited Norwich in 1934, and Mr. Le Grice shot some Dufaycolor film of Norwich and the display at Mousehold. Here are more aerobatics and shots taken from one of the aircraft of the countryside below. Sidney Mann of Colchester filmed the "**National Aviation Day**" at Colchester in 1935. Sidney used 9.5mm film to record shots of the display on the grass airfield near Ardleigh.

"**Luton Airport**" was opened on July 16th 1938, and the film shows the aircraft there and in use at the time. A year later at Ipswich the RAF had taken over "**Ipswich Airport**" and moved some planes to the grass site. These were shown off at an open day on July 9th 1939, and a Mr. Barnard filmed in colour on 16mm various planes lined up, the public looking round the new buildings, and Wellington bombers flying.

Ipswich Airport was the home of Suckling Airways who began flying scheduled services to Manchester and Schipol in Holland in 1986. Don Chipperfield was there with his camera, and sequences exist in the "**Don Chipperfield Collection**"

Ipswich Airport's life was short, for in the 1990s the Council decided that it should close, and the last plane to use the airfield took off in January 1997. The site is now covered with houses.

Southend had had an airfield since the First World War when it was used as a training and defence centre. During the 1939-1945 war it was a fighter station, and in 1948 it became Southend's municipal airport with charter and

A Suckling Airways plane at Ipswich Airport in the 1980s. From the" ***Don Chipperfield Collection***".

scheduled services operated by several companies. In "**Sunshine on Sea**", a 1959 publicity film for Southend, there is a sequence of tourists trouping in a long line to a plane. "And they are just going to pop over to France" says Johnny Morris, the commentator. "From Southend it only takes a half an hour in an aeroplane. It doesn't matter how much you fly, I always think this is the most exciting bit – we're off, we're up – surging away from dear old mother earth. There's no doubt that the airport adds to Southend's happy holiday personality – a touch of gusto, a smack of adventure". The plane soars above and, looking down below, there are lots of small and large aircraft parked all over the airfield. Two other films were made of Southend's Airport – an 8mm film of "**Southend Airport Open Day**" which took place in 1968, and a year later "**Corridor to the Sky**" showing a Vickers Viscount landing, a Bristol Britannia, and a BAC 1-11. The control tower, planes re-fuelling, luggage control, and the general business of running a busy airport are shown in this film made by John Brown and Chris Taylor.

Wattisham in Suffolk is a small village with a big airfield. The USAAF were based here from 1942 to 1946, then the RAF moved back and meteor jets arrived. At this time experiments were being carried out with "**The Martin Baker Ejector Seat**". The first success came on May 20th 1949 when test pilot Joe Lancaster bailed out of an AW52 research plane. The 1953 film not only shows the locality, but the various tests carried out on this life saving apparatus. In June 2003 the company said its ejector seats had saved 7,000 lives. The airfield was still operative in the 1970s, when Concord was the star attraction of the "**Air Display**" in 1972.

"**Wings For The ATC**" was filmed in 1948 by Don Chipperfield at Martlesham Heath airfield, six miles from Ipswich. This colour silent film shows a glider being towed into the air. After a short flight it lands again. Ron Page of Woodbridge saved a film showing the training of a cadet at the Martlesham Heath Gilding School. The commanding Officer at Martlesham was Flight Lieutenant Arthur Price. The cadet, who came from Framlingham College, was trained by the Chief Flying Instructor on a course which started at Easter 1961. It was not long before the cadet went solo. "**Training Cadets at 612 Gliding School**" was made two years before the school closed down. The Martlesham site is now covered with light industry and housing.

The only other films of gliding are "**Eastern Gliding Rally**" and "**Gliding**" made at Swanton Morley in 1962. This shows a Tiger Moth towing a glider into the air. The pilot in the glider was Alfred Warminger, a well known Norwich businessman whose hobby was flying. He took his glider all over the country to pursue his passion for the sport, but kept it between flights at the back of his waste paper business premises in Ber Street, Norwich.

The De Havilland aircraft company built the Comet racer "Grosvenor House" which won the air race to Australia in 1934. This was piloted by Charles W. Scott and Tom Campbell Black, and the aeroplanes took off at dawn at Mildenhall in Suffolk on October 20th. "**The Great Scott**" shows the preparation for the race, with the mechanics tuning up, and the Prince of Wales inspecting the planes. At 6.30am the next day the race began. It took Scott and Black 70 hours and 54 minutes to reach Melbourne. Scott and Black and "Grosvenor House" had won, and claimed the prize of £15,000 given to commemorate the centenary of the city of Melbourne.

The De Havilland Company set up their business at Hatfield in the 1930s, and made many famous commercial and military aeroplanes such as the Mosquito, Comet and Trident. The company went through many transformations over the years, becoming part of Hawker Siddeley in 1960, which in turn merged with others in 1977 to form British Aerospace.

Before British Aerospace closed down in 1992 they donated some of their films to the Hertfordshire Film Archive. The Hertfordshire Film Archive was incorporated into the East Anglian Film Archive in the mid 1990s. The British Aerospace collection includes such titles as "**The Quiet Take Off**", "**Engine Maintenance**", "**Aircraft MK4**", "**Trident**", and "**Lightning Strike**", a film showing this particular aeroplane at Coltishall airfield.

Boulton and Paul of Riverside Works in Norwich listed themselves in the 1920s as "Constructional steel and mechanical

H.M. AIRSHIP R101

A triumph of Engineering

The detail design and construction of framework was carried out in the workshops of

BOULTON & PAUL LTD.

NORWICH

London • Sydney • Johannesburg

Makers of Steel & Timber-framed Buildings, Residences, Bungalows, Stables, Motor Houses, Kennels, Greenhouses, etc., etc.

Engineers, Designers, & makers of all-metal aircraft. Makers of 'Electolite' Lighting Plants, 'Boulton' Water Elevators, Power Pumps, etc., etc.

By Appointment

engineers, horticultural builders, manufacturers of portable buildings, iron fence and wire netting manufacturers, pump and petrol engine manufacturers, and designers and makers of all metal aircraft". We have seen that they were building aeroplanes in Norwich in 1922 but they sold off this side of the business in the early 1930s. However, in the mid- 1920s, they were contributing to the British airship industry, which at that time had a promising future. They were entrusted with the detailed design and manufacture of the all metal framework of the R101, as the accompanying 1930 advertisement shows.

However, things did not turn out as planned. In 1930 Bedfordshire was at the centre of a national tragedy when the Cardington assembled airship R101 crashed at Beauvais in France on her maiden flight. Six years before, the government had launched a new airship programme. Two five million cubic feet capacity of hydrogen airships were to be built, the R100 by a private organisation, the R101 by the government. Even though technical problems of the R101 had never been solved, preparations went hurriedly ahead for her maiden flight to India on October 4th 1930.

The 47 crew were commanded by Flight Lieutenant Herbert Irwin. There were also six VIPs on board including the Secretary of State for Air, Lord Thompson, and the Director of Civil Aviation, Sir Sefton Brancker. The R101 was inflated to the maximum, and loaded with 40 tons of fuel and over 8 tons of water ballast. That evening of Saturday October 4th the R101's engines were warmed up. "**The R101 Story**" shows the giant airship at her mooring mast and men loading stores and generally getting ready. The crew and passengers entered the lift that took them up the mooring mast into the airship. At 6.30, in the face of approaching bad weather, she left Cardington. Almost immediately the over heavy nose dipped and water ballast had to be quickly jettisoned to prevent her hitting the ground. The airship, fully laden, recovered, and was now hopefully on her way to India.

Crossing the channel the airship encountered heavy rain, which could, according to Geoffrey Chamberlain in his "Airships-Cardington", published in 1984, add up to 4 tons weight to the craft. The airship was losing a certain amount of gas through leakage, but all airships suffered from this to a certain extent.

The airship was nearing Beauvais, about 40 miles north of Paris, when she went into a series of dives, and ploughed into the ground. The airship caught fire, and of the 54 people on board, only six survived the inferno. One was the wireless operator, the others were five of the engineers. "**The R101 Story**" shows the burnt out mangled wreckage the next day, and the cortege of coffins at Beauvais to the sound of sombre band playing.

The bodies of the 48 dead were buried in a moving ceremony at Cardington on October 11th. The coffins were carried through the gate of the cemetery, while people walked across the fields from the airfield to the service. The crowds watched silently as the coffins were lowered into the grave. This is seen in the film "**R101 Funeral**", a newsreel with no commentary, just the sounds

Topical Budget newsreel item of October 8th 1925.

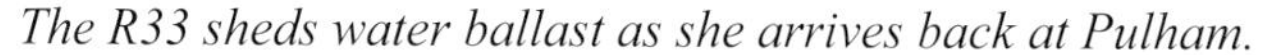
The R33 sheds water ballast as she arrives back at Pulham.

The ground crew helpers guide the R33 airship.

on the day, and the noise of the guns saluting. Today a tomb lists the names of those who died. "Here lie the bodies of 48 Officers and Men who perished in H. M. Airship R101 at Beauvais, France October 5th 1930". The disaster marked the end of the British dream of inter-continental travel by airship.

The government had given the go ahead for civil airship transport in 1924, and teams set to work at Cardington on the design of the R101, enlarging the hangars, and erecting the mooring mast. To obtain technical information, R33, built in 1919, and one of the most successful of these large rigid airships, was brought back into use as a test airship to gain data, knowledge, and further experience. Because the space at Cardington was needed, the R33 was sent to Pulham St Mary in Norfolk, where there was an airship station, in April 1925. Following pressure plotting and other experimental work, the R33 was moored to her mast. On April 16th at 9.50am a gale wrenched the airship from the mast, damaging the front portion. Fortunately there was a small crew on board, who managed to start the engines, so the airship was sort of controllable, but still at the mercy of the wind. She was blown over Lowestoft, and out to sea towards Holland. Eventually the wind moderated, and the airship was able to get back to Pulham 24 hours later. She was put safely away in her hangar, where the damage was repaired.

It took five months to fit a new nose, and at the beginning of October she was ready to fly again. The sun streamed into the hangar as she was revealed to the cinema newsreel cameras. A test flight took her to London and back, returning triumphantly to Pulham where the ground party caught hold of the ropes and returned her safely to her hangar. This is recorded in "**R33's Great Flight**". The mooring mast at Pulham was nothing as elaborate as that at Cardington. At Pulham the crews of airships had to climb a ladder on the outside of the mast. "**Airships as Aerial Airbase**" and "**Airship Stories**" show experiments of launching small aeroplanes and parachuting, the R80's maiden trip, and the visit of the "Norge" from Rome in 1926. This shows how important Pulham was as an airship base at the time.

The R33 safely back in a hangar. From ***"R33's Great Flight"*** *1925.*

"Your Film Show" booklet issued by the Electrical Development Association in October 1959.

*A black and white 405 line television camera in the new BBC Norwich studio in October 1959 from "**Opening of BBC Television News Studio**".*

Television Arrives

From 1959 the great recorder on film of life in the East of England was television. Both BBC East and Anglia Television began broadcasting in 1959, and soon built up a wealth of material of life, events, and happenings in the region. Right from the beginning, the BBC produced a short nightly news programme, and Anglia did also. But Anglia had more facilities, more staff, and more money. They also had a remit to produce a certain amount of local material per week. It took the BBC some time before they could produce opt-out programmes from their Norwich base on a regular basis, and even then, it was nowhere near the output of Anglia.

Television was a live medium, and when location material was required to insert in a studio programme, or a complete programme needed to be made in advance of transmission, the only way to do it was by using motion picture film. Video tape was just appearing in television, but the equipment was expensive, and the cost of the tape beyond most regional programme budgets. Anglia did have some video tape facilities as we shall see, but the BBC did not. So 16mm black and white film was used for news, which produced a negative picture when developed. This was fine for news where speed was essential, as the image could be reversed to a positive picture electronically. For feature programmes where there was more time to prepare the film, positive transmission prints were made.

When colour came in in the late 1960s there were two systems available. Reversal colour film for news, that is the original camera film was processed quickly direct to a positive; and Eastman Colour negative film for feature material. Here the cut negative could be printed to make a clean join-free graded and colour corrected show print for transmission. This latter system took time and involved the London film laboratories.

The two television companies used 16mm film extensively, and built up large libraries. This material could be used for follow-up stories, as stock shots, for repeat showings, or as 'archive' for the future. Unfortunately black and white film was not considered that important once colour had arrived, and much material was discarded. Producers, directors and reporters at the BBC in Norwich did keep some material on which they had worked either in their office or at home, and what survives from the black and white days has come from these sources. When colour came along, the BBC had a more systematic approach to keeping film material, and this now exists in the East Anglian Film Archive. Anglia had an organised film library from the early days, and as time went on this grew considerably. However, from time to time material was weeded out, and the Anglia collection today is only part of what once existed.

St Catherine's Close, Norwich, leased by the BBC in 1956 for local radio programmes, followed by the BBC East Television service which began in 1959.

Anglia began the change over to colour in 1969, but it took another four years before everything from the BBC in Norwich went out in colour. Equipping for colour was only one major task for the local broadcasters in the late 1960s; updating to 625 line quality (from the old 405 line system) also had to be carried out. It is worth looking at the history of the development of local television, especially as many film examples have survived from the BBC and Anglia, along with papers and documents, including a complete run of the Anglia edition of TV Times, which were saved by Jane Alvey for the East Anglian Film Archive.

BBC East

Viewers in the region could pick up the main BBC Television programmes in the early 1950s from a signal from the television transmitter at Sutton Coldfield, in Warwickshire. VHF channels reached a long way, and the route from the Midlands to East Anglia was fairly free from obstructions. Some people might have picked up a signal on channel 11 from London, but it is more likely that channel 4 from Sutton Coldfield provided the pictures. This is how viewers were able to see the Coronation in 1953.

The BBC began transmitting network television pictures for East Anglia from Tacolneston just outside Norwich on February 1st 1955. This was on low power from a temporary mast, for the main transmitter was not ready until October 1956. Now good pictures of BBC programmes were obtainable in the region. These came via Birmingham, and occasionally this centre for the Midlands made a programme on film in the East Anglia region for local viewers.

In 1956 the BBC leased a building in St Catherine's Close, All Saints Green, Norwich for radio work. A weekly magazine programme called "East Anglia Highlights" was broadcast on VHF only for local listeners. Dick Robinson, later to become editor of "Look East", arrived in 1958 to launch a nightly five-minute news bulletin, again on VHF only. Later came a local morning programme for listeners. The BBC were to occupy this building, formerly a tea rooms, and before that the home of Jasper Blaxland, a surgeon at the Norfolk and Norwich Hospital, until September 2003. That is when they moved into the Forum in the centre of the city.

It was in 1959 when television really came to the region. Anglia Television had won the licence to broadcast in East Anglia as part of the Independent Television network, and planned to go on the air in late October that year. The BBC wanted to get in first with a regional programme, so they hastily prepared a television studio in their building in St Catherine's Close. They installed cameras and associated equipment, trained newsreaders, set up a cutting room for film in the attic (incidentally where 25 years earlier the young Christopher Blaxland had a home cinema where he edited and showed his amateur films), installed a simple telecine machine to transfer the film inserts, and arranged for the 16mm film to be developed at Coe's photographic business in Mountergate in Norwich.

On Friday October 2nd 1959, a trailer on film was transmitted telling people they were to get their own BBC local television news programme from Monday, for those living in Norfolk, Suffolk, Cambridgeshire, Huntingdonshire, and the Isle of Ely. So on Monday October 5th, BBC Television from Norwich began transmitting a nightly news programme that was the forerunner of "Look East". At first it was billed in the Radio Times as "Regional News for the Midlands and East Anglia", as there were no separate editions of the Radio Times for these two areas. The programme of about ten minutes had a news-reader in vision, and short 16mm filmed items played in from the telecine machine on cue.

In 1962 the programme was called "East At Six Ten", the words displayed on the screen one above another thus spelling out 'east' vertically. It was renamed "Look East" in 1964 when the programme was lengthened to 20 minutes, and included magazine items, news, and interviews in the studio.

*Geoffrey Harvey in the new BBC television studio in Norwich rehearsing for the start of the nightly ten minute news programme which began on Monday October 5th 1959 from **"Opening of BBC Television News Studio"**.*

Most of the film inserts from 1959 have been lost. One story that has survived in the compilation **"Look East News Stories"** is of a Russian ship at King's Lynn, a rather unusual visitor at the time. Ted Chamberlain, a journalist and reporter for the BBC, and proprietor of a news agency, interviewed the ship's captain who could hardly speak a word of English, only 'yeess', so they have a game of chess instead. Then Ted wishes the captain good luck. At the end of the first full year the small production team, mainly Desmond Cox, the film editor working in the attic, put the film inserts together to produce a **"Review of the Year"** transmitted at the end of 1960.

Soon feature producers were assigned to the station, and opt-out monthly programmes appeared running for 30 minutes. The first feature producer was Gordon Mosley, who specialised in farming programmes, then came Malcolm Freegard who produced general half-hour programmes. These feature programmes were often live from the studio, with film inserts. One series, which Malcolm Freegard produced and directed (and made sure the film inserts survived), was called "**Outlook**". This began with 'The Breck' at the end of 1960, of which only a fragment of film survives, **"Interview with a Warrener"**. This shows local celebrity Dick Bagnall Oakley interviewing George Buck of Great Cressingham who caught rabbits for a living. Dick Bagnall Oakley begins "I haven't seen George Buck since I was stationed on Bodney aerodrome during the war, and then he was doing the job of a rabbiter, but now I have come down to Hopton Farm at Great Cressingham to find him working as an agricultural labourer, so I asked him how the change had come about. "Well I thought I would have a change. I had been doing that job rabbiting on and off, on and off, in one way an another, and I just thought to myself well I don't think rabbiting going to be no more good, but I wish I had stopped on the battle area and then I would have got a staff job like some of the others, but I was in too much of a hurry".

"In those days they farmed rabbits didn't they?"
"Oh Yes"
"Did you get a living out of that could you"?
"Oh yes, a good living, I got a good living out of that, yes, yes".
"Well how many rabbits have you caught in a season?"
"Well the best season I had was 5,600".
"How long is a season?"
"From the middle of September to the latter end of March".
"What do you think about myxomatosis?"
"Well I think it is terrible, and I don't think, speaking to you, and telling the truth, that'll ever get wiped out. That seems to me you get a nice cluster of rabbits, they'll go on for about three weeks to a month, and then that will strike into them all at once. Clean them right out, and I have seen little rabbits about a month old with it. I think it is terrible I do myself".

There had been a rabbit dealer in Cressingham before the war, and about 1950 when myxomatosis killed off large numbers of rabbits, people stopped eating them.

Other stories that have survived include **"Franie Brooks",** one of those local characters who became famous on television for a while, talking in his typical Norfolk accent about clearing out ditches of rubbish around Belton, near Yarmouth.

"Cause us old marshmen, we don't carry no watches or nothing like that. We work so much a rod, or so much a score, and that's how we carry on. We work as long as we can. We know when we have done a day's work, and if we leave off afore we have done a day's work, well we're the sufferer. If that rain, pour, then we always say that's a day for the Queen, and that's the day we have our holiday. That's all we worry about. They say rubbish is a bad enemy, I don't know if rubbish didn't grow I shouldn't have a job, nor wouldn't a lot of people".

At Emneth, near Wisbech, John Seymour, a Suffolk based writer, talks with travellers in **"Gypsy Interviews"** about their life. Most of the men take casual work on the local farms, lifting sugar beet or potatoes. Bob Lamb has been travelling for many years with his horse drawn caravan. He always stays at the same places, so he is known, and does not encounter any hostility. An older member of the group, Mr. Smith, shows off the inside of his caravan. Mrs. Smith explains that there is no oven, and she doesn't need one. When it is suggested she might like to leave the caravan she is most indignant saying she will never live in a house. Mrs. Murkin, whose husband is out at a local farm helping get the carrot harvest in, is alone with her four children. She says she 'just about manages' the travelling life, but would prefer to live in a house. Her children wouldn't though, they want to continue the caravan life, even though it often means putting up with the cold, and walking up to half a mile to get a bucket of water. In the evening they all sit round a fire outside, as John Seymour plays his accordion, concluding this short insight into how the travellers lived and worked in the early 1960s.

In "A Tale To Tell", a live programme broadcast on November 1st 1961, Malcolm injected a little drama into a film insert called "**The Green Dress**". This has children from Whatfield Primary School in Suffolk acting out a story about a jumble sale. The children bring clothes and other things to store away ready for the sale. One girl spots a green dress and announces she is going to buy it. But on the day of the jumble sale another girl gets the dress, and an argument breaks out. After the school holidays, when the children return to school and all is forgotten, everyone is busy preparing for a puppet show, making things out of rags. In the rag bag is the green dress. This story was written by the head teacher, Gwen Dunn. Gwen was no

End of programme caption card.

stranger to writing, having worked on other films and written talks for the BBC. In 1977 she wrote about television and children in "The Box in The Corner – Television and the Under Fives".

Paul Jennings, a writer of humorous articles for the national press, went to Alburgh in Norfolk, to find out why part of this hamlet is called **'Piccadilly Corner'**. Actually he doesn't really find the origin of the name at all, though one old chap does offer a plausible explanation. "I heard a family moved into the cottages opposite from London. The family included two daughters, smart girls they were to, so he said, and their hair-do had a fringe on their forehead, and the village girls, they copied it, they had fringes. And so, no doubt from that, their Piccadilly fringes, came the name Piccadilly Corner".

At King's Lynn in the episode entitled 'Brightfields', the Lynn harbourmaster Captain Nicholson explains the complexities of his job. He oversees the work of a steam tug, the harbour launch, and the Utility Barge, which is used to re-position the buoys which mark the channel. Bad weather, swell and other factors result in the sands moving all the time, and the channel had to be marked for the safety of the shipping. Local knowledge is very important, and "all shipping coming into Lynn has to have a pilot" says Captain Nicholson in "**Interview with Harbourmaster**". Ships anchor up to 15 miles away and wait for a pilot to be brought to them. The pilot scrambles aboard and safely brings the ship into port. On leaving, the pilot takes the ship out, and then has to be picked up and brought home again. For this there are two pilot cutters kept at Lynn. The pilot, who must not be more than forty years old, has to know every shifting sand, every buoy, every hazard that presents itself, particularly in rough weather, pitch black dark, or both.

Others in this 'Outlook' series running to twenty three programmes are "The Two Stages" with a report on amateur dramatics in the theatre in Tower Street, Ipswich, with an interview with an actor manager; "Beside The Seaside" which includes a boat trip on Mr. Earthroll's *Lady Maud* from Felixstowe pier; "Hook, Line and Sinker" with reporter Ralph Tuck talking to anglers taking part in the Henson Memorial Cup competition along the banks of the River Nene, and "The Hateful Thing" a programme about East Anglian legends. In this, John Saltmarsh, a fellow of King's College, Cambridge, talks about how to obtain the **"Witchbone"** of a toad. His story goes that after the toad had been buried in an anthill until all the flesh had rotted away, the bones were then placed in a stream at night, and the bone that floated up-stream was the witchbone. The possession of this bone would then give the horseman power over his horses.

Also in this programme broadcast on April 9th 1961, was the story of "**Black Shuck**", the mysterious and legendary large dog of North Norfolk, told by Tom Starling of Sheringham. "Old Shuck, yes I see him about 30 years ago, and where I see him was coming from Salthouse into Kelling. What a wonderful night it was, I always remember, the moon was at its fullest. In fact I had never seen such a beautiful night. And as I was a pushing the old bike, I hear the rattling of these chains, and I thought, that's nothing, that's just a matter of a horse straying off the marshes. That kept coming nearer and nearer, and I thought I had better stop here, and let it pass. Well, as I got on the corner to let it pass as I thought, it passed me in the shape of a big black shaggy dog. And do you know what, there was a gate dead opposite, and that passed right through this gate. Well, being inquisitive, I thought to myself, I'll see where it had gone.

Malcolm Freegard on the right making final arrangements for a programme from the banks of the River Waveney, a live programme that was never recorded, so is lost forever.

*Tom Starling telling his story of "**Black Shuck**".*

*Tense part of the story of "**Maria Martin**".*

Well, when I got to the gate, that never had been opened. So I said to the villagers the next night when I got there the whole story, and they said 'well that's nothing, that's what they call Black Shuck. He roams these roads pretty frequently, he's been seen many a time'. Well I said I had never seen anything like that before".

The series also tried drama, bringing to life the story of Maria Martin and the Red Barn Murder at Polstead, though with the small budgets of the time, production was not easy. Part of the programme was live, part on film, including the gruesome deed carried out in a Suffolk barn with a very 1960s looking Maria.

"Hidden Treasure", another in the 'Outlook' series transmitted on March 28th 1962, was what Malcolm Freegard, and in this case Ralph Tuck, were good at – getting the best out of people. Tuck interviews some children at **"Fakenham Primary School"** to find out their favourite things and what they have brought in to show their teacher. One girl has brought in a jug which was given to her by an elderly friend who then died, so the jug retains poignant memories for the girl. Another has a piece of coal, because it has interesting patterns, and a boy has a policeman's helmet he found in a hedge. What does a boy have in his pockets? Ralph Tuck finds out when a boy produces, sometimes

*A schoolboy emptying out his pockets for interviewer Ralph Tuck in "**Fakenham Primary School**", a short film insert in a live programme of 1962.*

***"Samphire Picking"** with 'Screw' Palmer, who is walking barefoot through mud on the marshes between Blakeney and Morston on the North Norfolk coast to collect samphire.*

with difficulty, piles of football cards, a matchbox, books, a fossil, numerous badges, a set of playing cards, bicycle clips and part of a bicycle chain. Asked which of these is his favourite he says the army badges, they belonged to his father, and he wants to join the army when he is old enough.

Another of Malcolm's finds was 'Screw' Palmer, who collected samphire from the Blakeney and Morston marshes. This luscious plant, tasting slightly salty, is at its best in July and early August. Samphire can be eaten straight out of the ground if you so wish, or as Mr. Palmer says in his voice-over at the end of the short film called "**Samphire Picking**", "When I get home, I put it in a big bath of water, give it a good wash, then drain it. If you are going to eat it as a vegetable, you just wash it, put it in a saucepan. I like it when it is hot with some vinegar. Other people like it cold. But if you are going to pickle it you wash it well, lay it out, get it right dry. We lay it on a clean sack, get it right dry. When that's dry, that'll take the vinegar a lot better, and that will keep for years."

Malcolm Freegard was fascinated by East Anglia and its people, and tried where possible to get its characters into his films. Malcolm first came to Norfolk from London when the family went on holiday to Sheringham. The next time was in the war, when flying Wellingtons with the RAF he had to ditch 60 miles off Cromer, and was then rescued and brought ashore. He survived many missions, though eventually ending up in Stalag Luft III camp. After the war, and after a spell at Cambridge, he became a master at Greshams School, near Holt. In 1956 he joined the BBC as a talks producer in London. Of all the radio scripts that came his way, the one he could not put down after reading the first eight words was "The second time I was struck by lightning…" He never mentioned what the rest of the story was about, but always said that that was an opening sentence that hooked the listener straight away.

Malcolm worked on the old 'Tonight' programme, and 'Panorama', then came to work as a producer at Norwich in 1960. He worked as required on the nightly news programme, produced feature programmes for the region including 'Outlook' and 'Eye on The Countryside' series, and occasionally made films for BBC 2 such as

*From **"A Kingdom of My Own"**, the story of John Constable.*

"A Kingdom of My Own" about the life of the Dedham Vale artist John Constable.

In this film readings from Constable's letters and diaries help to build up the story of his career with dramatised sequences that contrast with the tourism and motor traffic of the 1960s. In fact the A12 was being built past Dedham when the film was being made. This was a time of expansion of towns, and one of those selected was Diss in Norfolk. This quiet country town was threatened with an influx of new building and people in a proposed overspill plan, and so Malcolm Freegard thought that a film should be made before this happened. He invited John Betjeman to spend a day walking round Diss to see what he thought. John Betjeman gets off the train and says "Here's the station, where's Diss?" The reason for this is that in those days there were fields between the station and the town, with a ramshackle farm in the middle. You could just about see Diss in the distance. After trying to gain entrance to the Jolly Porters pub outside the station, Betjeman gets into a taxi, and travels to the town, noting that industry close to stations often gives the approach a rough appearance – which was true at Diss then as there was a tar refinery and gas works.

In **"Something About Diss"** John Betjeman explores the town. He looks at the houses, the Mere, the Corn Hall where a corn sale is in progress, and discovers Jacobean relief plaster work in the Greyhound Public House in St Nicolas Street. He goes to the church where he learns about John Skelton, a one time tutor to Henry VIII and

John Betjeman trying the door of the "Jolly Porters" pub next to the station – but no one in.

*John Betjeman spent a day looking around Diss for the film "**Somthing about Diss**".*

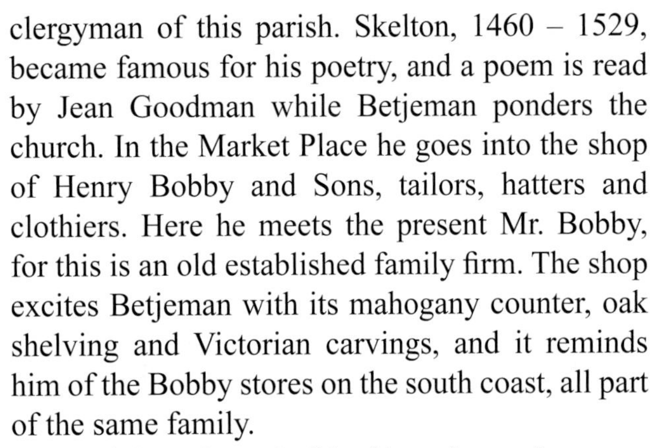

clergyman of this parish. Skelton, 1460 – 1529, became famous for his poetry, and a poem is read by Jean Goodman while Betjeman ponders the church. In the Market Place he goes into the shop of Henry Bobby and Sons, tailors, hatters and clothiers. Here he meets the present Mr. Bobby, for this is an old established family firm. The shop excites Betjeman with its mahogany counter, oak shelving and Victorian carvings, and it reminds him of the Bobby stores on the south coast, all part of the same family.

Right at the end of the film, after seeing some dilapidated and disused old buildings, as well as some put up in the 1960's which he compares with Slough, John Betjeman mentions the horror of the impending overspill plan – which in fact never happened. This is a delightful film, mainly because of the way it was made. Malcolm Freegard only had Betjeman for a day, so all the filming was done quickly and with a silent camera. Later, when the film had been edited, John Betjeman viewed it in a London sound studio, where he then read his commentary to the pictures as he saw them on the screen. This gives a very relaxed atmosphere to the film. The only problem was, when completed, the film was not long enough for the half hour opt-out slot. So Malcolm appeared live in the Norwich studio at the beginning of the programme to introduce it, then "**Something About Diss**" was shown. Malcolm liked to tell the story that a review in the paper said how good the film was, except "for the tedium of Mr. Freegard's introduction".

"Midsummer" transmitted on June 26th 1966 in the 'Eye On The Countryside' series, begins with Gwenn Dunn taking her class from Whatfield School out into the countryside to see butterflies and wild flowers, and collect small creatures from a stream for the children to look at in a glass jar. At the Ship Inn at Blaxhall, in Suffolk, traditional singing and step dancing is introduced by chairman Alf 'Wickets' Richardson, and Sam Friend sings 'Jim The Carter's Lad'. Richard Seabrook from Bury St Edmunds demonstrates sheep shearing, and the 127th Agricultural Show at Hadleigh is visited. Finally, at a pond at Little Glemham near Saxmundham, Hugh Barrett, a BBC East presenter, goes hunting in the dark with the Earl of Cranbrook for bats.

Throughout Malcolm's career at Norwich, he was ably assisted by his PA, June Lewis. In 1967, just before Malcolm left the BBC to run the University of East Anglia's Audio Visual Centre, he made **"A Couris Thing"** for BBC 2, a look at English windmills. Some of the mills were still working when this colour film was made, but it is the little asides which make it interesting, such as the carving on a pew of a post mill in All Saints Church at Thornham in Norfolk, and a boss in the cloisters of Norwich cathedral of a mediaeval windmill. The oldest surviving post mill, built in 1636, at Bourne in Cambridgeshire, is shown along with the smock windmill at Drinkstone in Suffolk. The later is owned by Mr. Clover, who demonstrates the canvas covered sails and how the shutters work.

A "Look East" sound crew in the 1960s. The camera is capable of recording sound on a narrow magnetic stripe down the side of the film. The cameraman is A. E. 'Mac' Claridge and the sound recordist is Eric 'Hank' Hancock, later a cameraman himself. On the right is Dick Robinson, who became editor of "Look East" from 1967, taking over from Kenneth Mathews.

The film ends with the enemy of all windmills, fire. All millers dreaded the mill catching fire, so a fire is shown - very obviously a model burning - but it does give the impression of how quickly these mainly wooden buildings could burn.

Most films sequences, particularly for the nightly news programme, were shot silent by BBC or freelance cameramen known as 'stringers'. There was a sound camera crew in the early days with cameraman Fred Viner at first, followed by A. E. 'Mac' Claridge, using a 16mm camera supplied from Alexandra Palace (where BBC News was based at the time), capable of recording sound on a thin magnetic stripe down the side of the film. This was used for all sound interviews. From 1970 sport was covered on a Saturday with 'Weekend Extra' – a short programme which included the local football results as well as a round-up of news.

In the early 1960s, there was a fairly regular opt-out of the main transmissions from London (not every week) on a Wednesday night around 10 pm. There would be programmes from Norwich as already mentioned, and the occasional programme from Birmingham such as "Scan" which "looks at life for the Midlands and East Anglia". An example is **"The Singer and The Song"** which featured two Norfolk folk singers - Harry Cox from Catfield and Sam Larner from Winterton. Harry Cox was born in 1885 at Barton Turf, and went to school until the age of twelve and a half. "I never learnt nothing" he says. "I learnt more when I left". He then worked as a farm labourer and remembers earning 'nine bob' (45p) a week. There was very little money about then as Harry remembers. "No Sunday suits. You were lucky to have a shoe on your feet at all. They were the times, they were". He shows off his

Sam Larner of Winterton, Norfolk.

'dancing doll' as he called it, a home-made doll on a horizontal stick which is held over a short wooden board. With his right hand Harry taps the board making the dolls legs, which are suspended over it, dance, like the men in the pubs of the time he says. He learnt his songs from other people, and from his mother and father, beginning when he was eleven years old.

10.10

PETERBOROUGH, TACOLNESTON
MANNINGTREE

FARMING CLUB

for East Anglia

Club Host, **Gordon Mosley**

IT MAY SURPRISE YOU

A collection of unusual farming stories exchanged with **Henry Teverson**

Film cameraman, John Lawes
Film editor, Desmond Cox
Directed by KEITH CLEMENT

HOLME MOSS
10.10-10.40 *Points North*

Farming Club for Wednesday January 10th 1963.

Sam Larner was born in 1878 and first went to sea in 1892. He did twenty weeks as a cabin boy and earned £5. A large number of Winterton men and boys were employed in the fishing business at that time. The year of 1894 was a bad one for the fishermen, and Sam remembers them making up a song "A penny towards the pot my boys, a penny towards the pot" and going round the village singing for beer money. He tells of bringing in the herring nets, and singing "Windy Old Weather" as they hauled. Sam talks about his life and his favourite songs he learned from the other fishermen when he was young.

Gordon Mosley, the Norwich based producer who first worked in radio, specialised in agricultural matters, and made regular contributions to the schedule with "Farming Club" (beginning January 11th 1962), which he also appeared in, and later "In The Countryside". His monthly farming programmes, which alternated with 'Outlook' at first, were later moved to Sundays at two in the afternoon.

About 1967 a series was introduced called "On Camera", an overall title proposed by Gordon Mosley and approved by John Johnston, the new Regional Television Manager for

Norwich at the time, which embraced any subject put out from Norwich. This became a weekly programme, so more producers were necessary. One was Douglas Salmon, who turned out to be a prolific producer. In 1972 he made a half-hour film called "**The Stanfield Horror**", a story of Victorian murder. It happened at Stanfield Hall, near Wymondham, the residence of Mr. Issac Jermy, the Norwich Recorder.

James Blomfield Rush was the illegitimate child of Miss Mary Blomfield and a 'gentleman of Wymondham'. Mary Blomfield then married a Mr. Rush, and the two year old boy James assumed that surname. As he grew up, he became interested in agriculture, and in 1835, hired a farm at Felmingham for a rent of £110 per year. Then, in 1836, James obtained a twelve-year lease from a Mr. George Preston on the 683 acre Stanfield Hall farm for £500 per year. In 1837 Mr. Preston died, and the Stanfield Hall estate passed to his son, Mr. Issac Preston, who changed his name to Jermy. Issac Jermy wanted the lease re-written, which it was. Rush was now being employed by Jermy as an agent, and when a local farm came on the market which Issac Jermy wanted to buy, he asked Rush to get it for him. Rush went into negotiations and bought Potash Farm – for himself. He then asked Jermy to lend him the money to pay for it. The bad feelings that ensued between the two men obviously got worse as Rush got deeper into debt.

On the night of Tuesday November 28th 1848, Issac Jermy and his son, blessed with the unimaginative name of Issac Jermy Jermy, and his wife were having dinner. Also at the table was a Miss Jermy, aged fourteen. After they had eaten, they retired to the drawing room. At half past eight Mr. Jermy senior went out of the Hall door for a breath of fresh air, as he usually did at this time. After a short time he returned, and as he entered the porch, he was shot through the heart, and collapsed on the floor, dying. The assassin, who had been hiding in the porch, then went down the corridor with arms outstretched with a pistol in each hand, passed the butler, who retreated into another room, and then came face to face with Mr. Jermy junior, whom he shot dead. His wife then came running through to see what the commotion was, and was shot in the arm, which later had to be amputated. The maid, Eliza Chestney, came running through to see what was happening, and was shot in the thigh.

The next morning the police arrested James Rush. There followed a lengthy trial, and on April 21st 1849, at noon, James Blomfield Rush was hanged. The execution took place on the bridge of Norwich Castle between the two gates.

Stanfield Hall near Wymondham in Norfolk.

*Another shooting in "**The Stanfield Horror**".*

Douglas Salmon dramatised the story of the Stanfield Hall murders, filming on April 28th 1972, with actors from the Maddermarket Theatre in Norwich, including Billy Wells as Rush. The budget was small - only £200, typical of opt-out programmes at the time. Made in black and white, with linking material from F. R. Buckley, an antiquarian from King's Lynn, this half-hour programme recounting the story is a compelling film to watch.

Douglas Salmon was brought up at Holland-on-Sea, between Clacton and Frinton, and even acted a small part in a film version of "**War of The Worlds**" made by the local youth club in 1952. He became a journalist, and joined Anglia Television, writing copy for the TV Times and working on Anglia's nightly news programme, About Anglia. In 1961 he left to join the news department of the BBC in London, and then went to the BBC regional station at Southampton. He came back to Norwich as assistant news editor of "Look East", and was made a features producer in 1970. He liked making films about East Anglia's past, and these included two programmes about airships – **"Skyliners"** in 1971, which deals with the history of airships, particularly in East Anglia where there were bases at Pulham in Norfolk, and Cardington in Bedfordshire, and **"Zeppelins"** in 1972 which recounted the raids on the Eastern Counties in

The hanging of James Blomfield Rush at Norwich Castle on Saturday April 21st 1849.

*Ian Masters in 1977 with members of the Theatre Royal Stage School who took part in filming comic sequences for "**Spot On**", a programme for younger viewers which was taken off as it was considered too 'middle class'. The man in the background is Tony Amies, who was cameraman for some of the filming.*

the First World War. He also made a film about the history of Clacton Pier, codenamed "**Number One, North Sea**". This 1972 programme traced the history of the pier, which was very much connected with the Kingsman family who owned and ran the pier between 1922 and 1971. Warren Mitchell talks about his days at this Essex seaside town, where he watched Clacton's own comedian, Clown Bertram, a popular performer who had his own theatre, entertaining children. Warren Mitchell talks warmly of Clacton, where his own career as an actor began.

BBC programmes from Norwich were still being made in black and white at this time, it was another year before they went fully into colour. Douglas Salmon made numerous other programmes, many done in the confines of a small studio in the BBC at Norwich. Live quiz programmes, "**Spot On**" for younger viewers, and "**Generations Apart**", where two people from the same profession were invited into the studio to talk about their lives and work from different times in the 20th century, were just some series Douglas produced.

Perhaps one of the more unusual programmes he made was about a wayward marshman and one time poacher, Mackenzay Thorpe. Known as "**Kenzie, The Wild Goose Man**", he lived at Sutton Bridge, close to the wild expanse of The Wash. In the 1940s, when he was newly married and money was short, he took to poaching. He preferred bad weather, even snow storms: anything that would keep people indoors. Early in the mornings, particularly Monday mornings when the keepers were still asleep after drinking on Sunday nights, was a good time he reckoned. Kenzie says his poaching record was 93 pheasants in one night. He did get caught on occasions, but always quickly gave himself up, handing over the 'bag' and gun, trying to make the best of a bad job. Kenzie kept records of his shooting, an example being January 1943, when he shot 146

"Kenzie, The Wild Goose Man" *outside his marsh home.*

Douglas Salmon (left) gets to grips with the postbag.

widgeon, 25 geese, 43 shelduck, and 11 curlew. He had a houseboat on the marshes which floated on big tides – his second home he calls it. It was fully decorated and furnished. From here he acted as a guide for shooting parties, and entertained a variety of famous people who came to learn from him the ways of the tides and wildlife. Amongst them was Peter Scott, the naturalist; James Robertson Justice, the actor; and Prince Charles, who talked about the gamekeepers at Sandringham, where once Kenzie went poaching – but he kept quiet about that.

"Last year I had the surprise of my life, the visitor was Prince Charles. I got hold of his hand, and shook his hand, and told him I had been following him about since he was so high on television and in different newspapers and books. And I pulled him into the front room where the wife was sitting, and said 'by jove, this is Prince Charles my duck'. 'There you are, I told you so' she said. And there was just a little lull, and Prince Charles says to me 'that's a lovely picture you have hanging over the mantelpiece Kenzie, what are those – mute swans?' I said 'no sir, they are hoopers, I painted that for the wife'. Then he said 'they tell me you can do about 80 different bird calls'. I said 'yes sir, plenty of them'. He said 'I wonder if you could do the old cock pheasant for me'. I said 'oh yes sir, I could. Do you want it in the spring of the year, or when it is standing in the wheat, or do you want it in the freezing loft at night, or do you want it going out of a covey?' He said 'you had better do the lot Kenzie'. I said 'thank you sir, I will do the lot.....".

Kenzie had many talents. He could paint, he had pictures of his beloved pink footed geese around his home and in his houseboat, he made films, and he could imitate the calls of animals. There are long sequences in the film of Kenzie 'calling' animals using his mouth and hands to simulate their sounds. He calls hares and partridges across the fields and dykes of this area which is half marsh and half cultivated land. Kenzie talks engagingly about his life, his love of birds, and, like many poachers turned conservationists, he has a go at people who let their dogs run wild frightening birds when they are trying to rear their young. They have enough problems from rats, weasels, crows, and gulls he says. Kenzie had the knack of finding nests, but always left them alone. He just liked to know the number of eggs, and where the nests were.

Kenzie was in his early sixties and already a celebrity when Douglas Salmon made the film about him. Colin Willock had written a book in 1962 called 'Kenzie, The Wild Goose Man', and he had appeared on Anglia Television as well. This may not be a film Douglas Salmon would have wanted to be remembered for, but it is a record of a man and his ways, a type of character they don't make any more.

When Douglas retired in 1985, a note from Alasdair Milne, Director General of the BBC, arrived saying "I am sure that you will derive great pleasure from knowing that the contribution you have made to the development and expansion of

English Regional Television has been greatly valued. It has been estimated that during your career at both Southampton and Norwich, you have produced around 1200 evening magazine programmes and 350 weekly opt-outs – an achievement of which you can be justly proud".

During the early 1970s, BBC Norwich went into colour. The studio was equipped with EMI colour television cameras, and a colour processing machine for 16mm reversal film was installed in the building. For a short time "Look East" was a mixture of black and white and colour, but by late 1973, everything was in colour.

The local news programme had a variety of 'anchors', including Hugh Barrett (he once did an interview around Steptoe and Sons without ever having seen the programme as he did not have a TV set at home), Ian Masters (who famously showed off a glass bottle with a model in it which he then dropped on the floor) and Stewart White. The very first "Look East" in 1964 was presented by Robert Dougall, the well known national television newsreader who had a home at Walberswick. The director of the nightly news programme at the time was Keith Clement, who suggested the name "Look East" after pressure from Radio Times who wanted a title. As there was already "Look North" in existence, Keith thought why not "Look East". Other directors were John Frost, David Spires, Mike Derby, and Paul Cort-Wright.

Working the 16mm sound camera was A. E. 'Mac' Claridge, with freelance cameramen employed when necessary. These included Peter Doubleday and John Lawes, with stringers in Yarmouth, Lowestoft, King's Lynn, Peterborough, Cambridge, Colchester and Ipswich sending in news and events shot on silent 16mm cameras. Among the reporters were Ted Chamberlain, Tony Scase, Brian Fawcett, Michael Cole, David Cass, Malcolm Allsop, David Richardson, John Myatt, and in 1962 for a couple of years, Martin Bell. David Frost contributed some stories from Cambridge in the early days, and he remembers getting his first ever BBC pay cheque for £2/12/6d. (£2.62p). There had been the occasional cookery item in the evening programme (with Zena Skinner), but it did not take off really until Delia Smith began her television career in Norwich. Jean Goodman did interviews for "Look East" and opt-out programmes such as '**In The Country**'. But she enjoyed making non-news items, particularly meeting people - such as Jill Goodwin who grew the herb "**Woad**" as a hobby at Ashman's Farm, Kelvedon. Jill shows the method of producing the blue wool dye and Jean Goodman watches, fascinated by the enthusiasm of this woman who had been dyeing wool since she was six years old. In 1939 she began spinning to make socks and jerseys for the family, and continued experimenting as her family of seven children grew up. Jill Goodwin became famous

5.55
THE NEWS

6.5
MIDLANDS TODAY
Regional news and topics
•
LOOK EAST
for the latest news and views
from the Eastern Counties
•
followed by
THE WEATHER

September 24th 1964.

*March "**Wheelwright**" Tom James filmed by "Look East" in 1970.*

for her work, even supplying dyed wool samples for the restoration of the Bayeux Tapestry. She wrote "A Dyer's Manual" in 1982, a book which has gone through many reprints.

In 1972 and 1973 Jean Goodman made a series of short films looking at villages throughout the region. The series was an A to Z, and included such places as **"Jaspers Green"** near Braintree in Essex where Dodie Smith, author of 'One Hundred and One Dalmatians' lived, and **"Hemingford"** in Cambridgeshire, where Jean Goodman met local people including Gordon Chambers outside the school, Jane Keane making puppets, Lucy Boston clipping her hedge, Mr. Webb outside the village hall, and the Rev. Don Brown rowing on the river by the church. This was the typical approach, - see and mention as many local residents as possible. Places like - O for **"Orford"** in Suffolk, P for **"Peakirk"** in Northamptonshire, and Q for **"Quidenham"** in Norfolk, were quite easy to find. Think of one for V and you eventually come up with **"Virley"** in Essex. U might be more difficult, but once again Essex has the answer – **"Ugley"**.

This village is between Bishop's Stortford and Saffron Walden. The Women's Institute at Ugley cries out for a joke, and Jean Goodman brings this up with Nancy Tennant while at a WI meeting at her house. "It's a ready made joke for visitors" says Nancy, and people have suggested altering it. "The Ugly Village Women's Institute – we found that very clumsy; some people would like to call it Oogly, and some years ago someone changed the name to Oakley, and we were very pleased when it was changed back to its original name". Jean Goodman also met Mr. and Mrs. Butterworth at their home, Orford House, where Charles I is said to have stayed when he broke his journey between London and Newmarket. Bert Little, who ran the Post Office, remembered that during the war servicemen would come and post a letter to themselves just for the stamp mark, and Mr. Wombwell showed pictures of carts in the olden days when he worked six days a week from five in the morning until 5.30 pm on the farm, all for 14/- (70p) wages. Finally Mrs. Gilby shows off her husband's collection of horse drawn waggons in the barns at Fieldgate Farm.

Jean Goodman seen here with Frederick Ashton, the ballet dancer and choreographer, one of the many celebrities she interviewed.

The films were normally shot silent, with Jean adding her commentary later, though there are some recordings of people talking. How about Z? Well there are no places in the Eastern Counties beginning with Z, so Jean went off to "**Zeebrugge**"!

Producing a half hour programme every night of the week required many people and a lot of skills. Programme meetings began about 9.30, sifting the news as it came in, deploying reporters and cameramen, arranging interviews etc. The running order would constantly change throughout the day, sometimes right up to transmission time. Film from all parts of the region had to be got back to Norwich by car or train, processed, edited, timed and assembled in the evening's film transmission roll.

To take an example of a "Look East" programme, on Tuesday April 3rd 1979, programme Number 3539 included five mute film sequences, which had to have a live commentary spoken as it was transmitted; five sound film sequences, where often the interview sound had been transferred to separate 16mm magnetic sound track so that the reporters commentary and any sound effects could be mixed in making a final smooth sound track; one video tape insert; and slides and captions. The programme link man was Ian Masters, with Rodney Burke reading the news. The mute film was run at the appropriate places as the news was

"LOOK EAST"

EXPECTED RUNNING ORDER

TUESDAY 3RD APRIL 1979

1500-1545: LOOK EAST REHEARSAL
1552.30-1554.40: AFTERNOON NEWS
1600-1700: LOOK EAST REHEARSAL
1700-1730: LINE UP
1738.53-1740.00: LINE UP
1755.05-1820.00: LOOK EAST

LINKMAN: IAN MASTERS
N/READER: RODNEY BURKE

TRAIL

	DM		SYMBOL (N/READER OOV)		
		L/O	NATIONWIDE TITLES		
		1	LINKMAN IN VIS	STUDIO	
		TK	CHILD GYMNASTS 12"	COMMAG FX FILM	
		L/O	NATIONWIDE HEADLINES		
1.	IH	1	LINK TO NEWS	STUDIO	4'00"
		3	NEWS		
		TK	UB PERKINS 21"	MUTE FILM	
		TK	TREES 23"	MUTE FILM	
		TK	200 SHOOTING CONTEST 23"	MUTE FILM	
		TK	100 EXHIBITION 23"	MUTE FILM	
		2,4	CAPTIONS, SLIDES		
2.	MD	1	LINK TO PRISONS 7'01"	STUDIO	3'15"
		VT	BOB + MUTE FILM + MR. DICKENSON (VTR 1600)	VT	
3.	MD	1	LINK TO BUSINESSMAN 5'00"	STUDIO	5'00"
		TK	650 BUSINESSMAN (ROGER OOV)	SEPMAG FILM	
4.	MD	1	LINK TO INDIAN BANKNOTES 3'02"	STUDIO	4'00"
		TK	600 INDIAN BANKNOTES (DUB 1630-COMMAG/SEPMAG FILM + GRAMS)	COMMAG FILM	
5.	BF	1	LINK TO CHILD GYMNASTS 4'26"	STUDIO	4'00"
		TK	CHILD GYMNASTS (JOHN OOV) (DUB 1645)	SEPMAG FILM	
6.	DM	1	LINK TO ANIMAL SANCTUARY J.K.	STUDIO	3'45"
		TK	500 ANIMAL SANCTUARY 3'25"	COMMAG/SEPMAG FILM	
7.		1	LINKMAN GOODNIGHT	STUDIO	1'00"
		4,2	WEATHER (LM OOV)	SLIDE + CAPTION	

GUEST: MR. GEORGE DICKENSON FOR BOB

NO NATIONWIDE INSERTS

*The running order for "**Look East**" No 3539, transmitted on Tuesday April 3rd 1979.*

read. The stories were about a strike at Perkins of Peterborough with 21 seconds of film, some trees that were chopped down in Northampton with 23 seconds of film, the Pioneer Corps training for a shooting championship at Brington near Northampton running for 23 seconds, and an exhibition by Essex University students at Colchester Castle running for 23 seconds.

A story followed about industrial action by prison officers with 31 seconds of mute film with voice-over by Bob Bufton, and 3 minutes of a recorded interview on video tape with Mr. George Dickenson who was a guest in the studio, but recorded earlier. The story is about one hundred and fifty prison officers who had begun industrial action in support of their national pay claim. The men were refusing to work more than five hours overtime. Mr. Dickinson was branch secretary of the Prison Officers Association, and spoke about the dispute at Norwich Prison which caused a 'declaration of a state of emergency'. After a link by Ian Masters, there was a five minute report on film by Roger Maynard about Neville Pedley and his factory at Saffron Walden. Mr. Pedley at first worked eighteen hours a day in a nissen hut, but with help and advice from the Council for Small Industries in Rural Areas, his company making television tables blossomed and "he now has a spacious factory with a turnover of a million pounds a year. Now he wants to help others starting small businesses using his own experiences". Another link, and we are into a three minute film from John Kiddy about Mr. Dick Leeder, a bank manager from St Neots, who collects Indian bank notes.

John Myatt then reports on young gymnasts from Icknield Primary School at Sawston, near Cambridge, where "they have carried off the East of England championship and compete against the top twelve in the nation at Gloucester on Saturday. Lessons are what they are here for, and gymnastics can only take an hour a week out of school time, but keen youngsters like Samantha Cole enjoy having the facilities they can use for as much spare time work as they want to put in. The school has only a couple of dozen girls from which to select its under eleven squad, and even fewer for the under thirteens. Much of its success is due to Alison Hawkins, a former teacher who coaches them, along with husband Forbes, and plenty of volunteer helpers." There follows an interview with Forbes Hawkins and headmaster Gavin Mann. This four and half minute film is followed by Ian Masters link saying "As regular viewers will know, I'm very much a dog lover, so I would be the first to congratulate a Bedfordshire organisation which for the past year has been saving unwanted and lost pets. Despite crippling financial problems, the home at Aspley Guise has survived to celebrate its first anniversary. John Kiddy again". There follows the three and a half minute film with reporter John Kiddy. At the end of this is the local weather. All this had to be carefully planned and timed to fit into the opt-out between 17.55.05 and 18.20.00.

These are everyday reports of events and happenings of life in the region. This is real local history preserved on film for us to see, and rich research material. All the above film inserts exist in the "**BBC East Collection**" kept at the East Anglian Film Archive along with many thousands of others. The stories, on 16mm film, survive from 1976 until film was ousted by the use of video cameras about 1985.

The weekly opt-out really took off with the introduction of **"Weekend"**, a magazine programme introduced by John Mountford and later by Roger Maynard, with a mixture of light items, personalities, regular walks and talks

John Mountford (on the left), the presenter of 'Weekend' with Ted Ellis at Wroxham. ***"Ted Ellis Walk"*** *at Hoveton Broad in 1980 was just one of many this popular naturalist did for "****Weekend****".*

with naturalist Ted Ellis, and of course things happening over the next few days around the region. This was a studio based programme with film inserts, which went out Friday evenings in the 1980s. There were many other factual programmes such as **"Variations"**. Produced by Christopher Lewis, this series looked at the artistic and aesthetic areas of the region and its people, and included beautifully shot and assembled films like **"The Five Burnhams"** about the villages of Burnham Deepdale, Market, Overy Staithe, Thorpe, and Westgate, on the North Norfolk coast. Christopher Lewis made a variety of documentaries during his time in Norwich (he moved on to become executive producer of the 'Antiques Road Show') including **"If There Are Ghosts"** in 1979, which recalled the Americans in the region between 1942 and 1945, using much archive film of the aerodromes and missions. This film was such a success that it was later networked on BBC 2, a sure sign of the quality of production.

Not much was known to the viewer about how programmes were made, but in **"A Day in The Life of Look East"** much was revealed of the behind the scenes organisation. There was one main studio at the BBC in Norwich, as well as production offices, a newsroom, library, video tape machine area, and cutting rooms for film. In **"Look East Film Editing"**, shot in 1985, the last days of 16mm film going through the system is recorded. By1986 virtually everything was on video tape. To preserve **"Look East Review of The Year"** for 1986 the East Anglian Film Archive transferred the tape programme to 35mm film to ensure its longevity, as well as some examples of Paul Baker's **"Day In The Life"** sequences made a few years later. All images were analogue until September 29th 2003, when BBC East moved from St Catherine's Close to the Forum in the centre of Norwich. Here they went digital. Cameramen sent in their video tapes, which were loaded into the server for editors and reporters to work on. Stories are transmitted direct from the server. Although it was supposed to be a tapeless environment, video tape was still being used at the time of writing to 'archive' stories for the future.

Anglia Television

The Anglia sign that introduced many of the local programmes in the black and white days. The full symbol, the complete Knight turning, was used on the more prestigious and networked programmes.

It took just over a year for Independent Television in Britain to become a reality following the Television Act which was given Royal Assent in 1954. On September 22nd 1955, Associated Rediffusion, the first of the commercial companies, began broadcasting to the London area. Five months later, the Midlands had their own ITV station, and in May 1956 Granada Television began transmitting to the North from Manchester, and six months after that, this service was extended to Yorkshire following the building of a transmitter to serve that area. Other companies followed in quick succession – Scottish Television in 1957, Television Wales and West and Southern Television in 1958, and Tyne Tees in January 1959.

It was now the turn of the East of England to have a regional ITV station, and the contract was awarded to Anglia Television by the Independent Television Authority in June 1958.

The group of people brought together by Lord Townshend, a farmer and land owner from Raynham near Fakenham in Norfolk, formed the first board of Directors, with Lord Townshend as chairman. They were Sir Robert Bignold, chairman of Norwich Union; Aubrey Buxton, a passionate lover of the countryside; Sir Peter Greenwell, chairman of Ransomes of Ipswich, and a farmer of Butley in Suffolk; William Copeman, chairman

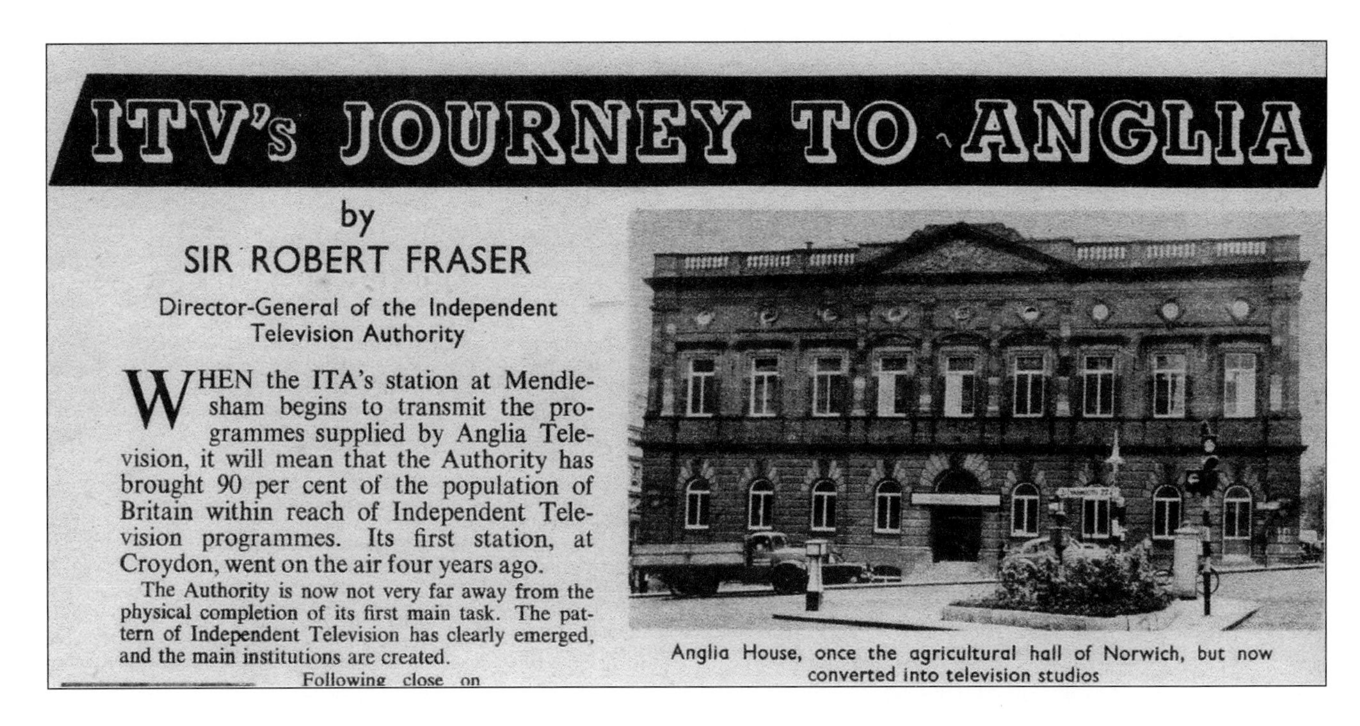
ITV's JOURNEY TO ANGLIA

by

SIR ROBERT FRASER

Director-General of the Independent Television Authority

WHEN the ITA's station at Mendlesham begins to transmit the programmes supplied by Anglia Television, it will mean that the Authority has brought 90 per cent of the population of Britain within reach of Independent Television programmes. Its first station, at Croydon, went on the air four years ago.

The Authority is now not very far away from the physical completion of its first main task. The pattern of Independent Television has clearly emerged, and the main institutions are created.

Following close on

Anglia House, once the agricultural hall of Norwich, but now converted into television studios

The Agricultural Hall in Norwich became the home of Anglia Television in 1959.

of the Norfolk News Co (publishers of the Eastern Daily Press and Eastern Evening News); Laurence Scott, managing director of The Guardian newspaper; John Woolf, chairman of the feature film company, Romulus Films; Donald Albery, head of a London theatre group; Professor Glyn Daniel, Fellow of St John's College Cambridge, and Dr Audrey Richards, Vice Principal of Newnham College in Cambridge. They decided to base their operations in Norwich, and secured a 75 year lease on the Agricultural Hall, a large building used for public events in the city.

This 1882 building was used for a variety of entertainments and events over the years, such as Blondin, the famous tightrope walker balancing on a wire stretched from one balcony to another; the GPO (who had the building next to it on the East side) using it as a temporary sorting office; a roller skating rink; and the ARP (Air Raid Precautions) in wartime. The inside is visible in a 1920 short newsreel film entitled **"Xmas Beef"**, showing cattle and stockmen in the main body of the hall at the regular fatstock shows.

Anglia Television acquired the use of the building from Norwich Corporation, and in 1958, work began on converting it into television studios, offices, and all the necessary rooms and departments needed by a television organisation. At the back, where a canteen was constructed for the yet-to-come staff, a high tower was built. As this was going up local people speculated that this was going to be for a transmission mast, but it turned out to be just a chimney for the heating arrangements.

There was much activity during 1959 getting ready for the opening in October. The new staff were trying to find an appropriate station symbol, and this is in evidence in a short film made by the Perkins Film Unit (Anglia did not at that time have a film unit ready) announcing the coming of the newest of the regional television stations. This 35mm film was made for a special television programme linked up with Eurovision. The film, **"Introduction to Anglia Television"**, opens with a designer going through various ideas for the station symbol. The film also shows the studios under construction, and Stephen McCormack, the first programme controller, introducing himself. But the station symbol did not come easily, and the story goes that Lord Townshend was walking down Bond Street in London and saw in Asprey's window a silver knight on horseback. This was bought to become the station's emblem.

The Anglia Knight is made of sterling silver and weighs over 700 ounces. It was commissioned originally by the King of the Netherlands.

The King was patron of a society called The Falcon Club which met once a year to compete in horse races, falconry and other sports. In 1850 the King felt so confident that he would win the contest that he commissioned a trophy from a London firm of silversmiths. However, to the King's dismay, it was won by an Englishman and brought back to Britain where it remained in the possession of the victor's family until 1959.

Aspreys, the Jewellers and Goldsmiths, was commissioned to make certain modifications – adding the Anglia swallow-tailed pennant to the lance head – and the magnificent trophy became the symbol of Anglia Television from 1959 until 1988.

During the summer and early autumn of 1959, Anglia was busy promoting their forthcoming channel across East Anglia. Over one million leaflets were distributed within two months informing people they should "see their TV dealer and get your set adjusted to receive the new Anglia programmes".

"From October 29th you'll see a wonderful difference to ITV entertainment....clearer, sharper pictures free from interference and easier to watch. You'll see your own exclusive programmes on local news and events. In addition to Anglia's incomparably better picture reception and local interest programmes, you'll see all your favourite shows too. This new and remarkable improvement in television entertainment will be brought direct to your screens from the highest mast in the country, Anglia's powerful new ITV transmitter at Mendlesham".

There were articles in the press and magazines, meetings, and special days when officials and the new presenters of Anglia met the people of the region. A helicopter, with 'Anglia, Your Own ITV' plastered on the side, landed at conspicuous spots. The new outside broadcast unit toured towns and villages, setting up cameras and monitors so that people could see themselves on closed circuit television screens. The purpose of all this was not only to let everyone know Anglia was coming, and to discover local talent, but also to be able to report to the advertisers the number of people likely to watch. It was important to get as many people as possible to have their television

The Anglia Knight.

sets and aerials ready to receive the new channel as the advertising rates depended on the number of viewers. Anglia set up an office in London to sell advertising time, and in Norwich a new advertising agency was born, Willsmore and Tibbenham, in Thorpe Road, specialising in making short advertisements for local clients.

Of any contractor so far appointed, Anglia had one of the largest regions to cover at that time, with the smallest population. It was estimated that there would be two million viewers. Anglia was advertised at first to go on air on October 29th, but this was brought forward to Tuesday October 27th 1959. Everyone in the region was excited by the new ITV channel coming to their region.

A multi channel television set was required to receive both BBC and ITV, so some people had to buy a new television equipped with channel tuning. Anglia was to go out on Channel 11 VHF. The transmitter required to broadcast the 405 line system to Norfolk, Suffolk, Cambridgeshire, and

The actual date of the opening was brought forward to Tuesday October 27th 1959.

Essex, was erected at Mendlesham in Suffolk during the hot summer of 1959. To cover such a large area, the mast had to be tall, and in fact it was the tallest television transmitter in Europe at that time – being 1000 feet high. "The possibility of causing interference to West German viewers in the established service area of the Langenberg station and to French viewers of the Amiens station demanded that the power radiated over a prescribed south easterly arc must not exceed about 15kw" says the ITA leaflet of the time, "Other complications included the need to prevent interference in the service area of Chillerton Down, which uses the same channel, and the need to observe the principle that ITA and BBC stations should not be adjacently sited". So, a mast at Mendlesham, 210ft above sea level, was the answer. A colour 16mm film was made by the contractors of the building of this transmitter titled **"The First 1000ft Television Mast"**. The broadcast area covered was small at first, as the map opposite shows.

There were four studios in Anglia House, Studio A (52ft by 62ft), Studio B (25ft by 41ft), Studio C (18ft by 13ft), and Studio D (9ft by 6ft). The two main studios, A and B, had Pye Mark V television cameras made in Cambridge. There were four telecine machines to transfer 16mm and 35mm film, and an Ampex video tape recorder. Anglia also had an outside broadcast van equipped with two Pye cameras and, unusually for the time, an Ampex video tape recorder within it.

For filming, there was a 16mm sound crew and one silent unit for feature work, and the same again for news. News could also call on 25 freelance cameramen with 16mm silent cameras across the region.

An important part of getting out information about programmes was the TV Times. "TV Times

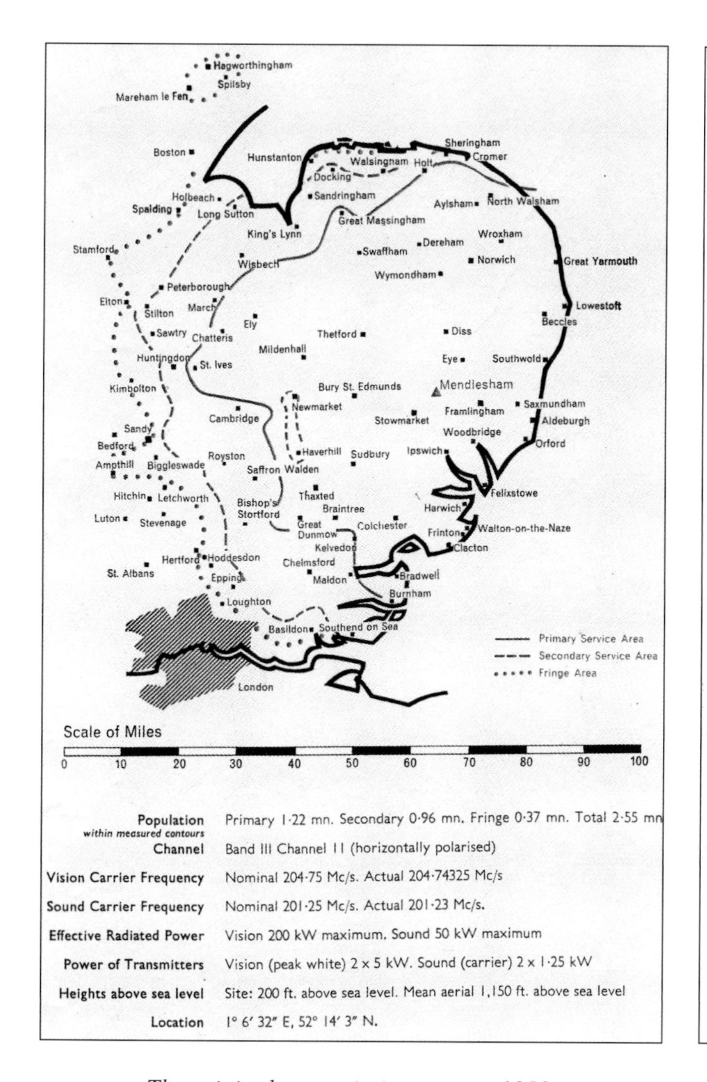

The original transmission area in 1959.

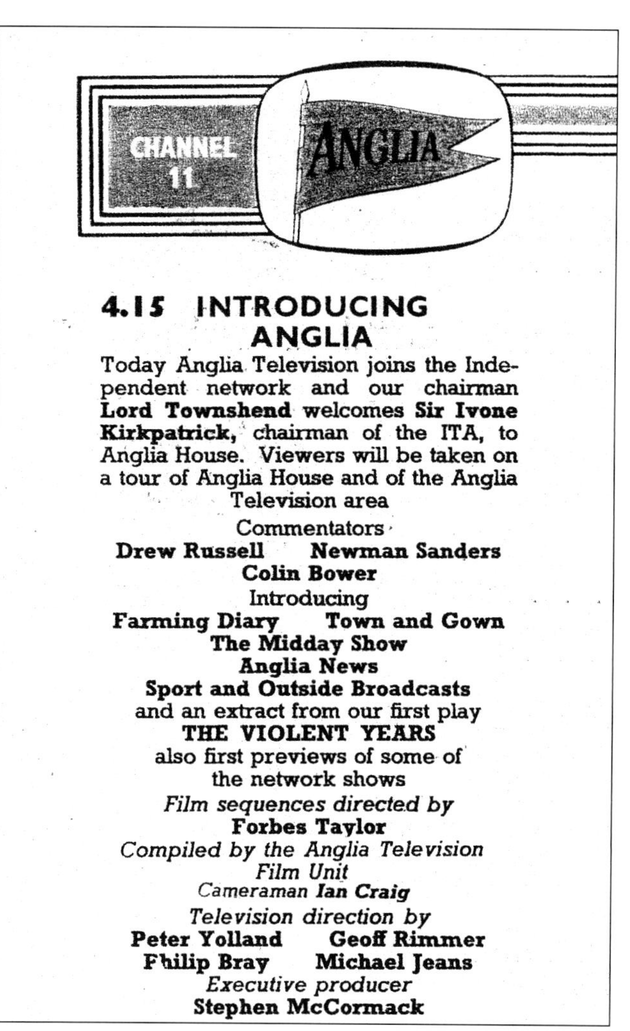
CHANNEL 11

ANGLIA

4.15 INTRODUCING ANGLIA

Today Anglia Television joins the Independent network and our chairman **Lord Townshend** welcomes **Sir Ivone Kirkpatrick,** chairman of the ITA, to Anglia House. Viewers will be taken on a tour of Anglia House and of the Anglia Television area

Commentators
Drew Russell **Newman Sanders**
Colin Bower

Introducing
Farming Diary **Town and Gown**
The Midday Show
Anglia News
Sport and Outside Broadcasts
and an extract from our first play
THE VIOLENT YEARS
also first previews of some of the network shows

Film sequences directed by
Forbes Taylor
Compiled by the Anglia Television Film Unit
Cameraman **Ian Craig**
Television direction by
Peter Yolland **Geoff Rimmer**
Philip Bray **Michael Jeans**
Executive producer
Stephen McCormack

Anglia's first programme on Tuesday October 27th 1959.

will help you choose from the exciting new programmes coming your way when Anglia Television opens. With TV Times you can plan your viewing so that you never miss a good programme. You can't get the best out of ITV without it. Order your TV Times - 4d every Friday". A new Anglia edition of the TV Times became available on October 23rd carrying several articles about the new station.

When the day came it was difficult to wait until Anglia began broadcasting at 4.15 on that Tuesday afternoon of October 27th. The live programme they opened up with was called "Introducing Anglia" (a video tape copy of this programme exists in the Archive). Lord Townsend and Sir Ivone Kirkpatrick, chairman of the Independent Television Authority, welcomed viewers at the entrance to Anglia House, as they had renamed the Agricultural Hall. Sir Ivone then operated a switch and Anglia Television began with "Introducing Anglia", a half hour programme, which took "viewers on a tour of the Anglia Television area". This showed extracts from forthcoming shows, and introduced the on-screen announcers Drew Russell and Newman Sanders. After this they rejoined the network for "Small Time, The Adventures of Twizzle" by Gerry Anderson at 4.45, then "Lucky Dip, The Junior Newspaper" from Associated Rediffusion; "Romance of The Railways" at 5.25, followed by the ITN news at 5.55. At 6.05, came the next programme from the Norwich based studios, "Anglia News". At 6.15 Scottish Television supplied "This Wonderful World" with John Grierson showing extracts from his favourite documentary films; then at 6.45, "**The Birth of a Regiment**", a film from the Anglia Television Film Unit of the new East Anglian Regiment, amalgamated from the Royal

Norfolk Regiment and the Suffolk Regiment. At 7.0 Anglia took from the network "The Song Parade" with Ronnie Carroll, and half-an-hour later, "Emergency - Ward Ten". This was followed by "Concentration", an "intriguing test of memory and observation. There are wonderful prizes for the contestants who can match up the boxes on the 'Concentration' board. Host David Gell". At 830 "Knight Errant 59" starring John Turner, Kay Callard and Richard Carpenter. This episode was called "Mediterranean Cruise". At 9.25 The News from ITN, followed by the big Anglia production of the night – Laurence Harvey and Hildegarde Neff in **"The Violent Years"**.

Right from the start Anglia had ambitions for supplying the network with programmes, particularly drama. On the board of directors was John Woolf, a feature film producer with an impressive record. He had produced (un-credited) in 1951 "The African Queen" with Humphrey Bogart and Katherine Hepburn (Bogart won an Oscar for Best Actor in a Leading Role), and "Room at The Top" with Laurence Harvey in 1959. Harvey won an Oscar also for Best Actor in a Leading Role. With Woolf's connections (he could just pick up the phone and get anyone he wanted – Joseph Cotton, David Niven, Rex Harrison) and an experienced team around him, Anglia built a formidable reputation for their networked dramas. This was difficult, for Anglia was looked upon as a regional company, and they were never able to breakthrough the ITV system of the big four (Rediffusion, ATV, ABC, and Granada) to become one of the networks main suppliers. John Woolf said in 1960 "Anglia is a regional station, and our main concern is with the people of East Anglia, but Anglia also has the talent and ability to produce programmes for the national network – in particular, plays. We should like to express our thanks to Associated Rediffusion for their continuous co-operation in the networking of Anglia drama".

*"**The Violent Years**", Anglia's first-night play.*

"**The Violent Years**" by Ladislas Fodor was directed by Peter Graham Scott, on loan from Associated Rediffusion, and was a great success that Tuesday evening attracting 4,752,000 viewers across the country. The next play, on December 15th, was done live from Anglia studios – **"Sweet Poison"** with Dawn Addams and John Ireland. The total audience figure for this play was 5,257,000 viewers. On January 26th 1960, "Carrington VC" with Richard Todd and Dorothy Tutin attracted over six million. This was directed by another well known and experienced director, George More O'Ferrall, who had been a BBC producer from the 1930s. Anglia was always good at getting talented people to work on their programmes.

But back to the story of the first night. At 11.8 came the "News Headlines, The latest from Independent Television News", and at 11.10, "Introducing Anglia" was repeated. This was followed by "The Epilogue" and 'close down'.

Actually the timings were not quite as those listed in the TV Times as can be seen from the technical programme rehearsal planning sheet from the master control room where the programmes were sent out to the transmitter at Mendlesham.

Master Control was where the daily transmission was assembled from network programmes coming up from London, Anglia produced programmes, Anglia acquired films, and the commercials. This master control room was just inside the main entrance, and was visible through glass windows. Some programmes came to Norwich on 35mm film such as shows of **"Ray Ellington Quartet"**, **"Dill Jones and His All Stars","** **Robin Hood"** and **"Encore"**, a programme of recitals by young artists. These were played in on Anglia's own telecine machines as the schedule demanded.

ANGLIA TELEVISION LTD — ISSUE NO: 2 — 6.10.59

PROGRAMME SHEET — WEEK NO. 44

	TUESDAY 27 OCT 1959		WEDNESDAY 28		THURSDAY 29		FRIDAY 30		SATURDAY 31 OCT
		1300	ITN NEWS	1300	ITN NEWS	1300	ITN NEWS		
		1302	THE MIDDAY SHOW ANG	1302	THE MIDDAY SHOW VTR ANG	1302	THE MIDDAY SHOW ANG	1340	ITN NEWS
		1345		1345		1345		1345	AFTERNOON OUT
		1443	SCHOOLS AR ALL x GR	1443	SCHOOLS AR ALL x GR	1443	SCHOOLS AR ALL x GR	1445	
		1550	INT. FOOTBALL England v Sweden AR ALL	1550	FASHION SHOW FROM RAGLEY HALL NR. ALCESTER	1550		1600	ATV ALL
1615	INTRODUCING ANGLIA F/A ANG							1640	PATRICK O'HAGAN SINGS ATV ANG
1645	SMALL TIME AR ANG	1650	SMALL TIME AR TTT/ANG	1645	SMALL TIME AR ANG	1645	SMALL TIME AR ANG	1655	ROBIN HOOD The Coming of Robin Hood ATV ANG
1700	LUCKY DIP AR ALL	1700	JUNIOR CRISS CROSS GR ALL	1700	ANIMAL STORY GR ALL	1700	PUZZIE PARADE AR ALL		
1725	ROMANCE OF THE RAILWAY AR ALL	1725	RIN TIN TIN (AR) Racing Rails ANG	1725	CISCO KID (AR) ANG	1725	MICKEY MOUSE CLUB AR ALL x ATV/GR	1725	LOCAL SPORT C ANG
1755	ITN NEWS ALL	1755	ITN NEWS ALL	1755	ITN NEWS ALL	1755	ITN NEWS ALL	1740	NEWS & SPORT ITN ALL
1808	C LOCAL NEWS ANG	1806	C LOCAL NEWS ANG	1808	C LOCAL NEWS ANG	1806	C LOCAL NEWS ANG	1800	THE INVISIBIE MAN Secret Experiment ATV ANG
1815	THIS WONDERFUL WORLD STV ALL	1815	FLYING REPORT ITN ALL	1815	CLOSE UP AR ALL x STV	1813	RIGHT TO REPLY ATV ALL x SOU/TTT		
1845	BIRTH OF A REGIMENT F ANG	1830	IVANHOE (AR) Free The Serfs ANG	1845	SEE FOR YOURSELF A ANG	1830	EDUCATING ARCHIE AR ALL	1830	BOY MEETS GIRLS ABC ALL
1900	SONG PARADE GR ALL x SOU/TTT	1900	MARK SABER ~~Sing Softly Sister~~ The Root of All Evil ANG	1900	RAWHIDE Incident of The Curious Street	1900	JACK HYLTON PRESENTS AR ALL x TT/TWW SOU	1900	TOMBSTONE TERRITORY ATV ANG
1930	EMERGENCY WARD 10 ATV ALL	1930	SKYPORT GR ALL x TTT		ATV ALL x SOU/TTT	1930	EMERGENCY WARD 10 ATV ALL	1928	ATV ALL
2000	CONCENTRATION GR ALL	2000	SPOT THE TUNE GR ALL	2000	DOTTO ATV ALL	2000	TAKE YOUR PICK AR ALL	2000	SATURDAY SPECTACULAR ATV ALL
2030	KNIGHT ERRANT '59 GR ALL	2030	NO HIDING PLACE AR ALL	2025	THIS WEEK AR ALL	2025	THE ARMY GAME GR ALL		
				2055	THE DEPUTY Badge for a Day (AR) ANG	2055	GUN LAW Renegade White (AR) (ANG)	2055	ITN NEWS ALL
								2100	FOUR JUST MENT Battle of the Bridge (AR) F ANG
2125	ITN NEWS ALL	2125	ITN NEWS ALL	2125	ITN NEWS ALL	2125	ITN NEWS ALL		
2137	THE VIOLENT YEARS (AR) ALL	2135	FILM Close Quarters AR /ANG	2135	VAL PARNELL'S STARTIME ATV ALL	2137	TELEVISION PLAYHOUSE Movement of Troops AR ALL	2130	GT MOVIES OF OUR TIME NURSE EDITH CAVELL ATV ANG
				2230	WHAT THE PAPERS SAY GR ALL x ATV/SOU/TTT	2235	MANTOVANI MUSIC FROM AROUND THE WORLD (ABC) F ANG		
		2250	MUSIC SPOT Let's Put Out The Lights VTR ANG	2245	LOOK IN AR GR/STV/ANG				
2308	ITN NEWS ALL	2305	ITN NEWS ALL	2300	ITN NEWS ALL	2305	ITN NEWS ALL	2300	EPILOGUE
2310	INTRODUCING ANGLIA VTR ANG	2307	EPILOGUE	2302	EPILOGUE	2307	EPILOGUE	2303	F ANG
2340	EPILOGUE F ANG	2310	F ANG	2305	F ANG	2310	F ANG		

Anglia programme rehearsal planning sheet for the first week of transmissions from Norwich.

The commercials, the life blood of the station, were all on 35mm film. These came from the advertising agencies in various lengths. Anglia Television fed these into their own schedules of networked and Norwich based programmes, so timings had to be precise. Not more than six minutes of advertising was allowed in every hour, unless there was something that could not be interrupted, then a minute could be carried over to the next hour, making seven minutes the absolute maximum. The commercials had to be assembled for each commercial break. This assembly work was done by a handful of people compiling each commercial break with the right number of advertisements to fill the time exactly. Each commercial came in several lengths depending on the time available and what the sponsor was actually paying for. The 35mm prints were assembled into a roll, with the correct leader on the front for running in, and the square burst flash of about a third of a second that separated each commercial. This was a busy department, as there were up to four commercial breaks in every hour, so a large number of advertisement had to be joined up for the day's transmissions by the staff.

To enable advertisers to see what their commercials looked like (there were no easy ways to view film in the days before VHS and DVD), new advertisements were joined up and shown continuously on a Monday morning at 9.30. This was not an advertised transmission, it was just for the agencies and advertisers to see their commercials on a TV screen. The public knew nothing of it, unless they happened to switch on their TV set.

Wednesday October 28th was the first full day of Anglia transmissions. ITV went on the air at 1.0pm with the "News Headlines", followed two minutes later by the Anglia production, "The Midday Show". This was one of Anglia's big daily productions. Philip Bray, the main producer, introduced the shows, which starred Susan Hampshire and Norman Hackforth, a veteran broadcaster and musician. Every day the audience came from a different town in the region. On October 28th they came from Haverhill, the next day from Cromer, and the following from King's Lynn.

One of the directors of Anglia Television, Aubrey Buxton, asked Ted Eales, the warden of Blakeney Point, to do a natural history spot in the programme. Because Ted had taken 16mm film of wildlife, and was experienced in talking to people about his work, his short piece in the show worked well, and it was to be the beginning of a career that Ted never envisaged. "The Midday Show" was popular with audiences, it was full of music, singing, dancing and above all fun. It ran for 43 minutes, and then at 1.45pm, the channel closed down for an hour. From 2.43 there were programmes for schools from Associated Rediffusion until 3.50, when "Remote cameras visit Wembley Stadium for part of the England v Sweden match". Children's programmes began at 4.45 with "Small Time", "Junior Criss Cross Quiz", and "The Adventures of Rin Tin Tin".

Staff assembling 35mm commercials in Anglia House.

At 5.55 The News from ITN, followed by Anglia News from Norwich. No more Anglia programmes until 10.50 in the evening, when Philip Bray produced "Let's Put Out The Lights" with "Norman Hackforth at his piano". This had been recorded on video tape earlier. So Anglia was now well and truly on the air.

A year later, Aubrey Buxton wrote of October 27th: "It was a day which all of us at Anglia Television are unlikely to forget. It was the day we began a new independent television service for more than 2,000,000 people in the Eastern Counties. Starting modestly with "The Midday Show", while the staff were getting in their stride, Anglia is now screening 10 hours local programmes a week. From sport to religious broadcasts, ballet to "pop", music, farming to topical events… all are tackled. Recently, "About Anglia" had the distinction of being the first Anglia local programme to appear in the weekly Top Ten. Regarding the plays which Anglia has networked throughout Britain, one remarkable factor testifies to our notable success. All Anglia's "Play of The Week" productions have reached Television Audience Measurement's network Top Ten".

Some plays were done in Associated Rediffusion studios at Wembley because of pressure on studio space, and because of the agreement that AR would network the plays. Lois Singer, who worked for a time with Associated Rediffusion, remembers that the company "lent" some staff to Anglia "to get things moving". One such was Paul Bernard who was working for AR at the time. His design plan for Anglia's "Their Obedient Servants", an Anglia play broadcast on June 5th 1963, survives and shows the layout in studio 5B at Wembley.

Anglia continued this schedule of a play every four to six weeks with an outstanding array of stars

Studio A, Anglia's largest studio.

and subjects. Luckily a few of these early plays were telerecorded. Basically a telerecording was achieved by pointing a 35mm or 16mm film camera at a TV screen, filming and recording the sound as the play happened. There were two ways a play could be telerecorded. One was that the play was telerecorded in sections, and these joined together, to form the complete film. The other way was for the play to be performed live from beginning to end and the telerecording made in one go. Sometimes the play would be transmitted live, and telerecorded for later review purposes, or for overseas sales. Telerecording was not of high quality, especially when a filmed insert was included in the play, which was then re-filmed by the telerecording. Video tape recording was still new at this time, and expensive.

Some of the Anglia plays from these early years that have survived either whole or in part include:- "**Square Dance**" with Hy Hazel, Keith Baxter and Lola Brooks; **"The Man Who Understood Women**" with Jane Asher, Tony Britton, Maxine Audley; "**The Two on The Beach**" by N. J. Crisp with Pauline James, Joan Hickson and Derek Francis; **"Better Dead"** with Ron Moody, Ann Lynn and Edward Fox**; "The Successor"** adapted by Troy Kennedy Martin with Rupert Davies and Felix Aylmer**; "Goodbye Johnny"** with Edward Judd**;** and **"The Move After Checkmate",** written by Barry England, and starring Robert Brown, John Collin, Michael Crawford, Donald Pleasance, Peter Vaughan, and Dorothy Allinson.

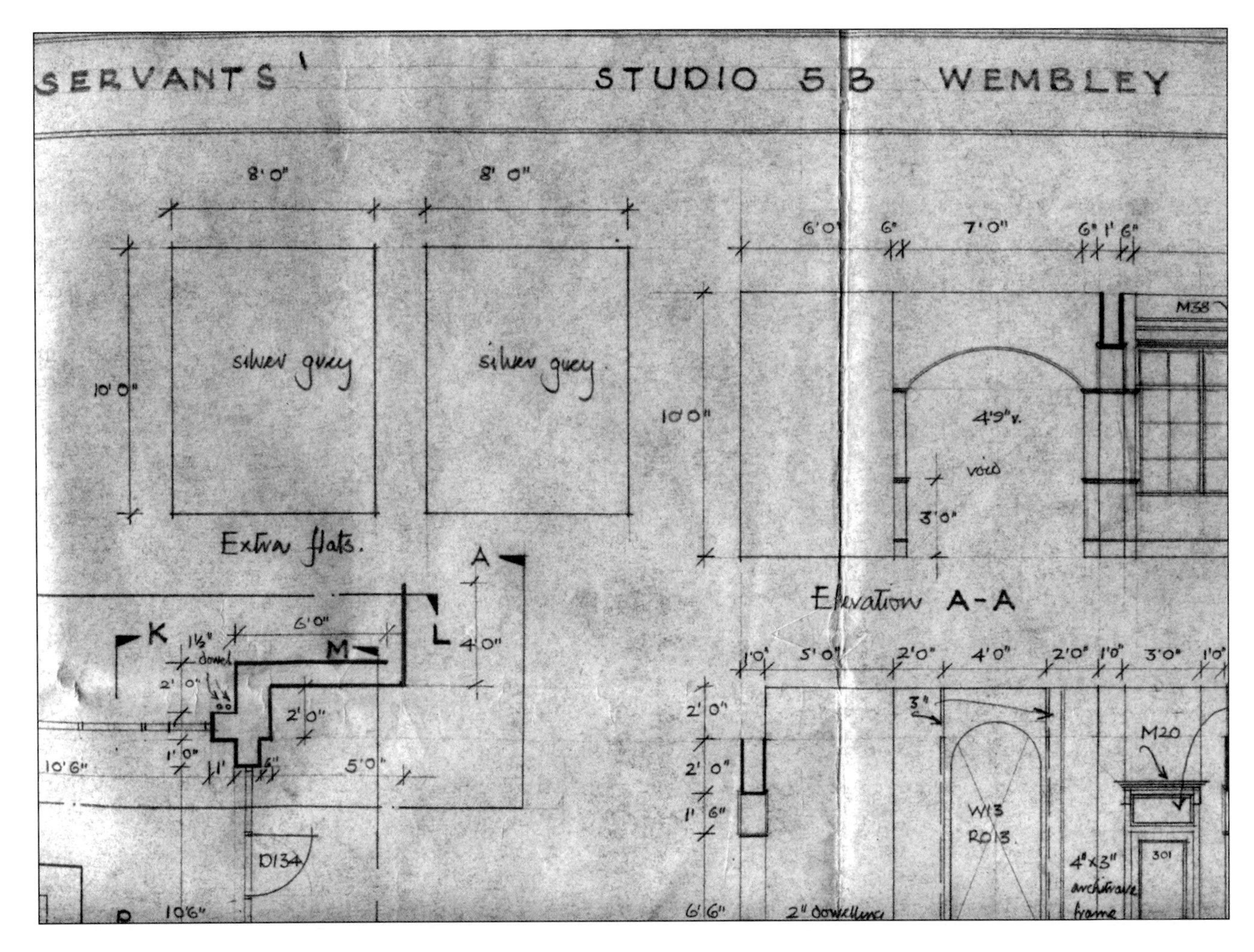

Part of the floor plan for "Their Obedient Servants" at Wembley studios.

The plays continued on into the 1970s, but in the meantime Anglia started another drama that was networked – the soap "**Weavers Green**", which began on Thursday April 7th at 7 pm in 1966. From an idea by Dick Joice, it was a sort of 'Archers of the screen' twice a week. In the East Anglian Film Archive, two telerecorded episodes exist on 16mm of "**Weavers Green**", which show the mixture of location (recorded on video tape) and studio content. The programme had trouble finding suitable slots in the network and after fifty episodes, Anglia decided to drop it.

Let's look now at a typical week of transmissions of local programmes for the week of June 25th 1961. "Farming Diary", hosted by Dick Joice, a farmer from Raynham in Norfolk, was on at 1.50 on Sunday, and later that evening "Guest Countryman" at 5.50 just before the news. This programme, directed by Ron Downing, was introduced by Philip Wayre, a film maker and wildlife enthusiast. "In this, the last of the present series, viewers will meet "Pooh Bear" at home at Great Witchingham, together with some other animals". Philip loved animals and was an enthusiastic film maker. Many of his films exist in the East Anglian Film Archive including **"Pooh Bear"**, part of which was shown in the programme. Finally, at 11.0pm "The Epilogue" by the Rev Colin Stephenson of Walsingham.

On Monday June 26th at 4.40 in the afternoon, and every day at this time, was "Afternoon Club" introduced by Valerie Oldfield, Anglia's first woman announcer. At five minutes past six, just after the ITN News, came "Anglia News", followed ten minutes later by "About Anglia". This was one of Anglia's most popular programmes. Introduced each evening by Dick Joice, the programme's reporters were Dick Graham, Peter Le Marchant,

John McGregor, and Bob Wellings. At 7.0, just after "The Flintstones", came "Is The Law A Ass" as it is billed in the TV Times. Devised by Woodrow Wyatt, journalist and politician, with a script by Anglia's Peter Le Marchant, this was "an investigation into the laws we live by – No 1, The Sale of Goods Act 1893". The only other Anglia programme that day was the Epilogue from The Very Rev. J. A. H. Waddington, Provost of Bury St Edmunds, who did all the epilogues that week.

"Afternoon Club" on Tuesday had John Seymour explaining how to make the Anglianaut aeroplane (I'm not sure what this was), and after Anglia News and "About Anglia", a programme on the "Royal Norfolk Show" introduced by Kenneth Horne. Wednesday June 28th had the usual Afternoon Club, Anglia News, and About Anglia, then at 6.53, "Take a Look - An Anglia Advertising Magazine". Peter Tuddenham, an Ipswich born actor, and Brenda Ralston "invite you to an interesting guide to the latest shopping news". These short advertising programmes (only about five minutes) promoted certain products direct to the viewer, the presenters going from one item to another as quickly as possible. Eventually these types of programmes were banned from ITV.

Cavendish Morton, a well known artist, conducted the painting competition in "Afternoon Club" on Thursday June 29th, and after Anglia News, a 'New View' programme in place of "About Anglia" - "I Packed My Bag", directed by Peter Joy. From an idea by Betty Marsden, and fronted by Kenneth Horne, this "new light-hearted game in which competitors pack an imaginary bag with articles beginning with a letter… and try to remember them" had "Prizes for Everyone". There was one other feature programme that evening from Anglia's production team, "Omnibus", which "takes a look behind the headlines in Anglia's weekly newspaper of the air".

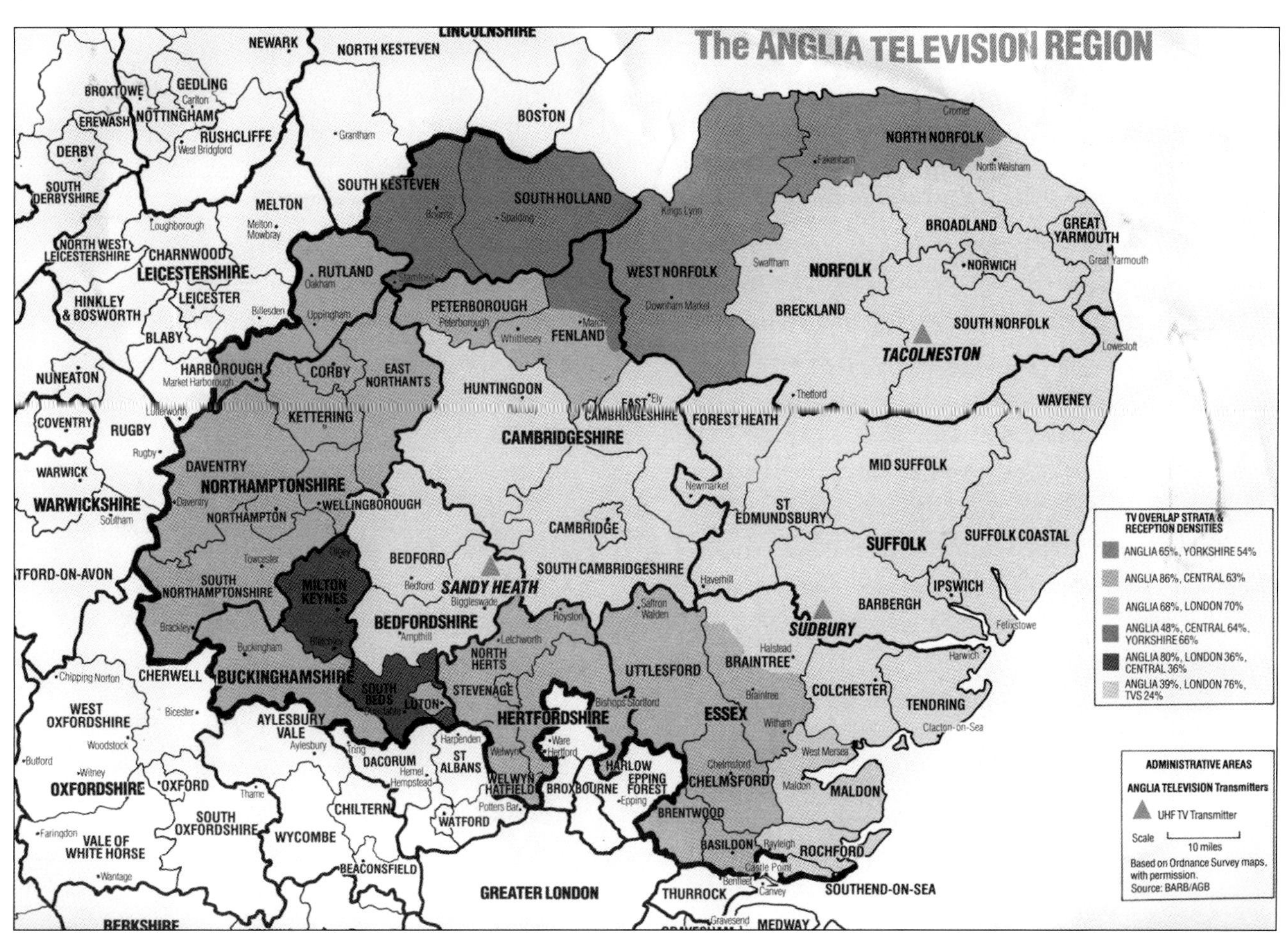

A later, revised map showing the Anglia region fed by the transmitters at Sandy Heath, Sudbury and Tacolneston.

Friday saw "Afternoon Club" with George Metcalf talking about lions and tigers, and after Anglia News and "About Anglia", another edition of "Take a Look", the advertising magazine. On Saturday the schedule was quite different - sport and family entertainment; the only Anglia programme being the Rev Waddington giving his last epilogue of the week.

The transmission area covered soon expanded with the opening of the Sandy Heath transmitter in Bedfordshire. Another transmitter was put up at Belmont near Louth in Lincolnshire, and in December 1965 Anglia included this area in its region. This was to cause a lot of disagreements with the Independent Broadcasting Authority over the next few years after transmissions were transferred to UHF in 1971, which increased the area to the North considerably. From 1965 Anglia was covering a vast area, and that is why the "**Anglia Collection**" contains many Lincolnshire items. Eventually this was sorted out by the Independent Broadcasting Authority (as it became in 1971), and with Yorkshire Television coming on the scene, Anglia lost the Lincolnshire area in 1974.

From 1959 to 1978, Anglia was contractually obliged as part of public service broadcasting, to show seven and a half hours of locally made programmes a week, raised to eight and a half in 1978. In many cases Anglia exceeded these minimum requirements.

One of Anglia's popular presenters was Bob Wellings, who was out and about on September 28th 1963 at the new University of East Anglia over shots of the temporary buildings at 'The Village' in Wilberforce Road, a site donated to the UEA to be used while the main buildings were constructed. "There are only a few finishing touches left. Tomorrow afternoon, Sir Keith Murray, retiring chairman of the University Grants Committee, will officially open this remarkable university. In October the first intake of undergraduates, perhaps a little nervous, perhaps a little uncertain of what they will find, but proud to be here, at the beginning of an educational venture as original as any that has been undertaken in the history of British universities". Bob, like his colleagues, also did longer reports to form programmes in their own right. One of these was called 'The Fast Ones' in the **"Here and Now"** series. This was transmitted on September 30th 1963, and the subject was sports cars. This was a time when petrol was just five shillings and a penny ha'penny a gallon. (about 26p). Bob interviews people, interspersed with his own commentary.

Over shots of a sports car rushing through a village, Bob begins "The car this man is driving has four wheels, two headlamps, a gear lever – all the things my car and your car has. The one thing that makes it different from your car and my car is that it is made to go fast, very fast. Tom Cook is a farmer. Why do you drive a fast car?"

"Principally because it is essential to my business, and secondly I get a great deal of enjoyment out of travelling at speed".

"What sort of enjoyment?".

"I think the sensation of being at the control of a potentially powerful machine".

"This car is capable of 150 miles per hour, do you really want a car that goes that fast?"

"I don't think the top speed is of any great importance. The advantage is that it is capable of travelling at fairly high speed for an indefinite period, also that it has got very good acceleration".

"Is any part of this showing off to other motorists on the road?"

"I don't think so, I wouldn't like to think so".

"Now if you had seen a pretty girl on the road driving in a sports car, do you feel you must overtake her?"

"No, I feel I would be more inclined to follow her and see where she is going to".

Over further shots of sports cars, Bob says "But what does it do for the woman? Shirley Cant is a painter. Why do you drive a sports car?"

"I feel it gives a bit of zest to life".

"What do you mean by zest?"

"Well, it is very dull these days, one has got to make as much interest as possible".

"Now, when you are on the road, do you challenge the men who are driving sports cars?"

"Oh, certainly I do".

"Do you think it is important to beat them?"

"Yes to a certain extent, it gives a bit of competition".

"What's the real pleasure you get out of driving a sports car?"

"Oh, on a nice day like this, the hood down, wind in one's hair, sunshine, fresh air".

"How much do you think you are muscling in on the male world?"

"Well of course the male world, it is so much more interesting isn't it".

"Do you regard your sports car as a sex symbol?"

"Well I suppose so, but if you are thinking of sex, of course a saloon is much more convenient".

"David Rand is a 26 year old lecturer. He likes to be called by his surname. Why do you drive a sports car?"

"Jolly nice, the speed is great, faster than British Railways, far more convenient".

"What particularly appeals about it?"

"Generally overtaking other people, being able to cruise at speed, in excess of our top speed".

"Is it important to be able to overtake other people?"

"Yes really, I like to go faster than other people. I travel over 500 miles in a week in the course of work".

"And you get a kick out of it?"

"Oh yes".

"Have you ever wanted to be a professional racing driver?"

"Oh yes, ever since I first learnt to drive. I am now taking a course of driving lessons at a racing school".

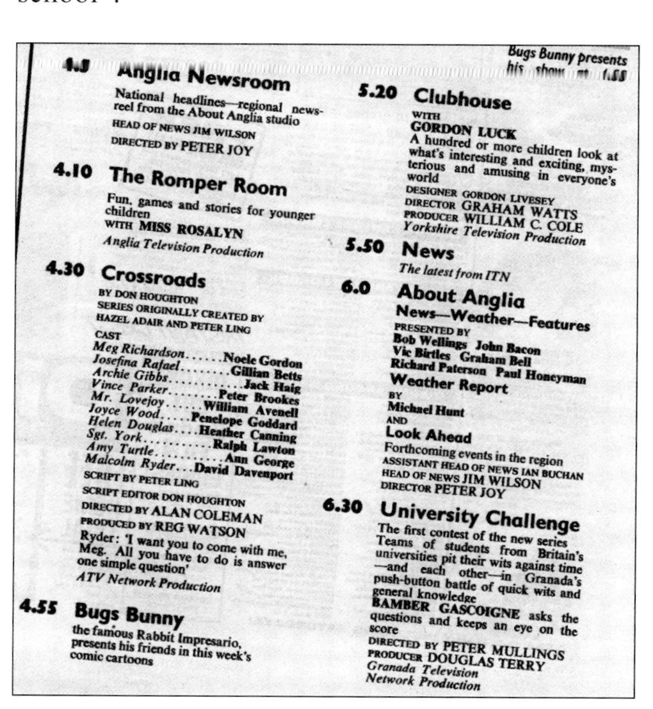

Bugs Bunny presents his show at 4.55

4.5 Anglia Newsroom
National headlines—regional newsreel from the About Anglia studio
HEAD OF NEWS JIM WILSON
DIRECTED BY PETER JOY

4.10 The Romper Room
Fun, games and stories for younger children
WITH MISS ROSALYN
Anglia Television Production

4.30 Crossroads
BY DON HOUGHTON
SERIES ORIGINALLY CREATED BY HAZEL ADAIR AND PETER LING
CAST
Meg Richardson......Noele Gordon
Josefina Rafael.......Gillian Betts
Archie Gibbs...........Jack Haig
Vince Parker.......Peter Brookes
Mr. Lovejoy......William Avenell
Joyce Wood.....Penelope Goddard
Helen Douglas....Heather Canning
Sgt. York..........Ralph Lawton
Amy Turtle..........Ann George
Malcolm Ryder...David Davenport
SCRIPT BY PETER LING
SCRIPT EDITOR DON HOUGHTON
DIRECTED BY ALAN COLEMAN
PRODUCED BY REG WATSON
Ryder: 'I want you to come with me, Meg. All you have to do is answer one simple question'
ATV Network Production

4.55 Bugs Bunny
the famous Rabbit Impresario, presents his friends in this week's comic cartoons

5.20 Clubhouse
WITH
GORDON LUCK
A hundred or more children look at what's interesting and exciting, mysterious and amusing in everyone's world
DESIGNER GORDON LIVESEY
DIRECTOR GRAHAM WATTS
PRODUCER WILLIAM C. COLE
Yorkshire Television Production

5.50 News
The latest from ITN

6.0 About Anglia
News—Weather—Features
PRESENTED BY
Bob Wellings John Bacon
Vic Birtles Graham Bell
Richard Paterson Paul Honeyman
Weather Report
BY
Michael Hunt
AND
Look Ahead
Forthcoming events in the region
ASSISTANT HEAD OF NEWS IAN BUCHAN
HEAD OF NEWS JIM WILSON
DIRECTOR PETER JOY

6.30 University Challenge
The first contest of the new series
Teams of students from Britain's universities pit their wits against time—and each other—in Granada's push-button battle of quick wits and general knowledge
BAMBER GASCOIGNE asks the questions and keeps an eye on the score
DIRECTED BY PETER MULLINGS
PRODUCER DOUGLAS TERRY
Granada Television Network Production

The film now shifts to a race track. "Here at Snetterton in Norfolk, there is a school for the aspiring racing driver. It is run by Jim Russell, a garage proprietor and himself a racing driver. How do you select your pupils?"

"Well Bob, we have a trial, about three trials a year, and we put them on a very safe circuit. What I am looking for is keenness, somebody with above average reactions, good sense of balance, and above all, somebody that really wants to drive a racing car fast but safe".

"Do you find that people who drive sports cars on the open road make the best drivers?"

"No, by no means, we've got many drivers that arrive here in a sports car who think they have the makings of a good racing driver, but at the very beginning we have to get them out of some very bad habits".

"Are they a bit stubborn to?"

"Oh yes they are, they think they know most, but we soon prove to them that they're wrong."

"Have you ever had pupils who have not driven at all and done well here?"

"Well one of the most outstanding drivers we have had at this school arrived on his bicycle, put his bike against the pits, took his cycle clips off. He turned out to be one of the best club drivers we have ever had at the school".

There follows sequences of cars driving round the track at Snetterton, then Bob continues "but for the sports car enthusiast, there are snags. In a few days' time basic insurance rates are going up by 30%. Loading on top of the normal premium for sports cars, can be up to 400% of the basic, that is if the insurance company consider insuring at all. Conclusions are difficult. The sports car does not seem to belong exclusively to the vital world of youth or to the world of dashing young men. It belongs to the breed. Today the modern sports car is a mecca of soft carpeting, heater, weather proofing, sound deadening, and wind up windows". Bob in vision now finishes "and the people who drive them vary from the local vicar to the housewife out shopping. The fast breed is being invaded by outsiders, and the British motoring scene will be more colourful as a result. Good night".

Bob drives off and the captions appear – Interviewer Bob Wellings, Camera Ian Craig,

Film Editor Paul Shortall, Directed by Harry Aldous. This report was networked by Associated Rediffusion.

Anglia productions on film, whether inserts, short films or features, amount to many thousands of cans of film in existence today in the East Anglian Film Archive. It is impossible to mention them all here, but what can be said is that it is a treasure trove of local history and life of the region from 1959 until film ceased to be used in the 1990s.

Popular and much loved Anglia programmes, and on-screen personalities, have been documented in two books produced by Anglia Television. In 1980, editor Anthony Davis produced "The First Twenty One Years", and in 1999 Tom Walshe and colleagues brought together material for "A Knight on the Box", though by this time the Anglia Knight had been discarded in favour of computer designed triangular logo. But memories of famous programmes linger, such as "Bygones", and its many spin-offs. These were fronted by Dick Joice, a Norfolk farmer, at first an unlikely choice as a presenter of programmes.

Richard Joice was helped by his father to become a farmer in his own right at the age of 25 at Hall Farm, East Raynham, as a tenant farmer on Lord Townsend's estate. Dick was an energetic man, with lots of interests. He not only had the farm to run, but built up a milk round with about 20 vehicles, took up photography, and set up, with Ernest Swain of Hunstanton, a mobile cinema circuit showing films in village halls. He bought a 16mm cine camera and started making films. The 16mm projector he also acquired was capable of recording sound on magnetic stripe, so Dick added commentaries to his films about farming, and took these round to schools and Young Farmers Clubs. His farm was written up in the Eastern Daily Press early in 1957, at a time when Dick built a 'down the row thinner', a new type of farm implement which thinned out the young sugar beet instead of the slow and backbreaking job of 'chopping out' the excess plants manually by hoe.

*Bob Wellings at Snetterton for his report for "**The Fast Ones**".*

It was with these credentials behind him, that Dick Joice was picked by Lord Townsend to present "Farming Diary" each Sunday on Anglia Television. As Dick states in his book "Full Circle" published in 1991, he never thought when he walked into the unfinished building to be called Anglia House, that he would spend the majority of his time there over the next thirty years.

Dick went on to present "About Anglia", "Bygones", and many other Anglia programmes. One of these in the early days was **"For Those in Peril"**, a film about Cromer's famous lifeboat coxswain, Henry Blogg. Henry Blogg had died in 1954, but many of his friends and colleagues were still alive, their memories of the great man vivid, so it was a good time to record what they had to say. Dick Joice talked with Jack Davies, his half-brother, asking him what Henry was like as a boy. "He was alright as a boy, but he didn't have time to play. He went to sea at twelve". Henry Blogg was born in 1876, and just wanted to be a fisherman. In those days the fisherman were busy practically all the year round, after crabs, mackerel, herring and cod. Henry joined the lifeboat crew at the age of 18, and became coxswain of the Louisa Heartwell in 1909.

Dick asked Henry 'Shrimp' Davies, so called because when Henry saw him as a baby he said "he looks like a shrimp", what impressed him about Henry Blogg. "Stubbornness I suppose, he'd never give in, if he started a job, it had to be done, no matter if that was a small job, or a big lifeboat job, in the wartime salvage operations, we would be on. He would not give up until it was finished" "What about his wife, what sort of person was she?".

"In the first place, a very frail sort of person, but a good wife for him. A good coxswain's wife. When a lifeboat goes off there are telephone messages - wives, friends, other lifeboat men want to know what's going on, and she was a good'un for that".
"Did they have any children?"
"Yes, they had two, a small boy, died about two years old, and a daughter they called Queenie, died about 27. Just about broke Henry's heart".
"Was he a very talkative man?"
"No. The only time when he talked was when he criticised you, and then he could talk"
"Did he ever lose his temper?"
"Yes very often. Not in the latter part of his life. When I first went to sea with him in 1928, he used to lose his temper, and get really angry. Then after Queenie died he was a changed man. More subdued, quiet, and more reserved". When Dick asked 'Shrimp' what was his most memorable rescue operation with Henry, he recalled the "*English Trader*", a 3,953 gross ton steamer aground on Sunday October 26th 1941 on Hammond Knoll, a sandbank close to the Happisburgh Sands. 'Shrimp' takes up the story.

"Those sandbanks, the sea doesn't obey the rules. Tide as much as anything creates the rough water. And as soon as the sea is running before the wind, as they do in deep water, they are all ways. The ship was being absolutely pounded to pieces by the sea. Henry described it later as the most appalling sight he had ever seen. We couldn't get nearer than a quarter of a mile. We made a few attempts, and tried to fire rockets to them, but couldn't get near her. He decided to lay off, beside the sands in deep water, till slack water, when the tide would be easier, change of tide, perhaps no tide at all you see, and the sea would be less rough, and we would have a chance.

"We young'uns thought we could get them, but no, he said we ought to wait. Well, we were laying there waiting and watching this ship being smashed to pieces. We suddenly thought we were going to lose the crew aboard her, 44 chaps. We pleaded with him to have a go – no, slack water would be the best time. Slack water would have been somewhere about four. The ship was getting such a hiding that we eventually persuaded him, against his better judgement, to have a go. I can tell you the time, twenty five past two. We got to within a quarter of a mile of her again, and the biggest sea I have ever seen in my life came up our port side, hit us, and the next thing I know we were in the water.

"Henry was washed overboard, and the second coxswain, and four of the crew. The second coxswain and Henry were the first to be picked up, and took command of the boat, and picked up the others. We were all pretty well done for, so we left for Gorleston. Unbeknown to us the Gorleston lifeboat was already on her way to the ship. They arrived at the time Henry wanted to attempt his rescue – at slack water. They did manage to get alongside the ship, but it was still too rough to take anyone off. They had to clear away and leave it until next morning.

"Had we had waited and listened to Henry, and waited until slack water, then we would have rescued that crew. That's what I mean when I say his judgement and calculation about the sea – I think that day proved it more than anytime". The commentary takes over to tell us that Blogg went back, came alongside the almost submerged ship, and took off the 44 crew.

This is more than a television film, it is an historical document told by the very people that were there. The film was directed and edited by one of Anglia's longest serving film makers, David Kenten. David is a remarkable director. He has the ability to carry the whole film in his head from the

*Dick Joice at Cromer for the making of "**For Those in Peril**".*

moment he thinks of it. He seldom wrote anything down, and often had many films on the go at any one time. He took on the role of studio director as well when 'Bygones' was being recorded.

David Kenten began as a projectionist in a south London cinema, then moved to the British Film Institute's National Film Archive, where he had the opportunity to view and evaluate hundreds of historical documentaries, newsreels and feature films before moving to television at the BBC. He worked at Lime Grove and Alexander Palace, and then joined ITN in 1955. Here he became a film editor, cutting black and white negative news film for transmission. Sometimes the film was still being cut while the programme was on air which "shaped instant decisions" he says. After a brief six months at Tyne Tees Television, he joined Anglia Television in March 1960. David recalls "when I arrived, there was one full time editor, Harry Aldous, who had come from Ealing Studios together with Ted Roberts, as his assistant. Ted was devoted to film, and later went on to found a successful film production company in London's Wardour Street. Within six months both David and Harry were made film directors".

At that time the sound feature unit consisted of director, PA (Production Assistant), cameraman, assistant cameraman, sound recordist, boom operator, electrician, driver, plus a 'mute unit' – mute denotes a camera not recording sound. "The management proposed upgrading the mute unit into a small sound unit if we agreed to drop the boom operator. The proposal was accepted as it meant a positive advance for technicians".

David would put forward ideas, the "basic concept being to explore 20th century history. This in reality meant extant locations and eye witnesses to events plus the inclusion of library cine films and stills". This often took him outside the Anglia region, sometimes even abroad. David continues "When 'Bygones' was established, Dick Joice was executive producer, he in turn was a can-do man who abhorred wasting time on endless paperwork. When, for instance, I verbally put the idea of making a feature on the life of Ted Ellis, the much revered naturalist, it was agreed in fifteen seconds flat. The resulting documentary included a visit to his childhood days in Guernsey, and ran to the agreed budget of £20,000. It stands today as a true record of this remarkable man's life".

Every programme had a budget which had to be kept to. "My problem of budget control was overcome by bolting on a couple of short sharp one-day shoots around the main 3 or 4 day feature, i.e. Isle of Man – 5 days on the horse trams, with half-a-day each on the camera obscura and the Laxey Wheel (on the Isle of Man). We then evened out the budget over the three stories, and in most cases came in on budget. Feature documentaries often came out of initial research, for instance, when I would value the story in minutes. In the case of the Blogg film it was going to be a half hour, but grew in editing to fifty minutes. When this timing was put to the management the answer was "on your head be it"! So I stuck to my belief in the documentary. Final endorsement came by record viewing figures, a repeat screening, and the RNLI buying 30 copies for showing around the country".

Dick Joice tried his hand at everything. If he was talking about trams at Carlton Colville Tram Museum, he would dress up as a tram driver. He made speeded-up films with Bob Wellings, chasing bicycle riding Bob through the streets of Norwich in his Jaguar. He fooled with Mr. Pastry (Richard Hearne who, incidentally, was born in Norwich) outside the Anglia building, he dressed up as a tramp and spoke in Norfolk dialect, and played Parson Woodforde in a re-construction from the diaries of the 18th century parson of Weston Longville, the Rev. James Woodforde.

He loved talking to people about the region's past and how things were done years ago. In 1982 at the Norfolk Rural Life Museum at Gressenhall, he interviewed the land girls who had come together for a reunion – an active reunion at that, of the land girls - "well I say girls", Dick says at the beginning of this Bygones Special, "because obviously they are no longer girls". He asks Pauline Watson what it was like. "We went right up to the top of the field, to get a load of turnips, and this old horse, he used to go up the field all right. But when we turned him round to come home, he knew he was going home, he come like the clappers. He knew I was a greenhorn, I didn't know the first thing about horses, and that old horse would come home like you know what, the cart a-rattling and turnips everywhere".

The film, also made by David Kenten, of the reunion of 300 girls, traced the history of the land girl in the First World War, and the re-formation in June 1939. Many girls came straight from towns and cities, and had to be trained so they knew a bit about farming. Archive film, liberally scattered throughout this half-hour programme, put the work of the women's land army in perspective. "Did you get up to any capers" ask Dick. Queenie Sizemore replies "Well, some of the young lads on the farm, they'd get us and stuff corn and chaff down the back of our necks. One time we did get the bull out and ride around the stockyard, which when he was put back kicked the door down".

The women are shown tackling some of the jobs they did forty years before, such as sugar beet topping, carting, sheep dipping, and helping with the threshing. The men watch. One says "They could milk cows, feed pigs, plough, and all the work they did they enjoyed. Some could use a pitchfork as good as the men, once they got over the mice running over their toes. They were very good. In fact I married one". **"They Did Their Bit"** is a delightful film of a forgotten part of the wartime story. Everyone has heard of land girls, but as Dick says at the end of the film "You did as much as the airmen, the sailors, the merchant navy to make sure we got through the 1939 fracas. But I always feel you did not get as much credit as you deserved". "**They Did Their Bit**" puts this right.

"About Anglia" was the regional news and interest programme that went out just after six o'clock every weekday night, running at one time for almost an hour. Some news was shot by "stringers" – freelance cameramen dotted around the transmission area. In the 1970s, there were two news sound film units, and 30 attached cameramen.

*David Kenten at the Menin Gate in Ypres directing the half hour programme "**Out There**" which was about the one hundred and forty World War 1 veterans visiting The Salient in 1964. The cameraman is Peter Fuller using an Auricon 600, recording sound on magnetic stripe. The assistant cameraman, Ken Little, is in the background, and the sound recordist on the left is Mike Tomsett.*

News film came in from all over the region – by train (being picked up at Norwich station), by road, and at one time, when Lincolnshire was part of the region – by aeroplane. The stringers often had Bolex or other small 16mm silent cameras, which held 100ft of film on a spool (two and a half minutes), which could be loaded into the camera in daylight without too much of the film at the beginning being "fogged". The black and white film was developed by Anglia's own film processing machine, and the editors cut the negative according to the time allotted to the story, together with the reporter's or editorial staff's requirements. The sound unit would send in one or two stories, and these would be treated in the same way. The 16mm sound cameras, often Auricon or similar make, held 400ft of film. This had to be loaded into 'magazines' in the darkroom back at base. 400ft of film lasted approximately ten minutes.

Normally, for news, the sound was recorded on the side of the film, on a thin magnetic stripe. Known as combined magnetic, sometimes "commag" for short, this "mag stripe" was unaffected by the developing machines, but the editors had to be careful how they cut the story, as the sound was recorded 28 frames in advance of the picture. This meant that the editor had to cut his film 28 frames in advance of where he would really like to cut the action, so that no sound was lost. This accounts for sometimes a sort of static hold of about a second before someone speaks.

*'Land girls' being interviewed by Dick Joice at Gressenhall from "**They Did Their Bit**" in 1982.*

Likewise at the end - it was easy to cut the picture on action, but there was still a second of sound while the film ran down to the sound head.

If there was time, then the way round this restrictive editing was to transfer the sound track to separate 16mm magnetic coated film, then the editor had control over the picture and sound separately, and could cut as he wished – even substituting a shot over a person talking without losing the sound.

The film sequences for that night's programme would be assembled in the right order – either on one telecine roll, or split so that alternate stories were on separate telecine machines. The negative picture was electronically reversed to positive. After transmission the rolls would be broken down, catalogued and canned.

The film was at first joined with cement splices – that is by using a solvent to weld the two pieces of film together once the emulsion had been scraped off one piece of the overlapping film. Cement splices could be made in about 15 seconds. In the mid-1960s tape joiners began to be used. These used special adhesive tape which the editor pulled across the two pieces of film to be joined, pressed it down with fingers to make good contact, and then quickly lowered the splicer handle. This forced punches in the handle assembly to go through the perforation, cutting the tape as it went, and at the same time cutting the tape at the edge of the film, so that as the handle came up, the two pieces of film were accurately joined with adhesive tape which was cut and perforated in one go. The film had to be taken out, turned over, and taped on the other side. If this was not done, the film could 'fold' in machinery, and might break. The visibility of either of these two types of joins was more prominent when the film being transmitted was a negative that was electrically reversed – so that a white flash occurred at the bottom of the picture on a cement join (though often obscured by peoples televisions where the picture was cut off at the bottom and sides) or in the middle of the picture when tape was used – both on the outgoing frame and the incoming frame.

In February 1971 a report in The Eastern Evening News stated "For the first time, ITV programmes in colour were today being beamed from the Sandy Heath transmitter which serves the

Cambridgeshire area. The original date for ITV colour transmissions to start in this area was January 18th, but because of a technicians' pay dispute, this had to be delayed until it was settled. A spokesman for ITV at Norwich said "some programmes this morning were in colour, and from now on almost all our filming will be in colour". For news 16mm colour reversal film was used. This was processed in a Photomec colour processing machine using the Agfa Gevaert system in about 25 minutes, and the film was then cut by the editor. The only difference from black and white work was that the film had the advantage that the picture was a positive image, the right way round to look at, making it easier for the editor and reporters to recognise faces. The sound colour reversal film again had magnetic stripe for the sound track when required. Grading shots had to be done by the telecine operator while on air, judging, after a rehearsal, what was needed concerning brightness and contrast. Unfortunately, this was sometimes noticeable on the screen by the viewer. The news story, if taken under changeable lighting conditions, often came on the TV screen momentarily too bright or dark, and there would be a sudden change to a reasonable picture as the operator corrected the problem as it came up on the screen. Film for news continued being used into the mid-1980s, when video cameras began to take over.

For feature production, whether a film insert or whole programme on film, Eastman Colour negative film was normally used. This is a much easier film to use from the cameraman's point of view, as it has more latitude than reversal film, and grading and colour corrections can be made when a print is produced from the negative. The normal procedure was for the exposed colour negative film to be sent to a London film laboratory for development, and a rush print made. The negative was stored, and the rush print sent to the film editor. The sound, recorded on quarter inch wide audio tape on location, was transferred within Anglia House to 16mm fully coated magnetic film stock. The 16mm rush print and the 16mm magnetic sound track were then edited on a 'Steenbeck' or other make of editing table. Here the two films were put in sync using the clapper board. The visual clap on the picture, and the sound of the

A can of rushes ready for editing. The numbers refer to the 'slates' or the identification of each shot. The picture would have the visual information on it of the clapper board, and the operator would say the number out loud so that it was recorded on the separate sound recording. That made possible easy synchronisation of the action and the separate sound track when editing.

clap on the sound track were synchronised, and the two films run together on the editing machine. The editor could cut the rush print and the sound track independently in any way he wished, or was instructed to do. When the editing was complete, and the various sound tracks that had been 'laid' on separate rolls of 16mm magnetic film, these dialogue, commentary, music, and sound effects tracks were then mixed together in a dubbing theatre to produce the final fully balanced sound track. In the meantime the final cut of the picture was sent to the negative cutter. Here the original negative was matched exactly to the cut rush print. From this cut negative a nice new clean graded and colour corrected print could be made for transmission by the film laboratory. The 'cutting copy' and the various production sound tracks were no longer needed, as now there existed a new colour print without joins, and a 'final mix' of all the sounds on one sound track. These two items were laced on the telecine machine in synchronisation ready for transmission or cued into the studio production which was being recorded on video tape. In the mid-1970s, Anglia had two feature sound units, six film cutting rooms, and a four channel dubbing theatre in Anglia House.

A Steenbeck editing table with a roll of picture and a roll of separate magnetic film stock. The two rolls would be run in synchronisation.

Major documentaries filling an hour slot were being made, such as **"No Lullaby for Broadland"** produced in 1979 by Geoffrey Weaver. This looked at the state of the Broads and what could be done. The Broads Authority was formed in 1978 to bring together the various responsibilities of county and district councils, Anglian Water Authority, the Port and Haven Commissioners and others. However there was much controversy over the suggestion that had been put forward that the area should be made a national park. Norfolk County Council was opposed to the idea, other organisations for it. Geoffrey Weaver's film examines the Broads with its large number of boats, water pollution, and floating rubbish, as well as its wildlife amid lyrical scenes of beauty of this unique part of England. The film looks at why the Broads are worth preserving, and why management so far had failed. James Hoseason maintains that conservation and navigation can work together so that damage by motor cruisers is kept to a minimum. Ted Ellis, the naturalist talks with local farmer Charles Wharton, Dr Martin George of the Nature Conservancy Council examines the water meadows and dykes, and Alan Skinner of Anglian Water Authority talks about financing conservation and efforts to improve the water quality.

Another big project Anglia undertook was a film of the life and work of Stephen Hawking, the Cambridge author of **"A Brief History of Time"**. Thousands of feet of 35mm film were shot for this ambitious programme which exists in the East Anglian Film Archive.

The late 1980s were the beginning of a time of change for Anglia. "Bygones" was taken off the air in 1988, and the company introduced their new identity in the form of an electronic, three coloured, A-shaped symbol. In 1994 Anglia Television was bought for £292 million by MAI plc, who themselves became part of United News and Media two years later. By 2000 many of the regional stations, including Anglia, were owned by Granada Television. Others were part of Carlton Television. Then Granada and Carlton merged in 2004 to create one ITV company. Since that time there has been a steady decline in regional programming.

After fifty years, local interest programmes from Anglia had virtually ceased by 2009, ending an era of material about the region for its people. Many of the films of this time are kept in the East Anglian Film Archive.

Stephen Hawking.

Network Television

Network television, whether the BBC or parts of the ITV network, frequently made films in the eastern region, and these survive in the company's archives. An example is a BBC Television film of 1965 called "**The Million Pound Grave**", which eight million people watched on August 12th 1965. This is a full account of the 1939 excavation of the Sutton Hoo ship burial in Suffolk. There was a story in Woodbridge that an old man had said there was untold gold in a series of low hills on the opposite bank of the river Deben, on land owned by Mrs. E. M. Pretty. These Sutton Hills, as they were known locally, intrigued Mrs. Pretty, and she contacted Ipswich Museum, who sent along a part-time archaeologist, Mr. Basil Brown. With the help of a couple of assistants provided by Mrs. Pretty, Basil Brown started his excavation. It was in July of 1939 that the real significance of the contents of the mound was realised, and the British Museum sent a team to Suffolk. Undisturbed for centuries was the remains of an Anglo-Saxon warship of the seventh century complete with a burial chamber containing a fabulous treasure. Many of those who took part in the dig just before war broke out recall the excavation that yielded one of the richest and most important archaeological finds ever made in Britain. The ship's contents, including armour and regalia, silver tableware, gold jewellery, and much more, are now in the British Museum. Replicas of the treasure are now on show in the Sutton Hoo visitors' centre close to the original site. A revised version of the BBC programme was shown twenty years later.

A couple of schoolteachers, Miss Barbara Wagstaff and Miss Mercie Mack, who happened to be on holiday in the area at the time of the excavation, took many photographs, but more importantly for us, a small amount of black and white 8mm cine film. Part of this movie is included in the BBC programme, and the whole roll is also preserved in the East Anglian Film Archive under the title "**Sutton Hoo 1939**".

"**A Man with a View**" is a 1966 film for BBC 2 made by Malcolm Freegard about King's Lynn. Our guide is Nicholas Wollaston who looks around the town and calls it a 'significant place, historic, aristocratic'. As he is driven around the taxi driver says "it's a friendly place, years out of date. It just wants somebody with vision and the go to get it going, because the town has very near everything". Actually that very nearly did happen, for as Wollaston says, "a few years ago there was a survey by the County and Borough Councils to recommend a plan for preserving, adapting, and redeveloping it. The report made recommendations which startled some of the residents of Lynn, who said it was much too drastic, which disappointed some town planners who said it did not go far enough" There are shots of houses which are empty "built with the help of Greater London Council for that vague and sinister thing called overspill – which never came".

Wollaston admires the architecture, the alleyways, the historic houses, and asks leather-clad motor-bikers what they think: "The old buildings should come down to make room for new buildings, for more entertainment for the young person". "If the old houses were knocked down it would lose much of its atmosphere. I think at the moment the old houses distinguish it from any other town" said another.

Nicholas Wollaston looks at the livestock market, the ferry to West Lynn, industries including Campbell's Soup factory, the docks where 1000 ships pass through every year, at the King's

*The shape of the Sutton Hoo ship is evident in this picture from "**The Million Pound Grave**".*

Lynn Festival which has a week of concerts and exhibitions often attended by the Queen Mother, and the thriving market, where you can buy washable 'walk on air' socks for a shilling (5p) a pair.

This, and other films, were made for showing on BBC 2, which had opened on April 20th 1964. Another was "**Good Old Knocker**", about Arnold Bennett, the prolific writer of novels and essays. Amongst his many books he wrote were 'Anna of The Five Towns' (1902), 'The Old Wives' Tale' (1908), 'Clayhanger'(1910), and 'The Card' in 1911. 'The Card' was made into a film with Alec Guinness in 1952, and a long section was included in **"Good Old Knocker"**, the title Malcolm Freegard gave to his 1966 film of the writer's life. Bennett was born in Stoke on Trent, and some of his novels are set in that area, but he lived much of his early life in Paris. He left his wife in 1921, and moved to London with a country house in Thorpe-le-Soken in Essex. 'Comarques' was the name of the house on the outskirts of Thorpe, which he shared with actress Dorothy Cheston and their daughter until he died of typhoid fever on March 27th 1931. Malcolm's film is a comprehensive story of the writer's life, and is in the East Anglian Film Archive not only because of the Thorpe-le-Soken connection, but because it is part of the output of Malcolm Freegard's television career. The film used a student to link the sequences, and Malcolm chose Germaine Greer in one of her first ever television appearances.

Television at this time was a huge complicated system, with large amounts of technical equipment and personnel. This is evident in "**The Dream Machine**", Denis Mitchell's film of the putting together of a light entertainment show at ATV in 1964. The film follows the booking of artists, a budget meeting, building sets, and rehearsals with three of the girls, Millicent Martin, Honor Blackman and Cleo Lane. Francis Essex, the producer and director, oversees the studio rehearsal where the six girls drive into the studio in sports cars. This is a good example of the complexities of a light entertainment show performed in front of an audience in one go even though it was only being recorded on video tape. There are many different skills involved, from music arrangements

*Nicholas Wollaston, "**A Man with a View**", looking at King's Lynn in 1966.*

to script writing, from choreography to timing. Denis Mitchell, using the fly on the wall approach, follows every part of the planning of the show, and uses a recurring theme of time throughout, with shots of clocks with the seconds ticking away. Denis's intention in making the film was to take a serious look at the state of television at that time. He used two very different characters throughout the film, Francis Essex the producer, and Roy Knight, a lecturer in Film and Television at Durham University. One reviewer said about the film "on one level it projected glamour and on another level it exposed glamour to value judgement".

Denis Mitchell began in radio, making programmes like 'People Talking', where he could record voices on the new medium of audio sound tape using portable tape recorders like the battery operated EMI L2 instead of the old disc system. Denis recorded onto the quarter inch wide magnetic tape, and then cut the tape physically to form the final programme. "I had fallen in love with the human voice" he once said. Moving over to television in 1955 he incorporated his sound techniques into his films. He let the subjects speak for themselves by creative use of sound, often overlaying sound tracks over the picture. First he worked with bulky 35mm film cameras on location, later with lightweight 16mm cameras then coming into use for television filming, making a less rigid approach possible. His "**Morning in The Streets**" made in 1959 was so successful that it was still being shown nearly fifty years later. The film, impressions of life just after

*"**The Dream Machine**", Denis Mitchell's record of the production of an entertainment television programme in 1964.*

dawn and throughout the day until children came out of school in Liverpool and Manchester, won an Italia Prize in 1959.

Later he made extensive use of 16mm synchronised sound filming, as the technology improved and became easier to use. Denis made over eighty films for television using his observation technique, including in 1970 a film of "**Quentin Crisp**" talking about his life in his Chelsea bedsit. He never dusts his flat he states, as after so many years he found the dust did not get any thicker.

In 1976, with his wife Linda, Denis made a record of people and places around his home at Great Massingham in North Norfolk. He called the film "**Never and Always**", and it took a year to make. Granada networked the programme in June 1977. There is no commentary, just the occasional question from behind the camera from Denis. One subject in the film is Stanley Smalls, a basket maker from North Creake. Smalls lived alone, with only his caged birds for company.

"I left school when I was twelve. I have been a working seven days a week ever since. I like work, I mean, I am not forced to do this, if you understand that". As he continues basket making Denis Mitchell asks "Well you have got to make a living haven't you?"
"No, I'll soon be eighty. I am very strong. I carried a tree weighing five hundred weight. Quarter of a ton"
"Carried it?"
"Yes, carried it on my shoulder. Yes. No day too long for me, no work too hard or too dirty. I don't never tell anybody no. If I don't intend to work for them I hide up so they can't find me.
"I'm psychic. I can forecast things that are going to happen. If anything is going to happen I either see my father, sometimes my father and mother when I sleep abed. The night when my mother died I see my father, and I said 'hello, you're back'. He said 'Yes, I have come to take mother away from you, cause she's getting too much trouble". She was gone in the morning. Yes. And that was the 25th June, exactly ten years after he died".

As Stanley Smalls lights up his pipe Mitchell asks "What time do you get up in the morning?"
"Between half past three and quarter to four. Go to bed at half past ten. I am a porridge man. Porridge and taters. Porridge twice a day. No meat, no sugar, no tea, nothing but water".
"Do you fear death yourself?"
"No. No. No. When my father in heaven think I am no more use, and a nuisance to anybody, he will take me home. Or my father come".

"**Never and Always**" is a fascinating and gentle film with many aspects of Norfolk life. Stratton Long of Blakeney tells of how he became a boat builder, and Richard Davies, coxswain of the Cromer Lifeboat and fisherman, tells of catching crabs for his wife to sell in her shop. Villagers talk of Great Massingham, and how it once had six pubs, two chapels, four bakers, three grocers, three carpenters, a tailor and two blacksmiths. T. S. Elliot's poem of 1942 called 'Little Gidding' provides the title – "Here the intersection of the timeless moment. Is England and nowhere. Never and Always".

In 1981 Denis Mitchell made a series of ten minute films for the BBC under the overall title of 'Impressions'. Four were made in the East Anglia region. "**Flying Start**" was shot at the now defunct RAF Coltishall airfield. Here Mitchell captures the exhilarating impression of flying from early morning through the busy routine of the day. The camera concentrates on the men, getting up, having breakfast, and getting ready to fly.

"**Harwich**" town archivist Len Weaver recalls the history of this ancient East Coast port, with scenes of Harwich, the ships, and the people.

"**The Old Rectory**" is about the antiques and collectables that restorer Bryan Hall had built up over the years. It is said that in his youth Bryan went round on a bicycle with a carpet bag collecting anything and everything. Many years later he had a great auction, and most of the collection was sold off. "**Retirement – Tulley George**" is just that – a day in the life of Tulley George of Great Massingham. Tulley had been a farm labourer from the age of 13, and had worked in many different places. His day begins with the making of a cup of tea for his wife. He does not drink tea himself. He cooks his own breakfast, and then works in the garden of his bungalow. He cuts firewood. He goes to the "Fox and Pheasant" for a drink, then off to Brancaster to dig some lugworms. Back in Great Massingham he cuts the grass round the gravestones in the churchyard. He tells a story of a one time rector of the parish who, after his wife died, fell in love with a choir girl. She was 22 and he was 82. They married and went to live at Bexhill on Sea. They had two children. He laughs. Tulley says he is "always busy, I never get bored".

"**We Can Say We Left Something Good**" is the title in the "Built in Britain" series made for the new Channel 4 in the early 1980s of a film about buildings along the Suffolk-Essex border. In Bridge Street, Saffron Walden, David Lewis is doing some pargetting. This is the ornamentation of a blank area of plaster with some form of patterning. David is using a simple mould carved by himself to impress a series of patterns into the wet plaster. He presses the mould gently and it leaves a series of curved lines known as the Essex pattern, as it is most common in this part of the county. David presses again into the plaster next to the first one, and continues in this fashion horizontally until the end of the plaster is reached. Then, the next impressions are made just below, interlocking into the first ones above, thus forming a complete overall piece of pargetting. "You must keep them even. Often I put some on, and I don't get it quite even, and I have to rub them out and start again" says David Lewis. He shows another pattern, commonly called the 'basket maker' pattern. This is a mould of four or five straight lines. This is pressed in so the lines are vertical, then next to it another impression, but with the lines horizontal. Then vertical, then horizontal and so on.

For certain areas of plaster, such as a triangular piece near the roof, perhaps overall pargetting would look wrong, but a single simple impression or relief would be right. For this David has a large rose pattern and other designs. He obviously loves his work as he says he is going to go on doing it until he is ninety. "I think it makes the building look interesting. There's going to be people here when we have all gone. If we can say we left something good, it should last 200 years".

The film goes on to show brick making at Bulmer where Peter Minter runs his farm and brick making business. It is farm work in the winter, but

Denis Mitchell on location at North Creake with basket maker Stanley Smalls.

*An Air-Sea rescue helicopter at Coltishall airfield from "**Flying Start**", 1981.*

*"**Tulley George**" at home.*

in the summer they make all types of hand-made bricks, mainly for restoration purposes. The clay is dug, wetted, and fed into the pug mill. This extrudes a continuous stream of malleable clay which is thrown into the brick moulds by hand, the excess cut off, and the formed brick tipped out. After drying the bricks are stacked in the kiln, the entrance bricked up, and then continuous coal fires burn for a week.

Restoration work at the time of filming was being carried out on Erwarton church near Shotley, using the local building material septaria, also known as cement stone. This has always been collected from the foreshore just below the church.

*"**We Can Say We Left Something Good**" includes a demonstration of pargetting by David Lewis in 1983.*

Another film in this series was made at Sheringham, where many of the local houses were built of stones from the beach. "**A Stone's Throw From The Beach**" looks at the fishermen's cottages and how they and other houses in the area were constructed of flint.

On April 14th 1964 Granada television networked "**The Three That Got Away**", a film about the coypu which at that time were eating the farmer's sugar beet, destroying river banks, and ruining drainage systems. The furry, rat-like animal with webbed hind feet grew to about two feet long. It was introduced into this country from South America in the 1920s principally for the fur which was valuable for the coat trade, but in 1937 three escaped from their cages at East Carleton in Norfolk.

Coypu quickly became a pest as they spread into Suffolk and Lincolnshire, and particularly the Norfolk Broads, and a campaign to eradicate the animal began in the 1950s. In 1962, 18,000 were killed. The film traces the work of the Ministry of Agriculture Fisheries and Food during their systematic trapping and humane killing of the creatures. According to the film, one farmer tried to exploit the remains of the coypu by selling the pelts, and making sausages out of the rest! Ted Ellis, the naturalist, tried cooking the animal. "Take the legs from half a grown coypu, fry lightly on both sides, then casserole for two and a half hours". Best not try it; anyway, the coypu have now gone.

The film was made by Douglas Fisher, a renowned wildlife film maker living at the time in Suffolk. Douglas had joined Dr. Desmond Morris at London Zoo in 1957 to make animal behaviour films under the title of "Animal Story" for the ITV network. In 1960 he formed Douglas Fisher Productions, and was contracted for five years to make a series of films under the title "**Another World**". Douglas was now completely in charge, filming animals in their natural surroundings. He photographed, directed and produced the films himself. Because he lived in East Anglia, several of the films were shot in the region. Another in the series was "**Feathered Hordes**", a film about starlings. There are wonderful shots of the magical patterns made by thousands of birds as they swirl around the dusk sky. Douglas recalled "In 1963 I

10.40 Another World
NEW SERIES
The Three That Got Away
The Story of the Coypu in Britain
What is a coypu? And what can happen when a few animals escape from a fur farm? This film tells an unusual story about an unusual animal
RESEARCH BY EDWARD A. ELLIS
COMMENTARY WRITTEN BY CLIFFORD DYMENT
SPOKEN BY MICHAEL SMEE
FILM EDITOR PETER NEAL
PRODUCED AND FILMED BY DOUGLAS FISHER
Granada TV Network Presentation

*"**The Three That Got Away**" began a new series of "Another World" in April 1964.*

was filming starling roosts near Colchester when I heard that Dr Eastwood and members of his team at the Marconi Research Laboratories were recording the movements of birds at their 23cm radar station at Bushy Hill near Chelmsford. We compared notes and found that we were both filming the same starling roosts. We subsequently combined our films and the result can be seen as an interesting sequence in "**Feathered Hordes**". The film, running 25 minutes and 32 seconds, as was required by Granada at that time, was one of three films chosen to represent Britain for the 1964 European Grand Prix for television films at Cannes.

Other films which Douglas made in this series and shot in the region include "**The Awakening Year**" about spring, and a film about "**Swans**" in East Anglia. As "Another World" became popular, Anglia television was developing "Survival" out of its own local programme about wildlife called "Countryman" which Aubrey Buxton introduced in 1960. One of the early films in this series was about wildfowlers versus birdwatchers. Filmed at Blakeney, local personality Stratton Long takes part in a staged meeting of local wildfowlers and birdwatchers, followed by Stratton going on an early morning shoot on the marshes between Morston and Blakeney. A further shoot is shown where the wildfowler is deliberately distracted by a birdwatcher. "**Shotgun Wedding**", as this film is called, was transmitted in 1963. "**Survival**", under the guidance of Aubrey Buxton, grew and became a separate company making films for the ITV network.

Rural parts of East Anglia have often been used by television when exploring village and country life. In 1971 the BBC made "**The English Village is Alive and Well**" showing life in the picturesque village of Peasenhall in Suffolk, with local people talking about their village, the people in it, and stories past and present. Granada Television made "**Working The Land**", a film that looked at the working conditions of farm workers who at the time did a 42 hour week. Filmed at Knettishall in North Suffolk, this shows the farm workers, all smoking cigarettes, starting work in the early morning before light. Over atmospheric shots, they talk about being farm workers earning just under £15 a week. Some lived in tied cottages, that is a house given to them while they worked for their employer. This had always been a problem for many who worked on the land, for if they were made redundant, or left their job, they had to leave their house as well.

"**The Burston School Strike**" is the story of Annie and Tom Higdon who were teachers first at a school in Wood Dalling, then at Burston, both in Norfolk. Some of those they taught just before the First World War are interviewed and describe the Higdon's strict but fair approach. They wanted the best for their pupils, and tried to improve the school and the childrens' wellbeing there. Annie got into trouble with the guardians of the school at Burston when she lit a fire to dry out the wet clothes of the children without permission. Tom found it difficult to accept the management's authority, and he upset them when he stood for election to the parish council, and got in. Eventually the Higdons were given three month's notice to vacate the school.

The schoolchildren went on strike and refused to be taught by a new teacher. The Higdons set up a temporary school and the children attended. The parents were happy, and the children enjoyed the pleasurable lessons of their favourite teachers. In time, enough money was raised for a new building in which the Higdons to carry on teaching, and this was opened in Burston in May 1917. The Strike School, as it was known, continued under the Higdons until 1939, when Tom died. Stephen Peet's film traces all the troubles and difficulties the school faced during the 25 year strike. The film, in the "Yesterday's Witness" series, was transmitted in 1974.

The same year another BBC producer, Eddie Mirzoeff, completed "**A Passion For Churches**" with John Betjeman looking at Norfolk churches and the people and places around them. This was a time when there was great interest in the wellbeing of churches, and the Norfolk Society Committee for Country Churches published a booklet entitled "Norfolk Country Churches and Their Future". This was written by Wilhelmine Harrod, who guided the production crew round the best and beautiful churches of the county. It is obvious Betjeman loved making this film, which begins with him rowing on the river Bure where, many years before, his parents had taken him on holiday. He visits a variety of churches, pointing out architectural features, goes to fetes, travels on the North Norfolk railway, and observes the Nuns at All Hallows Convent at Ditchingham. The working title for the film was "**Failed in Divinity**", but Eddie Mirzoeff changed that before the film was completed. Many of the out-takes from the film were saved by Lady Harrod who deposited them in the East Anglian Film Archive. Some have been made into a separate film by the Archive which shows Betjeman at work. "**John Betjeman Rushes**" show the poet standing patiently until the clapper board is removed from the shot so he can begin – though often another take is required because it did not quite work. As he rows a boat on the River Bure, several takes are required for the introduction to the film. A voice from behind the camera says "You have got about four strokes before you start". The clapper board appears in picture "307 take 1". After the necessary four pulls on the oars, John Betjeman begins "I was 8 or 9 when I used to come here to Norfolk, rowing and sailing with my father, and I think it was the outline against the sky of the church at Belaugh which first gave me a passion for stopping at every church I saw, and going in and having a look". Not quite what Eddie Mirzoeff wanted, so another take was necessary.

Thames Television made "**Dear Mum, Love Andrew**" in 1975, a film showing handicapped children on holiday at the "Break Children's Holiday Centre" at Hunstanton. The film begins with Andrew at home in Hounslow talking about the attitudes of able-bodied children towards disability. At Hunstanton children arrive at the home in a Break minibus, which was sponsored by the ITV programme "Magpie" (of which this film is an offshoot), and settle in. Andrew talks to the others about their disabilities, and enjoys outings arranged by the Centre. On Hunstanton Green in front of the pier, they watch and listen to a Radio One Road Show, and have a race in their wheelchairs.

In the 1960s Harlow was a recently built new place to live, and BBC Television's Panorama visited the town to see how things were going. Woodrow Wyatt interviews Sir Richard Costain, chairman of the Harlow Development Corporation, who says there are forty firms of architects, who, with a great deal of freedom, are building over 400 houses. Woodrow Wyatt then talks to some of the new inhabitants who mostly have come from London. One woman thinks their children will have

*John Betjeman in an out-take from "**A Passion For Churches**", though the working title was "**Failed in Divinity**".*

*The Punch and Judy man on Cromer beach in 1978, from "**Now and Then**".*

*Tony Amies, David Cleveland and David Wyatt filming "**The Prof**" at Lawford in North East Essex.*

a better life in Harlow, another contrasts her family living in one room in Forest Gate to that of a house in the new town. In "**Panorama, Harlow**", where workers have easy access to factories, the chances of work are discussed. One man, a clerk from Peckham, is keen to move to the town. If he finds a job, a house will be found for him, so keen are the developers to make this new town a success. The local vicar says he is busy with many christenings, a few weddings, but no funerals! Another film following the same lines, and promoting Harlow, is "**New Towns in Britain**", made by Transatlantic Televiews, presumably for transmission in the United States.

The BBC had a series running on children's television in the 1970s called "**Now and Then**", which looked at places and people, with an eye on the past. In 1978 they filmed at Cromer, where Henry "Shrimp" Davies talked about Cromer as it was in the 1890s, when there were bathing machines on the beach. This is contrasted with Cromer in the 1970s, showing the crab boats, a Punch and Judy show on the beach, and the fishermen relaxing by singing and dancing in a pub. 'Friday' Balls sings a catchy tune about the bottom of the boat falling through, and Richard Davies demonstrates step dancing to the accompaniment of Percy Brown on the accordion.

"Vision On", a very visual and artistic BBC programme for children with Tony Hart and Pat Keysell, included a white coated character known as "**The Prof**", who joined the programme in 1968. The Prof film sequences were filmed mainly on a farm at Lawford in North East Essex, and combined surreal comedy and animation. Made by Tony Amies and David Wyatt, with The Prof played by David Cleveland, one, two, or three short films were included in Vision On every week until the programme was taken off in 1976. The same character, this time trying to play a piano and called "**Piano Prof**", popped up in a short BBC East series called "The Tuesday Music Show", and again disguised as "**Cid Sleuth**" in BBC's "Jigsaw" series in the late seventies and early eighties.

In 1965 the BBC Schools Department made a recording of the Essex Youth Orchestra rehearsing and then performing the Overture to 'Hansel and Gretel' by Humperdinck, the Slow Movement of the 'Concerto for Trumpet and Orchestra' by Haydn, and pieces from 'Façade' by William Walton. All this was divided into two telerecordings called "**Youth Makes Music**". The first part looks at the rehearsal of the musicians who are all under twenty-one years old, and the social side of their lives where they play football and go to dances. The next part is the performance itself which takes place in a studio under the conductor Raymond Leppard.

The music of Benjamin Britten is heard in two films about the man himself. "**Benjamin Britten and His Festival**" was made by the BBC in 1967. Directed by Tony Palmer the film shows Britten's home town of Lowestoft, the local fishermen, a farmer who sings, the 1967 Aldeburgh Festival at Snape Maltings, Henry Moore talking to Britten about the siting of his sculptures, and Peter Pears discussing the acoustics of the new concert hall.

"**A Time There Was**" is a much longer and more ambitious film made by London Weekend Television in 1980. Running for 103 minutes, this was also directed by Tony Palmer. It is a profile of Britten, a chronological view of his life using many personal photographs and archive film with colleagues and family reminiscing, and with rehearsals and performances of his works.

George Ewart Evans is known for his pioneering oral history work in and around the village of Blaxhall in Suffolk. George was born in the coal town Abercyon in Wales in 1909, read classics at Cardiff University, and had an urge to write. At Sawston, in Cambridgeshire he met and married fellow teacher Florence Knappett, and in 1947 they moved to Blaxhall where Florence taught in the local school. George listened to the local people, the farm workers, the village craftsmen - listened to what they had to say. Once he had got to know them, he recorded them. These tape recordings became the basis for a number of books such as "Where Beards Wag All" published by Faber and Faber in 1970. "..the book's main concern is to illustrate the importance of the oral testimony of those people who grew up under the old culture.." he writes in the introduction. "Oral testimony can help the researcher… by giving flesh to the material he has gathered from other sources" he wrote elsewhere. From these conversations he unearthed forgotten ways and routines. He found out about the farm labourers leaving Suffolk in the late autumn seeking work in the maltings at Burton upon Trent. The story of the men and their work there is told in Anglia Television's 1975 "**Gone To Burton**", a film that could not have been made without George's extensive research. Farm worker James Knights of Little Glemham recalls that he exchanged his Suffolk winter farm wage of 12/- (60p) for 38/- (£1.90p) when he first went to Burton in 1899. He and others reminisce about the hard work, the conditions, the fights, and the accidents that befell some of their colleagues. Their first purchase at the end of the malting season was usually a new suit.

In "**A Writer's Suffolk**", directed by John Archer, George talks about his life, looks at the present state of farming and rural life, and compares it with what he has learnt from the people he talked to over a thirty year period. He visits a farm where heavy horses are kept working by Cheryl Clarke of Weylands Farm at Stoke by Nayland, and sees the modern computerised combine harvester spare parts department of Mann's depot at Saxham near Bury St Edmunds. At Hollesley in Suffolk young offenders work with horses as a form of therapy. He watches a horse being shod, and a huge eight-furrow mounted plough and a large combine harvester at work. George watches the old and new and tries to sum up his feelings about life and the land.

Television in the Eastern Counties brought to everyone the stories, the events, the happenings,the lives of the region over nearly a half a century of time. We are much richer in our knowledge and understanding of the area we live in through the work of BBC East, Anglia Television, and the major broadcasters who went out with their film cameras into Bedfordshire, Cambridgeshire, Essex, Hertfordshire, Norfolk and Suffolk and captured the life, the fabric, the land we live in. Thousands of these films from the broadcasters are preserved in the vaults of the University of East Anglia's East Anglian Film Archive at the Archive Centre in Norwich.

For further information of films mentioned in this book, and the Archive's holdings, please contact:

The East Anglian Film Archive,
The Archive Centre,
County Hall,
Martineau Lane,
Norwich NR1 2DQ

Telephone 01603 592664

The film vaults at the University of East Anglia's East Anglian Film Archive.

List of Films Mentioned in This Book

with dates where known

C

D

E

F

G

H

I

N

O

P

Q

R

S

T

U

V

W

X

Y

Z

Acknowledgements and List of Individual Film Makers

Many people have helped towards this book, some directly and some indirectly, some in the planning stages over the last few years, and some in the past. These include in alphabetical order Jane Alvey, Phillip Armes, Mikael Barnard, Jane Blanchflower, David Butcher, Richard Carr, Maurice Dale, Douglas Fisher, Jean Fox, Ieuan Franklin, Malcolm Freegard, Roger Gillham, Joan Hammond, Peter Hollingham, Dicky Howett, David Kenten, Tanya Knighton, June Lewis, Bob Malster, Emma Manning, Linda Mitchell, Brian Pritchard, Ken Rickwood, Dick Robinson, Richard Taylor, David Tilley, Rodney Tuck, Robin Williams, and Brian Woods-Taylor to name a few. Here is a list of individual film makers mentioned in this book, some of whom I was in contact with and they passed information to me about their films, others I found out about through relatives, friends, organisations, and my own research. Some however were untraceable, and others were unknown to me, though their films survive.

J

K

L

M

N

O

P

R

S

T

U

W

Note.
Television reporters
listed in main index

SELECT BIBLIOGRAPHY

Alvey, Jane, and Taylor, Richard, *East Anglian Film Archive-The Collections*, East Anglian Film Archive, 2008

Banks, Ivan, *Rails to Jaywick Sands*, Plateway Press, Croydon, 1988

Bloom, Alan, *The Farm in The Fen*, Faber and Faber, London, 1944

Bloom, Ursula, *Rosemary For Frinton*, Robert Hale, London, 1970

Boswell,V.C, *The Eastern Chronology*, Ipswich, c1932

British Film Institute, *National Film Archive Catalogue*, London, 1980

British Sugar plc, *A Short History of British Sugar*, c1995

Brown, R. Douglas, *East Anglia 1939*, Terence Dalton Ltd, Lavenham, 1980

Cambridge & Isle of Ely Territorial Army Association, *We Also Served*, 1944

Chamberlain, Geoffrey, *Airships-Cardington*, Terence Dalton Ltd, Lavenham, 1984

Croston, Eric, *Television and Radio 1985*, Independent Broadcasting Authority, London, 1984

Davis, Anthony, *The First Twenty One Years*, Anglia Television Group Ltd, Norwich, 1980

Day, J. Wentworth, *Farming Adventure*, George G. Harrap and Co. Ltd, 1943

Eales, Ted, *Countryman's Memoirs*, Jim Baldwin Publishing, Fakenham, 1986

Elliott, Christopher, *Aeronauts and Aviators*, Terence Dalton Ltd, Lavenham, 1971

Fream, W, *Elements of Agriculture*, John Murray, London, 1919

Geddes, Keith, *The Setmakers – A History of The Radio and Television Industry*, Brema, London, 1991

Gifford, Denis, *The British Film Catalogue Volume 2 - Non-Fiction Film 1888-1994*, Fitzroy Dearborn, 2000

Howett, Dicky, *Television Innovations*, Kelly Publications, Devon, 2006

Independent Television Authority, *ITV 1972*, 1972

Ipswich Engineering Society, *The History of Engineering in Ipswich*, 1950

Jaffa, Harold, *Norfolk Events*, Norfolk News Company, 1950

Jenkins, Frederick, *Story of Southwold*, F. Jenkins, 1948

Joby, R. S., *Forgotten Railways: East Anglia*, David and Charles, Newton Abbot, 1977

Joice, Dick, *Full Circle*, The Boydell Press, Woodbridge, 1991

Kemp, P. K., *The Bentall Story*, Bentalls of Maldon, 1955

Kinsey, Gordon, *Aviation – Flight Over The Eastern Counties*, Terence Dalton Ltd, Lavenham, 1977

Kinsey, Gordon, *Seaplanes-Felixstowe*, Terence Dalton Ltd, Lavenham, 1978

Low, Rachael, *Documentary and Educational Films of The 1930s*, George Allen & Unwin, London, 1979

Malster, Robert, *Ipswich, Town on The Orwell*, Terence Dalton Ltd, Lavenham, 1978

Malster, Robert, *Saved From The Sea*, Terence Dalton Ltd, Lavenham, 1974

Maritime Trust, *The Story of The Lydia Eva*, 1975

Meadows, Eric, *Hertfordshire, A Pictorial Guide*, White Crescent Press Ltd, Luton, c1977

Mitchell, Vic, and Smith, Keith, *Branch Line to Southwold*, Middleton Press, Midhurst, 1987

National Film Archive, *Catalogue of Viewing Copies*, British Film Institute, London 1971

Ormes, Ian, *From Rags to Roms – A History of Spicers*, Granta Editions, Chesterton, 1996

Peart, Stephen, *The Picture House in East Anglia*, Terence Dalton Ltd, Lavenham, 1980
Pollard, Michael, *North Sea Surge*, Terence Dalton Ltd, Lavenham, 1978
Potter, Jeremy, *Independent Television in Britain, Volume 4,* Macmillan, 1990
Reed, John, *Moving Images*, Capital Transport, Harrow Weald, 1990
Rickwood, Ken, *Stour Secrets*, David Cleveland, Manningtree, 2008
Simper, Robert, *The Suffolk Show 1831-1981*, East Anglian Daily Times, 1981
Stratton, J. M., *Agricultural Records A. D. 220-1977*, John Baker, London, 1978
Walshe, Tom, *A Knight on The Box*, Anglia Television Ltd, Norwich, 1999
Walthew, Kenneth, *From Rock and Tempest*, Geoffrey Bles, London, 1971
Weaver, Carol and Michael, *Ransomes – A Bicentennial Celebration,* 1989
Williamson, Henry, *The Story of a Norfolk Farm,* Faber and Faber Ltd, 1941
Willock, Colin, *Kenzie The Wild Goose Man*, Andre Deutsch, London, 1962

with Kelly's Directories of

Bedfordshire
Cambridgeshire
Essex
Hertfordshire
Huntingdonshire
Norfolk
Suffolk

and the files of the East Anglian Film Archive

General Index

E

F

G

H

I

J

K

L

M

N

O

P

Q

R

U

V

W

Y

Z